Moscow Believes in Tears

Moscow Believes in Tears
Russians and Their Movies

Louis Menashe

Washington, DC

Copyright © 2010 by Louis Menashe

New Academia Publishing, 2010

All rights reserved. No part of this book may be reproduced or transmitted in any form or by any means, electronic or mechanical, including photocopying, recording, or by any information storage and retrieval system.

Printed in the United States of America

Library of Congress Control Number: 2010930182
ISBN 978-0-9844062-0-3 paperback (alk. paper)
ISBN 978-0-9844062-4-1 hardcover (alk. paper)

New Academia Publishing
P.O. Box 24720, Washington, DC 20038-7420
info@newacademia.com - www.newacademia.com

For Leah and Ben

Contents

Illustrations	xi
Preface: Responsibilities	xiii
A Note on Contents	xvii
Acknowledgments	xix
Prologue	xxi

I I Found it at the Movies: *Kinojournal*, 1991-2004 1

Passport. Black Rose the Emblem of Sorrow.... Swan Lake: The Zone. Days of Eclipse. The Second Circle. Satan. Hey, You Wild Geese! Raspad. Go Away! The Stone. Close to Eden. Shy Boy. La Chasse Aux Papillons. The Chekist. Anna. The Thief. Brigands, Chapter VII. A Friend of the Deceased. Some Interviews on Personal Matters. In the Dark.

II Close-ups on the Past 43

1 On Stalin and Stalinism 45

Two Portraits, A Servant and a Victim of the Tyrant: *I Was Stalin's Bodyguard* and *The Akhmatova File. Repentance. Burnt by the Sun. A Trial in Prague.*

SHORT TAKES 67

Widow of the Revolution: The Anna Larina Story. East-West. Eternal Memory: Voices from the Great Terror. The Fall of Berlin.

2 On Russian Battlefields 71

Chapayev and Company: Films of the Russian Civil War. Tinker on the Roof, or *Commissar:* Jews and Russians in the Russian Civil War. *Commissar:* Another Take. Patriotic Gore, Patriotic Gauze: Films of The Great Patriotic War. *Stalingrad. Prisoner of the Mountains.*

viii   Contents

SHORT TAKES   105
Blockade. Zelary. 100 Days Before the Command. The 3 Rooms of Melancholia.

III Fragments from the Russian Experience   109

Nostalgia for the Homeland: Tarkovsky, *Oblomov* and Svetlana Alliluyeva. Filming Sokurov's *Russian Ark*: An Interview with Tilman Büttner. *Rasputin. One Day in the Life of Andrei Arsenevich. Siberiade. Stalker.* The Lonely Voice of Sokurov: Documentaries on the Russian Experience from a Russian Master.

SHORT TAKES   153
Wings and *The Ascent*

IV *Glasnost* Galore: Cinema in the Soviet Twilight   155

From Stagnation, *Perestroika: The Mirror, Oblomov, Autumn Marathon, Scarecrow, Little Vera.* Discovering the "Unknown Cinema." Some Perspectives on Soviet Cinema in the *Glasnost* Era. *Sideburns.* Woman with a Movie Camera: The Films of Marina Goldovskaya. *Adam's Rib.* Historians of the USSR Cross Over into Filmmaking. Requiem for Soviet Cinema 1917-1991. Anna Lawton Trailer, 1: *Kinoglasnost: Soviet Cinema in Our Time.*

V Transitions   205

Out of the Present. What is There to Celebrate? The Russian Documentary and the Petersburg Festival, "Message to Man." Moscow Believes in Tears: Problems (and Promise?) of Russian Cinema in the Transition Period: A View at the Turn of the Century. Border Crossings in the Baltic: The "Transit Zero" Film Conference. *The Return. Last Resort.* Buttons, Buttons, Who's got the Workers? A Note on the (Missing) Working Class in Late- and Post-Soviet Russian Cinema.

SHORT TAKES   264
4.
Anna Lawton Trailer, 2: *Imaging Russia 2000: Film and Facts.*

VI A Concluding Montage Across Time and Borders 267

Monuments and Musicals as Mementoes of Communism: *Disgraced Monuments* and *East Side Story*. From the Caucasus 1: *Vodka Lemon*. From the Caucasus 2: *Pirosmani*. Poisoned by Polonium: *The Litvinenko File*. *Nostalghia*.

SHORT TAKES 282

Animated Soviet Propaganda. Theremin: An Electronic Odyssey. Kolya. Transsiberian. Letter to Anna. The Lady with The Dog.

VII Soundtracks: Interviewing the Filmmakers 289

1 Andrei Konchalovsky and *Siberiade*, 1982 291

2 *Perestroika*, 1986-1991 300

Alexander Askoldov. Dmitry Astrakhan. Mikhail Belikov. Nana Djordjadze. Elem Klimov. Irina Kupchenko. Gleb Panfilov.

3 After the Fall, 1993-1994 357

Leonid Gurevich. Yuri Khashchavatsky. Mikhail Litvyakov. Alexander Rodnyansky. Aleko Tsabadze.

Index 403

Illustrations

1. Other kinds of "Responsibilities"	xii
2. Enthusiasm for the *glasnost* films	3
3. From Tengis Abuladze's *Repentance* (1984)	42
4. From Alexander Askoldov's *Commissar* (1967/1987)	82
5. At the Hermitage for Alexander Sokurov's *Russian Ark* (2002)	114
6. Catherine the Great, from Sokurov's *Russian Ark*	114
7. Program cover for the *Glasnost Film Festival*	154
8. Program cover for the "Message to Man" Festival	210
9. From Andrei Zvyagintsev's *The Return* (2004)	244
10. *A Family Celebration* by Niko Pirosmani	274
11. Irina Kupchenko	339
12. Leonid Gurevich	371
13. Anne Borin and Misha Litvyakov	371

Cover: A concerned Katya tries to calm her husband, an angry Peter the Great, in Alexander Sokurov's *Russian Ark* (2002).

Illustrations 1, 3, 4, 5, 6, 9 and Cover: courtesy of *Cineaste*. Illustrations 2, 7, 8, 12, 13: courtesy of Anne Borin. Illustration 10: from *Niko Pirosmani 1862-1918* (Leningrad: Izdatel'stvo "Avrora," 1984). Illustration 11: from a Sovexportfilm publicity calendar, Moscow, 1991.

1. Other kinds of "Responsibilities": The Bolsheviks demand, "Have you volunteered?" to fight on their side in the Russian Civil War.

Preface: *Responsibilities*

I am not a film critic, though I have written a lot on Russian films. Neither am I a film-studies academic, though I have spent my adult life teaching in academia. In my articles and reviews you won't find the specialized jargon and post-modern vocabulary that spackles the prose of critics and scholars—no conceits, discourses, situatings; no reifications or oneirics, please. The inimitable writer and critic James Agee explained to his readers what qualified him to write on film. He was, he told them, "in your own situation: deeply interested in moving pictures, considerably experienced from childhood in watching them and thinking and talking about them...." *Same here.*

Richard Schickel, another fine writer and critic of a later generation, called for more than "idle opinion-mongering" in reviewing films or other creative works; there has to be a "sense of responsibility" on the part of the critic, who must do "justice to the work at hand and to the culture in which it appeared." Here is James Agee again, on a different kind of "responsibility": Of John Huston's "pictures" he wrote that they "are not acts of seduction or of benign enslavement but of liberation, and they require, of anyone who enjoys them, the responsibilities of liberty. They continually open the eye and require it to work vigorously; and through the eye they awaken curiosity and intelligence." He might just as well have been writing of all good art and entertainment, not just John Huston's.

To those responsibilities must be added another when it comes to Russian and Soviet films (not fluency in the Russian language, though that would be very helpful). Film goers of a certain age will always identify Russian films with the Soviet Union, even long after the demise of the USSR. (I have friends who still say Soviet when they mean Russian.) If Soviet cinema was conceived and organized around a definite political purpose—not necessarily by the filmmakers, but by the State that financed them—then viewers and critics have the "responsibility" to learn something of the political or historical back-story behind the films.

For Soviet films, viewers in the West inevitably brought strong, pre-formed ideas and prejudices to the theater. These were *pro* or *contra*, rarely neutral, to what used to be called "the Soviet experiment," and to the character and intentions of the USSR. A bit of tempering of any hard and fixed attitudes from either perspective was not a bad thing. One of the reasons I introduced films in my classes on Soviet history (a time when, I admit, I held strong views of my own that were very sympathetic to Moscow) was to show students who were reared in the culture of the Cold War, with its images of Big Brother totalitarianism, that there were other sides to Soviet life that undermined the imagery. The films I showed communicated a different, benign story instead. "See!," the films would reveal, "Russians and Georgians and Ukrainians are just like us—working, loving, laughing, crying, going about the business of getting on with their lives with a hope we all shared, that of living in peace on our thermonuclear endangered planet."

But wait. Yes, those folks in the films were just like us, but they lived their real, non-celluloid lives within patterns that weren't up on the screen. Certain features of Soviet society were either lacquered heavily, or bypassed completely. Aspects of Soviet reality, whether pictured in daily life of the time, or in representations of the past in war and peace, came through in the films, but taboo after taboo handed down from above or internalized by the filmmakers themselves masked too much of that reality. The task of the "responsible" critic or film historian whose specialty was the Soviet Union was to peel away the masks and lead the "responsible" viewer to a clearer, more truthful understanding of what was going on over there: *My job.*

In other words, when it comes to Soviet cinema, a cigar is never just a cigar: a Soviet film was never just a movie. There were always political nuances that informed the films overtly or beneath the surface, and there were political attitudes held by the audiences that went to see them. Naturally, post-Soviet films may have a politics as well, and demand care with background and context too, but those old, very Soviet political and ideological overtones identifying all art and entertainment from the USSR, films included, are gone.

From lecturing about the films I showed in my classes on Russian and Soviet history, and discussing them with my students, I went a step further and began writing and publishing articles and reviews about those and other films. I also took part in several film projects about Soviet Russia, most notably as Associate Producer for two award-winning PBS documentaries, *In the Shadow of Sakharov* and *Inside Gorbachev's USSR*. (See my essay, "Historians of the USSR Cross Over into Filmmaking," in chapter IV, below.) My scholarly interest in the USSR began with a socialist edge, although reading Chekhov and Turgenev as a teenager also had something to do with my romance with the Russians. For an earlier me, the Russian Motherland was the Soviet Russian Motherland of Socialism that would help open our own paths to revolution and utopia in the West. When disillusion set in, a process that started with my first trips to the Motherland in the 1960s and climaxed with the failures of Gorbachev's *glasnost* and *perestroika* to put a human face on Soviet socialism, I turned more and more away from political concerns as such and retreated—advanced?—into the precincts of art, particularly film art. The emphasis on art is not amiss here. Soviet filmmakers in general, even without the promptings of the *kino* bosses, rarely conceived their work simply as entertainment; there was always a certain high-mindedness among them, as befitted the traditions of the Russian cultural intelligentsia.

The shifts in my personal and professional perspectives resulted in the materials assembled in this collection, a kind of commonplace book of reviews, interviews, reports, journal entries, long essays and short takes, written over a span of three decades, from the last years of the Soviet Union to the first years of the Former Soviet Union. Most of the writing was published in diverse magazines and periodicals, especially in *Cineaste*, which rightly describes itself as "America's leading magazine on the art and politics of the cinema," and to whose founder and Editor-in-Chief, Gary Crowdus, and his team of editors, I owe much gratitude for making their pages available to my critical views.

The work here will naturally interest the specialist, whether in film or Russian studies, though there is likely to be small and large disagreements over my presentations and interpretations, but I hope the non-specialist film lover will find them appealing enough to awaken a taste, if not already there, for watching and understanding Russians through their cinema.

A Note on Contents

Most of the articles and reviews that follow look at films with Russian or Soviet themes made by Russian or Soviet filmmakers. But I have also included reviews of films about those subjects by non-Russian, non-Soviet directors from abroad. The fascination foreigners have had with Russia, the Russian soul, or with Soviet history and its wayward paths, crisscrossed by trauma and triumph, is an enduring fact of modern times, and has found a place in filmmaking from different lands.[1] It deserves some attention here.

Reviews are indicated by the name of the film in italics in the Table of Contents, while titles of articles, essays and review-essays are in roman face.

All of the materials in this volume appear as originally published or presented, with only minor, primarily cosmetic or clarifying changes. Sources are indicated throughout. Since this is not a work of reference I have done very little updating, mainly changing a tense here and there, or noting the demise of a film figure. Some repetition and duplication is inevitable in a collection of this kind; my apologies. Thus, for example, Askoldov and his *Commissar* turn up in varying guises: in an interview (Chapter VII); in reviews (Chapter II, 2); and in several places in the historical essays.

---

[1] Hollywood's affair with Russians and Russian themes is deftly examined by Harlow Robinson in his *Russians in Hollywood, Hollywood's Russians: Biography of an Image* (Boston: Northeastern University Press, and Hanover, N.H. and London: University Press of New England, 2007). See also my review, *Cineaste*, XXXIII, 4, 2008.

Acknowledgments

I am grateful to the following publications and publishers for reprinting permissions (full citations appear in the text): *Documentary* (formerly *International Documentary*); Cambridge University Press, publisher of *International Labor and Working-Class History*; Wiley, publisher of *The Russian Review*; *Slavonica*; *Commonweal*; University of California Press, publisher of *Film Quarterly*; *Tikkun*; Cengage Learning, Inc. I owe a particular debt to *Cineaste*, where most of the reviews, articles and short takes in this volume originally appeared. I'm fortunate to have received support and encouragement from its Founder and Editor-in-Chief, Gary Crowdus, along with Editors Dan Georgakas, Cynthia Lucia and Richard Porton—themselves contributors *par excellence* to film criticism and film history. Gary is ever Mr. Reliable, no matter how busy, who always follows through with help when asked.

My thanks also go to Dr. Jeffrey B. Rubin, who planted the idea of a book; to Anna Lawton who proposed doing the book for New Academia, and whose talents as a publisher, film scholar, and novelist are matched by personal warmth and fine humor; to Gail Sinai, who got me started on the task of scanning and collating the materials that make up this collection; to Louis Evans and Laura Ciporen for their technical wizardry around the computer—I much valued their skills in formatting, etc., but it was also a pleasure working with them; to Helmut Gruber, who introduced the "Politics and Film" courses at Polytechnic; to Fred Ciporen, BP, for advice on some of the arcane ways of the publishing world, and for challenging opinions on film art; to Masha Godovannaya of St. Petersburg, always ready to answer whatever query I might send her way; to Anne Borin of New York, who helped connect me more closely with Russian/Soviet films and filmmakers back in the 1980s, and has remained an ever resourceful friend since; to Oleg Smirnoff, who I met on a Moscow tennis court in 1984, and who eventually came to New York where I regularly pepper him with questions of Russian language and contemporary culture; to the remarkable blues guitarist, Danny Kalb, who took an interest in my writing, and kept prodding me to produce; to Julia Arkhipova, now of New York, but once an excellent guide around her city, St. Petersburg, and its film festivals; to my friend, the writer and film critic, Leonard Quart, who always enriches our conversations on cinema and life; to Rubye Monet, for keeping me informed about Russian films on Paris screens; to my friend, the economist David Mermelstein, who values lay opinions as much as critics' views when talking about films; to Allis and Ronald Radosh, with whom I like to discuss movies, even as we disagree about political matters; to my friends Renée and Simon Dinnerstein, cinema buffs both, with whom I have shared many a discussion of Russia and Russian films. And thanks, too, to other non-professional cinephiles in my circle: brother Bob Menashe, Jan Rosenberg, Fred Siegel, Sima Szaluta, Mort Weiner, Elayne Archer, Manuela Dobos, the late Artyom Englin and cousins Jack Zaraya and Wendy Sabin. I am also very grateful to Birgit Beumers for her sharp editorial eye in matters of Russian film and filmmakers.

Sheila Menashe, always my first, critical reader, gets my very special, very big message of appreciation and affection. I'm glad my daughter Claudia, her husband, John Anderson, and my son, David, are film enthusiasts and I'm grateful for their attention to dad's writing.

Prologue

Russian films aren't what they used to be. Ask any filmgoer of that certain age mentioned above about Russian cinema, and the response is likely to include classics like *Potemkin* and *Ballad of a Soldier*. Such films earned attention and praise for political significance as well as artistic merit. Ask filmgoers of less than that certain age, and the response is likely to be a blank. How is it that the cinema of Eisenstein and Chukhrai, which once drew accolades from critics and public alike in the global theater, has not been, with some exceptions, followed by comparable successes? It's a long story. It involves a political and cultural history that spanned several decades and several upheavals, from the age of Stalin to the age of Putin.

That story won't be told here in simple narrative form, but by examining films from and about those eras we can sketch a picture of development and underdevelopment for Russian cinema and for the society out of which it emerged. The materials collected in this volume don't comprise film criticism in the usual sense, nor do they constitute history as such, but they draw on both realms and together help us locate the place and value of Russian cinema in modern times.

CHAPTER I

I Found It at the Movies: *Kinojournal*, 1991-2004

The great American film critic, Pauline Kael, "lost it at the movies" (the title for her book of dazzling reviews and essays has multiple shades of meaning).[1] *You might say, in my case, I* found *it at the movies — "it" being a rewarding way to illuminate Russian/Soviet life, culture and history; "movies" being, of course, the Russian/Soviet films themselves. From time to time, I tried keeping a journal of what I saw, making entries right after viewing. Some of these unbuttoned reactions are offered, unchanged, here, except for spelling and other like minor corrections. Programmers at different venues in New York — The Museum of Modern Art, the Film Society of Lincoln Center, and elsewhere — enjoyed a bounty of new films coming out or conceived during* **perestroika** *and after, and I always hurried to catch them there, or at press screenings. I've indicated location and date of screening (not the film's production date), just as they appeared in my* Kinojournal.

---

[1] *I Lost it at the Movies: Film Writings 1954 to 1965* (Boston: Little Brown & Company, 1965).

I Found It at the Movies

DATEBOOK Film *San Francisco Chronicle*

Two Russian Views From New Directors

Prison life, anti-Semitism explored in S.F. Film Festival entries

2. Continued coast-to-coast media and festival enthusiasm for the *glasnost* films that arrived after the collapse of the USSR. The *San Francisco Chronicle* reports on films by Lidiya Bobrova and Dmitry Astrakhan, April 26, 1992. I saw them in New York around the same time.

Passport: A Film by Georgi Danelia
6/19/91, Museum of Modern Art

I winced when it was announced that this was an Austrian-Israeli-French co-production. It showed: what a mess. Later Danelia told the audience the film was shot in ten days. That showed too. Everyone was wooden, everything weighed a ton, though the string of comic situations the film consisted of should have, on the face of it, been hilarious. Danelia later said the film was not a comedy but a "tragedy." It ends sadly, with people the victims of a world divided by borders.

Another problem: the film is overdubbed in Russian, so the usual Babel the result. Also, the English titles amusingly wrong; Jew appears often as Few.

D. said he conceived the film five years ago, but then it "was impossible to even utter the word Israel." Two Georgian half-brothers look like twins; one is Yakov, the other is Merab, i.e., one the son of a Jewish, the other of a Georgian mother. Yakov therefore entitled to emigrate to Israel with his wife and daughter, angering his Georgian father. At the airport Merab wants to celebrate with champagne, but since there is no alcohol at the regular counters, he gets into the duty-free area by borrowing his brother's ticket, passport, and visa. He gets the champagne but of course he can't get back into the airport and flies to Vienna. Query: how come the crew which is expecting him doesn't ask about the wife and daughter? But credibility is not one of the film's strong points. In Vienna he is put off by Soviet bureaucracy (Yevgeny Leonov plays a consular official in a wonderful cameo.) Along the way he picks up a Russian friend (Oleg Yankovsky), who hustles everywhere. E.G., he presents an American tourist with a balalaika at the airport, but reclaims it on the plane out of "nostalgia". In Vienna he pries it open to reveal stacks of dollars. Yankovsky turns up wherever Merab is, involved in one scheme or another. Last seen in an Arab headdress with a millionairess rug merchant in Jordan.

All sorts of characters appear—cousins in Israel, an American journalist, Georgian compatriots—in situation after situation, all unfunny, except for some anti-Soviet digs, as when he calls Tbilisi from Austria and is told to bring condoms and #10 screws, or when he's told to make a case of victimization, then worldwide Jewry will come to his defense through the UN, the Voice of America, etc., or when there's a discussion about declaring gold teeth.

The serious theme is that this is all a commentary on a world divided by borders protected by armed guards who send you to jail (he experiences them in the USSR, Israel, Jordan, and Austria). The film opens, inexplicably, with Merab laying a rose on the grave of a woman named Klein in Omsk. The conclusion of the film reveals the secret: Merab is taken across the Israeli-Jordan border by a hard-drinking Red Army veteran of WW II, the *émigré* Klein— who is killed by a land mine (in slow-mo). From comedy, bathos.

"Maybe we'll meet in another world where there are no borders," Klein had told him. As he crosses into Jordan Merab cries, "Don't shoot me, brothers!"

Danelia speaks of a specific Georgian sense of humor. It was there alright, but smothered by cheap comic situations.

Comrade Stalin Goes to Africa: A Film by Irakli Kvirikadze
7/16/91, Museum of Modern Art

Another absurdist Georgian comedy, not very good. A nice idea: a tale of preparing a Stalin look-alike to stand in for the dictator. Stalin can't bear sitting through boring ceremonial events, so he orders an occasional substitute. (I forget what the Africa in the title refers to; something Stalin said about some woman in Africa, vaguely salacious.)

The NKVD locates a look-alike, a Georgian Jew (the bosses are assured his name Pikhchadze can be Georgian too) who has a fabulous memory, hence can repeat Stalin's speeches word for word. (Is he the wonderful guy who plays Motyl in *IZ IDI*?) We are told—the NKVD knows everything—that he is impotent with his wife, but has a mistress named Fanya Kaplan. He is trained in some abandoned mansion where he has to relieve himself outdoors, and where the crew chief is always screwing his secretary, both fully clothed.

What kills what could be a mordant piece of work? Filmic shenanigans, basically. The usual alternations, b/w and color; self-references (the film opens with the narrator telling us the home movie we are watching shows us the director of the film shooting himself); lots of home movies; documentary intercuts—as usual for me the most fascinating part because they show shots of Stalin and the entourage I've never seen; here I spotted the young Kosygin and the young Suslov, and Mao himself; intercuts of US scenes like the Brooklyn Bridge and Broadway at night with Presley's "Jailhouse Rock" on the soundtrack [Nana Djordjadze, Kvirikadze's wife, explained to the audience that America was always a dream for all Soviets and there's irony here because it's Africa not America(?)];

disjointedness as a principle; shots repeated; and other such juvenilia.

As in the Danelia film, the comedy suddenly turns grim when Stalin dies and a *prikaz* comes down to eliminate the double. Shoot yourself they tell him but he asks, why not let me go? (I think they shoot him.)

There is something here—Stalinism *was* an absurdity, and it's good to be able to poke fun at its bizarre pretenses. But this amateurish treatment doesn't do the possibilities justice. At work again—busting loose from the old restrictions: sex, free form, mocking the icons. But all so flat....

Black Rose the Emblem of Sorrow, Red Rose the Emblem of Love: A Film by Sergei Soloviev
8/20/91, Museum of Modern Art

Another infuriatingly disappointing *glasnost* film by the maker of the popular *ASSA*, all the more disappointing because this has been touted as a supremely rich talented effort. There may be talent somewhere, there is vitality certainly, but the excess of everything—of costumes, of tired sight gags, of self-conscious, sophomoric absurdities (meaningless and uninteresting intercuts, directions to the audience, titles in several languages), of film-school camera tricks, and absence of real wit and subtlety make of this another boring effort to shock and break loose from the old conventions. Someone said the typical *glasnost* film is a nude woman smoking grass gazing at a portrait of Stalin. Yep, that's *Black Rose*...

The "story": A young woman is nailed into an empty flat by her father to make her study for exams. She lets herself out by the window, enters the apartment of an adolescent boy who shares it with a kooky but good layabout, calls her boyfriend, who comes over. (Example of excess: she can't just escape, she has to do it in an elaborate naval uniform with a fancy straw hat, net gloves, and what else I can't remember. It reminds me of that whacky loft *soirée* of the Russian *émigrés* I went to a few years ago.) From then on it's absurdist mayhem with no particular logic or feeling. (Well maybe the boy Mitya evokes some affection with his dreamy sensitive looks and kindness.) In the course of things a rock band appears, mama and papa appear, as does Mitya's guardian from Luber (translated as "the suburbs"), a nude woman, the boyfriend's father-in-law, a black man denouncing imperialism, and, in a dream sequence—how could he not appear?—Stalin himself with an entourage that includes the young Brezhnev and Beria. (The Stalin figure seems to an obligatory standard in all these films, usually, unlike here, in documentary footage.)

In the end, Tolik dies (he's the dotty dissident who brews moonshine just to retaliate against *them*; the jugs are capped by rubber gloves that balloon when the liquid ferments; he also likes to go around with balloons tied to him); Alexandra bears Mitya's (?) baby; Vova reforms; a priest baptizes Mitya who also joins the navy. Along the way a trenchant comment or two—e.g., grandpa, who is a White Guard aristocrat living in France, writes to Mitya to uphold honesty and truth, to distrust the lies of *perestroika* even more than the lies of Brezhnev; Vova comments that perpetual irritation is the common condition of all Soviets. An occasional amusing touch—the priest asks for stripping to the waist, meaning Mitya, but the guardian and his girlfriend do it. But for the most part bad farce, bad slapstick, bad put-ons....

Nudity, absurdity, sophomoric *épater le socialist realism*, misfiring critiques, and much wasted energy.

The frenetic pace reminiscent of Almodóvar.

Soloviev is an intellectual (that's the problem with these guys) whose declared esthetic is that art begins when meaning ends. One pictures him scurrying around the set or tearing through the script purging all meaning. Why a turtle in the death scene?, someone asks. No reason, he answers. Ditto in other cases. He is dedicated to beauty and love, and finds them in the seemingly ugly. This is, with *ASSA*, part of trilogy.

Soloviev had just arrived; awakened on plane with news of the anti-Gorbachev coup; quit kidding, and let me sleep, he replied.

Swan Lake. The Zone: A Film by Yuri Ilyenko
9/13/91, Film Forum

Again, trouble ahead: Canadian, Hungarian, U.S., Swedish, and Dovzhenko Studios all involved. But it's not joint productions they need. It's not technical hardware and Western sophistication they need. (Tarkovsky's greatest works made do with what he had at home.) It's talent they need. And discipline, and restraint, and overcoming the glee of doing whatever they want after years of ham-handed controls. It's art they need and not counter-statements and counter-esthetics.

Lots of promise here: It's Ilyenko after all, Paradzhanov's cameraman for the extraordinary *Shadows of Forgotten Ancestors* (speaking of making do), and, as the introductory title tells us, shot in Paradzhanov's prison camps. (A couple of times we see a magazine with Paradzhanov on the cover, under the heading "Maestro".) And an interesting idea, too: that of an escaped convict hiding out in the interior of, of all things, a monumental sheet-metal hammer-and-sickle, while life goes on along the highway below. This could have been, and was, up to a point, a kind of Slavic-absurdist Beckett in which the convict keeps returning to his peculiar haven. Instead, the convict leaves (made to leave? discovered? evicted?) for prison again, followed up by a couple of suicide attempts, one unsuccessful ending in resurrection, the other successful ending with his stiff cadaver standing against the bars of his prison. There are also sequences of is it real? or is it fantasy? often involving a blonde beauty (too gorgeously glamorous to fit in) who befriends him and wants to whisk him away. Here too, great possibilities: in the USSR love can only be realized in self-made havens like the convict's hammer and sickle interior. This is only partially fulfilled in a couple of surreal sections: she dresses for the "wedding", putting on, incidentally, hammer and sickle pendant earrings—are we supposed to laugh? In their erotically charged interior, however, they never do consummate things—once, effectively done, when her son refuses to accept their relationship and aims a barrage of sling-shotted pebbles at their metal exterior: cacophony and unrealized desire. Another time, an overdone picture of disappointment as she gets herself all messed up with the new silver paint the exterior has been painted with after his eviction. [One of these interior scenes shows the incredibly sloppy work they think they can get away with these days—it makes you want to scream, bring back the commissars! bring back socialist realism! She lights a candle then fumbles with the match-box, finally putting it down somewhere; she changes position and carefully tugs at her slip to keep it from climbing up her thighs; she wants to reach over but can't find something to lean on to support her weight: all these touches of clumsy improvisation and/or direction in a film of high surreal pretension.]

Here and there, as always, some powerful moments, aside from the overall powerful mood of despair: the convict running, running over barren rocks, the camera following him from above; the convict taking off his socks, revealing his horribly bloodied feet; the many ugly prison scenes, one with the caged convicts doused with a hose while swans waddle about. (Other swan images: in blue monotint they fly in formation; three dead swans on a flat-bed truck.) A "blood transfusion" in which not the blood, which spills inadvertently from the unconnected tubing, but an old woman's faith revives the dead man. This whole sequence something out of old Russian literature with its pain and pathos: the tipsy guard hauls the body on a horse-drawn cart to the old woman's on Easter night. The ugly terrain with some foul sulphurous water gushing from a sewer duct. The boy climbing into the convict's space....

But they don't all hold together. Perhaps Paradzhanov's different stories were woven too artificially around the one convict? Perhaps some linking sequences cut? (E.G., according to [Vincent] Canby, the program notes make it clear the boy turned the convict in.)

Reminiscent of *Stalker* (also taking place in a "zone"), but not as magical.

Days of Eclipse: A Film by Alexander Sokurov
8/29/91, Museum of Modern Art

A moody meditation in the Central Asian desert by the Tarkovsky-like Sokurov. S. is quoted as being taken by "the deep, difficult, painful impressions which Asia" made on him, and produced this reverie shot in a Turkmenia filled with heat and dust and poverty and suffering and the inability of a Russian to survive without some emotional or intellectual anchor. Reminiscent of the English-in-India theme and ambience. S. adds lots of strange images to the already exotic milieu. E.G., a lobster arrives in the post preserved in a gel; a lizard appears when there is food around; shots of the village structures in eerie light (eclipse?), and a shot of the lead figure (Sasha) walking among the miniature mock-ups that are the "village structures"; a clerk gets Sasha to fill out some forms, crossing his legs, seemingly desperate to urinate—when the forms are completed he rushes outside, flings the forms into the air and runs away. Lots of tight close-ups, slow pans, long holds; a horribly jangling phone, local folk music on the sound track (not often enough).

The film opens in amber, amber screen for the titles then amber sands shot from overhead. Somber Asian faces: a psychiatric compound? A Russian doctor—long-haired, arty, a Slavic Patrick Swayze—is there in a medical setting, but he never actually attends to patients; he taps incessantly at his portable typewriter, at work on his study of an Old Believer community in Turkmenia. There are political exiles here, including Seventh Day Adventists. Volga Germans are also mentioned, as are Crimean Tatars. There is no plot or real story line, only a series of scenes/images that have an emotional depth from the way they are shot. E.G., a Russian friend commits suicide. There is a long, long take against a silent soundtrack of the local police in the dead man's apartment, talking to each other, picking up items, looking around, they take the body out on a stretcher (the dead man's toes—a recurring Russian image?), and load it in the ambulance. (Later the dead man speaks to Sasha and he experiences a terror freak-out; this alienating place has gotten to him.) Another haunting scene, simply done: a maddened soldier is tracked down and shot by a patrol; the body is viewed by Sasha. Filmed from afar.

Sasha has a friend, Dima, a local Crimean Tatar raised by a Volga German family, and they have a tender (homoerotic?) relationship. A particularly beautiful/powerful scene: after the encounter with the talking corpse, Sasha goes to Dima, shaken. He is comforted by him, and without actually touching, they kind of embrace in a contorted way, their torsos horizontally parallel to one another. At the end of the film, they part sadly.

Besides the exiles references, there is another "political" moment in the film: Someone leafs through some pages of a book with Hitler photographs while the soundtrack has the hackneyed speech of some Komsomol official.

Other characters appear and disappear—Sasha's sister; an eccentric historian and his wife; an angelic boy nursed back to health by Sasha. (That kid, of beautiful visage of course, is the one cloying, annoying thing in the film.)

The script is based on a novel by the Strugatsky brothers, hence reasonable to assume sci-fi elements.

Sokurov's melancholic mysticism and relentlessly ominous mood doesn't always work, but he is still the most original voice in contemporary Soviet cinema. Despite the new freedoms, he hasn't gone haywire like some others, and remains true to himself. *Eclipse* has the look and feel of his *Lonely Voice*, made (and shelved) ten years earlier, pre-*glasnost*.

The Second Circle: A Film by Alexander Sokurov
12/13/91, Walter Reade Theater

Sokurov is certainly Tarkovskian (down to interior rain and the sounds of water), but without his dramatic and narrative style. This is a depressing, not quite real-time film of a son's arranging for a father's burial. The mood, like *Stalker*, is dismal, as much from the emotional material as from the squalid settings and the squalid interactions of the few characters. Overall, the film is compelling and intense despite the paucity of content. The son is grieving, clearly, for reasons we never know. We know neither son nor father, in fact. Hence, the film is almost a documentary of a death and burial arrangements in the contemporary USSR. (Seeing it now, one cannot help thinking it is a metaphor for the squalid death of the USSR itself.)

The opening is characteristic: a driving snow, a solitary figure bending and then kneeling into the wind. Silence, then a roar of the storm; fade. [Long list of credits follows, rather ruining the mood.] Soundtrack filled throughout, sometimes deafeningly, with ordinary effects—knocks, bundles hitting the surface of a table or floor, running water, radio static. Blue-grey colors alternate with greens, monotints, grey and white. A favored camera angle is from above. Some scenes shot from a peculiar vantage—e.g., when the 3 embalmers silently go about their business, injecting the cadaver with fluid (one gooses the other), applying make-up to its face, the son stands silently in the kitchen and the camera captures all four through the doorway.

The son, evidently not a professional actor, is just right as the anxious, inept, but still concerned only next of kin. He is probably everyone's idea of Raskolnikov—poor, distracted, feverish. Not an intellectual though. Emphasized throughout—as I noted for *Eclipse*—the dead man's toes. In fact, in one particularly pathetic episode, the son takes off his own socks to cover the feet of the dead man, patters around barefoot as the casket is taken out of the building with great difficulty, then asks the others to wait so he can put on his shoes over his bare feet. Oh, the flavor of Dostoevsky, Oh what a sad place our Russia is. When someone comes to wash the body and is told by the son the pipes have cracked, there is no water, he hauls the cadaver out into the snow to wash it there.

Oddly, there is emotional depth, despite our not knowing the faintest thing about the dead man or his surviving son, or of their relationship. We know each lived alone, the son in another town. Father was a military man, though there was some kind of falling out with his superiors. Did he fight at Stalingrad?—the son goes through some pathetic possessions; among them is a cigarette case with the Stalingrad monument on its face. From the moody stares and from the way the son does his best to care for the cadaver and see to a decent burial, we know he feels something at his father's passing. There is a strange and powerful moment when the son opens the dead man's eyes and stares into them for a long while, as if trying to see something there that he hadn't known in life.

There are some revealing portraits of Soviet officialdom in action. The local coroner who has to turn to a little boy (a rather beatific little boy, as in the *Eclipse* film) for the proper medical term for cancer (a diagnosis offered by the son). (The little boy also tries to comfort the son.) A wry exchange: the coroner, an old woman, cites "Ilyich" in the struggle against bureaucracy. What Ilyich are you talking about? asks the son. Lenin, replies the woman with a straight face. Then there is the undertaker, a big Russian woman who is impatient with her wimpy and impecunious client. She bosses him around with venom in her voice and gestures, and with total disregard of the dead man or the situation. [The archetypical unsentimental Soviet woman who really runs that miserable society.]

Some surreal episodes: a hand-held camera films the son as he gets ill in a crowded bus; jostling blurred images—a dream?, we wonder; no, it really happened, we find out later. A bobbing head-shot of the son as the background moves behind him—reminiscent of the wonderful scene in *Stalker* where we discover the young daughter is not floating but sitting atop her father's shoulders. Here we never see what the son is riding on. A huge incinerator seems to look down over the town below, but then the son, who is burning his father's clothes and bedding, appears and he is the same size as the incinerator. Hallucinatory. (Same trick in *Eclipse* where a figure strides among the miniature mock-up of the village.) This is the penultimate image. At the very end: the pathetic squalid empty room. Then the message:

Fortunate are the nearest and dearest of ours who die before us.

Satan: A Film by Viktor Aristov
3/29/92, Museum of Modern Art

Yet another filmic pop sociology from the moribund USSR with its usual graphic, painfully ugly representation of daily life. The difference here is that real EVIL is presented, not just loose living, corruption, alcoholism and the other standard blots we have come to expect from candid portrayals of Soviet life in the era of *glasnost* when filmmakers and other creative people overdosed on telling things as they are. Here, the corruption is on a scale that takes it out of just the Soviet ordinary. The main character, a blandly handsome young man in his 20s, is a psychopath, clinically speaking, or if you like, an existential cold-blooded amoralist echoing memorable types in Dostoevsky, Camus, and Simenon. There is real depth here, unlike say *Taxi Blues* or *Little Vera*. The Dostoevskian echoes are especially strong in that the young man kills not for the money, just like Raskolnikov, although his motives are not intellectual as in

Raskolnikov's case, but personal—he wants attention, is tired of being a nobody. Other Dusty (Nabokov's wry name for Dostoevsky) echoes: his victim is a pre-adolescent schoolgirl, recalling D's grief at a world that allows the death of single innocent child. Also: a friend spouts some superman theory when he berates someone for maligning Stalin. Stalin, he says, belongs to a group of historic figures like Hitler, Solzhenitsyn, Einstein and Gorbachev (!) who comprise a special category.

The poverty and confined quarters, the feverishness, and also the detective story (though there are no detectives) aspect all also recall D. But though there is a real crime, there is no punishment and no redemption. Vitaly gets away with it, leaving a string of victims, not just the dead child. In the ending—a cheap shot that detracts—he smiles triumphantly, wickedly at the camera. Also the title is unsubtle and somehow diminishes things.

Reading the above, I find the film sounds a lot more powerful than it really is. The shooting style is very straightforward, naively so, the colors are those mousy blue greys we've come to expect from recent Soviet films, and all of the violent scenes—the murder, the two seduction/rapes are played without any dynamics or real shocking effects. It's almost as if Soviet filmmakers are still too prudish. The one exception: Svetlana Bragarnik's Alyona is chilling in her portrayal as the murdered girl's mother. Two highpoints: when she learns of the purported kidnapping—she wails and writhes on the floor, her back to the camera—and when she realizes her lover is the kidnapper/killer. But she also is good throughout as a high-powered woman in some vaguely powerful position with vaguely illegal connections (two burly comrades seem to know the underworld and promise to help her.) She looks a lot like Anna Friendlich, and even limps like what I remember Friendlich doing in some film (*Rasputin*?, *Stalker*?). Part of the absence of the shocking may have to do with rendering evil as matter-of-fact. That's certainly the way Sergei Kuprianov's Vitaly goes about his business. Whether he's hitting the kid over the head (we see this at a distance)—he does throw up, though; or enticing a bride, at her wedding, in full bridal dress to go off to some back hallway with him, then possessing her standing up (she has no choice he tells her, it would be too embarrassing, and no one will believe she didn't go willingly), or finally has his way with someone he's been after. When the mother resists, he simply excuses himself. "I have to go to the bathroom"—and disappears into the night. In between extortionist phone calls to the parents in disguised voices and his seduction/rapes he goes about things calmly, normally. Takes care of an old man in his communal apartment (shown for the hell such things are), pals around with an Armenian friend.

[Is the city Leningrad? No water though. He and his grandfather are from Buzuluk. A Bergman-like scene (from *The Silence*)—marching soldiers in the night, self-propelled guns.]

Opening: we know we're in for trouble and ugliness—dank colors, a fog, sinister percussion. Crowds. A pack of running dogs. A woman's body attended to by EMS. (Looks real.) The girl, innocently riding on the handlebars with him to school reports a plane crash locally, 200 dead. All of this means: Welcome to the Soviet Union! In the Era of Apocalypse!

Apparent throughout: sexism and the strong women, but even the strong ones are treated like shit. His Armenian friend is sleeping with someone whose name he gets wrong; she still wants to be with him, but he tells her to get lost. Vitaly picks up a homely woman at the wedding (after he's violated the bride, evidently a virgin); she's delighted by this, but he gives her the slip and she goes berserk in the city's night streets. (A street-fair/carnival *à la* Arbat is aswirl.) The strong single parent mother who resists him and threatens to call the police, finally can't fight him off. And there's nothing Alyona can do either: he's got too much on her. Even her husband didn't know she had all that money stashed away.

At the *poshlust* wedding, the father of the bride is a Pamyat type who rants about Jews and Israel and how all take advantage of poor Russia.

The only nice person in the film: the unnamed father, a two-bit actor, whose trips abroad Alyona cruelly tells him were her doing. Even the dead girl's younger sister, a mere toddler, is a selfish creature, who knows sister is dead and wants her toys.

At the end, Vitaly wanders into the night after his encounter with Alyona. Fade to morning: we see him with two girls aboard a trolley-bus. He's seduced them too. A triumphal smile (and the bush-league—self-referential—wave to the camera).

An existential thriller. Really among the most interesting films spawned by *glasnost*. Not saying much, but still....

[My friend, the *émigré* Artyom, reported that he was told it is a really good film, but he won't go see it, or others like it: too painful to recall the Soviet past, evidently.]

Hey, You Wild Geese!: A Film by Lidiya Bobrova
4/1/92, Museum of Modern Art

This, too, a piece of (what we may now call) late-Soviet filmic pop sociology. But with a difference, namely a severe almost modern primitive style that comes from straightforward narrative, the non-professional actors, the stark black and white, and the recurring folk-like title song (*Hey you wild geese, tell me what's my fate in this world/Am I ever destined to bear my pitiful lot?*). Another difference: this is not Moscow, but village or small town life in Southern Russia. The obvious reference is Shukshin, but with no romanticism. The film begins and ends with sepia tint: a musician, handsome, bearded in the peasant way, and his three sons, sometime in the 1950s when life was simple and signified hope. An outbreak of color with the showing of a typical Soviet triumphalist/sentimental propaganda documentary on the 1980 Moscow Olympics with tears and Mischa the Bear. Moscow's food, hospitality, and the enthusiasm of adoring foreigners contrast against the squalid lives of the locals watching the film.

It is the 80s. The sons have grown up: Mitya the child-like invalid simpleton (he has one lung and can't find work; he has an invalid's pension of 21 rubles) with a wife who drives herself to fainting spells trying to make ends meet for her husband and daughter by taking in sewing. (A problem: locating needles for her sewing machine.) Petya, an alcoholic stoker with a melancholy temperament and a powerful unhappy wife. Sanka, a hulking ex-con (manslaughter), given to drink and an occasional catatonic fit. What ties them together is not only their pitiful lives, but their shared memories of a happier youth. The accordion Mitya plays is papa's; it symbolizes the old family and its hopes. It is almost expropriated by the militia when Mitya is driven to play at the marketplace for money. The policeman has pity on him and lets him have it back. [Mitya looks remarkably like the White officer's Cossack orderly in *Chapayev*: full head of dark hair and beard, sad eyes, and broad face. Bobrova's camera loves to linger in close-up on his sad visage.]

Just a series of situations, no real plot—adding to the old-fashioned look and feel of the film. Almost like a silent film—even an episode out of Chaplin in which Sanka picks up an alcoholic tramp with a front tooth missing, feeds her, dresses her, takes her to the bath-house. There's a peculiar shift in the film's focus from Mitya to Sanka when the latter suddenly appears, looking a bit like a menacing Raymond Massey in *Arsenic and Old Lace*. Sanka almost runs off with Petya's wife, who was, obviously, his old girl friend. The note of menace continues with a bunch of ex-cons with ugly mugs sitting around drinking and singing with Sanka at Mitya's house. But nothing horrible happens, only daily life. Even the stray animals look beaten, as do the old folks sitting around waiting for dinner at some center. The closing: the older Raya still at her sewing machine, still looking for needles, Mitya feeding slops to the pigs and breaking out into song.

Oi, what a sad place our Russia is….

Bobrova worked up the script in 1981 and never dreamed then it could be filmed. It's a diploma film for Gherman's workshop. Taken from life, not fictitious. Not happy, unfortunately, "but that's our life."

Someone in the audience from Ukraine asks, does this really exist in Russia? Never saw in Ukraine! Someone else: yep, I saw it. Bobrova says, what's this, Soviet patriotism?

Distributors don't like the film, not commercial enough.

"Women not more aggressive, but stronger." It's true women in Soviet society the dominant force, "history shows it."

Raspad: A Film by Mikhail Belikov
4/14/92, 1600 Broadway Screening Room

Unfortunately, another misfire. An ambitious piece of work by an angry Ukrainian filmmaker determined to use Chernobyl as metaphor for the collapse of Soviet society and morality (see the interview with Belikov, Chapter VII, 2). Curiously, *Raspad* is never translated for western audiences: it means collapse, breakdown, disintegration. Not a bad idea in that Chernobyl did in fact reveal the Soviets' lousy technology, lousy maintenance, lousy deceitful and selfish authorities, and their lousy capacity to hide the dangerous truth even from (especially from!) their own people. And Chernobyl finally forced Gorbachev to really open things up and give meaning to *glasnost*—the candidness and de-moralization that characterized the USSR in the ensuing period certainly contributed to its collapse. Add the many fascinating real-life personal stories that unfolded during the disaster. And FINALLY, the apocalyptic overtones of this "wormwood" event...add all of this and there is potentially an engrossing docudrama with large emotional resonances.

Belikov tries to achieve all of this but the problem is the film is neither gripping docudrama nor effective melodrama. The characters are stereotypes without any depth and their stories are integrated poorly. Special effects and the docudrama format (time and place titles at lower left) are not up to the technical levels to have a real impact, despite the assistance of US co-production (e.g., post-production at Lucas's Skywalker Ranch). Some of the crowd and panic and evacuation scenes work well enough, as do some initial on-site shots—burning graphite on the ground, Reactor No. 4 spouting fiery radioactivity into the night sky, etc. But there is no tension and no spectacular impact. Even when the journalists climb to the roof of the reactor at the end the effect is wooden. (The program notes describe actual filming at the reactor site—Belikov even got a dose of radiation sickness—but I suspect that scene was a studio shot.)

As for moral decay, this theme centers principally on the journalist's family—he forgets to bring back soil from his father's ancestral Greece (and improbably faints when he remembers this at a party) but his carousing friends assure him if he shovels some local dirt papa won't know the difference; his wife is having an affair with a local influential pretty-boy (this is never really spelled out, and there is no dramatic development); a young couple getting married wants a doctor to hospitalize his dad so they can have some privacy; an operator tries to sell over-priced tickets at the RR terminal as thousands are desperate to leave. Even the priests are anxious to get away. Not very powerful stuff. The atrocious behavior of the authorities is shown in their arriving in limos at the airport making their getaways with their families even as they are lying to the public; in a local editor refusing to run anything on the disaster, preferring feel-good news; and in a spokesman denying anything major at a news conference (a cute touch: he tells an American journalist "did the Soviet public suffer any consequences from the Three Mile Island event?").

The best sequences involve the young married couple on a motorcycle seeking privacy in the countryside but only suicidally (and improbably) getting deeper and deeper into the contaminated zone, but we never know what happens to them, and some of what could have been tender moments are clumsily handled. Also a little flat: the helicopter shots of the deserted Pripyat below, and the little boy who stays behind waiting with his cat for his mother. (On the soundtrack: Albinoni's *Adagio*, endlessly used by Soviet filmmakers.) Both cat and boy are fatally radiated.

Overall, especially in the crowd scenes (and especially when in one of them a couple is fornicating standing up), and in the party drinking scenes (someone comments on the fatalist character of the Slavs), we do get a feel for a society going to hell with itself with the fire and brimstone of Chernobyl as the backdrop. And there is someone's bitter comment: "We are all to blame." Add also Vysotsky's mordant song rasping out at the end and you have the elements of a powerful statement. BUT only the elements.

Go Away!: A Film by Dmitry Astrakhan, Human Rights Film Festival
5/14/92, Columbus Circle Theater
[The Russian—*Izydi*—might be rendered as *Get Thee Out* (or maybe better, *Begone!*) as in *Izydi Satana!*]

A moving first film by the Leningrader Astrakhan set in Babel-Aleichem-Kuprin land before the Revolution in vodka-soaked *pogrom* time (see the interview with Astrakhan, Chapter VII, 2). Rich characterizations and rich social-cultural textures mark this yet another film in the modern Soviet series on Jewish themes flourishing under *perestroika*. Fiddler on the Roof without any gloss, but with tremendous vitality.

Motyl, a big man with lusty appetites, gets his Second-Guild Merchant permit to run a dairy in a village where he and his family are the only Jews living on very friendly terms among the gentiles. He has dreams of making it someday in Petersburg. There are nice family textures—his red-headed daughter (played a little too modernly) is the sweetheart of his Russian friend's son Petya; his wife's relatives come for a visit and never seem to leave; he lives it up with some prostitutes and his wife smacks him when she notices a hickey on his neck. But all of this is overshadowed by the *pogrom* we know is to come from the constant black and white visions that begin the film and are interspersed throughout. In a powerful denouement (real time now in black and white) Motyl decides not to run away, as his Russian friends encourage, but grabs an ax and marches alone to confront the Black Hundred mob that has already ravaged the Jewish population in town. His Russian friends, including the local constable, grab weapons and join him. This intense moment which builds from Motyl's other-worldly eye-bulging crazed peering into the distance is, I think, ruined by the cliché end: a freeze frame of Motyl's haunted face, then fade to white.

Some beautifully done moments:

- The tender nuptial scene in an old woman's cottage between Petya and Belka, now Yefrosinia. Just lie there and let him fool around, the old woman advises her.
- Motyl is enraged when he finds out. His mother tells him, I too went mad when your father first kissed me. Motyl: but that was Solomon Moiseyevich not Petya Ivanovich!
- After the shock and a moment's hesitation, Motyl's friend Ivan: "Motyl, we're relatives!"
- Motyl buys a cow for his drunken and treacherous neighbor (this guy is a bit overdone—constantly soused and ready to join the *pogrom* against Motyl, who is always kind to him).

Life was raw, colorful, dangerous. (A gypsy horse-thief is beaten to death.)

Terrific Motyl by the Georgian O. Megvinetukhtsesi.

The Stone: A Film by Alexander Sokurov, New York Film Festival Feature
9/28/92, Walter Reade Theater

I wish someone hadn't told the audience in a special announcement before the film at this press screening that the "ghost" described in the press kit was really Anton Chekhov. Would I have guessed it to have been him? Would it have been seen differently if we did not know it was intended as a returned Chekhov?

The answer to the first question is yes, I would probably have identified him as Chekhov—the actor [Leonid Mosgovoy] was a good image of the writer, particularly the writer we know from the photograph showing him in mid-years, with *pince-nez* and formal dress. The museum-house and its setting by the sea was also reminiscent of what I have seen or imagined as Chekhov's Crimean summer home. As to the second question, I'm not sure knowing or not knowing makes any difference. The film is so opaque it really doesn't matter whether it is Chekhov or some other ghost who has returned to his seaside house. This is Sokurov in his most riddle-like, impenetrable mode. There is no plot, no story, just a ghostly encounter in which nothing much happens, and rendered in black and white, with shadows, often through a distorted lens. There are several endlessly long, silent takes. I nodded off repeatedly, awoke, and discovered it was still the same scene. One of these was particularly moving, though, and remains in my memory: "Chekhov" stares, just stares intently for a long time at the close face of the young man who is evidently the night watchman. There is so much in that stare—amusement, love, curiosity, an intense curiosity like that of a person who can't take his eyes off a beloved son he hasn't seen in many years: how you've grown, how handsome you are, how you resemble my father, how is life treating you?....

The young man discovers an intruder taking a bath. The intruder acts as if he belongs in this fine old mansion. "How long are you here for?," he's asked. "Don't know. Maybe forever," he replies. He wanders around, plays the piano, tries on clothes, dresses (formally) for dinner. An egret appears. He advises the young man about his health (he is, after all, Dr. Chekhov). There's not much for dinner, just the young man's sausage to share. They drink from an old bottle (literally ink? or, it tastes just like ink?). A walk out of doors. Woods. The sea. Chekhov sits out a snowstorm on a bench. "There used to be an orchard," he observes a couple of times.

Back inside. Someone is at the door. Chekhov goes to see who it is. "I'm coming with you," says the young man. End of film.

At the end a dedication to Vladimir Soloviev (the pre-revolutionary mystic philosopher), and to a woman whose name I didn't catch. Hmmm.

An allegory here? With the end of the Soviet Union, the return of old Russia is inevitable and desirable. Shown here is the best of old Russian culture and thought, Anton Chekhov. He is amused and puzzled by the present; and of course by the nice Soviet touch—little to eat or drink. And they've destroyed the fine old orchard. He'll make the best of it; let's start all over again, with a cleansing bath. But hold on, there's an ominous knock at the door.....

Maybe.

Unfortunately, what is sometimes haunting here—in the silent, dark, visually riveting manner of Tarkovsky and Sokurov (more Sokurov)—is overwhelmed by tedium.

Close to Eden: A Film by Nikita Mikhalkov
11/14/92, Lincoln Plaza Cinema

Won the Golden Lion at the Venice Film Festival, 1991—Europeans are suckers for this kind of stuff, though the theater was packed on the Saturday night I saw it here, and it's been running for about a month. [Still running, 12/19]

Jointly produced with the French. The original title is *Urga*, the Mongolian word for the lasso-pole riders use for various purposes, including, evidently, capturing women—in the opening scene, a hooded rider, with blood-curling shrieks, chases another hooded rider with an Urga, successfully. The prey we discover is a woman; not only a woman, but the hunter's wife, who is boycotting sex because they have three kids already and besides, government policy, for the cities at least, limits families to one child. Also, the Urga, when driven into the ground lets people know that lovemaking is going on in the vicinity. The wife, whose beauty matches her handsome husband's, fights him off, and so begins a visually and anthropologically satisfying, but not very compelling tale of the clash between tradition (the Eden of the title) and modernization. And into a cluster of clichés enters a Russian, with all of his problems.

[Eduard] Artemyev contributes a haunting flute motif to the score. The script was jointly authored by Mikhalkov and [Rustam] Ibragimbekov, from an idea by Mikhalkov. Lots of sky. Frequent shots of the sun. The bare hills stretching to the horizon. The land of Ghengis Khan (no wonder he set out to conquer other lands: where's the Eden here?) [I had an amusing discussion of the new title translated back into Russian—there is a word for Eden, *Edem*, but no Russian would understand it.] The Mongol theme has of course a particular resonance for Russians, but not a pleasant one. Mikhalkov plays with this theme: Zomba wants another son, the child would be the fourth, like Genghis Khan. In a fantasy-dream sequence the great conqueror appears with his fierce retinue scourging all signs of modernity—a TV set, a truck; they wrap the Russian in a rug and drag him with their horses. This sequence looked so good that I thought perhaps this is the film Mikhalkov should have made—an old-fashioned adventure tale with the conquering Mongols, minus TV sets.

The handsome couple live in their yurt with their 3 kids and a grandma. A Russian comes their way when his truck gets stuck in the sand—he fell asleep at the wheel, and almost fell into a pond. They bring him home, he drinks their firewater, they slaughter and roast a lamb for him, and their daughter shows her skill with the accordion, playing and gesturing merrily like a seasoned performer (and in contrast to the primitive ambience), a *paso doble*, of all things. Sergei is good-hearted, sentimental, earthy—a Sibiryak who cries when the girl plays. He hits it off with Zomba. Anthropology: he finds a corpse rotting in the plain when he goes for help—it's only uncle, Zomba assures him, that's the way we handle our dead.

The wife is a city girl, and she wants a TV. Also condoms. So off Zomba goes to the city with her note about condoms (but he's too shy to get them at the local pharmacy). At the local hotel nightclub, with Zomba and a Russian pal (who wants to roll Zomba), Sergei asks the band to play "The Hills of Manchuria" and has them read the notes tattooed on his back. One hundred years ago my grandfather died for you (the 1905 War?). *Toska* amidst the disco dancing of the young folks.

Some nice sight gags back at the yurt. A Rambo poster. Grandma contentedly popping the bubbles of the plastic wrap for the TV. On the screen Gorbachev and Bush. And the Mongolian plains. The accordion whiz reads Sergei's tattooed notes.

The subtle as borshch flash-forward ending—the landscape defiled by smokestack and gas station; the narrator is the fourth son in a new modernized Mongolia.

Mikhalkov the social romantic, just like his brother in *Sibiriade*.

Shy Boy: An Uzbek Film Directed by Kamara Kamalova
7/26/93, University of Illinois, Urbana-Champaign

I know nothing about the film or the director, except what was printed in the Center's Calendar of Events: "...captures the awkwardness of adolescence and the challenges for those coming of age in the Stalin era of the 1940s."

Actually, I think from internal evidence the film is set [Tashkent?] in the early 1950s.

Moonstruck among the Uzbeks.

Elizabeth Talbott of the UI library told me it wasn't very good; what surprised her was how aggressive the women were portrayed in the film—unrealistically, she implied. But maybe not; this was still the post-war period (many references to men going off to the War), and there was a man shortage. Also, things were a lot looser on the frontiers for the Russians depicted here.

Not very professionally shot, and the sentiments and characterizations are rather primitive, but as usual with films from exotic places, there is a certain "anthropological" fascination. And several elements in the work impart a bit of depth and mystery, the lush, sad musical score, for one thing; the constant haunted, fixed stare of Alik the moonstruck young man infatuated with Maya, the saucy would-be actress. (Unfortunately, she is not as striking as his rapturous gaze suggests, nor is there much subtlety in her portrayal.)

There are lots of Russian-Uzbek overtones: mixed marriages, half-breed offspring, etc.—but this aspect was hard to follow. E.G., we know Alik's sister is married to an Uzbek, but is Alik himself a child of a mixed marriage? His father never came back from the war. His mother is clearly Russian—and she is rather strange, always working, charitably it seems, and this annoys Alik, who seems to hold things together.

Alik is handsome, and in the way Maya describes: powerful and gentle at the same time. He stares at Maya, follows her everywhere, can't bring himself to speak to her, and when he is to recite his lines to her in a rehearsal of a play they have parts in, he falls down in a dead faint. Finally, an aggressive Uzbek friend brings them all together for some sexual fun, and Alik pounces on Maya, to her horror. He retreats, and their affair is never really consummated, despite heavy breathing, some exposure of her flesh (she bathes in her underwear, while he averts his eyes), and his passionate declarations. A touching moment: he brings her his pet lamb.

In the busy courtyard where Alik and others live a subplot with a treacherous outcome takes shape. A local bully-bigwig lives there, and when he bruises Alik's sister (the big-wig's son pees on people below from his porch above), Alik is determined to right the insult, something his brother-in-law is too frightened to do. Finally, in a poorly realized scene (much tension had been building), Alik slaps the big-wig, who promptly has his thugs seize Alik and pile him into a waiting truck. Ominously, the big-wig calls for fetching Alik's "dirk" (a gift from his father) before they depart.

Next, Alik, wearing a workman's cap, clearly years later, returns from somewhere, staring at a mosque we remember from the opening scene, and heads first for Maya's; she is gone, he is told, and he notices a lambskin used as a doormat in front of what was Maya's apartment. Next, he heads for the courtyard. Everyone is at a wedding, the big-wig's older son's, Alik's grandma tells him, and pleads with him not to go there, to leave things be. But Alik goes, sees the merriment, watches the big-wig dance, his sister and brother-in-law too. What will he do? What has happened to him?

We wait.... and the credits scroll.

Was he castrated? I thought at first his tongue was cut out. You know, some Uzbek revenge blood rite. But we don't know.... And evil has triumphed—in the form of the big-wig's getting away with his crime, and the victims are silent and complicitous. A parable of Stalinism?

La Chasse aux Papillons: A Film by Otar Ioseliani
11/11/93, Lincoln Plaza Cinema

I'm glad I caught it on the last day of its New York run—[Vincent] Canby's mean-spirited pan, rather insensitive to its meaning, didn't help the film. I went in particular because a) it's Ioseliani and b) I wanted to discuss it with Aleko Tsabadze, a fellow Georgian filmmaker and exile (see the interview with Tsabadze in Chapter VII, 3). Aleko told me he didn't care much for it—and neither did I at first; I thought Canby was absolutely correct in his put-down of the film as third-rate Buñuel. There was about it that quality of what Soviet filmmakers think of as the kind of art they would make if only they could (and, unfortunately did, during the *glasnost* years)—non-narrative, full of disconnected images, absurdity displacing meaning, and, worst of all, NOT FUNNY, certainly not as funny as they think....

....But then.... I was soon caught up in the really underlying mood and meaning of the undertaking, the elegy for a world forever gone, remembered only in the daydreams of the *émigrée*. Of course, Ioseliani also takes not all too subtle pot shots at the moral squalor and greed of both the very rich—the French, Indians, and Japanese—and the very poor—the Russians. The first group at least have a certain, though faded grandeur, while the Russians have only squalor, material and moral. The moment I felt all this was when the film takes a sudden turn brought on by the death of the lady of the manor, an invalid Russian *émigrée* of great wealth, but not enough wealth to keep up the estate in really grand style. The news is telegraphed to her poor sister in squalid Moscow, and then begins the sad/funny tale of the distribution of the estate.

Up to that point I agreed with Canby: the pace was tortuously slow, and the satire heavy-handed, though very well acted, particularly by Narda Blanchet, playing the lady's cousin, an eccentric amid lots of other eccentrics. We are treated to a series of images, some of them quite beautiful, shot in a small French town. At the estate dwell a visiting maharajah, a band of Hare Krishnas, the Lady and her cousin, and a maid who doubles as everything else, including car mechanic. There is also a whiskey priest who has difficulty getting up in the morning and needs a pick-me-up to get him through mass. Cousin plays the organ at mass, and also trombone in a local band. Women come and go, riding their bicycles, capes billowing in the wind. The neighboring estate belongs to the notary, who complains that the Lady's gardener trespasses with his tractor. His son has a beautiful black girlfriend who periodically blows up at him; she throws an egg at him, hitting a fine old oil portrait instead. They ride, play boules and croquet, drink cognac, take target practice, and fish—cousin does this with a bow-and-arrow in the estate pond. They also steal—cousin too, placing silverware in the toilet tank—or does she do this to prevent the maid from stealing it? In any event, the black girlfriend pinches it. (She also acts as guide in the mansion of the notary, who also fancies himself an operatic singer.) Finally, a group of Japanese are on hand looking for a chateau to buy, and they have settled on the Lady's, nothing will shake them. All done in very nice deadpan, especially cousin's.

It all unfolds episodically in a gorgeous autumn, as befits the real mood of the film. Then the central story genuinely unfolds (all is merely preparatory): Mme. de Bayonette is reading some old letters and falls asleep. The ghost (played by Ioseliani) of her officer-husband hovers, lights a cigarette, and leaves it, lit, on an ashtray at her side. She dreams of a duel, beautifully shot, distantly, in which two young officers fell each other in the wintry morning. She awakes suddenly, feeling his presence, sees the cigarette, takes a puff and expires. The news is dispatched to various relatives, including the dead lady's sister in Moscow. This allows Ioseliani to have some sardonic fun: the telegram is received in an ancient telegraph office, a clerk uses some ancient glue to make two copies, one for the KGB file of course, the other is delivered to a communal apartment where the usual squabbles and shrieking among the communards fill the air. There, two old ladies, one of them Mme. de Bayonette's sister, read the news in her small room, decorated with old photographs. Her daughter, a dance instructor, is summoned; she walks through the queues-filled Moscow streets to the noisy apartment and learns of her aunt's death. "Now which one was she?," she asks, and is shown an old photograph. She calls France, the connection is lousy, and Ioseliani throws another barb: the KGB listening room. They arrange to go to France, and at the reading of the will sister learns she is the heiress to the estate. The relatives all leave, squabbling in their disappointment. How grubby are the rich, too. But the really incisive portrait is of the grasping niece who settles nicely into her new wealth: momma wants to clear the dishes, but she insists the servants are for that. She bosses the servant around. She savors the luxurious digs. Later, she pockets the money the Japanese pay for the estate, buys an apartment in Paris and throws a party for her Russian friends (one of whom is played by Alexander Askoldov). The vulgarity of the Soviet *petit bourgeois*. Meanwhile, poor momma sits in her new room, alone, discomfited, with only her memories. (Very nicely played by Alexandra Liebermann.) Much of this I got from the untranslated Russian.

In the end: the Japanese get their estate and practice village ways—bicycles to mass, etc.—and hang enormous banners in Japanese on the facade of the chateau. In the last scene the maid is instructed on how to operate the new massive gates with a remote. And, oh yes, the train carrying the Maharajah's private car, with cousin aboard, is blown up by unidentified terrorists (just as in Buñuel's film—was it *Discrete Charm*?)

So: a curse on all classes and nationalities; humans are a nasty quarreling, money-grasping lot. Or at least the modern species is. Perhaps there is a nostalgia here for the Russian aristocratic way of life long gone, existing only in fading photographs and in the memory of a poor old woman sitting in a lonely room.

In the end: I was moved.

Postscript: Why am I including this in my notes on *Soviet* film? Isn't this after all a *European* film, made in Europe, shot with an international cast, by a director who has lived and worked in Europe for several years? Well, you can't get the Soviet out of a former Soviet director. Or perhaps better: you can't get the anti-Soviet out of a former Soviet director. (Cf. the *glasnost* directors.) Absurdity that is humorless—fatal for the absurd. A huge cast of characters. A certain cold humor. What else? Very amateurish editing, seeking "European" effects like intercut images of no narrative import, middle and long distance shots. (Maybe this is a Georgian painterly dimension?)

Aleko Tsabadze, picking up my word, found the film irritating. He thinks Ioseliani, like many *émigrés*, smug and arrogant and derisive of others. [He thought this of the Georgian composer Kancheli whose work for viola and orchestra I heard at BAM last week.] His humor "cynical", his characters cold, his emphasis on "things" overdone. He also didn't think the shift to Moscow worked.

The Chekist: A Film by Aleksander Rogozhkin
3/21/94, Museum of Modern Art

This was a last-minute replacement for Sergei Ovcharov's *Drumroll*, which didn't arrive from Moscow. According to Kardish, this the first time in the 30-odd year history of the New Directors New Films festival that this has happened. Another sad commentary on the state of things over there....

The Chekist is a ...shocker is I suppose the *mot juste*. (Speaking of *mots justes*, I noticed at the end that the film was scripted by the French in this French-Russian co-production, which explains some of the heavy-handed political-existential themes informing some of the dialogue—"I hate; you philosophize," says the worker Chekist to the intellectual Chekist when the latter asks him if he ever feels any qualms about what he's doing.)

The theme: the constant bloodletting finally gets to Srubov, the intellectual, who goes berserk, inserts himself into the group of prisoners about to be shot, is only wounded, is committed to a psychiatric ward.

At first, the graphic grimy execution is powerful. The troika of Srubov, Katz, and the worker-Chekist coldly read off names of prisoners and describe them briefly (priest, anti-Bolshevik, aristocrat, merchant, *et al.*) : "Opinion?" Each answers: "Shoot!" Was there a single discussion or an exception from this routine? I don't think so. The prisoners, about half a dozen or so at a time, are told to strip—even the priest who begs exemption—to face a wall, then are shot by a group of Chekists with pistols. The corpses are transported by a flat dolly to another part of the basement, then hauled up to street level by rope, like so much cattle, dumped onto a truck, covered with tarpaulin, their limbs sticking out, and taken to be, presumably, incinerated. All this in vivid color. The blood and blood stains are then hosed down in preparation for the next batch. Often there are pleas to Srubov, sometimes by people known to him, but to no avail.

The action centers on the black-garbed chain-smoking Srubov who stalks about stonily. Here's the rhythm: troika says shoot; the cellar; Srubov watches; worker watches Srubov; Srubov stalks; repeat. After a while there is so much of this repetition, especially near the end with scene after scene of the executions that the effect is numbing and numbingly boring. All that nude hoisted flesh frontal and rear is shocking at first, but then... But then you realize that the intent is not to shock by piling it on, but to shock by the very ritualization of it all. (And I have no doubt that this is the way it very probably took place.) There are all sorts of moments: a bride and groom are married before execution; they hold hands as they are shot; a young man soils his underwear and a guard rubs his face in it; another man spits in the executioner's face, etc. Throughout, a heavy babushka cleans up (in one scene she polishes the floor with her foot *à la* the Cossack-orderly in *Chapayev*). She sees all, crosses herself when Srubov walks by.

In one startling scene I think was truncated, she is shown showering in all her blubbery flesh and watched by Srubov. He has just been asked by one of his victims, a doctor, "are you executing me because your wife told me you cannot consummate your marriage?" Did Srubov in the uncut version assault the babushka? Sex and violence, then, are related in the character of Srubov. As for the worker (Pepel? Pepelin?), he is accustomed to having his female secretaries run through rifle positions with him, after which they strip. One of them gets shot too, nonetheless. A petitioner brings her daughter into to see Srubov; she unclothes her and offers her to him; he is unmoved.

The executioner Chekists snort drugs. One of them refuses to shoot a priest. Later, he tries to hang himself.

Katz was responsible for shooting Srubov's own father. When S. brings him home for dinner, his mother is appalled. An interesting scene pitting Katz against an old Jew who knew him from the community. At one point Katz inserts Pepel's name into the list of prisoners: Pepel automatically responds: Shoot!

At the end, a dream-like sequence of men on horseback, b/w then color; an aerial pan; snow. The idealization of the Revolution.

We kill in basements says one of the Chekists, not publicly with the guillotine. The revolution is not clothed in Marx's white gown says Srubov, the angel of death. In one scene he releases a whole company after they have shot their commissar. A sign that he is cracking....?

Rogozhkin made *Karaul*, also about ugly Soviet violence (and sex).

For all its overt heavy psycho-political themes, the film is flat and uninteresting. But oh how once again it reveals what an abomination Russian filmmakers think The Triumph of October was.

Anna: A Film by Nikita Mikhalkov
10/31/96, Film Forum

I had heard quite a bit about this documentary shot by Mikhalkov over a 12-year period, each year filming his daughter and asking her the same questions. [What do you fear? What do you hate? What do you love? What do you want? What do you expect from life?] This is the Apted *7-Up* genre, but in Mikhalkov's hands the vehicle reveals less about his daughter—we hardly remember her answers, in any event rather banal, except her first answers (she would like a crocodile, she hates borshch), and learn little of her life and development aside from the visual indicators that she is growing up. (From these, she seems shy, and sensitive, unlike her self-assured kid sister Nadia—she of *Burnt by the Sun* fame—who is introduced at the end of the film as a possible subject for a similar chronicle.)

No, this is not a revealing longitudinal portrait full of intimate details. Actually, if revealing or intimate, it is about Mikhalkov himself, as might be expected, knowing his ego. And about the vast drama of contemporary history unfolding as the background to the chronicle. With, of course, Mikhalkov's commentary and preaching (and preaching) throughout. We hear of the Mikhalkov and Konchalovsky backgrounds, of his dear mother and her death, of his own happy childhood, especially at New Year's.

In part I guess his strategy was to use Anna's banal responses as evidence of the totalitarian state having captured her mind and soul. She fears wrong answers and worries about Brezhnev's health and peace and war. He had just finished *Oblomov* and began formulating the film in terms of Iliusha and Anna—and where did their convergence separate? (The opening shots of field and stream recalled immediately *Oblomov* and *Burnt*). They were both children of privilege growing up in Empires. He uses a lot of *Oblomov* footage throughout to parallel the chronicle. His conclusion: the divergence is accounted for by the loss of faith and God. (Does this mean the Tsarist Empire had God?) (The Soviet Empire had everything, he says, except God).

Narrated by M. in that sentimental slavophilic style. Shot, he says, or the press kit says, when home movies were forbidden. Mistake here: not home movies, but state resources (film stock, crews, archive footage, etc.) used without authorization is what was dangerous about the venture. Best parts, as usual, the documentary footage: a particularly pathetic episode—a trembling aged Suslov pins, tries to pin, I think Hero of the Soviet Union medal on Brezhnev's medal-heavy chest. (Kosygin glowers in the background.) The film, without Anna, could easily have stood up as a chronicle of those fateful years, from Brezhnev's doddering days and his death through the deaths of Andropov and Chernenko through Gorbo and *perestroika* and the coup and the death of the Soviet Union and the (what he sees as) moral Western-influenced degeneration of Russian society. The official public bombast of those years. A shot from a Lenin film. Pioneers. "Let there always be sunshine..." Brezhnev can hardly speak. Gorbo's provincial rhetoric (though M. admires for his achievement), and Yeltsin (a new Boss). Great shots of Red Square protesters shouting Resign! A sad Gorbo announces resignation. And no one, M. comments, fills his tea-cup.

Interesting also: banned footage from M.'s *Kinfolk*, referring to Afghanistan. And brief cuts of Russian soldier defectors.

A recurring image—a group of workers, waiting, waiting. Russian people's patience. The public life and the different private one.

At her last interview Anna, bound for Switzerland, talks of her love for this field, this wood and, with his prodding, says it's "better here" in our *rodina*, as a tear falls. Then: Nadya. Back to Anna: long shot walking down a road, her back to us. (An earlier touching moment: his son cries and turns away when queried on camera; M. comforts him fatherly.)

NB, he drives up to his dacha in his Mercedes.

All a testament to "the mysterious Russian soul."

Repeat: Best as a documentary of contemporary history, and certainly not as a portrait of his daughter.

The Thief: A Film by Pavel Chukhrai, 1998 (on video)

My general reaction was that this is a well-made "popular" film (with possible metaphoric overtones), but rather conventional-melodramatic.

A husband-less woman gives birth to a son on a dismal plain just after the War. We see them six years later on a train when their compartment is rudely entered by a handsome swaggering Captain in uniform who wastes no time in seducing the beautiful Katya. Sanya, the gorgeous little boy (who compares favorably with Kolya of *Kolya*) is transfixed by Tolyan—is he his real father? (In an early scene the boy imagines his father on the caboose of a train. This is repeated.). They are now a family and arrive in an unnamed town where they settle in a *communalka*. Sanya resents this wedge between him and his mother as they dance and make love (they shut the door on him during love-making). He begins getting into trouble, but "dad" stands up for him, and shows him how to be tough with bullies. He dazzles him with his Stalin tattoo ("my father") on his breast, and a jaguar on his shoulder. Oh, Tolyan is quite a charmer; he dances, plays the accordion, is generous…. but really, a talented con-man who gets the people in the apartment tickets to the circus. While they attend he empties the apartment of valuables. Katya objects but she is fatally hitched to him and his destiny. The three leave hurriedly. Next stop: the Black Sea (where he ignores a checkpoint shout for him to stop), and where they once again settle in as a family. This time he seduces a lonely neighbor so he can raid her apartment while she is at the movies with Katya. (He has

Sanya assist him in getting in.) Another get-away, but this time he is nabbed and jailed. Momma dies. Sanya is sent to an orphanage. As an adolescent he meets a wrecked alcoholic Tolik-drifter who doesn't recognize him. With the pistol he saved (along with Stalin's photo) he shoots him, fatally it appears. Next Sanya is a professional soldier in the killing fields of Chechnya. Is the old crazed man he meets Tolyan? No. He boards a train; a beautiful young woman asks for vodka (not to drink; for her infant). He gazes on the two; full circle.

The retro feel of the period well captured. Is it a subliminal spoof on *Fate of a Man*, and/or *Ballad of a Soldier*, or other Soviet films glorifying the ordinary soldier-Ivan? Some nice touches:

- Stalin toasts at dinners.
- Prisoners transferred to Black Marias; they run a gauntlet of guards and guard-dogs as their women watch and shriek. Here Sanya yells Papka! (as in *Fate of a Man*?).
- The feel of a Soviet train.
- Twice: as boy and adolescent Sanya pees in his pants in Tolyan's powerful presence.
- The recurring song: *La Paloma*
- A regular feature of Soviet films: the big dinner table loaded with food, drink, and merriment.
- Russian-film fascination with trains.
- Is his neighbor-victim stereotypically Jewish (big nose, sensuous, vulgar, rich)?
- The anti-hero. Or, hero as rogue. (Mashkov is clearly a box-office heart-throb, *à la* Menshikov.)

Up for academy award as best foreign-language film, but so far (March, 1998) no theatrical release here. Who was it that told me it was one of the best Russian films s/he had seen?

Brigands, Chapter VII: A Film by Otar Ioseliani
3/29/98, Anthology Film Archives

A multiple-source production (French, Georgian, Russian), ditto the cast. Locations in Georgia and Paris.

A disappointment: too long, too dull. The unimpeachable impulse is to mock men's follies and violence through the ages. We see medieval fighting aristocrats and their women (in Georgia?), the Bolsheviks/Chekists in the first years of Soviet rule (in Georgia), and the everyday street violence of civil war today, also in Georgia. All these centuries of bloodshed and greed have led only to more bloodshed and greed, its latest manifestations courtesy the new Mafiosi of the post-Soviet era. Naturally, Ios. chooses the absurdist style to show this within an unconventional structure—the episodes mix with one another, the same characters appear in each (men never change), and the whole thing is presented as a film within the film. At the outset, after the silent-film style credits, we see a vulgar crowd of strip poker players carousing; just as a woman tears off her bra, a young man from another room enters with an Uzi and mows them all down (even children are infected)—hold it, a woman tells a projectionist, you've shown the last reel first (a special screening for a group of big-wigs, smokers all; Ioseliani's producers?).

Then the film (within the film) begins—with the comic/absurdist street violence complete with tanks, high-powered rifles, and artillery (could apply to Sarajevo) in Georgia. The omnipresent hero (with a nose like Akhmatova's) wends his way unemotionally through all of this, revealing another trademark of the film—the matter-of-fact way everybody goes about their business killing, torturing, executing. Victims, too, are unemotional. (Yes, we do hear screams in the Cheka cellars.) Very reminiscent of Rogozhkin's *The Chekist*, and especially of Jansco's *The Red and the White*. Another stylistic affectation: speaking in soft mumbles, when anyone speaks at all.

Then back and forth in time, but always the same cruelties. With sword and axe if not AK-47s. The longest sequence involves the Red takeover and rule in Georgia. A pickpocket is recruited by the revolutionaries—we are communists they tell him, oh yes, he says, "freedom, happiness..." He becomes a commissar in the new regime (shades of Kamo and Koba-Stalin and the Caucasian bank raids organized by the Bolsheviks). Apartments are expropriated and re-expropriated, a father instructs a Pioneer-son on the instruments of torture and allows him to watch a session. "Was it interesting?" his mother asks. Silently he demonstrates nose pincers, ear gouging. But Pioneer also informs on his father and teacher (Pavlik Morozov!). Amusing sections here and there—an opera rehearsal, with Lenin and Krupskaya singing an aria, is interrupted by the arrest of Lenin. Later we see orchestra seats empty; players depleted by repressions. (In this sequence they speak Russian.) But all of this is shooting fish in a barrel....

Everyman appears in Paris, a *clochard*. (A survivor.) Meanwhile the New Russians when they are not killing each other are taking French lessons and learning the art of wine-tasting. (Mercedeses, Chrysler New Yorkers).

The final sequence sees the young man calmly calling the police to inform them of what he has just done. (The West is corrupt and deranged too?)

Some cute parts ribald and Monty Python-like in the Middle Ages section involving a virginal iron girdle.

At the end (phew!) the camera pans across the eternal mountain-filled horizon....

[Evidently the subtitle refers to his seventh film; all have been about Brigands.]

A Friend of the Deceased
A Film by Vyacheslav Krishtofovich
4/17/98, Sony Screening Room

I was very impressed by K's last film seen here, *Adam's Rib*, and looked forward to this (see my review in Chapter IV). I wasn't disappointed, but certain things got in the way and kept the film from being as successful as *Rib*. Present were the same lyrical-melancholic tones, but with none of the humor; rather not—this had a strong dark narrative; but the pastels were there, as was the simple sad sound track with its solo flute, solo piano, solo sax, and at the end, over the credits, solo voice in a plaintive folk song.

It is today's Kiev, where the young seem to be having a good time but others are in trouble, like the hero, the sad, dark, brooding, handsome Tolya (Alexander Lazarev—where have I seen him before?), an intellectual (translator) having a tough time finding decent-paying work and watching his marriage disintegrate—his wife is having an affair with someone at work. We never see him, but he has a flashy red Ford, symbolic of the aggressive "New Russians" or New Ukrainians who know how to make a "back" (they use the original in referring to money). He feels humiliated interpreting for a businessman (a nice scene: a tough dealer exacts a good price for oranges from an Indian exporter). Tolya runs into an old friend Dima who does well as a salesman at a shop with imported consumer items like Absolut. They drink together (a lot of drinking goes on) and Tolya lets him in on his wife's cheating. Simple solution says Dima; he has a friend who will off him for a price. (In today's Ukraine everything, including murder is a business deal.) He wouldn't think of such a thing, but when the guy calls him, he doesn't reject his proposal and remembers the details—a photograph of the intended victim, the bucks, and where and when the target hangs out, all to be placed in a postal box (query: would this professional killer reveal these instructions on the phone? or maybe he's not such a professional? The latter is plausible given what we see later, but maybe it's an irrelevant detail—it's very dramatic to only hear the killer on the phone—he sounds smart and very cool.).

Now here is the fascinating, Dostoevskyan twist on which the whole film should turn: Tolya, at the end of his rope, decides to offer himself as the victim. He has himself photographed, places the essentials in the postal box, and waits to be murdered at his favorite café. But he is fated to live: the café shuts down to accommodate a private birthday party. Now plastered, he celebrates his accidental reprieve from his self-imposed death sentence and picks up a jaunty young (and overplayed) prostitute for a night of sex—mercifully K. doesn't show us the usual boring scenes in bed, but he does reveal a lot of her flesh. The twist continues: he can't call off the original deal; it's just not done. Now he has to save himself from his own contract. His solution is to find another professional killer to knock off the first. He does, and it is done successfully. (The second killer is an older guy, an *Afghan* who does his executions with a six-inch knife.)

Now what? This is where the two elements of the film—his deep disaffection, and the thriller part, both working nicely together—

get scattered into a mess of new plot lines and characters, including a mawkish turn. The title of the film suggests that what turns up at the end, and offers an open-ended resolution, is really what the story should have been about. It is this: Overcome with sadness at what he has done, and having sifted through the dead killer's wallet (of course, a photograph of the wife and kid is there), he visits the widow, telling her he owed her husband some money. Naturally, she is very young and very beautiful and very grateful and very lonely with a cute young toddler to take care of, and what a way to wrap it up.... But not so fast: 1) Dima's shop is firebombed; 2) Vika the hooker reports physical abuse—I'll have him bumped off Tolya decides—he arranges it with his guy (whom we see again rather bitter and remorseful looking, sitting on a river bank fishing); 3) finding another "contract" in the postal box, he warns the intended victim of the coming hit.

All of this—overpopulation, excessive plots and story turns, and multiple possible endings, and several codas aggregate to undercut what could have been the neat concentrated power of the film, yet another example of the esthetic of the excess all too often wounding otherwise good efforts. (The otherwise is a real pity here because the film is so well made, with an economy of dialogue, fine acting, and effective, quiet camera work—medium shots especially.)

The press notes emphasize K's dissatisfaction with the crass current post-Soviet scene. In the old days, he argues, warm friendships made life bearable. Now business and profit rule. So his intent is to make a *chernukha* film about the present. I can do without this low-intensity nostalgia for Soviet times, though there is considerable merit in just showing how difficult it is for many—especially the sensitive "weak" types like Tolya—to fit in. Oddly, the overall mood of the film and its main character reminded me of the Cuban film, *Memories of Underdevelopment*. Oddly, because in the latter it is the socialist revolution that has destroyed the old society, an inverse of what has happened here.

Some items:

- He wears a cross. Throughout there are shots of the domes of churches. Cf. especially the beautiful opening shot of the gold

domes in medium range, then the camera pulling back to Tolya at his desk working the phone. The sad lyrical tone set at the start.
- Nice, underplayed set-up: we know with very little shown that he is disoriented and dispirited, and that his marriage is in trouble (they are not sleeping together; she keeps him away while she is in the bathroom, etc.).
- A beggar woman, a beggar child.
- Dima tells him he has a friend who "works with one finger", i.e., he pulls a trigger.
- A little too often, commentary: "who isn't a criminal these days?", "before we had friendships, now we have business relations".
- A cute reference to "Pavlik Morozov" (translated "as in Soviet times").
- The café carries only Gitanes and Gauloises, no Belomors. Vika brings him a bottle of Hennessey.
- Is it a tale of his learning the ways of the world the hard way, his own descent into corruption? Or is it left open-ended? (He calms the crying toddler who cries "Papa". Almost a freeze-frame last shot long held as he takes this in.)

Some Interviews on Personal Matters
A Film by Lana Gogoberidze
2/99, Brooklyn Academy of Music Women's Film Fest

Finally I got to see a film I heard so much about and wondered so much about. Not as radical as I thought it would be, but effective nonetheless as a daily life melodrama that raises pointed feminist issues within a nicely structured formal frame. Especially striking: "Sofiko" herself, played by the Garbo-like Sofiko Chiaurieli. The camera dwells often in tight close-up on her strong, knowing, suffering face. Gogoberidze introduced the film and pointed out that the reference to Siberian exile was omitted from the Soviet-Russian version. (In flashback, Sofiko's mother returns after a long absence.)

Sofiko is a hard-working journalist who juggles a full-time job with care for her family, whose husband complains of her neglect at home and who leaves her for another woman. Her current assignment is interviewing women about their lives—home, work, leisure, etc. Thus we get to meet a cross-section of types, including an independent feminist played by Nana Djordjadze, and there is much unhappiness. A wonderful queue scene opens the film as a woman moves from line to line asking others to hold her place. "What leisure time?!" she replies to Sofiko's question. Amid this we get glimpses of Sofiko's own difficult life and, through flashback, her mother's sad parting and sad return. In parallel structure we see the young and the old Sofiko seeking comfort from her young then old mother in mother's bed. Sofiko refuses an affair with a fellow photojournalist who adores her. (A touching scene at his apartment when he's painting the walls.) A very open-ended conclusion; nonjudgmental; the viewer decides what's wrong and who's to blame for the sadness in Soviet life.

Very slow-moving and much filler, but I liked.

In the Dark: A Film by Sergei Dvortsevoy
5/7/04, Tribeca Film Festival

Dvortsevoy's two previous documentaries I've seen were on nomads of Central Asia and on a remnant village in Russia populated by old folks. *Cinema vérité*; no narration. *In the Dark* follows suit, except there's a couple of self-references—D. inserts self into the action and we even see him once. In color.

Film centers on a blind old man living in an apartment on the outskirts of Moscow with his snow-white cat (Angora?). (He resembles a fleshier faced Sakharov.) He has a collection of spools from which he weaves net bags, the kind very familiar in the old days. He then tries to give them away to passersby, but gets no takers (at least on camera). Everyone passing by has at least one bag, usually the plastic kind, one with a Pepsi logo. Someone barks at him that the bags are old-fashioned. A woman stops to greet him then breaks into song (this felt very set-up). Most of the film—short, only 40 minutes—is taken up with the man (Vanya) slowly puttering about, locating his weaving staff, finding a spool, muttering

("Gospodi," most often; "Bandiuga!," to his cat.), weaving. All of this sad enough, but one sequence, unexplained, shows Vanya in close-up with tears flowing down his cheeks. Throughout, sounds of a schoolyard below.

Film cheapened I thought by too much following the cat and its mischief.

Neighborhood looks a bit like Moscow's Brateyevo—smokestacks, coolers in the background. Two homeless types, alcoholics both, it seems, gather bottles and cans. "Time is money," says one of them, an unlikely, ironic source for the adage that Weber defined as the essence of the capitalist sensibility.

All adds up to a sad portrait, not just of the old man Vanya, but of present-day Russia. Very reminiscent of lots of contemporary Russian documentaries.

3. Varlam's standing corpse shocks his son, both played by Avtandil Makharadze in Tengiz Abuladze's *Repentance* (1984)

CHAPTER II

Close-ups on the Past

One of the more mordant political jokes from the old Soviet repertoire, especially popular among scholars and journalists, had it that "the past is difficult to predict." The allusion was to the particularly Stalinist habit of making sure that writers of history stuck to Party- and State-dictated versions of the past, never mind the facts and objectivity—or else. And the official line was always shifting. Yesterday's heroes could become tomorrow's unpersons, as happened most notoriously to many of the Old Bolsheviks after the lurid Moscow trials of 1936-38. Major events and developments could be consigned to an Orwellian memory hole if they didn't conform to current politics and propaganda—accurate information about the scale of famine and carnage during collectivization of the peasantry, for example.

Officially dictated norms about the past continued well after the Stalin years. One of the welcome characteristics of **perestroika** *was a new willingness—at last!—to tolerate fresh views of formerly taboo subjects like the secret protocols of the Nazi-Soviet "Non-Aggression" Pact which sanctioned Moscow's takeover of the Baltic Republics, or the NKVD's responsibility, not the Nazis', for the Katyn forest massacres of Polish officers. On many controversial subjects, Soviet filmmakers of both features and documentaries during the* **glasnost** *period played an important part in reaching the public with alternative histories and honest investigations, as shown in several sections below.*

Not everyone in and out of government has, before and after the end of the USSR, favored the revisionist histories. The past remains controversial and politically edged well into post-Soviet times, into the age of Vladimir Putin, who called the Soviet collapse the "greatest geopolitical catastrophe" of the 20th century. Neo-nationalist or neo-Soviet attitudes have surfaced and persist today around such themes as assessing Stalin, or weighing Soviet vs. Western contributions in WW II and to the defeat of Fascism. Incorporating those attitudes into re-written school textbooks as officially mandated is a disturbing trend in the Putin era.[1] Like his Soviet predecessors, Putin has straddled the Stalin issue—yes, he committed crimes, but he industrialized the USSR, and led it to victory in WWII. Late-Soviet and post-Soviet filmmakers have preferred to stress the crimes.

---

[1] In 2009 the Russian government established a "Commission to Counteract Attempts at Falsifying History to Damage the Interest of Russia." In a letter to Russian Federation President Dmitrii Medvedev, the American Historical Association (AHA) decried what appeared to be the attempt "to prevent the expression and/or publication of historical judgments 'unfavorable' to Russia," and to even "criminalize historical thought." The American Association for the Advancement of Slavic Studies (AAASS) also wrote to President Medvedev, joining the AHA in "urging [him] to reassess the establishment of this Commission and to consider abolishing it."

1 On Stalin and Stalinism

I Was Stalin's Bodyguard and *The Akhmatova File*
Two Portraits: A Servant and a Victim of the Tyrant

The glory days of Gorbachev's *glasnost* unchained all forms of inquiry and expression, and one of the results was an almost obsessive—yet entirely understandable—confrontation with the ghosts of the Soviet past, especially Stalin's ghost. To their credit, Soviet filmmakers, through both features and documentaries, had a hand in the new historiography; in some sense, they even led the way, outpacing historians and publicists. Certainly, they reached wider audiences, especially through television. Back in those days, a Soviet viewer had only to flip the television dial to view yet another compilation of archival footage showing faces and scenes long shelved but once familiar during what used to be described euphemistically as the period of "the cult of the personality". There was Stalin. There were his adoring masses passing in review. There were his boys, the Berias, Molotovs, Kaganoviches and other political thugs enjoying themselves or carrying some comrade's coffin at a state funeral (probably enjoying that, too). And there were the victims—writers, generals, Politburo members, scientists, ordinary folk.

Two films offer American audiences the work of the Leningrad documentary filmmaker, Semyon Aranovich, who fashions those old images and other later ones into some fascinating portraits. In one film Aranovich focuses on an ordinary servant of Stalin, a member of his guard; in the other, on one of his famous victims, the poet Akhmatova. From different angles, both give us a good personal look at the special atmosphere and compulsions of the Stalin system.

The Russian subtitle for *I Was Stalin's Bodyguard* (1990) is "An Experiment in Documentary Mythology". Aranovich wants to show not only the forms of Stalin's rule from above, but the other side, the forms of obedience from below that contributed to legend-making. Alexei Rybin, born in 1908, is on pension, having begun his career in the Soviet security services in the early 1930s. We see him in his apartment, his chest full of ribbons, still proud of his past, and full of talk about it. (A mark of Soviet documentaries: the endless talk of the interviewee.) Or he plays the accordion, ending his days happily, teaching kids to sing in a chorus, "to create a person useful to our socialist society."

Often Aranovich gets Rybin's face in very tight close-up, as if the camera itself will reveal the secret of the man, the reasons for his love and devotion to Stalin. It is the visage of the people of Central Russia, with their straight dark hair, flat features and high cheekbones; there are gold teeth, and now many age marks. This ordinary Russian saw Stalin up close and revered him. Chatting away, anecdote after anecdote, Rybin describes the Good Tsar surrounded by Wicked Courtiers. Beria the lecher. Khrushchev the cheat. Kaganovich the "foul-mouthed." Vasily, Stalin's son, "the good-for-nothing." By contrast, Stalin himself was a modest fellow in his old boots and simple tunic. He knew all his guards personally, invited them to drink with him, gave pedestrians a lift, and increased his cook's pension. Stalin liked venison and fried eggs, and enjoyed playing skittles. Rybin, who was in charge of security at the Bolshoi, claims Stalin understood art better than any performer, and knew his *solfeggio* perfectly. When he had to be cruel, it was for the good of all. He could also suffer, as when his wife committed suicide. Rybin remembers a brooding Stalin sitting and smoking by her graveside at night.

Aranovich allows Rybin to tell his tales without commentary, intercutting often with old footage, much of it new for us. His portrait of Stalin rings true; it is consistent with other reports of people close to him. Stalin was plebeian by origin and in his tastes, and cultivated the populist style of an old true Bolshevik. Other tyrants too have been kind to their servants and shone by contrast to the vulgar toadies around them. Never mind Stalin's crimes. Never mind that certain personal features are left out, Stalin's temper, for example, or his inner vanity and his colossal suspiciousness and vindictiveness. That is not the point. By the end of the film we understand Aranovich's text: *it is not about Stalin, but about a Stalinist.*

Alexei Rybin, the bodyguard, is one kind of survivor of the Stalinist system. Mercifully, there were others, its victims, who outlived the tyrant and savored the attack on his reputation and the partial dismantling of the system associated with him. One such person was no ordinary Russian, but the great lyric poet Anna Akhmatova.

Anna Andreevna Gorenko, born in 1889, adopted the pen-name Akhmatova, derived from one of her Tatar ancestors. She published her first book of poems in 1912, as a member of the "Acmeist" school, and her subsequent work, sensuous and personal, established her as one of the very few great voices of Russian poetry in the 20th century. She died in 1966, having seen, as she wrote, "events unparalleled at any time."

That was a typical understatement. Not only did she witness the calamities afflicting Russia—war, revolution, civil war, the Great Terror, World War II, the culture of Stalinism—but she and her muse were its direct victims. Her first husband, fellow Acmeist Nikolai Gumilyov, was executed in 1921 (under Lenin). Her second husband, art historian Nikolai Punin, was arrested in 1935 (under Stalin) and subsequently perished in the camps (as did another celebrated Acmeist, Osip Mandelshtam). Her only son, Lev Gumilyov, was arrested four times and spent 18 years in the camps. Akhmatova herself was alternately silenced, tolerated, silenced. The most furious assault on her work came in 1946, when Stalin's culture boss, Andrei Zhdanov, described her as "neither nun nor fornicator, but really both of them, mixing fornication and prayer."

And through it all, Akhmatova wrote. Though not a political writer, probably her best known work is a grim cycle of poems, *Requiem*, bearing witness to the victims of the Great Terror from the point of view of their wives, daughters, mothers.

In *The Akhmatova File* (1989) Aranovich captures the somber mood of those years when writers were routinely assaulted as enemies of the state. Skillfully, he weaves together old stills, photos, documentary footage, and recurring shots of Akhmatova's funeral and lying in state. As in *I Was Stalin's Bodyguard*, there are many sequences of Stalin and later Khrushchev and their entourages in various settings. Structurally, the film is a kind of morbid contrapuntal drama in which the poets are in counterpoint to the bosses. Akhmatova, Mandelshtam, Tsvetaeva, Pasternak vs. Stalin, Zhdanov, Semichastny, Mikoyan. (There is a striking sequence from the 1930s showing the young Anastas Mikoyan, later associated with de-Stalinization, extolling Stalin and the NKVD, the KGB predecessor.)

The music synthesizer in the sound track may be excessive (another all too familiar and sometimes irritating feature of Soviet documentaries), but the voiced over cadences of Akhmatova's poetry and prose and the reminiscences of her friends are haunting. There is no narration, and the frequent flashbacks and flashforwards might confuse an American viewer who is not acquainted with Akhmatova or her fellow writers or the political figures who had the power of life and death over them. The documentary by Jill Janows, *Fear and the Muse: The Story of Anna Akhmatova* (1991), produced for the Center for Visual History and shown on PBS, is a more accessible introduction to Akhmatova than Aranovich's more complex film. (Janows used much of Aranovich's footage.)

Among the great pleasures of this sad film are the many photos of the young Akhmatova—dark, slender, sinuous—and her stunning profile with the geometric nose. If an artist were to imagine a Russo-Tatar poet of the first decades of the 20th century, she would look like Akhmatova. (Artists and photographers loved doing her portrait; Modigliani did a simple, expressive line drawing of her in 1911.) In her later years she had grown plump and matronly. But she had survived, her spirit intact.

[*Cineaste*, XIX, 2-3, 1992]

Repentance

In 1962, during the first bloom of de-Stalinization in the USSR, Yevgeny Yevtushenko openly assailed the "Heirs of Stalin" in a celebrated poem with that title. Stalin's corpse had just been removed from the Lenin mausoleum in Red Square and his remains reinterred beneath a simple slab at a more modest spot by the Kremlin wall. Yevtushenko used these events for his striking imagery:

I appeal to our government
With the request
To double
To triple
The guard at this slab
So that Stalin may not rise,
And with Stalin
The past...

In a new flush of de-Stalinization two and a half decades later, a Georgian cinema-poet, Tengiz Abuladze, resorted to the same imagery to make a similar point. Yevtushenko wants to keep his tyrant *buried*; Abuladze has his heroine repeatedly *disinterring* the dead tyrant of the film *Repentance*. (Or, alternatively, both want to keep their tyrants out of honored resting places. Yevtushenko: *As long as Stalin's heirs exist on earth/It will seem to me/That Stalin is still in the Mausoleum.*)

This is symbolism with a serious purpose, but there are also comic possibilities here, as Hitchcock showed in *The Trouble with Harry* (1955). For the first section of his film Abuladze, too, has some fun with the idea of digging up a dead body; we are in for a political comedy-satire, one might think. But it becomes clear that the heroine's body snatching is also Abuladze's clever McGuffin, designed to get her arrested and put on trial so she can unfold the criminal history of the local tyrant Varlam. Exit farce (temporarily); enter tragedy. Ketevan Barateli, the heroine (played handsomely with a quiet, cool bitterness by Zeinab Botsvadze, who looks like a Georgian cousin of Vanessa Redgrave), tells the court how Varlam terrorized her family and sent her father, a painter of religious themes, to his death in the camps. Varlam is still alive, she announces, for "as long as you defend him, he lives and corrupts society." (Yevtushenko: *We rooted him/Out of the Mausoleum./But how to root Stalin/Out of Stalin's heirs?*)

The setting is the present, and Ketevan's story tells of the not-too-distant past. Yet the guards and judges at the trial wear medieval vestments, as do Varlam's retinues in flashback. At a real trial in 1938, the climax of the Great Purge Trials staged by Stalin, one of his most prominent victims, the later rehabilitated Old Bolshevik Nikolai Bukharin, managed to allude to the "medieval form of jurisprudence" at work in the modern, progressive USSR, as in the "confessions" of the accused. Were Bukharin's words the idea behind Abuladze's puzzling medieval figures? Perhaps; an historically sophisticated viewer might read it this way. But even the unsophisticated could not fail to understand another reference: Ketevan's judges, "the heirs of Varlam," decide to put her away in a psychiatric ward, much as many dissidents had been disposed of under "the heirs of Stalin."

So Abuladze juggles past and present, juxtaposes different times, places, and moods; there are abrupt transitions, and dreams within a dream, and unmistakable historical references within a fantasy, or fantastic encounters within a history. Varlam is at once comic and demonic, a buffoon and a sadist; now you see him, now you don't. These rather self-conscious avant-garde, often stagy devices make it a difficult film at times, but not nearly so difficult as the matter of evaluating it, for there is *Repentance*, the Soviet movie, and there is *Repentance*, the Soviet Event. If the quality of the movie were equal to the magnitude of the Event, *Repentance* would be a very great film indeed. It is far from that, though there are many compelling moments in it. The performances are of the highest order. There are rich visual textures (a fondness for the color red). Given the Soviet context, Abuladze also took quite a few risks, esthetic and political. (Gruziafilm, the Soviet Georgian film studio where it was made, is known for its offbeat directors.) Still, too many seams show amid the range of styles—from the realistic to the satirical to the surrealistic. The humor is often heavy-handed and the symbolism is laid on with a trowel. And, somehow, this ardent indictment of political crimes—of Stalinism—is often boring and unmoving.

Nonetheless, *Repentance* had become a kind of flagship of Gorbachev's *glasnost* and *perestroika* campaigns, and not just in the arts. The film was emblematic of hopes for renewal in all institutions of Soviet life. To succeed, any genuine renewal had to shake off the past, first of all by confronting it honestly; next, by unapologetically condemning tyranny, whatever its ends and name; and last, by indicting complicity by silence, especially when the silent remain heirs and beneficiaries. This is strong stuff for a Soviet movie, but all of this *Repentance* does, more or less, directly or indirectly; there never has been anything quite like it, and like its impact, in the USSR. People wept and applauded at the first screening of *Repentance* in Moscow; 700,000 came to see it during opening week. It also captured much attention abroad, though hardly comparable to the reception at home. (One simply has to be a Soviet citizen, particularly of an older generation, to take its full measure.) It won a special award at Cannes and was the official Soviet entry for the 1987 Academy Awards.

Repentance took its place with other powerful Soviet works of art on the Stalinism theme that were once suppressed and then became available to the Soviet public. Like *Repentance*, such efforts as Akhmatova's grim poetic masterpiece, *Requiem*; Anatoly Rybakov's novel of the terror atmosphere of the 1930s, *Children of the Arbat*; and Vasily Grossman's epic set in World War II, *Life and Fate*, are all soaked in blood and tears. In the USSR, artists preempted the historians in stunning the public about the past.

How do you convey the experience of Stalinism in film? The hallowed traditions of Soviet cinema and literary realism might have pointed the way. Two wrenching scenes in *Repentance* are in this mode. In one, a dreary queue of women and children approaches an unseen agent at an information window for news of their imprisoned men. (The ever-waiting, ever hopeful women: the theme of Akhmatova's dirge.) In an unfeeling voice the agent provides just enough information to let the anxious women know whether the men are alive or dead. In another, related scene, women and children gather at a railroad siding where some timber has been dumped to search for messages which their imprisoned men in work camps might have carved into the logs. It is an anguishing sequence, shot from above without sound, except for some soft music by Arvo

Pärt, sad and stately as in a pavane. Suddenly, a woman comes upon a simple inscription from a loved one; she throws herself on the log, crying, and caresses it, slowly and lovingly.

All of this belongs to the wretched history of the Gulag, which could provide endless subjects for Russian filmmakers for years to come, just as it had already made its way into Soviet literature, officially published or in *samizdat*. It may be that the realist method is the most effective for capturing the emotions about such subjects, but Abuladze, save essentially for those two scenes, preferred to convey his argument in the poetic and surrealist language of Georgian and other Soviet cinema. Many sequences in *Repentance* will remind you of dreamlike passages in Tarkovsky; likewise the strong religious overtones and frequent Christian motifs and symbols in the film.

Above all, Abuladze cast his tale in the form of an absurdist fantasy, with comic moments jostling with tragic ones. There is a certain logic to this. The history of Stalinist and other tyrannies is full of the absurd, the irrational, and inexplicable. If everything is permitted the tyrant, then the arbitrary and the random come into play along with 'rational' policies of terror and intimidation. In one grotesque scene, the dictator Varlam has ordered everyone with a certain family-name rounded up; then he remands the order, professing ignorance of it and concern over its injustice; then he backtracks and lets the order stand. The Soviet record in the Stalin years was filled with such absurdities. (Abuladze has said characters and incidents in the film were drawn from life, including this one about the victims with the same family-name.) Moreover, in an atmosphere of institutionalized terror, the security forces get carried away, as do gossips, grudge-bearers, paranoids, and plotters coveting the victims' jobs and apartments.

There is another challenge: How do you portray Stalin-Beria? Historical figures in general are notoriously difficult to limn. Too much imaginative license may strain credibility, while striving for historical accuracy may yield lifeless stereotypes. Sometimes the most effective technique is the full-blown, uninhibited caricature. Humor is also a fine weapon against tyrants, as Chaplin understood in *The Great Dictator*. As played very broadly by Avtandil Makharadze, who also doubles brilliantly as his son, Varlam wears

Hitler's toothbrush moustache, plus a version of Beria's pince-nez, and Mussolini's black garb, with black leather belt and suspenders. The physical resemblance to Stalin is negligible, although Varlam's corpse in profile occasionally recalls the aged Stalin. Abuladze has said Varlam is timeless and serves as a composite for all tyrants. I don't believe that for one minute; and try telling that to old Soviet audiences, especially those in Soviet Georgia where Beria terrorized people for years, rising up the ladder of the security organs to a position of Party chief, running things as if in his own fiefdom. From Georgia Beria climbed to positions of Party and government power in Moscow over, in Khrushchev's words, "an untold number of corpses." Beria had a reputation for personal brutality and lasciviousness, and pretensions of culture, with a liking for classical music. Many of these qualities are brought out in the film. Varlam sings Italian arias, and ogles the artist's wife. Varlam also exudes an "innate oily cynicism," as someone said of Beria, but he never forgets a slight and has a nasty vindictive streak, features Beria shared with Stalin, whose faithful servant he remained until the latter's death in 1953.

All in all, far from being a vicar for all tyrants, Varlam is really Beria, who was Stalin's vicar. Why not then portray Stalin directly? Stalin was a much more interesting and complex figure than Beria, as countless biographers, historians, and memoirists have shown. The best portraits capture the undeniable stature of the man, but a stature built largely on personal cold-bloodedness, and great political agility. He had none of the pretensions and hysteria of Hitler and Mussolini, and displayed large doses of crude humor, of the gallows sort. (There is much of all this in Varlam.) Revealing profiles of Stalin appear in such works as *Conversations with Stalin* by the Yugoslav ex-communist Milovan Djilas; Solzhenitsyn's novel *The First Circle*; the reminiscences of Stalin's daughter, Svetlana Alliluyeva, *Twenty Letters to a Friend* and *Only One Year*; and an uncanny exploration, part fancy, part fact, that bears a spiritual kinship to Abuladze's concoction—*The Red Monarch*, by Yuri Krotkov, a Soviet émigré from Georgia. None of these works were published in the USSR before *perestroika*, although they were hardly unknown. Besides, there was plenty of home-grown material available on Stalin lying around in private drawers and restricted archives, and in people's memories.

In 1984, a direct portrait of Stalin was still impermissible, hence perhaps Abuladze's somewhat evasive approach, despite the conceptual boldness. Even most of the enthusiastic contemporary Soviet press discussions of *Repentance* I read were less than candid and had a self-congratulatory tone about them—"See, we now have been honest with our past; look at Abuladze's film." These reviews were clouded over with platitudinous generalizations about tyranny and avoided *naming* Stalin and Stalinism as the issue, though those subjects were clear as daylight to Soviet filmgoers, certainly of the over-thirty generations. There were reports from the USSR that youthful audiences there did not get it; they remained, thanks to the big memory holes that defaced official Soviet history, ignorant of the enormity of Stalin and Stalinism. A young Soviet *émigré* I knew was angry at Abuladze's film for precisely this reason; why all this allegorical beating about the bush, he wanted to know, when a straight-forward indictment that named names and used the S-word would have done the job? Did the form of the film reflect an assessment on Abuladze's part of what the political climate would permit, or was it purely an esthetic option? So often in the past Soviet filmmakers seemed to have entered into parallel, unacknowledged bilateral agreements with their political bosses and their audience: to the former they promised a respect for certain proprieties; of the latter, they asked, look for the subtext behind the proprieties. (Seeing a Soviet movie is such a complex business!)

In any event, things changed during *perestroika* and, of course, after the collapse of the USSR. Real biographies of Stalin began appearing, unlike the ritualistic hagiographies of the distant past, and in contrast to the absence of any biography in the more recent pre-*perestroika* past. Filmmakers, too, offered their portraits. There is a sense, however, in which Abuladze's expressionist composite, with Stalin immanent in Varlam's Hitler-Beria-Mussolini character, is even more devastating than a direct portrait, for it links up Stalinism with Fascism and Nazism, something considered quite anathema in official Soviet and even post-Soviet ideology.

Lavrenty Beria was executed not long after Stalin's death, while Stalin himself, so far as we know, died conventionally of a stroke. Abuladze's Varlam succumbs after a terrible fit of paranoia and guilt: poetic justice, if not historical accuracy here. (Stalin may have been paranoid, but the record reveals not a trace of guilt.) Varlam's heirs are happy to bury him and go about their comfortable philistine lives. After they deal with the grave-despoiler and her taunts, Abuladze's fantasy-farce turns soap-operatic. The denouement is a let-down, a series of somewhat clumsily constructed episodes in the present by which Varlam's grandson finally exacts his own and his father's *repentance* for the tyrant's crimes.

A weak ending, a confusion of forms, and much structural incoherence: no matter. Whatever its defects, Abuladze's film has a moral vitality that merited the gratitude of the Soviet public. For the Soviet and post-Soviet film industry, it was the brave harbinger of the long overdue reevaluation of buried heroes and buried demons. Can you imagine what a rich source for screenplays Soviet history can be, free of falsifications and official dictates?

[*Cineaste*, XVI, 3, 1988]

Burnt by the Sun

One of the murkier chapters in the history of the Soviet security services relates to their activity among 'White' *émigré* groups, especially in the two decades after the 1917 Revolution. The capitals of Central and Western Europe pulsated with the anti-Red politics of the *émigrés* in those days, and Moscow riddled them with agents, often recruited from among the *émigrés* themselves. Decisions to turn coat were not easy, and often complex in motivation. Some of the *émigrés* had a change of heart about the Soviet regime and were willing to work for it; others, ardent patriots, placed Russia above their politics, even if it was now *Soviet* Russia. Then there were others who simply wanted to get back to the motherland, and were willing to contract with the devil to realize that wish, which may have meant agreeing to assist in the "liquidation," as a Politburo directive put it in 1923, of "especially dangerous enemies of the Soviet regime."

One of the most scandalous of such cases centered on Sergei Efron, husband of the great lyric poet, Marina Tsvetaeva. Efron fought for the Whites during the Civil War, made his way out of

Russia, and eventually settled in Paris, writing and editing, and even working as an extra in French films to make ends meet. But politics was his passion—politics and Russia. His political sympathies flip-flopped, and he was active in trying to reconcile the *émigrés* to the Soviet regime, encouraging a back-to-Russia movement. His own attempts to return were denied by Moscow. Perhaps he was already an agent and this was part of his cover? Perhaps he was forced to do a little dirty work in exchange for permission to get back? We don't know. What is known is that in a celebrated Swiss trial for the murder of Ignaz Reiss, a former Soviet agent and defector, Efron was named as a Moscow operative, something long suspected by the *émigrés*. (He was also implicated in the murder of one of Trotsky's sons.) Efron promptly disappeared, and turned up in Russia living in a government dacha outside of Moscow. Later, he disappeared again, this time for good, probably into the dungeons of the Lubyanka.

There is wonderful dramatic and psychological material embedded in this sordid stuff, and not just for the historian. Parts of this story are depicted in Nikita Mikhalkov's engrossing *Burnt by the Sun*, winner of the 1994 Oscar for Best Foreign Film.

Mikhalkov is a resourceful and prolific filmmaker. Not all of his films have been shown here, but those that have reveal an ability to reach Western audiences shared by few modern Soviet and post-Soviet directors. He gets magnificent performances from his actors, often in virtuosic ensemble efforts. His films look good; they are painted in rich colors, and his camera and editing are always lively. He is a romantic and a Slavophile who dotes on sentiment, and his vivid characters inhabit melodramatic scenarios frequently drawn from Russian literary sources. *"A Slave of Love"* (1976), *Unfinished Piece for Player Piano* (1977), *Oblomov* (1980), *Dark Eyes* (1987), and *Close to Eden* (1992) display a talent for successfully uniting very 'Russian' themes with the conventions of global cinema.

In *Burnt by the Sun* Mikhalkov gets very Russian indeed; he manages, mostly successfully, but sometimes irritatingly, to fold Chekhov into the terror-ridden atmosphere of the Stalinist 1930s. The result is a compelling historical melodrama, but one quite reckless with clichés. Deadly Russian Roulette? Yes, the film begins with such a sequence. The beloved bathhouse? That's next. Indolent gentry hanging about the dacha? The mix of humor and pathos—the laughter through tears? A Gogolesque touch or two—a poor lost truck driver wandering around in circles? Yes, it's all there. It would all be shameless were it not redeemed by the film's powerful emotional crosscurrents of an unusual love triangle tinged by sinister purpose, and—especially—by a terrifically explosive denouement layered with psycho-political complexity. And this is Russian, too: everyone gets it in the end; there are *crimes* and there is *punishment*.

The monstrous evil of Stalinism, 'burning' even those who worshipped its radiance, certainly comes through in the film. (Mikhalkov quotes a popular tango of the day throughout the film to make this bitterly ironic point. He converted the name of the tango, *The Wearied Sun*, into *Wearied by the Sun*—or as in the English title, *Burnt by the Sun*.) But some of the details may be lost on the Western viewer. Mitya, the returned *émigré*, played brilliantly with a combination of charm and menace by Oleg Menshikov, is modeled on the Efron-like *émigrés* described above. Through a series of devices, sometimes very strained, amid the Chekhovian goings-on at the beach, or in the richly populated dacha, we are fed bits of information letting us know that after fighting against the Bolsheviks and surviving the Civil War, he emigrated to Paris where he knocked about, sometimes earning money from his musical and dancing talent. At one point he tells someone that he works for the NKVD (a Stalinist predecessor of the KGB), a jest of course.

Of course it's not a jest. Mitya was recruited to finger White officers in Paris for the NKVD. His reward—he is allowed to return to Russia. More, he is asked to supervise the quiet arrest of a Bolshevik Civil War hero, Colonel Sergei Kotov, at his country dacha. Remember, this is 1936, the high season of Stalin's terror, when even revered party, state, and military officials were mowed down by the security apparatus. Contrary to what many viewers concluded from the documentary-like title cards at the end of the film, Kotov was not a historical figure, but, like Mitya-Efron, a historically-based composite evoking the memory of many larger-than-life Soviet military heroes victimized by Stalin's murderous paranoia. (One example: the dashing and innovative Marshal Mikhail Tukhachevsky, Civil War hero and Deputy Commissar of Defense—arrested, tried, convicted *in camera* on trumped-up charges, and executed in 1937.)

In the film, Mitya and Kotov are no strangers. Cunningly, the screenplay by Mikhalkov and Rustam Ibragimbekov, has them doubly connected. Mitya was recruited to the NKVD by Kotov. More important, Kotov is now married to Marussia, Mitya's former lover back in the days of the sweet life among the gentry-intelligentsia before the Revolution. It so happens that Kotov's arrest will take place in the very dacha that was the site of Mitya and Marussia's happiest hours in their former lives. The film filters these script contrivances through an evocative overall mood (behind the jocularity, we know something terrible is in the offing), and through superb acting. Some of the best comes from Ingeborga Dapkounaite who creates a wholly believable Marussia—slender, handsome, quietly expressive, at once seductive and girlish, and very vulnerable. She is at the center of the strange choreography played out in the course of one sunny day that pits Mitya on his ominous mission against the older Kotov, who not only knows what the younger man is up to, but is suspicious that he has rekindled Marussia's affection. There are some effective touches conveying Marussia's inner anxiety over Mitya's mysterious reappearance—not very subtle, but effective, in the Mikhalkov cinematic style. When Mitya asks her for water to drink, the camera comes in close to show how she overfills the glass, dazed, letting the tap run on and on. When Mitya chronicles his life in the form of a puppet fable for Nadya, the Kotovs' six-year-old daughter, again the camera dwells on the tea cup in Marussia's trembling hands.

Nadya is played by Mikhalkov's own daughter (remember how he brought her on stage to accept his Oscar?), and Mikhalkov himself plays Colonel Kotov, a decision I think a casting mistake. Mikhalkov is a supremely gifted actor, sensuous and louche, a kind of Russian Jack Nicholson—his part as the footloose oil field worker in the epic film, *Siberiade*, directed by his brother, Andrei Konchalovsky, is a good example of his skill. Mikhalkov has said that he gave himself the part of Kotov only because he was determined to cast his daughter as Nadya, and he wanted her to be comfortable. She is not the problem; he is. She does very well as an engagingly precocious wiseacre who is immediately won over by the charming

Mitya (another source of tension between him and Kotov.) She is all the more poignant since we know that, like all relatives of 'enemies of the people,' young and old, she too will be a victim of the Stalin machine. But Mikhalkov's considerable talents work against the story here; he is too full of himself, somehow too overwhelming a performing presence for our comfort. He and his daughter show off too much. Yes, the bigger the Soviet hero he is, the harder he will fall. But there are, in Mikhalkov's rendition, several notches more glamour than the gruffness needed to realize a big Soviet hero.

There is something else about Mikhalkov-Kotov that skews the political moral of the story, or masks its complexity. Our sympathies go out to him when—in the best scene of the film—he is brutally bludgeoned by NKVD thugs in the back seat of their black limousine. This, after he expresses his cocksure certainty that a simple telephone call to the private number of his good friend Stalin will clear up this mistake. "If only Stalin knew," was often the last desperate cry of Stalin's victims before they got a bullet in the back of the head. Kotov's bloody face grabs our attention more than the extraordinary reaction of Mitya to the gruesome spectacle. He sits coolly in his elegant whites, to Kotov's left, and looks away, through the car window, in supreme indifference to the Colonel's ugly fate, almost as if he is bored. *What a monster.*

But there is a more subtle meaning in that look, one which disburses moral responsibility for the violence a little less one-sidedly. It is this: You, Kotov, served the Bolsheviks willingly, and helped put them in power; this whole system which now devours you is of your own making. What did you expect? I, Mitya, had my life shattered by you, in the deepest personal, not just political, sense; because of you and your bloody Bolsheviks, what hurts most came to pass—I was, as he tells Marussia, "obliterated" from her memory. I assisted in this crime against you to get one last look at the world taken away from me. Pardon me, Colonel, if I look away; I can't pity you.

Paradoxically, Mikhalkov's own sympathies as a Russian nationalist and monarchist (this despite his belonging to the old Soviet cultural elite) probably lean to Mitya, but his own powerful presence in the film tilts reactions in favor of Kotov. The film could also have done without two dubious devices, one the periodic appearance in and out of doors, of a moving fireball; the other, a large portrait of Stalin hanging from a hot-air balloon rising suddenly from the countryside. (Mockingly, Mitya salutes it.) Both devices are flat; they might have worked better to convey the surrealistic atmosphere of the times if some very special effects were available to the filmmakers. As it is, the times and the story told here are, in themselves, surrealistic and nightmarish enough.

[*Cineaste*, XXI, 4, 1995]

A Trial in Prague

Zusana Justman's film (2000) is another documentary from the depressing annals of Stalinism in Eastern Europe and the USSR. The setting is Czechoslovakia, the land of Kafka, and the sad, grotesque story recollected here imparts a murderous political spin to the idea of the Kafkaesque. (Probably not accidentally, the title of the documentary recalls the title of Kafka's most famous novel.) But then Stalinism, wherever it held sway, was always more than a little Kafkaesque.

A title card with a simple statement of historical facts introduces the film: "In 1952, fourteen leading Czechoslovak Communists, including Rudolf Slansky, the former General Secretary of the Party, were tried on charges of high treason and espionage. Eleven of the fourteen were Jews. This is the story of believers, men and women whose lives were caught up in this event—the biggest show trial of the Cold War." On the sound track we hear a muted rendition of the great inspirational hymn of the working class, *The Internationale*. Gritty black and white footage filmed at this deadly parody of a trial shows the prosecutor in the earnest pathological style practiced by the Soviet prosecutor Andrei Vyshinsky at the Moscow show trials, 1936-1938, the archetypes of these macabre political pageants. The Czech prosecutor proclaims "The Communist Party crushed this gang of traitors in time!" and calls for their death. In the front row facing him are some of the defendants looking on meekly, dejected. They had outdone each other in public declarations—scripted for them under torture, and endlessly rehearsed—of their own guilt and of their betrayal of party and state, and they know, more or less, what awaits them—the hangman's noose? lengthy prison sentences?

Sitting there is Slansky himself, and we get a good look at him, then and later in the film. In Costa-Gavras's *The Confession*, his riveting dramatization of the painful ordeal of one of those defendants, Artur London, Slansky is shown repeatedly in intriguing back-of-the-head shots only. Costa-Gavras's ingenious device was a way of calling attention to the central victim of the politics that also ensnared London without diverting us from the London story. (It also points up one of the differences between the historical documentary and the historical film dramatization; certain imaginative directorial options are not available to the documentarian) The Slansky story deserves a documentary or a dramatization in its own right; there is enough color and pathos in it. Of his Moscow comrades, who were the real masters of Czech politics and society for four decades after the Red Army drove out the Nazis, Alexander Dubcek, who came to lead the ephemeral "Prague Spring" crushed by Soviet tanks in 1968, had this to say: "That they should have done this to me, after I have dedicated my whole life to cooperation with the Soviet Union, is the great tragedy of my life." Slansky might have said the same pathetic thing, except that unlike Dubcek, he was no liberal-minded reformer enjoying great popularity. He was a loyal Stalinist who had spent the war years in Moscow, and then led the Czech party with all the ferocity of a mini-Stalin. In and out of the party he was disliked and feared. And, unlike Dubcek, who was simply shoved aside after the Prague Spring was shut down, Slansky paid for his devotion to Moscow with his life. With ten others convicted at the Prague trial of 1952, he was hanged. This, not long after party leaders had congratulated him on his fiftieth birthday as the party's "faithful son and warrior, filled with love for the working classes and with loyalty to the Soviet Union and to great Stalin."

A Trial in Prague dwells on such bitter ironies through the stories of some of Slansky's co-defendants, like him, loyal communists all. The stories are movingly told by an array of survivors of those nightmarish times, including the widows of the condemned men, Artur London (sentenced to life imprisonment), Otto Sling (hanged), and Rudolf Margolius (hanged); and the son of another communist forced to testify at the trial against his comrades, Pavel Kavan. (More irony, or historical justice works in mysterious ways: Kavan's eloquent son, Jan, became Minister of Foreign Affairs of the Czech Republic after the Communist collapse.) The documentary is narration-free; the survivors speak for themselves amid archival footage, family photographs and other stills, and of course, the dreary clips from the trial itself; intertitles fill in historical details. Some of the most compelling and thoughtful recollections come from Eduard Goldstucker, who had been the first Czech ambassador to Israel, and was another figure forced to level concocted charges against his comrades at the trial. (He was also—gulp—a Kafka scholar.) At one point Goldstucker breaks down on camera as he describes the beatings he endured.

Collectively, the testimonies of the survivors portray the anguish of those days, how large political events they little understood, or understood badly, convulsed their personal lives, and they address, directly or indirectly, the big questions bound to gnaw at all communists—Why were they victimized by the very party they gave their bodies and souls to? How did a party driven by noble ideals descend to lies, torture, and crimes that—all the victims agree—made the Gestapo gentle by comparison? What prompted Moscow to launch the whole heinous enterprise? What made the victims confess to preposterous charges—espionage in service of Anglo-American imperialism; bourgeois nationalism; seeking to restore capitalism; undermining the socialist state; and other absurdities? And what of the ugly anti-Semitic currents openly marking the trial and the pre-trial interrogations, but often masked by the coded term "Zionism"?

Several of the testimonies here emphasize the attraction of communism in the years before and during World War II. Lise London, daughter of a militant Spanish miner, speaks of the working-class experience as a formative influence. Maria Sling, Otto's English widow, cites the threat of fascism, and the natural drift to communism among intellectuals at Oxford. (Both Maria and Lise, incidentally, believed their husbands' confessions at first, and thought them guilty, a good indicator of the zealous party frame of mind. How could the party be wrong? If even their wives believed the nonsense, it was easy for the party to sell their guilt to the public.)

Heda Margolius, an Auschwitz survivor, offers the altruistic impulse, especially among intellectuals, as a factor in the communist temptation. Goldstucker sees the universalist ideals of socialism as particularly attractive to Jews. Besides, he adds, there was the glorious Soviet Union already demonstrating that socialism was being built. And then there was the Spanish Civil War, seen at the time as the first major anti-fascist battleground, with communists prominently engaged in the struggle. Never mind what Stalin's real agenda was for intervening in Spain; the international brigades organized by Moscow seemed to validate in self-sacrificing practice those universalist, altruistic ideals. Another sad irony, bearing the Stalinist fingerprint: many of the accused at the Prague trial had fought in Spain. Or fought in the resistance during the World War. Or spent time in Nazi camps—London was at Mathausen, for example. In other words, the best, most devoted, most militant communists, especially those with experiences abroad, were most suspect in the paranoid political theater staged in Prague, directed by Moscow.

The Moscow trials of the 1930s offered many precedents for the Prague event two decades later—the same wild charges and wilder confessions, the same lethal results. They worked for Stalin earlier, why not use the same script, updated and modified according to the Czech scene, again? (Remember that even Hollywood had contributed a positive take on the Stalin script. Michael Curtiz's Warner Brothers' production of *Mission to Moscow*, 1943, campily amusing today, justified the Moscow trials as a lawful endeavor to quash a monstrous anti-Soviet conspiracy.) The Moscow trials put Old Bolsheviks in the dock, many of whom had indeed mounted political opposition to Stalin, when such a thing was still possible and natural in the Soviet party. The trials and the many death sentences was Stalin's brutal way of settling scores with the old opposition, and preempting by terrorist precedent any potential opposition. The Prague defendants, however, were not oppositionists. But Tito, the Yugoslav communist leader was; he had defied Stalin in 1948. The Prague trials, as several sources in the film and elsewhere speculate, were the Stalinist way of disciplining the Eastern European party-regimes, of terrorizing them away from any Titoist dreams of independence from Moscow. (The Czechs were not alone in experiencing the crackdown; there were arrests and trials in all the capitals of the Eastern European "Peoples Democracies" from 1949 through the early 50s.) For good measure, along with the charge of Titoism, the Prague defendants were also accused of Trotskyism, a charge that always carried a sinister resonance among the orthodox communist faithful.

Confessions from the accused were needed for public relations. How did the interrogators get them? Koestler's *Darkness at Noon*, his fictionalized account of the arrest, interrogation, and confession of a composite Old Bolshevik, explains devotion to the party and its progressive historical mission as a primary source for the willingness to accede to the party's request for self-incrimination. There is a sliver of plausibility to this explanation as it might have affected some victims, but for most there were simpler reasons. Sleep deprivation, beatings, threats, degradation, and isolation got the desired results from even the most determined resisters. (Costa-Gavras's *The Confession*, based on Artur London's memoir of his prison and trial experience, presents all this with great power and relentless, stomach-turning detail. London is played by Yves Montand.) Otto Sling's widow in *A Trial in Prague* cites humiliation and loss of dignity as the operative reasons for confession. Goldstucker emphasizes sleep deprivation. In his *The Confession*, London remembers he "was ready to sign anything for five minutes of sleep." He also offers the poignant insight that it was relatively easy to be heroic against one's fascist enemies, but one was psychologically disarmed when it came to facing your own party.

At the trial, each of the defendants was identified by nationality, as in "Artur London, born 1/2/1915, of Jewish origin... ," and "Zionism" figured prominently in the charges, but the ugliest manifestations of anti-Semitism came during the pre-trial prison ordeals. Jan Kovan reports in the film that his father was told by one of his guards that they "would finish Hitler's job." After an anti-Semitic crack from his guard, Kurt London in the film, *The Confession*, snaps, "How dare you say that with a party pin in your lapel!" Unfortunately, anti-Semitism in the communist parties was all too common. An anti-Jewish purge was underway in the USSR in the late 40s, and the campaign ballooned into the notorious "Doctors Plot," when a group of Kremlin physicians, most of them

Jewish, were arrested for purportedly planning the assassination of Soviet leaders. Stalin's death in 1953 saved them and the "plot" was eventually dismissed as a fabrication. These eruptions of crude anti-Semitism in the communist world didn't stem from ideology (as in Nazism), but in great part from Cold War politics, when the new state of Israel was perceived to be in the American camp. Goldstucker alludes to this in *A Trial in Prague*, while Jan Kavan speculates that the Moscow-directed anti-Zionist frenzy was a way of sending a friendly signal to the Arabs. It was just as easy—easier—to tag Jewish communists as "Zionist" as it was to label them "Titoist" or "Trotskyist". (Across the ocean, another trial of Jewish communists, under very different auspices, was taking place, that of the Rosenbergs, who received the death sentence for atomic espionage. The world communist movement garnered much Cold War capital from this by mobilizing public opinion against the Rosenberg trial and their sentence; one of the benefits was distracting attention from the Slansky trial.)

A Trial in Prague is a solid, even essential, piece of work on an important, but little remembered, dark episode of 20th -century history. It may not be the fullest, most comprehensive account—there is none on film, so far as I know—but it tells us enough in its 83 minutes to let us know the main story in a strong, if understated way. A Czech friend who grew up in Prague then and knew many of the victims and their families, told me the film was accurate for what it did, and it brought back painful memories. What it did, she thought, was concentrate exclusively on the trial at the expense of exposing the wider terror afflicting all of Czech society at the time and for several years after the eleven communists were hanged by the communist regime. Ultimately, the victims were posthumously exonerated, "rehabilitated" in communist jargon, the process beginning with Khrushchev's anti-Stalin efforts in the USSR. *A Trial in Prague* concludes with a touching moment as Heda Margolius visits the family gravesite. She had a simple inscription dedicated to her husband on one of the stones, even though Rudolf Margolius was not buried there. The story is that his ashes, together with those of the other victims, were scattered on an icy road outside of Prague soon after they were hanged.

A Trial in Prague ought to be supplemented with some collateral materials. Costa-Gavras's *The Confession* (1970) is a must for graphically recreating some of what can only be reported in the documentary. The film is based on Artur London's book of the same name. Other accounts by survivors are *Stalinism in Prague* by Eugen Loebl, and his *My Mind on Trial; Report on my Husband* by Josefa Slanska (Slansky's widow); and *Under a Cruel Star: A Life in Prague* by Heda Margolius Kovaly.

[*Cineaste*, XXV, 4, 2000]

SHORT TAKES

Widow of the Revolution: The Anna Larina Story

Lenin once described Nikolai Bukharin as the darling of the whole Soviet Communist Party. That counted for little later on when Stalin, once Bukharin's close friend and political comrade, put him in the dock at the last of the grotesque Moscow show trials, and had him executed in 1938. The "Widow of the Revolution"—an awkward and melodramatic title—of Rosemarie Reed's informative historical documentary (2001) is Anna Larina, the unfortunate wife of the unfortunate Bukharin. As the widow of "an enemy of the people," she had her infant son taken away from her, and Stalin consigned her to two decades of labor camps and internal exile. It is an intriguing story, told here with archival footage, photos (including what is possibly a shot of the arrested Bukharin being taken away to the Lubyanka), and Larina's own recollections and commentary on camera before her death in 1996. Bukharin's biographer, the historian Stephen F. Cohen, who also became close to the family, narrates, and excerpts from Larina's memoir, *This I Cannot Forget*, are voiced over by Vanessa Redgrave. (Redgrave is an amusing, ironic choice. Politically, she has leaned to Trotskyism, but Trotsky was a chief ideological rival and political enemy of Bukharin.) Not all viewers will share in the idealization of Bukharin, but compassion for Larina is inevitable. She was still in her teens when she married the older Bukharin, and at the time of his arrest he apologized to her in tears for "ruining her life". The story has a comparatively happy ending, though. Larina survived Stalin, was re-united with her son, remarried and raised a family, and lived to see her enduring hope of Bukharin's rehabilitation realized, thanks to Gorbachev. A Widow of the Revolution vindicated by the Last Heir of the Revolution.

[*Cineaste*, XXVII, 3, 2002]

East-West

Another grim, lesser known story from the Soviet past is the subject of this French-Russian co-production directed by Regis Wargnier, whose *Indochine* won a best foreign-language Oscar in 1993. (*East-West* was the official French entry for the Oscars for 1999.) The film teeters between grand political melodrama and occasionally clunky soap opera, but its riveting narrative, solid performances from an international cast, and a thriller climax overcome its many contrivances. And you cannot help but appreciate Wargnier's earnest, ambitious effort on behalf of the theme of human decency against a repressive state. Stalin's USSR invited Russian *émigrés* living in France to return to the motherland at the end of World War II. Many accepted, to their eventual regret; awaiting them was imprisonment, Central Asian exile, even execution—the paranoid Stalin suspected espionage as their reason for returning—or, as in *East-West*, they faced the hardships of living in squalid communal apartments. The talented Oleg Menshikov, who played the morally ambiguous NKVD (KGB) mercenary so effectively in Nikita Mikhalkov's *Burnt by Sun*, is equally effective here as the *émigré* who persuades his French wife (Sandrine Bonaire) to return with him, and then, apologetically, pleads with her to stick it out. "Every prison has a way out," she responds, and resolves to flee. There ensue many complications in their private lives, in a land and time when private lives were never really private, and always subordinated to the political compulsions of Party, State, and a suspicious tyrant. The plot twists twist a little too much, and some of the heavies are cartoonishly so, but the general story, drawn as a composite from real tales, is entirely believable. Handsome cinematography (by Laurent Dailland) helps. As does the appearance of Catherine Deneuve, who always gives fresh meaning to the role of celluloid Grande Dame, as a sympathetic visiting French actress.

[*Cineaste*, XXV, 3, 2000]

Eternal Memory: Voices from the Great Terror

The "voices" in the title of this poignant and instructive historical documentary from The Cinema Guild, directed by David Pultz, are voices from Ukraine, where Stalin's terror machine broke and took more lives than in any other non-Russian territory of the Soviet Union. The focus is on an effort that began during the Gorbachev years as part of a giant reclamation project to bare the terrible truths of the past—the discovery and exhumation of anonymous graves in those mass burial grounds where the Soviet security apparatus dumped its thousands of victims. Pultz takes us to Lviv, Kiev, Vinnitsa, and Lutz for personal testimonies from survivors and witnesses, and from tearful relatives of the dead, now honored with collective monuments or simple hand-written epitaphs hung on trees. Meryl Streep narrates in soft, understated style, and there are many archival clips to illustrate the history, including a risible excerpt from an old Soviet documentary (read: falsification)—just look at our jolly peasant women harvesting in Ukraine! What was really a many-years harvest of sorrow is commented on by several authoritative figures, among them Sovietologist and former National Security Advisor Zbigniew Brzezinski. What they say is unexceptional, but the film could carry itself without their often intrusive talking heads. A dramatic and unresolved issue is aired at the end: Should the still-living executioners be brought to justice? Yes, says former Ukrainian President Leonid Kravchuk, citing Nuremberg. No, says a contemporary Ukrainian prosecutor, citing statutes of limitations. After seeing this film, how can you not agree with Kravchuk?

[*Cineaste*, XXV, 1, 1999]

The Fall of Berlin

Mikhail Chiaureli's birthday present to the 70-year old Stalin (1949) is the quintessential cinema contribution to the cult of the dictator. Seen today in a newly restored release (by International Historic Films, Inc.), it also stands at the summit of old Soviet kitsch.

Chiaureli, a fellow Georgian, pulls out all the stops in this Adoration of Stalin (played by another Georgian, and Stalin's favorite, Mikhail Gelovani). We first see the benign General Secretary puttering in his arbor as the soundtrack (score by Shostakovich) swells with hymnal, devotional sonority. Here Stalin dispenses sage counsel to an awed aw-shucks love-sick Stakhanovite steelworker. Later, and throughout the film, with infinite calm and wisdom, Stalin's steady presence guides, advises, gently prods all those around him, and ultimately leads the epic march of the Red Army to Berlin. Completing the heavenly portrait, Stalin descends by air to the conquered German capital to receive the grateful hosannas of the victors below. (Never mind that this never took place. The successor General Secretary Nikita Khrushchev singled out the film for its fictionalized idolatry in his famous "Secret Speech" denouncing the Stalin cult in 1956.) Chiaureli cross-cuts the Stalin and battle sequences with footage of Hitler, the anti-Savior, as a lampooned hysteric, no match for the warlord Stalin. Intimations of the Cold War to come appear in images of a porcine, disagreeable Churchill at Yalta, and Hitler's counting on a deal with the approaching Americans. This digitally remastered DVD improves the quality of the original Agfacolor (a trophy form the Germans), and includes an illustrative historical slide show. P.S. Stalin liked his birthday present.

[*Cineaste*, XXXII, 2, 2007]

2 On Russian Battlefields

Chapayev and Company: Films of the Russian Civil War

"Beware of terrible times," wrote Anna Akhmatova in her *July 1914*, "the earth opening up for a crowd of corpses. Expect famine, earthquakes, plagues, and heavens darkened by eclipses." World War I is the immediate reference, but her chilling words offer poetic insight into several other blood-soaked events in Russia's experience of the 20th century. Scholars are still counting the number left dead by World War II (the "Great Patriotic War of the Soviet Union," as it is known there), with ca. 25-30 million in the latest estimates. Precision is missing from the total body count of Stalin's terror and Gulag, but many millions is not far fetched. Then there is the Russian Civil War, a traumatic time of troubles in the inevitable wake of the Bolshevik Revolution. There were probably about 800,000 military-related deaths, as the new Soviet regime battled enemy arms, while close to 10 million perished from what might be called the war's collateral damage—disease, hunger, repression, economic dislocation.

It took the collapse of the Soviet Union to bring some real measure of Stalin's terror to Russian screens—Nikita Mikhalkov's Oscar-winning *Burnt by the Sun* (1994) is one riveting example. Some of the best known Soviet films at home and in the West highlight the Great Patriotic War—*Ballad of a Soldier*, *Fate of a Man*, *The Cranes are Flying* are among the most familiar. *[See "Patriotic Gore, Patriotic Gauze: Films of the Great Patriotic War" below.]* Soviet films of the Russian Civil War, however, are not as well known in the West;

there are also some legendary favorites among Russian audiences that have either been forgotten here or never even reached U.S. theaters. But now, thanks to the efforts of several U.S. distributors, and especially to the Russian Cinema Council (Ruscico) and its frequent outlet here, Image Entertainment, the Russian Civil War is becoming an important part of the DVD repertory.

And properly so, for filmic as well as historical reasons. The Civil War in Russia not only secured Bolshevik survival, but it had significant ripple effects on the Soviet future. Stalin was active on several fronts—the former Tsaritsyn where he served was renamed Stalingrad—and he became a popular figure in the communist lower ranks; at War's end he was named General Secretary of the Party. The conflict helped shape his ruling style and that of the Soviet regime for years to come—the necessity for terror and violence directed at real or imagined enemies was a salient lesson of the Civil War for Soviet political culture and statecraft. The appearance of foreign troops on Russian soil during the Civil War, including U.S. contingents—what was really a minor intervention favoring the "Whites"—assumed major symbolic meaning, used as evidence of militant imperialist hostility to the encircled Soviet state.

As with Soviet films of the Great Patriotic War, the Civil War films elide many issues and details, the conflict's great savagery on both sides, for example. The ferocity of the War is better rendered in a literary work like Isaac Babel's *Red Cavalry* than in most of the films discussed here, which are more like tales of heroes and adventure that happen to be set against the backdrop of the Civil War than honest pictures of those years. They were Soviet films, after all, inescapably constructed according to the rules mapped out by the political bosses. But creativity slipped through those constraints, as it always did in one form or other, and some terrific cinema was the result, even if filmmakers kept mum about certain things. Trotsky as organizer and head of the Red Army? A bloodthirsty Lenin? Stalin's bungling on the Polish front? Anti-Jewish pogroms by pro-Bolshevik Cossacks? Peasant attraction to the anarchists? The anti-Bolshevik uprising at Kronstadt? Such a list can get quite long, but you won't know it from Soviet films. Contemporary, post-Soviet filmmakers might want to point their cameras at those once forbidden themes. Alexander Rogozhkin did in his *The Chekist* of

1992, which is almost unwatchable for the brutality it shows of the newly formed Soviet security forces in action.

The War had a direct effect on Russian filmmaking in interesting ways. Many in the pre-revolutionary establishment—directors, producers, actors—fled from the old centers of production and headed south; they were more comfortable there under the rule of the anti-Bolshevik Whites. Mikhalkov drew on this development for the inventive narrative of his *"A Slave of Love"* (1975). The young Soviet regime meanwhile grasped the virtues of the new medium for political education and produced short agitational films—the famous *agitki*—conveyed by train and ship to remote towns and the peasant countryside. Here was the school for a new generation of Soviet filmmakers, Dziga Vertov among the most famous. Others witnessed or took part in Civil War campaigns, identified with the goals and spirit of the Revolution, and went on to build careers with international reputations.

One such figure was Vsevolod Pudovkin, whose *Mother* (1926), *The End of St. Petersburg* (1927), and *Storm over Asia* (1928) comprise a classic trilogy in tribute to the Russian Revolution and Civil War. All three silents rely on a similar central story line, the growth of revolutionary consciousness—for a working-class mother, a peasant, a hunter—but *Storm* is far and away the most colorfully set and visually arresting, its exoticism virtually overwhelming its political message—the awakening of an East newly energized by Moscow. Pudovkin and Anatoly Golovnya's cinematography bring a sensuousness to the tale of a young Mongol hunter victimized by English traders and their military protectors. There are beautiful long shots of sky and steppe and silhouetted figures, alternating with numerous close-up reaction shots of Buryat-Mongol faces as they gaze on a sword dancer, or watch a mother breast-feeding her infant, or show their appreciation of the gorgeous, undulating fur of the silver-fox hide that springs the plot into motion. An actual mass religious ceremony at a Buddhist lamasary featuring strange masks and costumes is integrated into the narrative, which ends with a memorable set-piece as a devastating windstorm sweeps away the alien occupiers, figuratively and literally. A peroration by the hero became a commonplace of the Soviet war film, as either a warning or an exhortation. In *Storm*, the hero Bair (Valery Inkizhinov, a

Yul Brynner before Yul Brynner) proclaims "O my people, rise in your ancient strength and free yourselves!" The film's original title in Russian was *The Heir of Genghiz Khan*. (The Image Entertainment DVD is about a half hour longer than VHS versions I have seen.)

Alexander Dovzhenko, another master of Soviet silents, treated Civil War themes in his *Arsenal* (1928) and *Zvenigora* (1927), but they are odd works, reflecting the director's preoccupation with visual poetry at the expense of coherent narrative or clear ideological instruction. Yakov Protazanov's 1927 silent, *The 41st*, on the other hand, addresses one of the moral issues raised in civil wars, conflicts which often pit brother against brother, or as in this case, lover against lover. A Red Army sharpshooter with 40 notches on her rifle is thrown together on an isolated isle with a White Guard officer. After political sparring they cross the ideological divide and let their feelings take over. But will revolutionary duty succumb to love when it appears the officer will be rescued? The film's title gives the ending away. A stern morality in defense of the revolution in time of civil war teaches there is little place for sentiment. The tale was later filmed in color by Grigori Chukhrai, with lyrical camera work by the masterful Sergei Urusevsky (1956).

Some Soviet critics attacked Protazanov's film as reflecting bourgeois values in its moral nuancing, but the real ideological bulldozing of filmmakers as well as other artists into conformity came with the Stalinist 1930s, especially upon the proclamation of "socialist realism" as the official guiding esthetic in 1934. No moral ambiguities, comrades. No bourgeois experimentation. Let's just have straightforward stories with positive, inspirational heroes. That same year the Soviet public got one in the persona of the Red Army commander and Civil War martyr, Vasily Chapayev, destined for immortality thanks to the film directed by the Vasilyev "Brothers" (Sergei and Georgy, who were not related). *Chapayev* was a splendid achievement, an enormously popular film, then and for years to come, chock-full of earthy humor, adventure, lovable characters, a dose of melancholy (the hero sings doleful Russian folk songs), and a work boasting the proper political credentials. Chapayev (a moustachio'd Boris Babochkin) and his sidekick Petya (Leonid Kmit) give their lives fighting Admiral Kolchak's White forces. Yet simple courage in the struggle for Bolshevik victory is not enough. The unpolished hero has an appealing rough-and-ready style of military leadership that suits his men, but he has to be disciplined into correct comportment by his political commissar, Furmanov (whose novel was the basis for the film). In the Leninist canon spontaneity must surrender to Party guidance. Whatever the political pedagogy, the public embraced this filmic Chapayev enthusiastically as a folk hero, located somewhere, as a Soviet critic put it, between Tarzan and Jesse James. Dovzhenko was later commissioned—by Stalin personally, no less—to create a "Ukrainian *Chapayev*," but the result was his leaden *Shchors* (1939), based on another Civil War hero who died in combat.

We have to leap ahead three decades for another good Civil War film that also matched *Chapayev* for popularity with the Soviet public—the rather more sophisticated, rather campier *White Sun of the Desert* (1969), directed by Vladimir Motyl, hardly known here, but now available, unlike *Chapayev*, on DVD. Both films are Soviet versions of genre Westerns—outdoor settings, fearless heroes overcoming impossible odds, shoot-outs, touches of romance, the battle between the clearly good (red hats) and clearly evil (white hats), and much comic relief. Both films feature a Soviet everyman in uniform. Fyodor Sukhov (Anatoly Kuznetsov) of *White Sun* is a simple stouthearted fellow with a generous soul returning home at the end of a Civil War campaign in Central Asia. In his voiceover we hear the letters he writes to his dear wife Katerina back home whom we meet as in a vision at the opening of the film—a stereotypically strong, handsome Russian woman, blonde and blue-eyed, with an ample bosom and voluptuous thighs. This is 1969, remember, when restraints on film culture had been considerably relaxed—still, studio bosses refused to permit Katerina's bare buttocks in the scene. Motyl in fact was asked to cut many scenes from the film before its release but reportedly Brezhnev himself saw an uncut version, loved what he saw and greenlighted it, though it was finally issued with some alterations.

Evidently based on a real incident during the Civil War in Central Asia, when the Soviets battled opponents known as "Basmachi"—a Red Army contingent took a harem under its wing, but it's not what you may think—*White Sun* shows its hero swashbuckle his way through dangerous encounters, all the while overcoming temptation and guiding the harem—"Comrade Girls," he calls them—to safety. One concern of the censors was that officials of the Central Asian Muslim republics of the USSR might be offended by a demeaning portrait of their region. Fortunately, there was enough ideological propriety in the film to overcome such qualms. Equality of women was a strong plank in the Bolshevik program. In the film, the harem members post a sign outside their quarters reading "First Free Women's Commune of the Orient".

The message might be politically correct on its face, but that's not what accounts for the film's strength and huge popularity. Soviet cosmonauts ritually watched *White Sun* before their missions; some took it into space with them. While *Chapayev* is earnest, and its humor old-fashioned and folksy, *White Sun* is bathed in modernist irony; its tongue-in-cheek abandon exudes mockery, not only of Westerns and the Hollywood hero, but, between the lines, of official ideology itself. In good cult fashion, Soviet audiences have memorized certain lines of dialogue from the film, including a customs officer's "I feel sorry for the State". (Modern Soviet audiences do their own mocking of *Chapayev* in another way, coming up with a whole bagful of jokes built around the hero. Sample: Petya tells Chapayev there are Whites in the woods. Chapayev: "This is no time for mushrooms, Petya.")

Irony has no place in several of the Civil War films produced to honor the 50th anniversary of the Bolshevik Revolution in 1967. The only irony lies in the fact that some of the best were immediately shelved for taking impermissible liberties. Larisa Shepitko's *Motherland of Electricity* and Andrei Smirnov's *Angel* were two parts of a trilogy, *The Beginning of an Unknown Century*, deemed too dark or unconventional for release.[1] Alexander Askoldov's *Commissar* suffered a similar fate. All three were only released in 1987, during Gorbachev's *glasnost* period, when many earlier banned films finally reached public screens. *Motherland* and *Angel* are short, half-hour works; *Commissar* is an ambitious full-length feature which received considerable attention when released theatrically in the West, and merited it. Inevitably, the story of a Civil War commissar who is sidelined by a pregnancy and quartered in the crowded home of a poor Jewish tinsmith would run into trouble in Moscow. The theme of Jewish suffering was never acceptable in modern

Soviet cinema. What's more, the pessimistic Magazinnik, played brilliantly by the late Rolan Bykov, muses on an "International of Kindness" as opposed to the commissar's strict understanding of the need for struggle and blood. But the commissar, a terrific Nonna Mordiukova in the role, has her rougher edges softened by motherhood, and even entrusts her infant son to the Jewish family when duty calls. Askoldov's black and white film went overboard for a kind of '60s-style wide-screen expressionism. There are strange hallucinatory sequences during the childbirth scene, and even an odd, anachronistic flash-forward showing Jews trudging to a death camp, all of which was not likely to win over studio bosses back then. (Ruscico has brought out *Commissar* on DVD; see below.)

Yevgeny Karelov's *Two Comrades were Serving* was an entirely more conventional effort, set in the Crimea as Red forces prepared to assault General Wrangel's Whites, but it has some interesting takes. The cast included many luminaries of Soviet screen and stage, with a standout performance by the great bard Vladimir Vysotsky, who plays a complex White officer—one of the film's welcome wrinkles. Another is the way filmmaking is worked into the narrative, as Mikhalkov was to do with much greater skill in his *"A Slave of Love"*. In what is essentially a buddy film, two soldiers are assigned to do some aerial reconnaissance when a French movie camera falls into Red Army hands. The buddies are a study in contrasts—Baryshkin (Bykov again) is a gung-ho fighter for the Revolution, proud of having personally executed a suspect "military specialist," as Tsarist officers recruited by the Reds were called; Nekrasov (the young Oleg Yankovsky) is sensitive and thoughtful, and less convinced of the communist Eden that Baryshkin believes will result from the war—another wrinkle. He even annoys Baryshkin by reminding him Lenin came from a gentry family. Their plane stalls and crashes in territory controlled by the rebel followers of the anarchist Makhno (who are convinced the Bolsheviks have sold out the Revolution). They escape, but only to be taken mistakenly as White spies by the Reds. Commanded to be executed (by, incidentally, a tough woman commissar), Nekrasov tells his buddy that perhaps he too, had made a mistake when he shot the military specialist.

Such moments and characterizations are the redeeming elements of an otherwise standard Soviet war film, albeit this is the Civil War. There is that emotional pull, however, as in the classic Soviet war films, when we realize the song Nekrasov keeps singing, "Two Comrades were Serving..." foretells the death of one of them. Their reconnaissance mission didn't succeed because of a film malfunction (another interesting touch), but Nekrasov did manage to capture a parade celebrating the 3rd anniversary of the Revolution—the sequence is shown as a postscript to the film, artfully spliced with, I think, some real newsreel footage.

Another kind of Civil War buddy film—buddies, actually—came from Nikita Mikhalkov, starring in his directorial debut, *At Home Among Strangers, a Stranger at Home* (1974). Two years later Mikhalkov, ever the Russian patriot, again chose the Civil War for the setting of his *"A Slave of Love"*. The latter is a much more disciplined and mature work than the mixed-genre, over complicated *At Home* (even the title is complicated), a knock-off of sorts of the modern Western. Think *Butch Cassidy and the Sundance Kid* of 1969 on higher ideological ground. (A sentimental song about the old and the new at the opening even sounds a bit like "Raindrops Keep Fallin' on My Head.") "Thank God it's not an American Western," opines Mikhalkov's favorite cinematographer, the late Pavel Lebeshev, in one of the bonus sections of the DVD. There are enough art-house devices in the film to validate Lebeshev's statement, though I wouldn't brag about it. Monotint sequences, flashcuts, chiaroscuro interiors, crane and overhead and angled shots, fantasy inserts—all abound in this adventure story about Bolshevik efforts to save a shipment of gold from the clutches of the White remnants and bandits who roam the Northern Caucasus at the end of the Civil War. *I simplify*. Moscow needs the gold demanded by the League of Nations in exchange for food to relieve widespread hunger. (Let's not quibble over the historical details.)

There certainly is a lot of verve here, amidst a spectacularly effective train heist, a cliff-hanging chase, a traitorous murder, and Mikhalkov playing the bandit chief with his trademark raffish charm and insouciance. He wears a big tan slouch hat and we first meet him biting into an apple as he nonchalantly walks along some train tracks. Hats are important—the head Chekist supervising the gold transfer wears a black Homburg. He is played by Anatoly Solonitsyn, who was Andrei Rublev in Andrei Tarkovsky's masterpiece of the same name (1966). Solonitsyn's acting and a Tarkovsky-like long, long take in a silent, darkened room partially lit by afternoon sun as the opening credits scroll are among the many features that lend a sort of existential gravitas to the film. It feels misplaced, clashing with the purely thriller aspects of the (complicated) plotline. The ending has the band of brothers from the Civil War rejoicing in their survival and recovery of the gold. The scene is a reprise several years later of the film's first shots as the buddies, fused in friendship in Civil War combat, celebrate the triumph of Equality! Brotherhood! Peace! I found all this, at beginning and end, full of a self-conscious actorly-false hilarity. At least those scenes weren't shot in slo-mo.

"*A Slave of Love*" has its arty elements as well, but Mikhalkov brings it off with virtuoso performances and a clever, tightly knit narrative. Its film-within-a film construction is intriguing—a cinema crew forced out of its natural Moscow waters by the revolution is shooting a silent titled "*A Slave of Love*" somewhere in a southern area controlled by the Whites. The star of the film and the "film" is Elena Solovei, who plays the temperamental diva modeled on the real goddess of early Russian silent film, Vera Kholodnaya. (The DVD includes a biographical short about her.) The cast does some great ensemble work, something the Russians do best—an anxious director, a ditsy scenarist, an impatient producer. They know nothing of the confused politics of the time; Bolsheviks, Makhno, Petliura, Denikin are just groups and names they are mystified by. Another cinema self-referential: the crew's cameraman (Rodion Nakhapetov) is an undercover Bolshevik who does revolutionary moonlighting—he secretly films White atrocities to offset negative images of the Reds in world opinion. (His confederate is played by Mikhalkov.)

There is one brilliantly realized scene after another, starting with the disorienting opening: we watch a silent film, then realize it is being watched in a theater, when suddenly a White security officer breaks things up and arrests someone, flinging him against the glass of a storefront outside. The Whites, too, understood the strength of film in the propaganda war. (It's reported that they publicly burned Soviet *agitki* when they captured Odessa.) White counterintelligence has a suspicion that someone from the film crew is filming illicitly, and this provides one plotline. They finally get their man, but not before he has enlisted the film star in the cause—is it real love for her, or seduction in service to the revolution? Is she "a slave of love"? She may be dotty and demanding, but she recognizes a higher calling and is thrilled to participate in a noble adventure. Once in a public square outside a theater she beseeches the crowd to consider those suffering from hunger and poverty, only to quit her harangue abashedly as she is enveloped by adoring fans. She sits sipping tea in an outdoor café after she has been entrusted with some dangerous film, then she watches in horror as the cameraman in his auto is riddled with bullets by the Whites—we see the action in a long shot, then in a reverse long shot we watch her trembling, silent reaction. A daring operation by Bolshevik raiders rescues her on the film set, and the White agent is gunned down.

All these wonderful scenes are capped by a wonderfully ambiguous ending, as she fades into the distance aboard a runaway trolley, chased by Whites on horseback. Where will she end up? Whither the Revolution?

An ambiguous ending—and not only the ending—also marks the extraordinary work by Miklos Jancso, *The Red and the White* (1968), a Hungarian-Soviet co-production, also designated to mark the 50th anniversary of the Revolution. Like the other films, its subject is the Russian Civil War, but compared to them it might well have come from a studio on a different planet. Not only does Jancso subvert the idea of a simple contrast between a good and a bad cause, but he delivers the material—Hungarian soldiers stranded in Russia after the First World War are fighting on the Red side—in a series of severe, highly stylized often enigmatic episodes. Wide angle shots, and a slow fluid camera filming in black and white, supplemented by only natural sounds add to the disquieting feel of the film. (Cinematography by Tamas Somlo.) There is little dialogue; commands are barked softly in a ritualistic execution scene; the choreography of violence throughout is hypnotic. Most of the cruelty may be on the White side, but a White officer abides by a military honor code when he has a Cossack shot for abusing a woman. The only genuine hero of the film is a head nurse at a field hospital who invokes Hippocrates, not Lenin; she sees no Whites or Reds, only patients. Jancso, too, it seems, does not distinguish between the combatants; he sees only victims.

All of this might have been the stuff of some of Jancso's striking films in Hungary, but it didn't go down well with the Soviets. What's more, there was a subtle imbalance in language and nationality, sure to upset the Russians. The Hungarians fighting with the Reds speak Hungarian, while the Whites speak Russian. The film climaxes with a big battle scene (a long shot of the two forces arrayed impersonally in distant geometric formation) with the Red side singing, "We Renounce the Old World" (also known as "The Workers' Marseillaise"), an old favorite of Russian revolutionaries. It is sung in Hungarian. There is more eroticism, even more nudity in the film than in Soviet cinema, not to mention cinema of the Civil War. A promiscuous nurse is Russian. A not very attractive Red commander is a Russian, full of hard bitten bravado, who needs something before dying—he grabs a nurse and plants two mighty open-mouthed kisses on her lips.

No, the Soviets picked the wrong man to direct a film paying homage to the triumph of the Reds in the Russian Civil War. The film ends with a quiet coda, as a young Magyar surveys the killing grounds after the battle. He raises his sword in tribute to the fallen. The Reds have won, but the look on his face bespeaks anything but triumph; it is a sad look and seems to ask the question, "What was all this for?," as the screen fades to black. Not a very acceptable look; not a very acceptable question. The film was denied distribution in the USSR.

The Bolshevik Revolution and the triumph of the Reds in the Russian Civil War were the twin pillars of the "foundation myth" of the Soviet state. The collapse of the USSR, and with it the erosion of old formulaic dogmas, have freed up perspectives on the past. Russian filmmakers, always a kind of community of alternative historians, are sure now, one hopes, to look upon the past and its myths through a new glass, darkly.

[*Cineaste*, XXX, 4, 2005]

[1] See Leonid Gurevich's discussion of the trilogy in the interview, Chapter VII, 3.

Tinker on the Roof, or *Commissar:* Jews and Russians in the Russian Civil War

4. In the childbirth scene the Bolshevik commissar Klavdiya (Nonna Mordiukova) has visions of her campaigns in the Civil War in Alexander Askoldov's *Commissar* (1967/1987)

Was *glasnost* good for Soviet Jews? The answer is *da*, if only because Jewish themes were at last beginning to appear on those "blank pages" of the Soviet historical record that Mr. Gorbachev said needed filling. Recovering the Jewish chapters of the national memory was good not only for the Jews; it was good for the nation's moral balance, for the general process of renewal, for the tattered banner of Soviet socialism. It also was good for Soviet-American relations, since the U.S. government's attitude toward the Soviet Union was influenced by the way Soviet Jews were being treated.

There were a lot of Jewish chapters to recover—many tales to be told. As usual in the USSR, artists led the way. In the past, there was the occasional *cri de coeur* by some righteous gentile, as in the celebrated "Babi Yar," in which Yevtushenko did what official history and official monuments failed to do—highlight the brute fact of Jews as special victims of Nazi terror on Soviet soil. Or the occasional novel, as in Anatoly Rybakov's *Heavy Sand*, which offered a rich tableau of Jewish life in Ukraine from before the revolution through World War II. (The same Rybakov's evocation of the purge period, *Children of the Arbat*, finally appeared in the USSR, two decades after it was written.)

Since *glasnost*, the appearance of works with Jewish subjects became a more regular feature of the Soviet cultural scene. For example, another frequently iconoclastic poet, Andrei Voznesensky, wrote a harrowing article in the youth magazine *Yunost* about a German massacre in the Crimea. As at Babi Yar, the existing monument fails to mention that Jews were the primary victims. Voznesensky's anger was directed especially at a different kind of atrocity—the continuing plunder of the mass graves by local citizens without interference by the authorities. The monthly *Oktyabr* began serializing *Life and Fate*, Vasily Grossman's long-suppressed epic novel set at the time of the Stalingrad battle. Among other Jewish themes in the work, its scenes of victims heading for the gas chambers are as powerful as anything ever written on the Holocaust. The magazine *Druzhba Narodov* ("Friendship of the Peoples") published the "Doctors' Plot," the memoirs of Yakov Rapoport, a survivor of one of Stalin's most notorious frame-ups, in which the accused, mostly Jews, were charged with seeking to take the lives of the high-level officials they were treating.

Making all of this information public in the Soviet Union was a striking development. A certain low-level anti-Semitism, together with the official Soviet ambivalence about ethnic particularism, traditionally kept specifically Jewish themes and Jewish grievances from being aired in the media. Cinema was no exception, although this wasn't always the case. There were several Soviet anti-Fascist films that focused on Jewish subjects. Among them were *Professor Mamlock* (1938), the story of a renowned German Jewish doctor hounded by the Nazis, and *The Unvanquished* (1945), the tale of the awful fate of the Jewish population in Ukraine under the swastika. After World War II, but especially after the emergence of the state of Israel in 1948, the situation for Soviet Jews became more complicated; Jews and Jewish themes all but disappeared from Soviet cinema, even after Stalin. Here and there, especially in films about the war, one learned from cinema that Jews existed in the USSR. *The Theme*, a fine film by Gleb Panfilov, made in 1979, but released only later thanks to *glasnost*, contains a powerful sequence involving a contemporary Jewish writer who has decided to emigrate in order to preserve his artistic integrity. This positive portrait of the writer, along with the sensitive subject of emigration itself, may have accounted for the film's shelving when it was first completed.

A similar fate was prescribed for Alexander Askoldov's riveting and unique *Commissar*, completed in 1967. Imagine making a film about Jews, Jewish suffering, Jewish humanism, and a Jewish plea for tolerance and amity among nations; and imagine making this film just as the Israelis gained victory in the Six Day War, when the USSR was about to break off relations with Israel, when Zionism was being associated more and more with imperialism (and worse) in official Soviet doctrine and policy, and when Soviet anti-Zionism was merging increasingly with anti-Semitism. Making such a film in those days is what is known as bad timing. That the film was made at all, and that it amounted to a major production no less, is something of a small miracle. The head of the state film agency responsible for budgeting, approving, and supervising production was called on the carpet about the film and explained that Askoldov—who is not Jewish—somehow tricked everyone about the real character of his work. It was Askoldov's first film, and it was to be his last. Cinema bosses accused him of promoting Zionism and other evils, and they threw him out of filmmaking. He was also ousted from the Soviet Communist party. For the next twenty years Askoldov made a living by directing variety shows and doing occasional television work. Now in his late seventies (he was at Moscow University with Gorbachev), he bears all the traces of one of those rock-hard, principled, antiestablishment, "difficult" types who, though isolated, stuck to their guns in Soviet society—figures as ideologically diverse as Andrei Sakharov, Alexander Solzhenitsyn, and Roy Medvedev.

Through another small miracle, Askoldov's film was preserved. In other times it might have been destroyed. ("Wipe it out!" Stalin sometimes would order.) Askoldov's wife preserved a copy by hiding it in her closet until another miracle—*glasnost*—brought it to the screen at the Moscow Film Festival in 1987.

Askoldov uses "In the City of Berdichev," a simple, Isaac Babel-like short story by Vasily Grossman set in Ukraine during the Russian Civil War, as the basis for a cinema meditation on human warmth, or as the director likes to say in interviews, on the true meaning of "internationalism." It is 1920 and a tough, no-nonsense commissar (Nonna Mordiukova), built like a sturdy Mother Russia from some revolutionary poster, arrives with her cavalry unit in a silent, bullet-marked town. We know she is tough because without flinching she orders the execution of a deserter. He had "traded the revolution for a woman's bed," she bellows at him. The irony of this order becomes immediately apparent, for the tough, committed commissar has to reveal to her unit commander that she herself is with child and is too far along in her pregnancy to do anything about it but go through with the birth. She is lodged during her confinement with a poor Jewish tinker named Yefim (Rolan Bykov), his six children, his wife, and his mother-in-law. The shtetl meets the Red Army: Tevye confronts the commissar. After initial suspicion, the Jewish family and the Russian woman get along together. The family members are tender with her and help her through a difficult delivery. She loves them and doffs her military garb in favor of maternal dress. But these are terrible times. Revolutionary passion and duty compel the commissar to rejoin her unit, and, in an act of love and trust, she leaves her beloved infant behind with the Jewish family.

The film often has the clean, earnest, black-and-white look of early Soviet cinema set during the revolution and civil war. But, from the beginning, we know we are in for something else. A statue of the Virgin gazes at a bone-weary cavalry group slowly riding into town. It is misty, and we hear a woman singing a soft, haunting Russian lullaby. (Later, the same lullaby will blend with a Yiddish one.) Flashcuts of a church and a synagogue complete the setting. There will be a flashback death in slow motion, dream-like sequences of the battlefield, a terrifying flash-forward vision of the tinker and his family marching to a death camp, a hyper-realistic children's reenactment of a *pogrom*, and a macabre dance of hope under artillery bombardment—all intercut into the simple story. This is 1960s cinema; it is Chagall spliced into the Soviet screen.

But *Commissar* displays more than just the stylistic cinematic mannerisms of the 1960s. The USSR was also then undergoing a breakup of Stalinism as an ideological system, a process muffled but hardly arrested by the complacent Brezhnev decades, as later developments attest. All sorts of challenges to cliché, dogma, and official history began to surface. Askoldov's film belongs to that process. First, it refreshes the Soviet memory about Jewish life in the western regions of Imperial Russia, where patience, faith, and the gentle/comic sense of the absurd made poverty and pain endurable. Granted, Askoldov's portrait of Jewish virtue—honest toil and earthy, life-affirming joy amidst the squalor and the peril—skirts close to patronizing caricature: The solid natives teach the sophisticated commissar a thing or two about life. Nevertheless, such elements make for good cinema. When we meet Yefim's wife, a stunning dark-haired beauty (Raisa Nedoshkovskaya), she is lustily scrubbing clothes at her washboard. When Yefim leaves for work in the morning, he greets the day merrily by peeing outside his door and dancing and humming down the lane.

Second, and perhaps what makes this less of a "Jewish film" than a general political statement (for which Askoldov might have gotten himself into as much trouble as he did with the Jewish dimension), is the film's support for soft humanism over the hard revolutionary mentality. Askoldov has said that his film honors internationalism and berates chauvinism—unimpeachable Leninist qualifications. But it also honors motherhood, family, and mutual caring over the imperatives of class struggle. In one exchange, Yefim tells the commissar of the need for "an International of kindness." She reproaches him for his naiveté and asserts that a true International must bear the blood of workers and peasants in hard struggle. A very solitary, very mournful trumpet intoning "The Internationale" at the end of the film is a good clue as to which side of the dialogue between Yefim and the commissar Askoldov is on.

Soviet authorities, cultural and otherwise, probably still had many reservations about the film. Isn't the civil war presented in an insufficiently triumphant mode? Aren't Jews presented excessively favorably in comparison with other nationalities? But *glasnost* is *glasnost*, comrades, and the film came out of the can. Unfortunately, *glasnost* has also meant opening up public debate to reactionary voices, such as those in the Pamyat group with their primitive conspiracy theories and good old-fashioned Russian anti-Semitism. In the notorious critique of *glasnost* by a Leningrad chemist, published, with probable support from above, in *Sovetskaya Rossiya*, liberalizing trends were assailed as "cosmopolitan" tendencies, the traditional coded attack on Jews and Jewishness. This sort of attack led many Jews to worry about a film like *Commissar*: better not to rock the boat, they say. At the time, Pamyat was ridiculed in the Soviet press, and *Pravda* sternly rebuked *Sovetskaya Rossiya*. That is what candid debate was all about in the Gorbachev era. The cure for *glasnost* was more *glasnost*. And Askoldov's *Commissar*, like Abuladze's anti-Stalinist film *Repentance*, stand, in retrospect, as important markers in the USSR's incomplete quest for honest historical self-exploration.

[*Tikkun*, III, 5, 1988. Reprinted from *Tikkun: A Bimonthly Interfaith Critique of Politics, Culture, & Society.*]

Commissar: Another Take

This welcome two-disc set from Kino International is a beautiful black and white widescreen restoration of Alexander Askoldov's one and only full-length feature—a minor masterpiece—and adds some fascinating reminiscences by the film's principals, Askoldov included, that comprise sad commentary on Soviet cultural politics of the time (1967). Askoldov based his screenplay on short story set in the Russian Civil War by the Soviet/Jewish writer Vasily Grossman, *In the Town of Berdichev*, and from it took off on his humanistic concerns about the thwarted ideals of revolutionary "internationalism". A tough female commissar with a Red Cavalry unit is too advanced in her pregnancy to abort, so she quarters in the crowded home of a poor Jewish tinsmith for her confinement. From this odd arrangement a loving relationship develops between the commissar and the family, and they help her through a difficult delivery. In the end, she has to decide between motherhood and fighting for the Revolution. What's wrong with this picture in the eyes of Askoldov's political and film bosses, who caused him an emblematic Soviet ordeal? On the face of it, nothing—Askoldov's pitch got clearance for a major Gorky Studios production. (Among important talent was the composer Alfred Schnittke who scored the film with original music, added some klezmer, plus a haunting blend of Russian and Jewish lullabies.) But Askoldov strayed too far from political and stylistic conventions. For one (big) thing, he stressed Jewish suffering and compassion, a Soviet no-no. (Askoldov is not Jewish, but in the interview here he remembers the Jewish family that sheltered him after his parents were hauled off to the Gulag.) Moreover, his sympathetic tinsmith, the brilliant Rolan Bykov, also interviewed here, suggests an "International of kindness" over the militant, Leninist version. Then there are some surreal flashbacks, and a startling, anachronistic flash-forward of Jews marched to a Nazi death camp. Results: Askoldov ejected from the Party, banned from film directing, banished from Moscow, and his film shelved until *glasnost*, twenty years later. A miracle this stunning work survived.

[*Cineaste*, XXXIII, 1, 2007]

Patriotic Gore, Patriotic Gauze: Films of The Great Patriotic War

In an earlier age, before thermonuclear-tipped ICBMs altered military planning, Field Marshal Bernard Montgomery cautioned battlefield strategists against marching on Moscow. "Invading Russia," he said, "is always a bad idea." Just consider the most notable modern failures: Hitler's "Operation Barbarossa" of 1941 ended ingloriously for his mighty *Wehrmacht*, and Napoleon's *Grand Armée* of 1812 was shredded on the plains of Imperial Russia. *The Great Patriotic War of the Soviet Union* is the chin up, hortatory way Russians officially describe their part of what we call World War II, an updating of the title Tsar Alexander I's government gave to the campaign against the French, *The Patriotic War*.

Russian patriotism may indeed have been what mostly animated soldiers at the front or populations in the rear, a primal emotion encouraged by the rulers, Tsarist and Marxist alike. Stalin famously invoked the great national heroes of the pre-Bolshevik past—Alexander Nevsky, Dmitri Donskoy, Minin and Pozharsky, Alexander Suvorov, Mikhail Kutuzov—before mentioning "Lenin's victorious banner" when he addressed Soviet troops as the German army threatened the gates of Moscow. The Soviet film industry played its patriotic part even before the German attack, and dutifully offered biopics of many of those iconic Russian figures. Alexei Tolstoy, author of the novel *Peter I*, who co-scripted Vladimir Petrov's film (1937–1938) of the same name based on the book, defined its "central idea" as showing "the might of the Great Russian people and the indefatigable nature of their constructive spirit." Eisenstein has his hero declare at the conclusion of *Alexander Nevsky* (1938), "He who comes to us with the sword shall perish by the sword. The Russian land lives and shall always live by this!" Part warning, part prophecy as it turned out, but remember that the film was shelved because of its anti-German message after the Nazi-Soviet Pact of 1939. When the Germans broke the agreement and attacked two years later, *Alexander Nevsky* returned to Soviet screens in all of its inspirational anti-German patriotism.

All this suggests the ways in which the Soviet film industry—it couldn't be otherwise—zigged and zagged with the appropriate turns in Party-State policies. But portraying the suffering motherland under Nazi savagery was an undertaking that made any directives from above superfluous; in the period 1941–1945, as Jay Leyda writes, "Soviet cinema had declared war." The great exhortation of the day, "All for the Front! All for Victory!" meant turning out war films from the studios as vigorously as Stalin T-34 tanks and Katiusha rockets rolled off assembly lines. Newsreels and documentaries shot by intrepid Soviet filmmakers on the battlefield were among the weapons, but there were first-rate features as well. They dramatized very vividly the cruelty of the invaders, and also the avenging intervention of the partisans, or the heights of patient heroism scaled by ordinary villagers. The moral of these films was the simple, harsh message: Hate the Germans. Leo Arnshtam's *Zoya* (1944) was one such powerful work, a dramatization of the real-life partisan Zoya Kosmodemyanskaya, brutally executed by the Germans. Mark Donskoy's *The Rainbow* (1943) was another in the same vein, widely shown abroad and capturing several prizes in the U.S. "They're Germans and that's why they kill," says someone in the film. At the end, one of the village women calls for no mercy to the occupiers: "Let them suffer their fate. Let them taste it to the last drop.... Let them see how their cursed generation, their wretched country, will be beaten into grief..." And grief was certainly the German fate everywhere from Stalingrad to Berlin. (The historian Antony Beevor relates how a victorious Red Army soldier told German POWs amidst the Stalingrad rubble, "This is how Berlin is going to look.")

After 1945, the Stalin cult overwhelmed Soviet cinema of the war; partisans and soldiers and villagers triumphed thanks to the mega-genius of the Generalissimo. Stalin of course loved this stuff about himself, and he had final cut over all films. One such piece of Great-Leader kitsch was Vladimir Petrov's *Battle of Stalingrad* (1949). Another was Mikhail Chiaureli's idolatrous *The Fall of Berlin* (1949), later criticized by the arch de-Stalinizer, Nikita Khrushchev, for its neglect of those around Stalin (like Nikita Khrushchev): "...only Stalin acts, issuing orders from a hall in which there are many empty chairs... And where is the military command? Where is the Political Bureau? Where is the Government?... There is nothing about them in the film.... Stalin acts for everybody...." At war's end, the film has Stalin, counter-factually, flying into defeated Berlin—having descended from the skies in a sequence recalling the Führer's arrival at Nuremberg in Leni Riefenstahl's *Triumph of the Will*. (One always wonders with Soviet cinema—is the director making a sly, Aesopian point to get past the censors, or perhaps here he was thumbing his nose at Riefenstahl?)

One Russian film historian has described Soviet post-War cinema as "the worst—the most false and mendacious—of any period." Fortunately, the period was comparatively short-lived. While Cold War cinema temporarily displaced the Great Patriotic War, and the wicked Germans were displaced by cartoonish portrayals of wicked Americans, the death of the tyrant in 1953 and the cultural "Thaw" that soon followed brought a new look and temper to Soviet filmmaking about WW II. Cinema of this period, being Soviet cinema, paralleled Moscow's political agenda of the day, which gave a new slant to Soviet foreign policy and sought "peaceful coexistence" with the imperialist West, the U.S. in particular. What we think of as Soviet *war* films of this period are really *peace* films, and in a double sense. They projected the goals of Soviet foreign policy—to advance the USSR as a peace-loving great power—but they also amplified the deepest feelings of the Soviet population, who now looked upon the ordeals of 1941–1945 in the reflective spirit of mourning and introspection, instead of the earlier biliousness and triumphalism, almost as if the fruits of victory were too bitter to enjoy. They didn't exactly forgive the Germans, but the message of these films seemed directed at war itself, echoing the popular desire for peace. The Party, the State, military leaders disappeared from the narratives (even the Germans disappeared from some of them). Stories of the war's ordinary heroes and victims were told in very human terms, often away from the battlefield, in a sad, lyrical key; with greater honesty, they also showed the seamier side of life on the home front. Moreover, these war films blazed a trail in developing the new film language that graced Soviet screens for the next two decades.

Two offerings from the Criterion Collection are among those classics, in stunning black-and-white digital transfers. The Italian director, Pier Paolo Pasolini, called this Soviet new wave "neo-romantic," and Mikhail Kalatozov's *The Cranes are Flying* (1957), with its dazzling cinematography by Sergei Urusevsky, was the emblematic feature of this period, defining the whole era. Using the script by Viktor Rozov from his own theater piece, Kalatozov once commented that he was inspired as well by Tolstoy's *War and Peace*, the epic novel which, among many other things, dwells on the effects of war on relationships—not only did his military obligation separate her husband-to-be, Prince Andrei, from Natasha, but it drove her into an adulterous affair with the womanizer Anatole Kuragin. In *Cranes*, the lonely Veronika, separated from her beloved Boris who went off to war without a proper farewell, falls for the overheated overtures of the draft-dodger Mark. Their physical consummation takes place in a (literally) lights-out, over-the-top scene juiced up with pounding piano, billowing curtains, crashing glass and piercing sirens during a Moscow air-raid (whew!). That bit of melodramatic excess is offset by other more restrained scenes, among them the profoundly moving, underplayed moment when the hauntingly beautiful Tatiana Samoilova, in the role of the doleful Veronika, hoping against hope for Boris's survival, gets the news of his battlefield death. (The only war-front scene in the film concludes with Boris, played by the talented Alexei Batalov, in a frozen, dying gaze at the skies imagining, in Felliniesque slow motion, the wedding celebration that never took place.) The film also points up the corruption of local officials and their hangers-on enjoying themselves far from the front. A victory speech at war's end—a convention of the Soviet war film—emphasizes the new aims of peace, reconstruction and reconciliation, symbolized by Veronika's simple act of distributing flowers one-by-one to the returning soldiers—as the cranes fly over Moscow. Saccharine, yes; but effective nonetheless. There are no supplementary materials on this DVD, but some scenes under the opening credits have been restored.

Another major contribution to the new cinema of the war—leaving aside Tarkovsky's idiosyncratic *Tarkovskian* treatment in his moody *Ivan's Childhood* (also known as *My Name is Ivan*, 1962)—was Grigori Chukhrai's *Ballad of a Soldier* of 1959, with its memorable tale of a young soldier returning home, a theme as old as *The Odyssey* and as recently told as Charles Frazier's *Cold Mountain*. Here, the teen-aged Alyosha Skvortsov, the quintessential common Russian soldier of peasant origins, has only a few days to visit mother on the collective farm to repair a leaky roof. That sounds so Soviet, so trite and sentimental, but Chukhrai brings it off thanks to a smoothly paced and emotionally packed series of diverse adventures and mis-adventures mixing grief, humor and adolescent romance. There are some gauzy bits, but from the terrific opening sequence shot dizzily from above and rolled over, showing Alyosha fleeing from a German tank, to the denouement—"*Al YO sha!*" screams mother (Mother Russia?) after her breathless run through the wheat fields to reach him (I confess my eyes are never dry when I watch that scene)—*Ballad* sweeps you, with feeling, into the physical and psychological world of Russians at war.

As in *Cranes*, *Ballad* highlights some of the less heroic aspects of the war. There is the extortionist train guard who demands some provisions from the stowaway Alyosha—the tins are clearly marked MEAT, acknowledging a direct U.S. contribution to the Soviet war effort that Russians in their inventive sardonic fashion called "the second front". Then again there is the painful subject of women at home taking up with other men. (One of the most popular wartime poems was Konstantin Simonov's plea of the soldier, *Wait for Me*.) In *Cranes*, besides the Veronika-Mark liaison, a hospitalized soldier is shown crazed by the "Dear Ivan" letter he receives. In *Ballad*, Alyosha delivers some soap, a precious wartime commodity, as a gift from a front-line soldier to his wife, then angrily snatches it back when he discovers there's another man in the household. Such episodes were in line with the new candor of the period's war cinema, but honesty had its limits in the eyes of Soviet film bosses. *Ballad* ran into trouble because of that remarkable opening sequence—a Soviet soldier shouldn't be shown in a cowardly fashion, running away from a tank! Other films were deemed "too pacifist," as was Alexander Alov and Vladimir Naumov's *Peace to Him Who Enters* (1961), which has a Soviet soldier assisting a German woman in childbirth. A decade later Alexei Gherman's gritty *Trial on the Road* (1972) was shelved after production for the way it handled the touchy theme of desertion to the German side. (Another popular film of the new wave, Sergei Bondarchuk's *Fate of a Man*, 1959, deals with another delicate subject, the fate of escaped Russian POWs, by showing the hero, Sokolov, welcomed by his buddies. In fact, they were not tenderly treated; according to grim Stalinist battlefield codes, they were usually branded deserters or collaborators. Or cowards, who should have chosen death on the battlefield over surrender. Stalin disowned his own captured son when the Germans offered a prisoner swap.)

An amusing sidelight of our own: When *Ballad* was shown in the U.S., it opened with a kind of disclaimer from its distributor, J.J. Frankel, as if to reassure American audiences that this wasn't some piece of Red propaganda catching them unawares. The statement alluded to the recently signed cultural agreements between the U.S. and the USSR and that, consequently, American films were being shown in Soviet theaters as well. That scroll doesn't appear in the Criterion DVD, but the extras include some other curiosities—audio interviews (heard over stills) from Gideon Bachman's Film Art program on the old listener sponsored station, WBAI; Chukhrai is heard, as are the two young leads, Vladimir Ivashov (Alyosha) and Zhanna Prokhorenko (Shura), all in New York for the screening.

Criterion has also added an opening sequence missing from both 16mm and VHS versions of the film I have seen—Mother is shown in a post-war village scene walking sadly past a neighboring couple and their infant; her Alyosha never returned from the war.

Lesser known, and not quite up to the achievements of *Cranes* and *Ballad*, but a significant part of the same ensemble of Soviet war films is Rezo Chkheidze's folk-flavored *Father of A Soldier* (1964) from Soviet Georgia, available on DVD from the Russian Cinema Council. Chkheidze was a student of Dovzhenko; that plus the "poetic" traditions of Georgian cinema explains some of the visual appeal of the film, with its panoramas of vineyards and cornfields, and the solicitous attention to them by its grizzled hero, the Father of the title, whose massive mustachioed face we often see in tight close-up. Like *Ballad*, this is a journey film—of a peasant father setting out to find his wounded son. Along the way, father co-opts himself into the Red Army and fights with them all the way to Berlin; never mind his age, Georgians are known for longevity—his own father, he tells an officer, lived into his 100s. In episode after episode, amidst the killing fields, father shows a loving concern for his son, tenderness toward nature and its bounty, and a deep regard for his fellows, whom he cautions not to behave like fascists. The humanism and patience of this ordinary peasant have the Tolstoyan dimensions of simple grandeur that not even the cruelties and disappointments of the German-Russian war can diminish. There is triumph at the end, but sorrow as well, in keeping with the elegiac disposition of war films of the Thaw. This Ruscico DVD supplements the film with a generous dose of documentary footage from 1941–1945.

For many years all Soviet studios and many Soviet directors felt an almost religious urge to do war films, either out of a kind of civic duty owed the memory of the dead (the number is now placed at 27,000,000 million), or from the need to memorialize their own experiences. Official reasons prevailed as well. Hence Yuri Ozerov's bloated, 5-part *Liberation* (1968–1971), typical of the bombast of the Brezhnev years, and specifically mandated to counteract any impression fostered by American films like *The Longest Day* (1962) that ignored the Soviet contribution to victory over the Third Reich. That it was the Soviet fighting machine that, in Churchill's words, "tore the guts out of the German army" is undeniable. For the Soviet people to survive the traumas of war and its aftermath was also part of the triumph. To honor those achievements in cinema art without the clichés of the war-film genre was something only a few films succeeded in doing after the justifiably celebrated products of the Thaw. Alexei Gherman turned to the war again in his wonderful *Twenty Days Without War* (1979), based on a Konstantin Simonov story, the chronicle of a melancholy journey (again a journey) of a war correspondent from the front to far-off Tashkent for the all too brief pleasures of love and peace. Pyotr Todorovsky's *A Wartime Romance* (1984) is a bittersweet evocation of life after the war, where some hearts would always bear the emotional wounds of war. The poet Yevgeny Yevtushenko's autobiographical *Kindergarten* (1983), is rather overwrought but still conveys effectively the many sides of Soviet life during the war as witnessed by a boy on a long journey from Moscow to Zima Junction in Siberia. (Yes, yet another journey film. The pre-revolutionary scholar Kliuchevsky wrote that the history of Russia is the history of a people in motion.) Larisa Shepitko's *The Ascent* (or *Ascension*, 1976) is another partisan and German-occupied village film, set in Byelorussia, but unusual for—as the title suggests—its spiritual, even Christian overtones.

Shepitko's life was cut short by an automobile accident on location for the film *Farewell*, completed by her husband, Elem Klimov, in 1982. Klimov, who died in 2003, was born in Stalingrad in 1933 and remembers as a boy seeing the Volga in flames during the great battle there. For his war film, *Come and See* (1985), however, he picked another event, the hideous massacre of villagers in Khatyn, Byelorussia, by a special German commando unit as punishment for partisan activity in the region. Countless other villages suffered the same fate, but there has been little awareness in the West of such horrors. In his majestic study, *Russia at War*, Alexander Werth comments, citing two well-known locations of German atrocities in France and Czechoslovakia, that there were "in the Soviet Union, not *one* Oradour, or *one* Lidice, but hundreds" of villages where men, women and children were exterminated. In the horrifying climax of *Come and See*, wailing villagers are forced into a barn, which is then set afire and blasted with machine guns and grenades: a scene out of hell. (Klimov's title—perhaps more biblically rendered as *Come and Behold*—comes from the Book of Revelation with its visions of the Apocalypse—"…behold a pale horse; and his name that sat on him was Death, and Hell followed with him.") *Come and See*, based on Ales Adamovich's *Story of Khatyn*, stands alone, almost unbearably powerful, among Russian films of war, very far from those discussed above, which are creampuffs by comparison. For that matter, it stands apart from films of war from most other modern sources. Klimov's method differs from the severed limbs and gushing-blood style found in Spielberg or Stone, and closer to the incantational, surrealist modes of Coppola or Malik. (But there is plenty of burnt flesh and bloody torsos in the film too; the realist, hyperrealist, and surrealist operate in equal measure.) When I once mentioned to Klimov that I thought *Come and See* had the qualities of a thriller or horror film—the ominous, persistent drone of a German reconnaissance plane overhead; the buzzing flies and Glasha's vomiting before a flashcut of executed villagers (Glasha is the young woman living with the partisans); the German column on its way to hellish deeds coming out of morning mists—he objected to the characterization. "Hey," he said, "this is WAR! Total horror, everywhere. To recreate the sensual image of war, to convey this to the viewer, especially the young viewer who has never seen war, but plays at war. That's one of the aims of our work."[1]

He succeeded, all right. Klimov did it by using color; the cinematography of Alexei Rodionov, especially his Steadicam; non-professional actors for his villagers; the bravura performance of Alexei Kravchenko as Flyora, the teenager who "got his gun" to fight with the partisans, his face lined and his hair turned gray in the process; and an unflinching attention, without commentary, to ugly details. The film ends with victorious partisans exacting justice on the German beasts, but the effect is somber; oh, the cost! *Come and See* stands very high in the war-film roster for its undiluted, frightening power, nightmarish in its assault on the senses. The Kino Video DVD release has much informative bonus material, including interviews with Klimov and others associated with the film, production stills, and archival war clips.

One of the village victims in *Come and See* is a Jew. An old Jew appears in *Kindergarten*, and there are references to Jews in *Fate of a Man*, but for the most part, one wouldn't learn of the existence of large Jewish populations in the western regions of the USSR, much less their attempted annihilation by the Nazis, from Soviet cinema of any period. It's one of the many subjects, a very big one in this case, connected with the war that Soviet ideological/political imperatives kept from the screens. There are other subjects conspicuous for their absence from Soviet filmography. Oddly, the "Hero-City" Leningrad, blockaded for 900 days by the Germans and surviving unimaginable cold, hunger, disease and, as recently opened archives reveal, cases of cannibalism, has never received its full cinema due. It is Vladimir Putin's native city—his father was wounded during the siege, and his brother died there—so perhaps an official *ukaz* will pitch the idea of a Leningrad saga. Other unpleasant topics overlooked in Soviet times might also be addressed in post-Soviet cinema, from the activity of the notorious "blocking units" of Soviet security forces to forestall any idea of retreat or desertion, to the astonishing treason of General Vlasov and his army of anti-Soviet "volunteers" from German POW camps. And didn't Ukrainians and others greet the invading Wehrmacht with the traditional bread and salt, as a befitting welcome for the "liberators"? The rape of German women in massive numbers by Red Army soldiers is another ugly subject deserving attention. The list of such neglected script material could go on; there is much drama drawn from life here, and real-life tragedy, too. The Russian film studios shouldn't leave it to Western filmmakers, who continue to be fascinated by the Russian-German war, to take up such matters. (See Jean-Jacques Annaud's *Enemy at the Gates*, released in 2000; Oliver Hirschbiegel's *The Downfall*, 2004, chronicles Hitler's last days as the Red Army controls Berlin—ironically, much of the film was shot in St. Petersburg, the former Leningrad that withstood the "900 Days".) Two other releases were welcome signs that Russians hadn't forgotten the war—Nikolai Lebedev's *The Star* (2002), a popular action film which, shades of Tarkovsky's *Ivan's Childhood*, tells of young scouts operating behind the lines to gather intelligence for the advancing Red Army; and Alexander Rogozhkin's pacifist comedy, *The Cuckoo* (2002), set in Finland, a sector of the Eastern Front neglected by filmmakers.

With Soviet wraps off, the Russian film world ought to be capable of offering not only works highlighting once forbidden themes, but those that delve with greater depth and subtlety into characters, and into the moral issues they face against the background of war, that cauldron of challenges to personal honor and decency. Greater, that is, than even the films I have discussed above, laudable though they may be.

[*Cineaste*, XXIX, 3, 2004]

[1] See my interview with Klimov in Chapter VII, 2.

Stalingrad

This is an unrelentingly harrowing war film (1993), told from the German side, from the (frozen) ground up, focusing on an elite battalion as they are smashed by the Red Army into a cold and hungry remnant of deserters-stragglers. As with the riveting *Das Boot* (also a Bavaria Atelier Production), while I find myself not exactly rooting for the Germans—I know they were stunningly defeated, anyway, and got what they and their war aims deserved—I can't refrain from feeling some sympathy for some of them in their miserable end.

The director, Joseph Vilsmaier, has succeeded in eliciting that sympathy by using a conventional war-film scenario. There are the ordinary grunts with differing personalities—the Good Germans—and the bad officers; there is the gung-ho lieutenant who grows up morally in the course of the story; there are terrific battle scenes leavened by sardonic humor in the face of death; there are encounters with the very human Russian enemy, both military and civilian; there is the transition from the arrogance and confidence of these Young Lions to their humiliation on the Volga (the film opens with an effective sequence that contrasts the battalion enjoying wine and women during R and R on an Italian beach, to their anxiety as their troop-train crosses the ominous Russian steppe). But it is an honest portrait that highlights in miniature the larger grisly drama of Stalingrad. (A similar portrait is drawn in the famous German novel of the same name by Theodore Plievier. The epic novel by Vassily

Grossman, *Life and Fate*, tells it from the Russian side, as does the history by Alexander Werth, *Russia at War, 1941-1945*).

The city, an important trans-shipment point and rail center, was once called Tsaritsyn and renamed when Stalin led Soviet forces against the Whites during the Russian Civil War. The symbolism was immense as Hitler declared he "would not leave the Volga," and Stalin commanded "not one step back." The result was the encirclement of the German 6th Army and its pulverization leading to surrender. Much of this information is transmitted through title cards at the beginning and end of the film, and at key points in the story when it becomes clear there was no hope for German victory despite the mantra "In the Name of the Führer". Vilsmaier translates the vast scale of the battle into its reality as a series of house-to-house, virtual hand-to-hand confrontations amid the ruins of the city, what the Germans call "rat-warfare". (Down in a sewer we even see rats gnawing at the corpse of a soldier.)

The film is shot in color, but the primary hues are the field-grey of German uniforms, the white of snow and ice, and the red of bloody stumps, torsos, and smashed skulls. Striking, too, are the cold blue eyes of Lieutenant Hans von Witzland (Thomas Kretschmann), of an aristocratic warrior family, whose trajectory from a proud and demanding officer to a humbled deserter who joins his men in their private farewell to arms provides the dramatic spine of the story. Branded a "Russian-lover" when he deplores the brutal treatment of Soviet POWs, his honor and ethics as a soldier and officer are repeatedly put to the test. From the Nazi point of view, he fails; traditional ethics had no place in Operation Barbarossa, the savage campaign against the sub-human Slavic-Jewish-Bolsheviks. An emotional highpoint of the film: von Witzland's refusal, as he is paralyzed with moral horror, to order the execution of a group of Russian civilians. Another officer gives the command, and they are shot.

War-film gore and carnage can be banal; ditto stereotypical "moral" situations, as in this firing-squad scene. But Vilsmaier, with his superb cast and his own cinematography, brings it off convincingly here in this powerful film, from its ironic sunny opening to the long grim fadeout of a frozen Witzland cradled in the arms of a soldier. It is a strong feature-film complement to the stark documentary compilation *Stalingrad* (1943), shot by many Soviet cameramen at the site, directed by Leonid Varlamov and Roman Karmen, some of which was used for the television series *The Unknown War*, narrated by Burt Lancaster. That this Stalingrad is German adds to its power.

[*Cineaste*, XXIII, 2, 1997]

Prisoner of the Mountains

Prisoner of the Mountains (1996) belongs in a way to that venerable genre, the Russian war film. Only things have been turned inside out. Russia's enemies here are not the ferocious counter-revolutionary White Armies of the Civil War (as in, say, *Chapayev*), or the savage German invaders of World War II (*The Rainbow, Fate of a Man*, and numerous memorable others). In Sergei Bodrov's film, Russians are the invaders, their Chechen opponents are tough, but noble, and war itself is the cruel enemy.

Bodrov (b.1948), formerly a journalist and scriptwriter, came to prominence as a director during the liberating, *glasnost* wave of the Gorbachev years, when once forbidden subjects and styles filled Soviet screens. To cite two of his best known films: *The Non-Professionals* (1987) follows a troupe of young amateur musicians through rural Kazakhstan in a detached, semi-documentary way, while *Freedom is Paradise* (1989) is an unadorned look at Soviet society through the eyes of a lad who escapes from his reform school to seek out his father in a distant prison camp. Bodrov is clearly animated by humanist concerns, and by a quality I've heard more than one Russian in the film world describe as essential for the health of post-Soviet society—*compassion*. The director has said that he wanted to make a film set in a contemporary battleground—Bosnia, for example, or the former Soviet republic of Tadjikistan—not in order to engage political issues or take political sides, but to claim eternal human values amid war's ravages. When the smoldering situation in the Northern Caucasus flared into a full-scale war of Chechen independence from Moscow, Bodrov had an ideal dramatic vehicle for expressing his compassion—that war plus a Tolstoy short story about an analogous war a century and a half earlier.

It took a certain amount of courage for a Russian director to craft a pacifist film about the Chechen war, and one, moreover, in which the Chechens are presented more positively than the Russians. (Many Russians have objected to the film on these grounds.) Passions run very high in both camps. The Chechens, a Muslim people numbering about a million and a half today have been battling Russian control since the early 19th century. In 1944 Stalin ordered wholesale deportations of the Chechen population to Central Asia for collaborating with the Germans. After the USSR broke up in 1991, they started their drive to independence. From the Russian side, the popular view of the Chechens is of a sullen minority involved in illegal activity (like other ethnic groups from the Caucasus, they are known derisively in Russian as "Blacks") and blamed for much of the organized criminal violence around such areas as drug trafficking and gun-running that have plagued major cities in post-Soviet Russia. From the official point of view, the Chechen quest for independence threatens, if successful, the unity of the fragile Russian Federation, made up of dozens of non-Russian minorities.

None of these issues appear in Bodrov's film, nor, consequently, is the exceptional ferocity of the two-year war explained. The Russians have resorted to massive aerial bombardment and artillery barrages, while the Chechen guerrilla campaign has seen mass hostage taking. The site of the film's action is not even identified as Chechnya. (It was shot in neighboring Dagestan.) It is a given that we are in Chechnya, and that the Russian army is there. Why it is there, and why the Chechens give battle is left to the audience to intuit. I see in these omissions not only Bodrov's above-the-fray pacificism (both sides are victimized by the war, whatever the issues), but the severe post-Communist "reaction-formation" of so much of the Russian intelligentsia, filmmakers included, against all "politics" and political ideologies. What counts for them are the "normal" human currencies of love, decency, loyalty, friendship, kindness—or Bodrov's compassion.

Which brings us back to Tolstoy, and another peculiar (minor) omission. The film credits the story to "an idea of Boris Giller," one of its producers and screenwriters, but any educated Russian knows it is derived from a spare and touching Tolstoy short story written for young people in 1872, based on the author's experiences as a Russian officer in the Caucasus a generation earlier. In the Tolstoy tale, *A Prisoner of the Caucasus* (subtitled, *A True Story*), two Russian officers are captured and held in shackles for ransom by a Chechen villager. One of them escapes with the assistance of the Chechen's young daughter, a girl of 13, who is moved by pity and compassion (and perhaps something else) for the Russian.

Flash forward a century and a half for Bodrov's film, based on the outline of the Tolstoy story, embellished and transferred artfully to contemporary Chechnya. (Bodrov's title in Russian is the same as Tolstoy's.) The Russians are still there, and the Chechens are still fighting them and taking them hostage. In some of Tolstoy's other works his descriptions of the hatred the Chechens felt for the Russians even read like the dispatches of journalists there in our own day.

Bodrov's film version is a handsome and melancholy war-drama set in the spectacular Caucasus, with Pavel Lebeshev's camera roaming beautifully in panoramic long shots across the flat-topped roofs of mountain villages. (Lebeshev was the talented cinematographer whose work may be seen in many of Nikita Mikhalkov's films, including *Slave of Love* and *Oblomov*). Bodrov's two captured Russians are a hard-drinking cynical veteran NCO played with effective swagger by Oleg Menshikov, the dark messenger of death in Mikhalkov's *Burnt by the Sun*, sporting a moustache here and looking like a carefree Russian Errol Flynn; and a young and innocent recruit — the late Sergei Bodrov, Jr., the director's son, not a professional actor but turning in a superb performance as a reluctant soldier who learns some life — and death — lessons in the Chechen killing fields. The two are brought closely together in captivity after a nicely shot opening ambush scene.

The film unfolds in a series of episodes that are paced briskly by Russian standards, rather glacially by Western norms, especially for an adventure film. But taking time with the story works to its advantage; we get the full flavor of several different relationships as they develop. There is the buddy aspect in the older soldier-young recruit pairing. They see the world differently, and get on each other's nerves, but they recognize they are in this thing together and must bear it with patience and humor — those very

Russian characteristics of endurance, and indifference to danger. In one scene they dance rollickingly to Louis Armstrong's *Let My People Go*. In another, the crusty Sasha (Oleg Menshikov) lapses into nostalgia and despair, and reaches to touch the young Vanya's hand as the soundtrack soars with the patriotic hymn *The Slavyanka*: a very moving moment. (Leonid Desyatnikov's haunting score alternates Caucasian motifs of reeds and woodwinds with Russian tunes, especially *The Blue Scarf*, a sentimental ballad popular during World War II.)

The second important relationship involves the two Russians and their captor Abdul (the Georgian actor Djemal Sikharuklidze), an imposing figure who wants to exchange them for his son, held by the Russian army, and who resists the demand of some elders to kill the two. His dramatic act of kindness in the film's denouement matches the tenderness shown by his young daughter. Her relationship with the young recruit Vanya is both central to the film's narrative and its emotional core. Played brilliantly by another non-professional (Susanna Mekhralieva, discovered by Bodrov in a Dagestan schoolroom), the dark-eyed Nina is captivated by Vanya, by his plight of course, but perhaps by budding romantic feelings for him as well. She talks to him, dances for him, dresses for him, and ultimately frees him in a courageous act of defiance against all the force of patriarchy and custom. (Unlikely? Well, Tolstoy wrote that it was a true story, and anyway it serves Bodrov's purpose well.) Vanya, fearing the trouble her act will cause her, refuses to escape. The powerful climax follows: a long, long walk past a cemetery (a nice touch) as Abdul leads Vanya to his execution ("dead man walking," Chechen style). Abdul is bound now to avenge the killing of his son by the Russians during an escape attempt, but in a heart-stopping moment as we wait with Vanya for the fatal bullet, Abdul fires into the air and walks away somberly, back to the camera. Enough of killing, that walk seems to say.

I should note that some have interpreted that last scene differently. Since we never see Abdul fire into the air, and since the traditional code of vengeance would strongly suggest otherwise—Abdul would shoot him, period—the alternate explanation has a now dead Vanya magically trying to wave off the Russian helicopter gunships overhead as they target the village. And in a ghostly voice-over afterword Vanya tells of trying to dream of the villagers "he came to love." This interpretation is fueled by two episodes in which the executed Sasha—Sasha's ghost—appears to Vanya. (Sasha had killed two Chechens cold-bloodedly in an attempted escape; his throat is cut in retaliation.) So why not have Vanya's ghost turn up as well? I think Bodrov's two brief excursions into magic realism are ill-conceived and clumsily brought off, but in that last scene, either way, the "real" Vanya or the "magic" Vanya conveys the same message: the merciful Chechens, people he developed an affection for, are repaid with brutality.

There is one other clumsy scene in an otherwise consistently moving and well-made film that amply earned its Academy-Award nomination in the foreign-language category. Bodrov stages a folkloristic tableau of Chechen warriors dancing, drinking, wrestling, and roasting some meat at a campfire. It comes off kitschy and patronizing. The film has plenty of authentic local color without it in numerous village scenes. The contrast between pre-modern village life shown in the film and the very modern instruments of war (on both sides, though the Russians have the overwhelming fire-power), is striking.

The guns were silent in Chechnya when this was written. A peculiar peace had materialized: the Chechens claimed independence and acted that way, while the Russians denied their independence but agreed to let them act that way. There were rumors in Moscow then that President Boris Yeltsin asked for a private screening of *Prisoner of the Mountains,* and was so affected by the film that it impelled him to redouble efforts for peace. Wonderful, if true. Now that would have been really good magic realism.

[*Cineaste*, XXIII, 1, 1997]

SHORT TAKES

Blockade

Soon after invading the USSR the Nazis printed invitations to an expected grand victory celebration at the famed Astoria Hotel in Leningrad. They never got their gala; Leningraders gave them 900 days of resistance. "The Great Patriotic War" has a canonical status in Soviet, even post-Soviet, film. Sergei Loznitsa's documentary (2005) is his contribution to the canon, and employs a very effective strategy to convey Leningrad's mortal struggle. He assembled old clips in a silent, episodic array—no narration or titles, with an added track occasionally simulating ambient sounds. An unspoken narrative thread arranges the found footage, beginning with a shot of the beautiful skyline at dusk or dawn (or is it during the "White Nights"?). But barrage balloons and gun emplacements tell us this is a city at war. Cruel scene after scene follows. Women trudge through icy streets hauling belongings—or frozen corpses—on sleds. The street dead are so common that passers-by hardly notice. German POWs are marched through the streets; save for a woman who spits and shouts at them, onlookers are impassive. The terrible reminders of death alternate with scenes of life—people gather at newsstands or bulletin boards, or they rip up stadium benches for firewood; they fill buckets of water from holes in the ice, or they clear rubble from bomb wrecked buildings. Finally, this grim minimalist montage yields fireworks of victory over the blockade. I offer a speculative cautionary note: at the end, the film's sole title identifies a clip of those hanged in public as Germans accused of war crimes. Could they have been Russian collaborators? We can't tell.

[*Cineaste*, XXXII, 2, 2007]

Zelary

A torrid lovemaking scene opens this at once strong and sensitive film from director Ondrej Trajan, set in Nazi-occupied

Czechoslovakia, 1943-1944. *Zelary* (2003) is a significant new contribution to the Eastern European war-film genre, and the war intrudes in several brutal ways, but its narrative heart is an unlikely love story pairing an unlikely couple. Eliska (Ana Geislerova), is a future doctor involved in the urban resistance; Joza (Gyorgy Cserhalmi) is a barely literate peasant from the Moravian mountain country. Physically, too, they differ. The vibrant young Eliska is pretty in a Julie Delpy sort of way—thin, with delicate features and red hair, while the older Joza is stolid and muscular, and has the craggy face you would expect of a man of the mountains. (An extracurricular contrast: Geislerova is a popular Czech actress; Cserhalmi is famous in his native Hungary.) A plot contrivance—the Gestapo is after Eliska—throws them together in a fictitious marriage to live in Joza's village, Zelary, in a beautiful valley, beautifully photographed by Asen Sopov. A series of short scenes structures the film as a kind of village epic—with many diverse, vivid characters and rich folkloric detail—that unfolds with the changing seasons. And the couple changes as well: In their chaste bedroom they become real husband and wife. Corny and you guessed it? Yes, but *Zelary* is handled throughout with such storytelling grace and understatement, plus skillful acting, that what develops is entirely welcome and believable. (The film is based on a true story, as told in the autobiographical novella by Kvita Legatova.) Another kind of contrast: the carnality of the bedroom scene at the beginning of the film (Eliska with her then lover) and the tender, emotion-filled unions between Eliska and Joza. The latter are infinitely more erotic—as always, less is greater. The menace of war is never far away from village life. The SS makes its appearance, and there is a sequence with villagers taking refuge in a swamp reminiscent of a grim scene in Elem Klimov's terrifying war masterpiece, *Come and See*. The real shocker here comes with the Red Army's appearance. A unit of Soviet soldiers fueled by drink, vengeance, and lust rampages Zelary even as they liberate it. Their loutish behavior inevitably affects the fate of Eliska and Joza. This whole section, incidentally, could never have been filmed when Moscow ruled Eastern Europe, its cinema included.

[*Cineaste*, XXX, 1, 2004]

100 Days Before the Command

Probably every recruit in every army in the world has at some time felt during basic training like the lowly invertebrate of Psalm XXII, 6: *But I am a worm, and no man: a reproach of men, and despised of the people.* That happens to be the epigraph for Hussein Erkenov's unconventional *100 Days Before the Command* (1990), a late Soviet *glasnost* film exposing the humiliations and cruelties inflicted on young men by their military superiors at a training camp in Central Russia. (The title is a misleading literal translation; better would be "100 Days Before Discharge.") The harshness of Soviet basic training was legendary, outstripping other nations in that regard, but it wasn't until the freeing up of the media in the Gorbachev era that such matters were openly broached in the press, literature, television and film. Harrowing tales of pent-up frustrations that led to breakdowns, suicides and fragging became common public knowledge. The novella by Yuri Polyakov was among the first to address the subject, and it is the basis for this film that he also co-scripted. There are plenty of ugly, graphic episodes—an officer urinates on a sleeping recruit, another dumps a bowl of soup on a table-mate at mess, and so on—but Erkenov conveys the terrors mostly in a moody, elliptical, and often incomprehensibly enigmatic style. He has obviously watched a lot of Tarkovsky, judging by the many long takes, the slow, *very* slow pans, the color alterations, and the plenitude of water and rain throughout the work. (The many scenes exposing male flesh, often full frontally—and a couple of a nude woman identified as "Death"—reminded me of Claire Denis's similarly elliptical film of a decade later, *Beau Travail*, set among French Foreign Legionnaires.) *100 Days* is uneven; by turns haunting and edgy, and irritatingly obtuse, but powerful overall.

[*Cineaste*, XXVI, 2, 2001]

The 3 Rooms of Melancholia

This powerful triptych with the odd, poetic title offers an unusual window on the two Chechen wars. Singular savagery has marked the conflicts. The Russians have violated Chechnya and its inhabitants with all the delicacy of a brutal occupying army, while the Chechens have resorted to the not very endearing tactics of mass hostage taking. Accounts of the wars are bound to be painful, whether from the Russian or Chechen point of view. The pain and the scale of violence have been shown in several films by some major Russian directors, but none comes as close to portraying the anguish of the war as this documentary (2004) from the Finnish directing and producing team of Pirjo Honkasalo and Kristiina Pervila, with camera work by Honkasalo. The film elicits some acute visual and emotional effects by understatement and from its stylized documentary form—long, silent tracking shots, very tight close-ups, mournful original music (by Sanna Salmenkallio), a sequence shot in black and white, very little dialogue, an occasional voiceover. There is no battle footage, no military or political talking heads, no narration for historical background and current developments, only the impact of the wars on what was once Grozny, the ravaged Chechen capital, and on war's most vulnerable victims, the children. Children occupy these "rooms" in different locations, the first, ironically enough (perhaps a bit too ironically) at Kronstadt, off St. Petersburg, where Russian cadets, many from broken homes themselves, are drilled in the arts of war and anti-terrorism. "Room No. 2" introduces us to Hadizhat Gataeva, a woman of mercy who combs the desolate remains of Grozny for the wretched children orphaned by the wars. She takes them to the comparatively safe haven of neighboring Ingushetia ("Room No. 3"), a setting allowing for some beautiful photography that could have come from a Tarkovsky composition. Gataeva's orphanage may provide the children some relief from war, but will their wounds ever heal? Filming in Chechnya remained hazardous; credits at the end of this disturbing documentary include the film crew's security and bodyguards.

[*Cineaste*, Vol. XXX, 4, 2005]

CHAPTER III

Fragments from the Russian Experience

From the West, and its Russophile (or Russophobe) fascination with Russia in her Imperial, Soviet or post-Soviet incarnations, have come floods of commentary and interpretation, at length and aphoristically. Winston Churchill famously described Soviet Russia as a "riddle, wrapped in a mystery, inside an enigma." The Marquis de Custine, in his much quoted musings following his travels in early 19th-century Russia, described an "Empire of Fear." Scholars and journalists also sought comprehension through travel and direct observation, plus research too—pioneering Russianists such as Bernard Pares and Mackenzie Wallace in Great Britain, Anatole Leroy-Beaulieu in France, among them. Their analogs in the U.S. included George Kennan, whose distant cousin, George Frost Kennan, had an enormous impact on U.S. policy toward the Soviet Union, having formulated what became known as the doctrine of "containment," based on his perception of the "sources of Soviet conduct," and what to do about them.[1] Russian/Soviet study centers and institutes proliferated in the U.S. during the Cold-War years; a publishing industry developed, and continues to this day, though not with the same volume and political urgency. (I and this book and perhaps you, the reader, are part of the phenomenon.) Popular culture as reflected in movies and music—from Hollywood's Doctor Zhivago *to The Beatles'* Back in the USSR—*has also shared in the fascination.*

Do we as a result have a clear, generally acceptable understanding that captures the "Russian soul," "eternal Russia," or "the Russian experience"? It should be obvious that there is no simple or single, free-standing answer. Scholars, journalists, educators, writers and other members of—to employ a widely used Russian term—the intelligentsia have displayed many divergent and often contradictory views. As for the general public, here or in other countries, words and names from the Russian/Soviet experience that have entered the global lexicon are a form of shorthand, convenient portals to certain mental images. Some, legitimately or not, bear benign, others sinister connotations. Think sputnik, Lenin, KGB, gulag, vodka, Dostoevsky, steppe, Stalin, kremlin, tsar/czar, Siberia, Rasputin, soviet...[2]

Get the picture? String those and other signifiers together and a rough history in fragments lies behind them, much as the following articles and reviews in this section comprise a kind of short tour d'horizon of some of the subjects that have captivated us—and the Russians themselves, filmmakers not least.

---

[1] Churchill uttered the celebrated epigram in a 1939 radio broadcast, but he quickly added a "key" that undermined much of the purported mystery: "That key is Russian national interest". Astolphe, Marquis de Custine's aphorisms appear in his *La Russie en 1839*. Anatole Leroy-Beaulieu published *L'Empire des tsars et les Russes* in three volumes, 1883-87. Sir Donald Mackenzie Wallace's *Russia* was published in 1877, while Sir Bernard Pares' many Russia studies include numerous editions of his text, *History of Russia* (originally 1926). George Kennan's revealing *Siberia and the Exile System* appeared in 1891. His cousin's argument was published as an article under the pseudonym, "X," in the journal *Foreign Affairs* in 1947. Kennan later held that his call for "containing" the expansion of Soviet power was misinterpreted in an exaggerated military direction by U.S. policy makers.

[2] I'm tempted to include Russian Roulette in the list, but no one is sure of its provenance, although a good case could be made that fatalism and a taste for risk become what we think of as the "Russian character".

Nostalgia for the Homeland: Tarkovsky, *Oblomov* and Svetlana Alliluyeva

It used to be that if you were Russian and you had abandoned the USSR you could forget about ever returning. A primitive, quite tribal vindictiveness guided the Soviet government in matters of repatriation. If you left, you were a traitor, period. One extreme manifestation of this ferocious demand for loyalty was Stalin's practice of punishing Soviet soldiers who fell into German hands during World War II and were eventually liberated. They went straight from German concentration camps to Soviet ones according to the logic that capture proved disloyalty. In the "Great Patriotic War of the Soviet Union" a true son of the fatherland would have courted death rather than risk capture.

Back in the 1980s, however, the Soviet government displayed an unaccustomed warmth toward some of its prodigals—repatriation with a human face. With suitable public repentance on their part, certain defectors and deserters were allowed to rejoin the fatherland after abandoning it. You could un-defect. You *could* go home again.

At least you could if you were the journalist Oleg Bitov, who claimed to have been kidnapped by British agents; if you were Igor Rykov, Oleg Khlan, and Nikolai Ryzhkov, who all deserted in Afghanistan; and of course, if you were Svetlana Alliluyeva, Stalin's daughter, who *defected*—no ambiguity about it—to the United States in 1967, her way of celebrating the 50th anniversary of the Bolshevik Revolution.

We don't know what negotiations, deals, plea-bargainings, and promises were concluded between these five individuals and Soviet authorities. We don't know if these examples represented the start of a major campaign on the part of the Soviet government to woo back the hundreds of cultural and political dissidents who defected, or who were handed one-way tickets to the West and stripped of their Soviet citizenship. We don't know if an even larger target was intended: the tens of thousands of Soviet Jews, Armenians, and Germans whose emigration was a palpable byproduct of *détente* and whose return, even in small numbers, would have been a triumph in those days of renewed Cold War. The re-interring of Boris Chaliapin's remains in Moscow even suggested that the acceptability of return was not limited to the living.

What we do know is that for many Russians, even non-ethnic "Russians," the fatherland exerted and exerts a powerful, mystic magnetism, like no other in the West.

A cliché? Part of the old nonsense about a purported Russian soul? Well, speak to any *émigré*, even the most anti-Soviet, and you will notice the eyes clouding over with tenderness for the homeland when the subject comes up. Some describe this Russian suffering as *toska*, a longing for the lost homeland. The late film director, Andrei Tarkovsky, among the most prominent Soviet defector-luminaries, called his penultimate film *Nostalghia*, and reminded Westerners that the word is pronounced in Russian with a hard 'g'. "To us," Tarkovsky said, "the word signifies a painful and destructive mood or feeling." The film is a bleak portrait of a Soviet scholar in Italy broodingly researching the life of an 18th-century Russian *émigré* composer who eventually committed suicide. His own condition as an expatriate was reflected in the film, Tarkovsky explained. So: a melancholic Russian director films abroad the story of a melancholic Russian scholar abroad researching the life of a melancholic Russian composer living abroad. This *nostalgia*, according to Tarkovsky, "mixes the love for your homeland and the melancholy that arises from being far away. It is an illness, a moral suffering which tortures the soul. It can be fatal if one is not able to overcome it, but it can be contracted only in a foreign country." Given this diagnosis and the self-evident cure, it would have come as no surprise if Tarkovsky had un-defected as well, especially if he had survived into the Gorbachev period.

Back in Moscow, Sergeant Rykov described his homesickness and despair while in England. "If previously," he said, our heads were burning with narcotics [in Afghanistan], now [in London] it was with thoughts of home. I came to understand clearly that I could live only in the land of my birth."

At her press conference in Moscow Svetlana Alliluyeva reported that two triggers helped push her homewards. One was what she saw as the absence of feeling, during D-Day commemorations in the West, for the Soviet dead in World War II. Forget for a moment her father's pact with Hitler or his peculiar reluctance to take Hitler's invasion seriously when it came; never mind Western losses or the vast Western contribution to the Soviet war effort in the form of lend lease and the Normandy invasions: that the USSR suffered some 20-30,000,000 dead in battling and defeating the Germans is a stark, awesome fact that no Russian, defector or loyalist, will allow anyone in the West to forget.

The other trigger for Alliluyeva was seeing the Soviet film *Oblomov* (1979). Who couldn't help wanting to go to Russia, even for just a visit, after seeing Nikita Mikhalkov's beautiful film? It is based on the great 19th-century novel by Ivan Goncharov about a title character who suffers from anhedonia and neurasthenia, a sort of Slavonic-aristocratic Woody Allen. The celebrated opening scene takes pages and pages to get Oblomov out of his divan-bed. For his torpor and indiscipline Russians have taken Ilya Oblomov to be a national type. Lenin condemned "Oblomovism." Yet the film amounts to a reverie for traditional Russia. On the soundtrack is an excerpt from Rachmaninoff's sublime *Vespers*. (Rachmaninoff: another *émigré* who died in the West. Will Holy Soviet Russia claim his remains too?) A sleigh glides along the snow past the pastel-colored facades of old St. Petersburg. And there is the broad, Russian *douceur* of Oblomov himself, who, after all, seeks only *pokoi*, an untranslatable word connoting unruffled serenity. He doesn't want any hassles, we would say. Alliluyeva would sympathize. Explaining that she sought private peace, not political freedom, she says that in the West she "was not free…for one single day. I was in the hands of businessmen, lawyers, political figures and publishers" interested in her as a commodity. (Alliluyeva has been unhappy everywhere; her most recent residence is in the U.S. again. See *Svetlana About Svetlana*, a short 2009 documentary by Lana Parshina.)

The last scene in *Oblomov* has a child, the son of the dead Oblomov, running across endless fields beneath a wide-open sky crying "Mama, mama, mama…" The boy had been adopted by Oblomov's friends; he was on his way to meet his real mother who visited him occasionally. She didn't say so at her press conference, but I'll bet Svetlana Alliluyeva, who longed to see her children and grandchildren, wept during this cinematic epiphany exalting reunion in Mother Russia.

If you want to understand Russia and the Russians, learn why they defect. Even more, learn why some go back.

[©1985 Commonweal Foundation, reprinted with permission. For subscriptions: www.commonwealmagazine.org.]

5. At the Hermitage, working on Alexander Sokurov's *Russian Ark* (2002). Sokurov is at right; his cinematographer, Tilman Büttner, center, in short sleeves.

6. Cinematographer Tilman Büttner's favorite scene: Catherine the Great watches a rehearsal in Sokurov's *Russian Ark*.

Filming Sokurov's *Russian Ark:* An Interview with Tilman Büttner

Russian Ark is not what you might readily identify as a film by the Russian master, Alexander Sokurov. The mood of Sokurov cinema, including the many documentaries, "Elegies," and features, is usually dreamy, vaporous, deeply spiritual; the look of his films matches their opaque story lines and their quiet characterizations—spare, gloomy, contemplative. *Russian Ark* is different; its parts are a movable feast bursting with color and energy and noise, a set of costume mini-dramas full of personality, an anti-Sokurov carnival. There is even—rare for a Sokurov film—some humor. And, wondrously, all shot in an hour and a half single video take.

What prompted Sokurov to pull off this stunt, a cinema highwire act performed in the elegant chambers and galleries of St. Petersburg's Hermitage, where filming is normally forbidden? His answers have ranged from the fatuous to the poetic. I got sick of editing, he is quoted as saying in one interview; I wanted a film that unfolded its subject in a single breath, he said in another. That subject, outwardly, at least, is history, Russian history to be exact, stretching from the time of Peter the Great in the early 18th century to the eve of Romanov demise in 1913, with a reference or two to Soviet times, and some glances at the present. (At one point, the Director of the Hermitage himself, Mikhail Piotrovsky, puts in an anachronistic appearance.)

Sokurov has always had a taste for history, his major at Gorky University, and much of his *oeuvre* dwells on historical themes. Three of his last group of feature films focused on Hitler (*Moloch*, 1999), Lenin (*Taurus*, 2001), and Emperor Hirohito (*The Sun*, 2004), a trilogy on 20th-century men of power. In *Russian Ark*, Sokurov conveys historical episodes and historical figures through a series of brilliantly realized stagings—here is Peter the Great yanking at the ear of an underling, while Katya, his wife, tries to calm him; there is Catherine the Great applauding a theatrical rehearsal, then running to take a leak; Nicholas I accepts the apologies of the Persian envoy for a massacre at the Russian legation in Tehran; Nicholas II, the last Tsar, supervises his large family at table. Historians of Russia, especially, will have delicious guessing-game fun identifying all the historical *dramatis personae* Sokurov parades before the viewer: Who was that woman wearing a nun's habit walking with the Tsaritsa Alexandra? Wasn't it Ella, her widowed sister? And why does the Tsaritsa say, "It's all my fault"? She's talking about carrying the fateful genes that gave her son and heir to the throne the dread bleeding sickness, hemophilia. That sailor standing behind the royal family while they dine is Nagorny, the faithful companion to the ailing heir. (Rasputin doesn't show up.) Is that dandy with curly hair and a dark complexion chasing someone supposed to be Pushkin? Who is that man dressed in black we see stalking the marquis on his journey through the museum? Probably an agent of the "Third Section," Nicholas I's secret police. (He is played by one of Sokurov's favorite actors, the very talented Leonid Mozgovoy, who has incarnated Chekhov in *Stone*, 1992, as well as Hitler and Lenin.) That Russian diplomat massacred in Tehran, wasn't he the celebrated dramatist Alexander Griboedov?

Non-specialists may have trouble picking out these things. No matter; there is enough visual splendor in the whole show to keep everyone enthralled. Besides, there are the fascinating verbal exchanges between the wandering, opinionated French aristocrat, who is seen, and his soft-spoken foil and companion, who is invisible. The aristocrat is based on Astolphe, Marquis de Custine (1790-1857), a writer and traveler with a gift for observation and aphoristic commentary that scholars and journalists have leaned on ever since the publication of his *La Russie en 1839* (it has appeared in English in several editions). His stinging remarks have entered the vocabulary of all writers on Russia, Imperial and Soviet: A society "not built on foundations of human dignity;" "Siberia, that indispensable auxiliary of Muscovite civilization;" "I was entering the Empire of Fear;" "Russia is a land of useless formalities;" and, one of his most quoted quips, "The Russian government is an absolute monarchy moderated by assassination." In *Russian Ark* he is charmingly played, with just the right doses of hauteur and kvetchiness by Sergei Dreiden, who resembles the great Swedish actor, Erland Josephson. The voice of the contemporary figure who mysteriously finds himself accompanying the marquis belongs to Sokurov himself. Many of their exchanges center on the marquis's unwillingness to credit Russians with originality or talent, a position

Custine sets forth repeatedly in his book. Their give and take also echoes the age-old debate Russians have tortured themselves with—are we part of European civilization or not? No doubt about where the marquis stands: "Raphael is not for you," he sniffs in the film. "Goodbye, Europe," says his companion, ambiguously (sarcastically?) at the end of their promenade—goodbye to the marquis, or to the great European treasures collected in the Hermitage?

Another of Sokurov's passions, of course, is art, and the Hermitage was a natural for locating this pageant of Russian history. The film was thus also a way of paying homage to the ineffable works hanging on its walls, many of which come into view. Sokurov seems to have had a similar intent when he set out on another film journey, the beguiling documentary, *Elegy of a Voyage* (2001)—in some ways foreshadowing *Russian Ark*—which carried him across European borders from Russia to Holland, where he lovingly settled in at a "Dutch Ark," Rotterdam's Boijmans Museum. So perhaps Russian history here is really Sokurov's way of meditating on the Hermitage's eternal art, and not the other way around. As history, after all, *Russian Ark* is rather incomplete, just a slice of it, a group portrait of a narrow stratum at the top; there are no peasants or proletarians here. And that group of bejeweled ladies and dashing, caparisoned officers, and the last Tsar and his whole family is marked for doom, even as they dance to Glinka's mazurka at a grand, joyous, spectacularly filmed ball in that dazzling penultimate scene. Above the music, though, you could almost hear the Great October Socialist Revolution crashing at the gates of the Winter Palace. But the unsinkable *Russian Ark* and its precious cargo will survive.

In the end, for all of its engrossing overt and latent themes, *Russian Ark* is a towering achievement of cinematography. (The irony: Sokurov, the spiritual filmmaker, is impresario to a bit of technical wizardry.) For helping realize that achievement, credit belongs to the Steadicam, and to its operator here, Tilman Büttner. Büttner, who handled the Steadicam for Tom Tykwer's popular *Run Lola Run* (1997), was born in 1961 in the German Democratic Republic (East Germany), and graduated from the Konrad Wolf School of Cinema and TV in Potsdam, 1988. He worked for East German television until the Berlin Wall came down, after which he and some colleagues organized the production company, Kopp Film. (A good account of the technical aspects of filming *Russian Ark* is the article, "Tour de Force," by Jean Oppenheimer in *American Cinematographer*, January 2003.) I spoke to Tilman Büttner in Greece for *Cineaste* magazine, at the Thessaloniki International Film Festival, where *Russian Ark* was shown to enthusiastic audiences. (Thanks to Irina Vosgerau for interpreting during the interview, and to Joel Agee for additional help with translations.)

Menashe: *I wouldn't have thought, based on the kind of film* Run Lola Run *was, that Sokurov would choose you for work on Russian Ark. Lola is rather different, to say the least, from what Sokurov had done in the past.*

Tilman Büttner: Yes, I agree with what you say, but Mr. Sokurov's idea for *Russian Ark* was for a single take by a good hand-held camera on Steadicam, and he was looking for someone who was good at shooting that way. I think that was the reason he asked me. His German production company had recommended me, and suggested working with me, so I sent him my demo reels, and his answer was "OK, we'll work together." Normally, I'm not the right man for Mr. Sokurov; his films are totally different, cinematographically.

How exactly?

His films have very fixed shots, shots of very long duration, and he himself wants to do a lot of the camera work...

He's used different filters, painted frames, distorting lens and mirrors....

Yes, but for this film it was impossible. He can't operate the Steadicam, and he can't interfere with the lens.

So, he needed you, and he needed the kind of work you do in order to realize the conception of Russian Ark—*one take, capturing the sense of motion from the initial arrival of the revelers attending the ball to the very end in the ballroom, and moving from one hall to another. And for a single, 90-minute take, he couldn't use film.*

Actually, his wish was to shoot in film, but technically this was impossible. I proposed using the Sony HD 24p camera. Using this camera you can adjust lighting to create a film look, if you work contrasts between shadow and light. I told him it was the right technology for the project, and that it would be good for later transfer to film, much, much better than 16mm, and much better than mini-DV or Hi-8. My company in Berlin was the first in Germany to buy a 24p camera and all its systems. This was very lucky for us; I could show it to Sokurov, and show him its quality. Lucky timing; a great coincidence.

You were the right person, with the right equipment, at the right moment. So he didn't have to be persuaded—he saw what you could do with this camera and he agreed to go ahead. You spoke of lighting. It looked like you used available light coming through the windows, and other light from chandeliers and fixtures. Was that so throughout, or were certain scenes specially lit?

Yes! Yes! (Emphatically.) The camera wasn't sensitive enough in the available light. In St. Petersburg on December 23 it's very dark and we needed a lot of light, although there were a lot of windows, big windows at the Hermitage. I had to create atmospheres, and wanted to avoid having the same atmosphere in each room. I had 40 electricians, and only 26 hours for light preparation in 35 rooms, big rooms. And for the first time in its history, the Hermitage closed a second day for us—usually they close only one day a week. We were given one day for preparation, and a second day for shooting.

There was a scene where Catherine the Great runs out into the snow. It looked to me very natural, using only the available light.

Yes, only what was available. But to give it a most natural look, we had to do a lot of things in post-production. Because of the limit on our time, we had to save a lot for post-production in many parts of the film, color correction, for example. We knew before shooting that we could adjust and correct later.

So it meant that you had an enormous amount of preparations—of the rooms, of the lighting for the rooms, not to speak of the hundreds and hundreds of actors and extras assembled for the action. How closely were you involved in the preparation of the action, or did Sokurov map out the whole sequence himself? The step-by-step, room-by room sequence.

A year and half before shooting, we had 7 weeks together; we walked through the halls and Sokurov showed me what he wanted. I tried to remember everything, and I also videotaped and took still photographs, especially for preparing the lighting. I and my German gaffer were in constant contact with Russian electricians and gaffers. The story was Sokurov's alone, but it was possible for me to point out how certain positions and movements would help the story.

So it was essentially Sokurov's idea to convey several hundred years of Russian history and some of its personalities at the Hermitage. Where you come in is, for example, when Sokurov wants to show Peter the Great chastising one of his underlings, you tell him we must have a certain kind of lighting, and we must have an exit strategy so I can maneuver to the next scene. Basically, is that the way you worked with him?

Yes, yes. I tried to understand his conception, and make suggestions on lighting and camera movement in order to come closer to his meaning. I always had this in mind—what did Sokurov want to express in this film?

You understood what Sokurov's conception was, what he wanted to achieve?

(Laughter)

Or did you?

I'm not sure. I'm not sure. I tried to understand, but I don't know if he understood me, and what I could do for him.

Hmm... You know, I first saw the film in New York with a Russian friend of mine. She's from St. Petersburg herself, and Petersburgers are very proud of their city, and proud of the Hermitage, and proud of how they survived the war, and so on. She said she liked the film, but she said she really didn't understand what the point of it was. What was he trying to say? And you can't figure that out either?

I believe only the director can answer this question! (Laughter) Well, Sokurov has given a lot of interviews about the film, and what he always says is that art is what lasts, art is the most important thing. At the beginning of our work, I asked him why is it we don't see the Soviet period, and revolutionary times—you know, Lenin was in the building too. That was all very important. He said, No! He wanted only the Tsars, and the gold, and the art.

Do you think Sokurov admires that period before the Revolution?

I think so.

Well, he's clearly anti-Bolshevik, and anti-Soviet. He has a line in the film where the marquis mentions the Convention in France, a bloody period during the French Revolution, and the narrator (Sokurov) replies "We had a Convention for 80 years."

He had no kind words about the Soviet period; you really couldn't talk to him about it. I tried several times to raise the subject. It was a hard time, a cruel time in the Soviet period, but it was also a time of electrification, of railroad building, of industrial progress. And what about the art of that period?

He does have one reference to the Soviet period in the film: the war with Germany and the blockade of Leningrad, when 1 million people perished.

Yes, in that connection you hear the sound of an airplane overhead, and you see 4 Soviet soldiers cross in front of me. Then there is a workshop scene—a long, dark room with snow falling within where coffins are being made—from the same period.

Clearly, you shouldn't have discussed politics with Sokurov; he has a different point of view. But did you have any serious artistic differences with him, any creative conflicts in shooting the film?

We really didn't have any conflicts as such, but by the end I felt there was a loss of trust. I did my best, but I think Sokurov wasn't satisfied. He didn't show or express that, but I felt it. I think he would have liked to run the camera himself, so in a way it was natural for him to be dissatisfied. But he isn't familiar with new camera technology; he thinks in terms of 35mm film. Exposure works differently with video, its reaction to light is different. When you work with it you have to consider lighting differently, and you have to think about what can be done after shooting, in post-production. He wanted to shoot without light. Impossible, I told him; you would have no picture on the monitor if you use no lighting with this camera. For Sokurov there was sufficient light in the building. But what's important is the relation between darkness and brightness. You have to create atmosphere, not just what's visible to the naked eye, and you have to think about what's possible after shooting.

Didn't Sokurov do his own cinematography for Taurus, *the film about Lenin?*

Yes, but not the lighting. He operated the camera, and moved the camera, but Anatoly Rodionov, his best friend and colleague, and a cinematographer, did the lighting.

You used a Steadicam, meaning that you were constantly in motion with this thing, running through the hallways, and following the actors—you were in good shape! And I don't think there was any tracking.

No, but for some parts I had a special dolly built. The Steadicam was always on my body, but occasionally for 30 seconds at a time I would have to rest and stretch by half sitting on a bar-stool placed on the dolly and wheeled over by a grip.

Bravo! You did an extraordinary job. How did the German and Russian crews work together, and how did you like working in a Russian setting?

It was wonderful working together with the Russian team. They took very good care of me in their beautiful city, and we did fine work together. I was very impressed by them. There were 40 Russian electricians, with a Russian and a German gaffer. The make-up artists and the 22 assistant directors were all Russian, and did very good work. Only I, my focus-puller, my gaffer, and the camera technician were German.

Placement was obviously very important. The ensembles of actors and extras had to be placed so that the camera could move around them and through them, and so on. Did you have anything to do with that, did you offer suggestions as to where they should be positioned?

The AD's were responsible for placing and moving. We weren't able to have a complete rehearsal. Only some parts were rehearsed, and only with the lead actor. It was only on the day of shooting that Sokurov, my shooting team, and I saw the full array of actors for the first time. The AD's had done good work with the actors and extras—in churches and gyms. But it was the first time we were all together in the Hermitage! Eight people were always behind me—Sokurov, translator, continuity people, my assistants. The dancers in the ballroom scene interacted beautifully with the camera and with our movements. You feel that only the camera alone was in the room with them. Sometimes the actors and extras had to improvise their movements and positions during the shooting because of mistakes we made.

Were there any mishaps? Did anyone trip or fall, or miss a cue?

No, nothing. But at the beginning of the film, we started continuous shooting only on the fourth take; there were technical problems with the first three. But we had to go with the fourth take—camera batteries for the whole film would not have lasted if we didn't. We also had to take advantage of the natural light; and—this was very important—Mr. Gergiev [Valery Gergiev, Conductor of the Mariinsky Theater Orchestra in the film] had to catch a flight back to New York! Later, there was a small problem with one of the lights. It came into the frame when one of the extras with her big costume walked into the room and knocked it over. I was very angry, and cursed…. [he laughs].

During the shooting, especially where there were lots of people, were commands shouted to the actors and extras?

Yes. Sokurov was always at my side, at the monitor. He had to speak his part of the dialogue with the marquis, and sometimes he gave instructions altering the actors' and extras' positions. He would shout "Now, move from left to right!" "Stop!" "Move Together!"

Well, it came off beautifully. It looked as if you had rehearsed repeatedly.

As I said before, we saw the whole thing only on the day of the shooting. When I arrived, I was fascinated by the beauty of the costumes; I saw the beauty of the scene, and the energy of the people. It gave me the energy to do my part. Midway, I was tired, very tired, and I had muscle pains, but I was so fascinated by the beauty and the novelty that I felt "I have to do this!" Before we entered the ballroom, at the doorway, I was totally overwhelmed by the mass of people, and the spectacle, and the sounds, and Gergiev. I was in pain, and I told my assistant, "Andrei, we can't get through; there are too many people, there's no space to move." He said, "Let's try. We'll make it!"

For me, one of the most impressive scenes of all was the final one where everyone is leaving, hundreds of people are leaving the Grand Ballroom. They've got their coats on, they're talking about how wonderful it was, and the camera is following them all along. How did it feel to shoot that?

I was very happy, because I knew that in five minutes it would be over! After the ballroom scene when I "danced" with the dancers, I was very exhausted. When the music ended, my feeling was "Ah, in five minutes…finished!" But before that, there was a very special sequence. I had to go down the steps with the departing guests, then reverse angle and go down the steps backwards. I had to feel my way onto the dolly below, and then my grip pulled me rapidly to the exit.

What were your favorite parts of the film?

From a cinematographer's point of view, my favorite was Catherine the Great's scene on the balcony, watching the theater rehearsal. We had good light, and it was prepared in a short time—four hours, when normally a 360-degree shot would require two days of lighting preparation. There was a nice feeling in that room. Another good scene was Catherine running outdoors, in the courtyard; a nice picture. Also the Persian ambassador reporting to Tsar Nicholas I. There were a lot of good scenes, but that theater rehearsal was best.

In that scene with the Persian ambassador, the grandson of the Shah, there's what looks like a long tracking shot, as you survey the courtiers—were you on that dolly for it?

No, I walked. We also constructed a special ramp behind the officials so that I shot them from above as I went up the ramp. That was Sokurov's idea.

In the final shot the camera pans and turns to a window, then goes through the window, and it's hard to see what's there—a fog, a river....

Yes, that's very interesting. Sokurov was not sure how to end the film. He told me we should go outside and see the river Neva, the snow and ice, and beyond the river, the city of St. Petersburg. He wanted the feeling of an ark, a ship plowing through the waves. I would have to go outside and swing the Steadicam. But after we finished the Hermitage shooting, his idea was to insert something else for the ending in post-production. What you now see at the end of the film is a shot of the Baltic Sea two hours before freezing, with mists rising. We shot that separately, and put it together with my shot from inside the Hermitage.

Meaning, we have seen paintings, culture and art inside the building and now here is the natural world?

Yes, it is indefinable space for the "Russian Ark" to sail into the future, as a kind of time-travel vessel carrying all history and culture with it, and not just the Russian.

What did you think of the dialogue between the narrator and the marquis? What was it all about?

Well, it was a constant mutual provocation. The main issue was does Russia have its own culture, or did it just imitate the French or the Italians.

I think the marquis is the chief provocateur. For example, at one point the marquis notices how well musicians are playing and affirms that they can't be Russian. The narrator quietly corrects him; yes they are Russian, he says.

Sometimes the narrator doesn't take the marquis seriously. And the marquis gets very picky at times. The narrator seems to be saying, in answer to the provocations of the marquis, that what we—the filmmakers—are doing is significant now and for the future, and it is indeed Russian art.

[*Cineaste*, XXVIII, 3, 2003]

Rasputin

In Renoir's *The Grand Illusion,* there is a wonderful scene where Russian prisoners of war welcome a gift from the Tsaritsa Alexandra. With great gusto, looking for food and spirits, they pry open a large wooden crate only to discover a random assortment of very ordinary books. (*Knigi,* they mutter.) Enraged by this insulting frustration of their expectations, they proceed to set fire to the crate, contents and all. Has there ever been better symbolic expression, in film or other medium, of the historical cliché about "the alienation of the Romanovs from the mood and needs of the people"? Or the mass anger that engulfed the royal house and plunged the entire nation into the flames of revolution and civil war?

The cliché is true enough, but behind it remains a certain human drama, a puzzle even, that has fascinated historians and filmmakers alike. There is the Tsar himself, a man who could enter the following in his diary, just after his abdication from the 300-year-old Romanov throne: "I had a long and sound sleep. Woke up beyond Dvinsk. Sunshine and frost.... I read much of Julius Caesar." (As a Russian officer of the time put it, he had "abdicated from the throne of Russia as if he were handing over a squadron.") Or take the Tsaritsa, the beautiful Princess Alix of Hesse-Darmstadt, reared by her grandmother, Queen Victoria, as an English lady at Windsor. She embraced wholeheartedly the triple creed of Autocracy, Russian Orthodoxy, and the Russian Nation associated with her consort's crown—and also developed a ruinous attachment to a

Siberian peasant-holy man. (Contrary to the whispers and rumors of the time, it was never a sexual attachment.) And this Rasputin—what was he up to? Lechery? Political power? Delusions of mystic grandeur? Pawn of others? This strange *troika* of Tsar, Tsaritsa, and Slavic *fakir* governed, during the Great War, the world's largest empire on the eve of its collapse. What a subject for a movie.

And so it has been, ever since the Russians themselves after the first (pre-Bolshevik) revolution of 1917 started turning out indictments of the lurid doings *chez* Romanov with such titles as *Dark Forces, People of Sin and Blood,* and *The Holy Devil.* The new Soviet regime's politicized aesthetics for the cinema eventually throttled such preoccupations. In the West, beginning with Lewis Selznick's grand production, *The Fall of the Romanoffs* (1917), the subject has endured to our own time. The list of Rasputins includes everyone from Conrad Veidt and Lionel Barrymore to Gert Fröbe and Christopher Lee.

These versions of Romanovs and Rasputin often hinge on a common theme of traditional historical writing, that the fate of the Russian empire was determined by a bizarre *starets* (religious elder) who enjoyed the fullest confidence of the Emperor and Empress. Sir Bernard Pares, a founder of Russian studies in the West, expressed the opinion that "the cause of the ruin came not at all from below, but from above" where "we are faced with the strangest of human tangles, the complicated and abnormal relations of three persons—Rasputin, the Empress and the Emperor: set in an ascending order of authority and a descending order of influence." Alexander Kerensky, in power for a few months before he was swept away by the Bolshevik revolution, later wrote, "If there had been no Rasputin, there would have been no Lenin."

From the official Soviet point of view, this is all bourgeois nonsense, reflections of a shallow understanding that individuals make history. The struggle of classes, the political action of masses make revolutions and topple empires. Before the inevitable tide of events, the behavior of the last Romanovs was of secondary significance. "There is no denying that Nicholas II ... was ungifted and dense," observes a text by Soviet historians, and the Tsaritsa "malicious and hysterical," yet "it was not against the physically degenerate Romanov dynasty, but against the whole obsolete autocratic system that the wave of popular wrath had risen."

Early into the Soviet period, directors themselves became exponents of what a Russian study defined as "the basic principle of the Soviet historical film.... The people [are] the major force in the historical process." Such a credo foreclosed any extended, not to mention nuanced treatment of the last Romanovs. There is no room for Nicholas and Alexandra in Eisenstein's mass epics *(Potemkin,* 1925; *October,* 1927), or in Pudovkin's ode to individual peasant and plebeian heroes *(The End of St. Petersburg,* 1927), to mention three classics that would outline the parameters for the Soviet cinema of the revolution for decades to come. As for Rasputin, perhaps the chaste traditions of Soviet film, and Soviet art in general, barred a frank treatment of his most remarkable characteristic, his powerful sexuality; better no treatment at all.

Among the several striking features of this intriguing film by Elem Klimov is, therefore, the subject itself.[1] In a film set in Petrograd in 1916, with revolution in the air, we get no positive heroes, no Lenin, no Bolsheviks, no sturdy proletarians, no aroused peasants. We have, instead, the royal family, Rasputin himself as central figure, many vividly sketched hangers-on, and lots of (by Soviet standards) sex and violence. For a film produced in 1975 for what could have been a Mosfilm contribution to the commemoration of the 60th anniversary of the Bolshevik Revolution, *Rasputin (Agoniya*—"Agony" or "Death Throes"—in the original), challenges some of the hoariest canons in Soviet cinema treatments of the Revolution. In Soviet society, the film-maker, like the poet or novelist, was often a counter-historian as well, someone who offers the public themes and interpretations not sanctioned by official ideology or historiography, often in hidden, "Aesopian" form.

As with many other directors of his generation (he was born in 1935), Klimov's talent spilled him into controversy, and his career was checkered by official wrath and official acceptance. His *Welcome (Dobro pozhalovat,* 1964) was criticized for its excessively satirical treatment of Soviet youth camps. Before its general release in 1985, *Rasputin* was allowed only an appearance or two at film festivals. In 1982 Klimov completed a film begun by his wife, Larisa Shepitko (killed in an auto accident during production), *Farewell,* based on a celebrated novella by Valentin Rasputin (no relation) about the deliberate flooding of an island-village in Siberia in the name of progress. The film was attacked for its "motif of gloom" and was even for a time barred from circulation abroad. By contrast, Klimov's last film, *Go and See (Idi i smotri)*, about the massacres of Byelorussian villagers by the Germans during World War II, received a wide global reception. The film captured the Golden Prize at the 1985 Moscow Film Festival.

For US distribution *Rasputin* was cut by 45 minutes from its original 150. In addition, oddly enough, there is a voiceover introduction and coda in the US version that conveys the standard Western judgment on Rasputin's responsibility for the revolution: "Never before had one man unwittingly unleashed such a cataclysmic chain of events." Now *that* would have amounted to a startlingly revisionist gloss had it appeared in the original. In fact, the Soviet voice, following a scrolled quotation from Lenin about the "corruption and foulness ... of the tsarist gang with the monstrous Rasputin in the lead," observes simply that Russia and the world had reached a turning point, and that a new history began on October 25, 1917. The original narration in Russian, incidentally, is soft and insinuating, as if letting the viewer onto some unpleasant secrets; it is just the right voice, for it segues perfectly into the atmosphere of strange and unearthly events that hangs over the film. The narrator in the American version, with his thick, almost comically Russian-accented English, belongs instead to some Movietone newsreel on the Russian Revolution.

Klimov's film is a sort of documentary or docudrama in its mixture of fact and fiction, with its narrator sketching in historical backgrounds, and—a favorite device of the last generation of Soviet film-makers—its intercut black-and-white newsreel footage. There are also monochrome montages of old stills. In the original, all major characters are identified in an elegant, *fin-de-siècle* script at the bottom of the frame. (Klimov's *Sports, Sports, Sports*, released in 1971 to widespread acclaim in the USSR, is similarly constructed. Contemporary interviews are interspersed with old films of sporting events and with acted sequences that recreate famous games or matches.)

The whole effect of *Rasputin* is of a loosely jointed series of colorful tableaux punctuated by visual references to the historical record. In one sequence, Tsar Nicholas (Anatoly Romashin) is working alone in a photography darkroom bathed in an eerie (hemophiliac?) scarlet. In the developing tray is a black-and-white portrait of the royal family, a real one familiar to us from numerous textbooks on old Russia. As the camera shows him looking at the photo, we recognize him as an exact likeness of the Tsar in the original. The scene is creepy, suggestive. We know what fate awaits him and the family; perhaps he knows too. (Klimov could just as effectively put Nicholas in a screening room; we know the tsar loved to watch films.)

Klimov portrays the last Romanov as an introspective and distant man occasionally escaping his terrible responsibilities as sovereign of a troubled land and father of a hemophiliac son. In his first appearance in the film, Nicholas is at an easel painting a richly colored bouquet of flowers. The scene is beautifully set up with long shots of ice skaters and a snow-covered royal playground. (How gorgeously and with what sweetness Soviet directors sometimes reconstructed old Russia.) Reluctantly and disbelievingly, Nicholas hears a lecture from the chairman of the State Duma (parliament) about the perilous state of things. Nicholas dismisses him with the announcement, "My people love me!" Cut to black and white: throngs are being fired upon by the Tsar's armed men in uniform.

So Klimov's tsar is not himself an evil or cruel man in the usual sense, not Nicholas the Bloody, as he became known in his own time, or as he was known in Soviet schools. Klimov's portrait is reminiscent of the old myth of the Good Tsar surrounded by evildoers. Nicholas seems exasperated by Rasputin's influence but also in awe of him, and incapable of challenging the Empress, who remains Rasputin's unswerving champion. Nicholas is troubled and needs a shot of vodka from time to time to keep him going. This relatively benign interpretation of the Tsar reportedly accounts for the trouble the film ran into in the USSR. Actually, there is an exoticism and a sort of abandon to much of the film that Soviet culture guardians might consider off-color. The decadence of the old order, particularly of its elites—the tipsy merchant, the hedonistic aristocrat, the cruel officer—is a commonplace scenario. But here Klimov has uncorked such a gallery of oddballs in an environment of such licentiousness, corruption, greed and religious hysteria that even Western audiences might squirm. The last line in the film belongs to the Empress (Velta Linne), who snarls, after Rasputin's burial, "I hate this country!" One can imagine a Soviet official being upset by this unflattering, disrespectful picture of Russia, even if it is pre-Soviet Russia.

From his first appearance in Petersburg early in the century, Grigory Efimovich Rasputin ("the dissolute one," is one translation for his acquired surname) gained a reputation, especially in high society, as a man of God gifted with prophetic as well as healing powers. Rasputin's hold over the royal family came from his uncanny ability to soothe the Tsarevich and arrest his bleeding during the frequent crises brought on by the dread disease inherited through his mother, the Empress. Inclined to religious mysticism to begin with, Alexandra came to see Rasputin as a blessing sent by God to heal her child. Reports of his sexual ramblings and alcoholic binges she dismissed as spiteful gossip-mongering. She saw in him as well a mystical link between Tsar and people overriding the threats to the throne organized by malicious politicians. Klimov compresses the whole drama of this abnormal situation in a brilliantly realized section early in the film. Once again, Nicholas listens, half attentively, as his officers and ministers expatiate on the menacing state of things at the front and at home. Chain-smoking, abstracted, his mind is somewhere else. Quietly, without warning, he slips away through a curtain of military maps leaving his chief of staff in mid-sentence. The camera glides us with him along a dark corridor. We are transferred in time and place: from the realm of the state to the center of the family, the nursery; from modern Russia at war to primordial Russia of icon, folk song, and mysticism. In the dim light the family witnesses a strange scene. Rasputin cradles the tsarevich, singing softly some peasant ditty. Soon the bleeding stops; the crisis has passed. The Empress, relieved, indulges a fit of hysterical praying to Rasputin's image. The Emperor stands alone at the end of the scene, isolated, uncomprehending, uneasy.

If Klimov has risked an almost Chekhovian reading of Nicholas, he has taken an even greater risk with Rasputin (Aleksei Petrenko). In scenes that alternate between *opéra bouffe* and *Grand Guignol*, Rasputin fills the screen with his wild vitality and coarseness. Petrenko plays him broadly, eccentrically, as a clown and put-on artist. When he meets some bigwigs, he enters the room crawling on all fours. When he spots a beautiful woman, he jumps out of his boots with desire. When he drinks the madeira laced with cyanide by his assassins, he burps loudly. In his apartment—a mad, disorganized interior crammed with servants, hordes of petitioners, and doting ladies, one of whom wears a beard like her master—Rasputin roams about, stuffing rubles into a pot, wringing the neck of a chicken (mercifully done), and almost ravishing a beautiful aristocrat who has come to offer herself to get her husband out of prison. (Another of Klimov's risks: she is shown nude from the waist up, and then in full nude in a flashcut.)

This is certainly an original portrait, powerful and frenzied. A comic, loutish peasant-Rasputin keeps the air of sustained mystery in the film from cloying, though some may find the portrait jarring. Perhaps there is a logic to it as historical explanation.

There is another healer in the film, a Buryat-Mongol named Badmayev who, in some of the weirder scenes, runs a curative spa and herbal center for the upper classes. The victim of a savage physical attack by churchmen, Rasputin turns to Badmayev: "They all want a miracle. They're tearing me to pieces. Some call me Christ, others—anti-Christ. For what? Why? Who am I, Badmayev?" To which the strange healer replies: "A son of a bitch and you'll croak like a lecherous cur." After that, the meticulously re-created set-piece assassination scene comes as an anti-climax. (Badmayev was a historical figure whose grandson was, until his recent death, an influential Kremlin doctor. Some Moscow rumors suggest the real reason the film was originally shelved was its satiric portrait of grandfather Badmayev.)

It is good to have a Russian *Rasputin* in the West, albeit in somewhat altered form. Apart from the historical insights, the film reminds us of the creativity of a whole group of Soviet directors—Klimov, Tarkovsky, Mikhalkov, Konchalovsky, Guerman, among others—who developed a new language for the cinema of their country in the 1960s and 70s. They liked big, often historical themes, they eschewed conventional narrative and plot in favor of mood and atmosphere, they offered ensembles of vivid characters, their sound tracks used silence and the synthesizer. (Alfred Schnittke scored Klimov's film.) Seeing *Rasputin* when it was finally released, some of the original '70s novelty had worn off. With *perestroika* it was time to enrich Soviet film vocabulary, and shake up cinema institutions. Klimov himself was appointed head of the Union of Soviet Filmmakers. It looked as if the new Gorbachev regime was positioned to support a general campaign against orthodoxy in the arts. The Soviet collapse made all of this a historic might-have-been. Tarkovsky died in 1986; Klimov outlived the Soviet regime (d. 2003), but, sadly, did not manage to extend his creativity into the new environment.

[*Film Quarterly*, XL, 1, 1986]

[1] Klimov comments on the film in the interview in Chapter VII, 2.

One Day in the Life of Andrei Arsenevich

The Andrei Arsenevich in the title of Chris Marker's documentary (1999) is the late Soviet film master, Tarkovsky (the patronymic is derived from the first name of his father, Arseny Tarkovsky, a Soviet lyric poet). A strange title for this exploration of Tarkovsky's film art, given the inevitable association with the title of Solzhenitsyn's ground-breaking novella, *One Day in the Life of Ivan Denisovich*. For one thing, the film, made for the French television series, "Cinema in Our Time," doesn't span a single day in Tarkovsky's life; it addresses a career and an *oeuvre*. For another, though Tarkovsky may have been subjected to the assorted humiliations and idiocy of Soviet bureaucrats that led him ultimately to West European exile, there is no comparison with the senseless sentences and the sadism inflicted on victims of the Gulag, such as those experienced by Solzhenitsyn's peasant anti-hero (and by Solzhenitsyn himself).

Another peculiarity: Chris Marker, the politically minded, left-leaning—Marxist?—documentarian, makes a deeply adoring film about the—spiritual? Christian? art-intoxicated?—exponent of 'difficult,' antinarrative fiction cinema, Andrei Tarkovsky. What an odd couple. But odd maybe at first sight only. A certain symmetry unites them. Marker's documentary work has also been inventive, idiosyncratic, and very personal. His signature style is the subjective film-essay. The one fiction film he directed, *La Jetée* (1962), mainly an assembly of still photographs, belongs to the genre of poetic cinema. Then there is Marker's interest in Russian themes and in the Soviet experience. Early in his film career, he directed *Letter from Siberia* (1958), and he returned to a Russian subject with *The Train Rolled On* (1971), working with the maverick Soviet director, Alexander Medvedkin, and exploring the latter's experiences as head of the agitational 'film trains' of the 1930s that visited and filmed at Soviet collective farms and industrial sites associated with the first Five-Year Plan. Medvedkin (1900-1989) was himself a fascinating figure, staunchly Soviet but quite unorthodox as a director of short fiction, and would likely have appealed to Marker for political as well as creative reasons. His first full-length feature was the quirky peasant folk-fable, *Happiness* (silent, though made in 1935), too unusual for Soviet film bosses of the day, but rediscovered and hailed by film students in Moscow three decades later. That still of those soldiers in strange masks on the cover of the 1983 paperback edition of *Kino*, Jay Leyda's classic study of Russian and Soviet film is from *Happiness*, aka *Snatchers*. Medvedkin is the eponymous hero of one of Marker's better known documentaries, *The Last Bolshevik* (1993), another loving tribute from one innovative filmmaker to another.

If you like Tarkovsky (as I do), you'll certainly like Marker's homage to him. Even if you don't, you might appreciate the Marker film for the handsome way it evokes, with generous clips, Tarkovsky's often undecipherable visual poetry, imparting to it lucidity and thematic coherence, and explaining its technical apparatus. One example: Marker points out that Hollywood loves the shot from below, silhouetting a hero against the sky (here Marker inserts a shot from a Western); Tarkovsky likes to tilt his camera downwards, bringing his subjects close to earth, at "root level" (Marker here illustrates with several different shots from Tarkovsky films). The elements themselves are virtual characters in a Tarkovsky film, and the (non) narratives are saturated with soil, grass, mud, water, rain. (As in Kurosawa, many have noted.) Fires—houses ablaze, fireplaces glowing—are regularly scripted into the action. There is little or no eroticism in a Tarkovsky film, but an almost tactile sensuousness is evident in the play of those elements, and in the way the camera pans slowly over material things. There is no mysticism here in the usual sense, only the mystery—and beauty—of earthly matter, or of art crafted by human hands (another favorite motif: the camera leafs through a volume of reproductions of great paintings, or scans paintings on a wall). Marker's narration, read by Alexandra Stewart, is mostly insightful and helpful, but not without the occasional overinterpretive gloss. The American searching the sky is "naive," in contrast to the Russian contemplating the earth. Marker attributes what he calls Tarkovsky's carnality to the Russian Orthodox sensibility, as opposed to the Roman Catholic suspicion of nature and the body. I wonder. Whatever the source, however you explain it (I can't), there is something undeniably very Russian in a Tarkovsky film, even when the characters speak Swedish (*The Sacrifice*, 1986), or Italian (*Nostalghia*, 1983). I think the most Russian moment in all of his work unfolds in the great climactic bell-casting sequence, an epiphany partly excerpted by Marker, of what no doubt will be Tarkovsky's most enduring opus, *Andrei Rublev* (1966; 1971).

Tarkovsky's body of work was not large, only seven films in a period of twenty-six years (1962-1986), not counting two student films that have survived. Life at Mosfilm was not easy for him. The director had more than the usual set of problems with Soviet philistines, and he was unusually adamant in rejecting proposed changes and compromises. Not a promising combination for productivity. Tarkovsky dabbled in the occult, and Marker cites his experience of channeling Pasternak during a séance in which the Soviet author tells the young Soviet director he will make only seven films. "Only seven?" asked Tarkovsky. "Yes, but good ones," came the reply.

Two of those films were made in Europe, after a frustrated Tarkovsky left the USSR for the West, at first as a visitor, then as a defector. According to the family-hostage policy routinely practiced by the Soviets, his son and his mother-in-law were denied permission to join him abroad. Permission was granted only when it was clear Tarkovsky was mortally ill with lung cancer. Marker has a wonderful way of handling this part of the Tarkovsky story, integrating several documentary techniques seamlessly. They also remind us of Tarkovsky's assertion that there were no boundaries between his life and his films. *One Day* opens with the beautiful opening scene of the waiting wife from *The Mirror*, a head shot from the rear, focused on the hair tied in a bun (the Russian sign of an expectant woman?). Marker then cuts to his own rear-head shot, bun included, of Tarkovsky's wife Larisa at a Paris airport waiting for the plane bringing her son and mother from Moscow. The tearful reunions are filmed, including the particularly poignant one of the bedridden Tarkovsky embracing the son he had not seen for five years. "Chris, did you get it all?" asks Tarkovsky in the Italian he learned when filming *Nostalghia*. The narration tells us two KGB agents had approached Tarkovsky on a Paris street to inform him his son and mother-in-law were coming, but when he spotted them, he thought he was about to be assassinated by two killers from Moscow. Now Marker intercuts some rare footage—a fragment by the film-student Tarkovsky, the opening scene of, yes, *The Killers*, based on the Hemingway short story, with those two intimidating strangers at the diner. Suddenly, Marker has the Russian dialog give way to American voices from the same scene of Robert Siodmak's film based on the same story. An added treat: the young actor (and jazz lover) Tarkovsky saunters into the diner whistling "Lullaby of Broadway,"

Marker's documentary ensemble of narration, direct cinema, and suggestive paralleling or illustrative intercutting from Tarkovsky films works artfully in other parts of *One Day* as well. Tarkovsky embraces his son—cut to like scenes of adult and child in several of his films. Larisa stands outside their Paris apartment, arms outstretched to the heavy rain, "Just like in a Tarkovsky film"—cut to numerous rain-soaked interiors and exteriors. Marker captures Tarkovsky in action with his cast, translator, and crew (including the regular Bergman cinematographer, Sven Nykvist), on the island of Gotland for the last, complicated scene of *The Sacrifice*, with its tracking shots of desperate characters against a unity of sky, earth, water, and fire. Marker records Tarkovsky's instructions for a particular action, and simultaneously keyholes the scene as filmed.

Filming the making of *The Sacrifice*—and of the big last scene that had to be shot again because of a camera jam—is a major part of another documentary about Tarkovsky, also very informative, though more conventional than Marker's, *Directed by Andrei Tarkovsky* (1988, by Michal Leszcylowski, who coedited *The Sacrifice*). It features narration drawn from Tarkovsky's book, *Sculpting in Time*, together with interviews of Larisa Tarkovsky, and excerpts from an Italian documentary in which Tarkovsky offers his observations on life, death, film, and art—the purpose of the last is to improve ourselves spiritually, he believed.

Marker notes that Tarkovsky's great hope was that film rose to the level of the other arts. I can think of no better introduction, for friend or foe of Tarkovsky's work, than Marker's profoundly moving film, an example as well of the short documentary in the hands of a virtuoso enchanted by his subject.

[*Cineaste*, XXVI, 4, 2001]

Siberiade

Siberia: imagine a modern tale of earth, forest, struggle, and community; a Slavonic saga, a *Siberiade*. That is the name of a prodigious film by Andrei Konchalovsky, one of the most gifted of the last generation of Soviet directors. The film won the Special Jury Prize at the 1979 Cannes Film Festival and had a run in the U.S.

Contrary to what one might have expected at the time, *Siberiade* is no long triumphalist hymn to Soviet socialist achievement. (Long it is, some three hours worth, even after Konchalovsky edited down the released version by half an hour.) The film is an often brilliantly realized historical tone poem with moods that are alternately lyrical, brutal, mystical, and frenzied; they reflect the bizarre textures and traumas of Russian 20th century history itself. Ultimately, the film bears witness not to progress, but to the *costs* of progress.

Siberia has had dreadful connotations in the Western perception—a vast hinterland, a continent of ferocious winter weather and penal servitude. We think of the lowest recorded temperatures of any inhabited place in the world, and also of the Gulag, great realms of unfreedom organized by Tsars and Soviets to confine political and other dissenters.

There is truth to this picture, but many Russians perceive Siberia differently, much as early settlers saw it—a land of pristine beauties on a colossal scale, and a realm of freedom far from Moscow's church dogmas, military recruiters, tax collectors, and bureaucrats. In early modern times Russian traders, fugitives, trappers, Cossacks, and adventurers crossed the low wooded hills of the Urals into the West Siberian forests and plains to establish outposts of Slavic culture among the sparse indigenous populations. It was a frontier epic not unlike the westward push across North America—with similar tales of heroism and the swindling of the natives. (Konchalovsky is quoted as having been struck by the idea of making a film about Siberia while flying across the United States.)

Where Russian trapper or trader traveled, the Tsars staked the claims of the Russian state. By the middle of the 19th century, the Russian continental empire embraced the whole of the Siberian expanse. Despite the huge distances, Siberia felt the economic and political pressures of European Russia. The Trans-Siberian Railroad, begun late in the 19th century, symbolized and facilitated contact. One of the last reform projects of the Tsarist regime brought thousands of land-hungry settlers into Siberia. The Siberian theater was one of the major fronts during the Civil War that pitted the new Red Army against the Whites and their foreign supporters.

Soviet victory heralded new and bigger development plans for Siberia. (Besides, Stalin, you might say, specialized in its colonization). Whole industries were moved there for originally protective reasons during the Second World War. The Soviets built giant hydroelectric dams and wood processing mills, tapped huge coal and iron deposits; they began adding a new northern stretch to parallel the old Trans-Siberian. In the 1960s came the dramatic discovery of oil and natural gas fields beneath the West Siberian marshes. (The gas pipeline from the Urengoi deposit to Western Europe angered Washington and produced some cracks in the Western Alliance.) The Old Siberia—its culture and ecology—was no match for the relentless rush of Soviet modernization.

This is Konchalovsky's raw material. From it he has distilled a tale of two Russian families in Siberia, one rich, the other poor, from before the revolution to the 1960s. Love affairs cross class and family lines, and the Revolution upends the old relationships. The poor Nikolai Ustyuzhanin runs away with the rich Anastasia Solomin; later he returns as a Bolshevik commissar to organize the village and bring the now *déclassé* Solomins into line. A poor relation of the

Solomins leaves Siberia behind him to become a Soviet military and political luminary. He too eventually returns to the village as a big shot from Moscow to check on oil prospecting.

Outwardly, this might be a conventional civil-war tale—class struggle, the Bolshevik Triumph, the coming of the Age of Oil. With the assistance of superb acting from his large cast, Konchalovsky yields the narrative iconically, through constantly shifting tableaus that are brilliantly, sometimes eerily, colored. Surrealistic, open-ended scenes are juxtaposed to straight story telling. The characters enter each others' lives, through their old and young selves, through their ghosts, and through their descendants. It is all as if Tolstoy were working with Robert Altman. In the last scene a rapturous/doleful dance of the generations recapitulates time, memory, and transformation.

These dazzling devices which comprise for me much of the cinematic virtue of *Siberiade* may be annoying puzzles for many viewers. Western audiences may also have a hard time keeping track of all the characters, their names, and their different incarnations. Konchalovsky was co-writer of Tarkovsky's controversial *Andrei Rublev* (1966). Those who were mystified by sections of that transcendent film of a monk's search for beauty in a ravaged medieval Russia will be uncomfortable with some similar techniques in *Siberiade*. There are unexplained silences and scenes that go nowhere. In one spooky sequence the last descendant of the Ustyuzhanin family, now a footloose chief of an oil drilling crew, wanders in a swamp remembered from his youth. He comes upon and enters an abandoned hut dominated by an old poster of Stalin, a famous one showing the General Secretary in his tunic with right arm outstretched (an interesting touch; Stalinism enters the film only allusively). A bottle disappears and reappears: Ustyuzhanin hears and sees someone stirring outside the hut—his dead father? He follows and drowns, although he is alive and well in the next scene. Was it a dream? Do Siberian swampy vapors trigger hallucinations? Or was it an intermezzo laced with symbolism, a possible allegory of Soviet history as a catalogue of feverish accomplishments, chased illusions, and anguish?

Konchalovsky avoids political simple-mindedness by making the clash between Ustyuzhanins and Solomins complex and full of paradoxes. The rich routinely practice violence and the poor routinely experience suffering. Yet there is a bonding between them out there in Siberia in a community living close to the earth. In different ways progress will destroy both of them. There is a spine-tingling moment in the film when the Bolshevik Nikolai Ustyuzhanin (Vladimir Samoilov) arrests his brother-in-law, Spiridon Solomin (Vitaly Solomin), as a counterrevolutionary. Spiridon breaks into folk song, the powerful, melancholic *Chorny Voron*, "The Black Raven" portending death. Suddenly Nikolai joins Spiridon in song: together, the commissar and his victim. It sounds very Russian, doesn't it? One thinks of pages in Dostoevsky, or of Ivan the Terrible slaughtering his enemies, then weeping and praying for their souls.

The themes of sanctity of nature and tradition abound in the film. There is mourning for a beautifully crafted old gate that is rammed down by an oil crew truck. When trees are bulldozed with abandon by the last Ustyuzhanin we remember early scenes in the film when his grand-father cut down spruces one by one, clearing a road leading mysteriously to the "brightest star," and listened to the sobbing of the other trees for their fallen sister.

The film also has its fun and high spirits, however, particularly when it's oil prospecting time in the Sixties. Soviet roustabouts, their good and bad times, a woman who complicates matters—it could all have come out of those colorful old Hollywood films about Texas or Oklahoma, complete with a spectacular gusher, explosions, and a raging fire. Nikita Mikhalkov, the director's brother (and himself a director of enormous gifts), plays the returned Ustyuzhanin with brilliant verve and flair. Liudmila Gurchenko is spellbinding as the aging, riverboat-smart, and sensuous woman with whom the last Ustyuzhanin resumes an affair. She is, naturally, one of the last descendants of the original Solomins.

Western audiences might have been put off by some of the impenetrably murky stuff in the film. Soviet audiences were amazed at the sex and violence in it, tame enough by Western standards or by comparison to films from Eastern Europe. Environmentalists and others troubled by the costs of revolution and modernization will be interested to learn that there was thoughtful concern over these matters in the heart of the Soviet cultural establishment.

(One of the great themes of the Soviet environmental movement was outrage at the pollution of Lake Baikal, the most famous body of water in Siberia, by mills on its shores.) The film is a visually rich and imaginative evocation of the glories and pains of Soviet historical development within a surprisingly neutral political framework. But whatever the political judgment, *Siberiade* is, as befits the subject, big and breathtaking.[1]

[*Cineaste*, XII, 4, 1983]

[1] See my interview with Konchalovsky in Chapter VII, 1.

Stalker

While other Soviet film directors tackled problems of daily life and reinterpreted Russian literary classics or historical subjects, Andrei Tarkovsky uncompromisingly staked out his own special zones, his themes anchored in dense enigmas.

The action and nonaction in *Stalker* occupy a mysterious landscape known as "the Zone," where regular causation and physics are thought to be inoperative. Yet the whole of *Stalker*, like Tarkovsky's other works, is a special film zone where normal laws are suspended and replaced by beauteous renditions of color, light, time, space, and sound. Straight narrative has no place in Tarkovsky's zones. In them, the distance between two points is always a curved line doubling back on itself. All that is solid melts into air, or to take Tarkovsky's favorite image, water. Symbols, visions, and riddles wander from frame to frame. A viewer is likely to become anxious, uneasy, sometimes exasperated—and never more so than in *Stalker*, which adds pictures of personal despair and industrial squalor of unmatched intensity. Amid the malaise, one senses that Tarkovsky is posing very large questions about existence. Even if his answers are not easy to decipher, the images and the questions linger and reverberate long after the viewing.

Stalker is based on a novel by the popular Soviet authors of science fiction, Arkadi and Boris Strugatsky. The work appeared in the Leningrad youth magazine *Avrora* in 1973, as *Piknik Na obochine*

(Roadside Picnic). Although the Strugatsky brothers contributed the screenplay, Tarkovsky took such liberties with the original that it earned the rebuke of some Soviet critics. (Tarkovsky's problems with Soviet authorities and critics were legendary.) Even before its first public showing, *Stalker* was attacked as "elitist"; only three prints of the film were released, without publicity, for Moscow. Within a short time, however, the film had attracted a wide audience, especially among the young. Tarkovsky altered the setting of the original from the United States to a nominally undefined locale that most audiences, especially Soviet audiences, cannot fail to identify as the Soviet Union. (The film was shot in Soviet Estonia.)

Tarkovsky confronted problems of universal, rather than merely Soviet, relevance in the modem epoch, with its cult of materialism and scientific-industrial progress. The main characters in the film are named after general categories—Stalker, Writer, and Scientist. Stalker's wife is never named, and their daughter is known as "Monkey." The English word "stalker" serves as the title of the film and is used throughout for the central character. The border guards preventing access to the Zone are not particularly Soviet-looking in their white helmets. Moreover, it is a certain "Professor Wallace," a "Nobel Prize winner," who signs the prefatory note that tells of this incomprehensible Zone, of unknown origin, possibly the result of some meteorite or unearthly visitation: "We sent in troops: no one returned."

Despite its Anglicisms and universalisms, *Stalker* has a distinctly Russian and Soviet feel. The theme of confinement and escape, of getting past barbed wire and armed border patrols, is a notable mainstay of modern Soviet history. Stalker is played with a feverish, truly Dostoevskian anguish by Alexander Kaidanovsky. With his shaven head and grimy clothes, he is a *zek* (prisoner) for life, a character out of Aleksander Solzhenitsyn's work, forever imprisoned in real and private gulags. Already having served a sentence for trespassing into the Zone, he tells his wife (Alisa Friendlich), who pleads with him not to go again, "I'm imprisoned everywhere."

The idea of a "zone" might also trigger special associations for Soviet audiences. In 1908, an object of immense size and extraterrestrial origin exploded over a Siberian forest. Traces suggest either a comet's tail or a meteorite as the source. A second real-life event, closer to the stuff of the film, is described in reports, never officially confirmed, of a huge, nuclear-related explosion in the 1950's in the Ural Mountains. After the accident, Soviet authorities are said to have evacuated the region and sealed it off. In the film, Stalker's daughter is described as a "Zone mutant," born without the use of her legs, and Stalker has suffered some kind of contamination from his forays into the Zone.

These unexplained catastrophes in the Soviet Union provide possible points of reference for the material in *Stalker*. They no more help one understand *Stalker*, however, than the Soviet experience in World War II "explains" Tarkovsky's *Ivanovo detstvo* (1962; *Ivan's Childhood*), or the Tartar invasion of medieval Russia explains his *Andrei Rublev* (1966, released 1969). These experiences are merely settings for Tarkovsky's real subject, humanity's fate in a harsh world that constantly challenges inner goodness.

In fact, much of *Stalker* is taken up with ruminations on matters philosophical and personal as the three characters spend a strange day together. Wordiness is an unavoidable characteristic of dramatic situations of the sort found in Samuel Beckett's *Waiting for Godot* (1952), to which the film has been compared. Stalker might also be called Preacher. He admonishes his fellow travelers that a man becomes kinder when he thinks of the past; that the most powerful things are abstract, such as music; and that the supple shall conquer the hard (the last sentiment is an unacknowledged paraphrase from the *Tao Te Ching*). Recited as well are some lovely verses drawn from the work of Tarkovsky's father, Arseny Tarkovsky, whose poetry also appears in *Zerkalo* (1975; *The Mirror*) and in *Nostalghia* (1983; *Nostalgia*), and drawn from the nineteenth century lyric poet F. I. Tiutchev.

The drift of Tarkovsky's thought may be gleaned from these passages, but it is not from words that *Stalker* derives its eloquence. More important are its moody silences and the nonverbal elements of the sound track—industrial sounds, such as the roar of a locomotive; the din of clanging metal; the clickety clack of a railroad handcar; as well as the synthesizer score of Eduard Artemyev, with its sinuous, vaguely Eastern, deeply melancholic lines suggestive of sitar and reed. (Artemyev also provided the music for Tarkovsky's space fantasy, *Solaris*, 1972.) Above all, there are the mesmerizing visual images. Tarkovsky is the most painterly of film masters.

Stalker begins with scenes of primordial despair. Credits appear over a blue-tinted monochrome portrait of a run-down cafe. A figure is hunched over a stand-up table to the left, and a bartender putters noiselessly to the right. The effect is like some daguerreotype portrait of desolation at an after-hours bar. The camera tracks into a bedroom through a narrow opening, overhead across three sleeping figures—a man, a child, and a woman—then across again in the other direction. The setting is seamy and industrial, as the viewer learns from the passing train that rattles the spare furniture and glasses. It is a dreadful morning. The scene concludes with the woman, Stalker's wife, writhing uncontrollably on the floor boards as he leaves, over her objections, to meet his clients at the café.

Scientist (Nikolai Grinko, who also appeared in *Ivan's Childhood*) and Writer (Anatoly Solonitsyn, a Tarkovsky regular who played Rublev) have hired Stalker to guide them through the forbidden Zone, where there is a spot in which one's deepest wishes may be realized. After some chatter that establishes Writer as jaded and skeptical, they set out on their quest. Writer had been chauffeured to the rendezvous by a beautiful young woman, elegantly dressed. She is not permitted to come along and is never seen again. She serves as a reminder of the opulent and frivolous world outside the Zone and its environs.

Led by Stalker, the trio eludes the guards, who take some shots at them. The escape is easy, even comical. It is not clear whether this is an unfortunate lapse in mood of the film or is intentional. Perhaps the nation's authorities permit access into the Zone as a kind of safety valve for yearning and discontent. In fact, the viewer soon discovers that the Zone, despite an unusual feature or two, is not very different from other terrains. The Zone may yield only a moral and psychological space, not a miraculous topography.

Individual head-shots of the travelers fill up and linger on the screen as the trio rides into the Zone; the silence is broken only by the sound of their handcar, regular and hypnotic. Signs of fear, curiosity, and expectation are on their faces. The film breaks into full color when they reach the Zone. It is very quiet, and the landscape is disappointingly dull. There are ruins about, including the shells of destroyed tanks. Flowers have been stamped out by "Porcupine," a former Stalker who got his wish, grew rich, and then committed suicide. The flowers have come back, but they lack fragrance.

Stalker knows his way around and never ventures without first throwing a crude probe, fashioned of a cloth looped around a metal nut. He is beside himself with anger when his clients ignore his instructions. They persist, but nothing terrible happens. Scientist disobeys the rule not to retrace one's steps; he goes back to fetch his knapsack, and to Stalker's consternation, he is later seen munching placidly on a snack and sipping from his thermos at a spot that the others have struggled to reach. Writer is constantly unruly. Stalker has to strip him of his liquor and pistol. At one point, he physically assaults Stalker—"Why did you hit me?" cries the guide from the depths of his frustration and pathos. The benign-looking Scientist suddenly assembles a portable nuclear device and announces that he will blow up the whole place. He does not, however, follow through. At the climax of their decidedly unheroic journey, which includes a long trek through a large drain tunnel, no one wants to go into the wish-bestowing room.

The Zone has turned out to be more mysterious for what is not there than for what is. This is allegory, not science fiction. It is the viewer who imparts the "special effects" through imagination and intuition, assisted by Tarkovsky's characteristic bag of wonders: alternations between color and monochrome; flooded, rain-soaked interiors; montage that disorients time and spatial relationships; a gentle black dog, wise and comforting, materializing from nowhere; a long, long, overhead track of water coursing over artifacts of civilization from the age of faith (an icon) to the age of self-destruction (a revolver, a syringe). At journey's end, the three exhausted characters huddle before a pond as the camera pulls back, and an eerie light bathes them first in blue, then in gold, then in blue again.

This powerful, silent moment of long duration is like an epiphany. Have the seekers won some special grace after all? Are they wise with their self-discovery or with the realization that the Zone, like the rest of the contemporary universe, has no miracles to confer, that there, as everywhere, men quarrel, cannot understand one another, have different temperaments, and are separated from the community and from the natural world by the implacable forces of egoism and technology?

It is difficult to say. They return to their sad, blue-tinted café, more desolate than at the start. Back home, Stalker is overcome with grief. He thinks that the mission was yet another failure; he blames the two intellectuals for lack of faith. Yet perhaps this guide is himself misguided; he tries too hard, forces his faith on others, and wants miracles. He is not free from illusions, intolerance, and selfishness, though his suffering is real.

Tarkovsky caps his tale with manifestations of devotion and transcendence. Earlier, Stalker's wife writhed at his departure, now she comforts him in his anguish. In a confessional soliloquy addressed to the camera, she declares her willingness to endure pain with him, abandoning both hope and happiness. She is like the wife of the seventeenth century Russian religious dissident and martyr Avakuum. When told that their suffering would last until death, she replied, "with a sigh.... 'So be it... let us be getting on our way.'" Stalker's daughter reappears in the final scenes. Resembling a young Madonna from an icon, she is prematurely sad; a gold scarf covers her head like a halo. The viewer sees her from the chest up; she seems to be walking or gliding, despite her deformity. The camera pulls back to show that she is only atop her father's shoulders. The real marvel comes later. The daughter is at home, reading from a thick book with black covers. She closes the book, rests her head over the table and stares at the glasses on it. White filaments float in the air; the black dog whines; something is happening. Again the locomotive comes roaring by. Beethoven's "Ode to Joy" (a motif of *Nostalgia*) mingles with the roar. The little girl has a special power; it is she, not the locomotive, who now moves the glasses without touching them.

With this breathtaking moment, Tarkovsky insists on an affirmation of the spirit as opposed to the material world. Like many Russians, past and present, Tarkovsky is a faith-intoxicated artist convinced of the powers of enchantment to awaken souls. One need not share that Russian sensibility to appreciate his films, nor does one have to share Tarkovsky's theology or pessimism. His work, and *Stalker* most bleakly of all, reaches out to audiences as provocative paintings in film of the contemporary condition.

[From *Magill's Survey of Cinema: Foreign Language Films*, 0E. © 1986 Gale, a part of Cengage Learning, Inc. Reproduced by permission. www.cengage.com/permissions]

The Lonely Voice of Sokurov
Documentaries on the Russian Experience from a Russian Master

The first time I heard of Alexander Sokurov and saw one of his films was back in 1989, thanks to the Glasnost Film Festival, which was designed by its U.S. and Soviet collaborators to introduce the American public to the bold new films coming out of documentary studios during Gorbachev's *perestroika* in the USSR. They were definitely not the old, officially sanctioned pap, and most were exciting not due to their stylistic innovations but because of their once-forbidden contents—they included candid exposures of what had been historical and societal taboo subjects, from the murderous repressions of the past to contemporary Soviet ills like poverty and alcoholism (See Discovering the "Unknown Cinema" in Chapter III).

One film stood apart from the others: Sokurov's ironically titled *The Evening Sacrifice*, made in 1984, released in 1988, is a short, unconventional documentary capturing from odd angles the look and spirit of crowds celebrating May Day in Leningrad. One learned that Sokurov was considered an "underground" artist in the film world, someone who had been making documentaries and features since 1978, all shelved by the culture bosses—until *perestroika*. Although he graduated from VGIK, the Moscow film school (in 1979), his original diploma submission was rejected—*The Lonely Voice of a Man* was an idiosyncratic rendering of several works of fiction by Andrei Platonov, himself an idiosyncratic Soviet writer. Since *perestroika*, and of course after the Soviet collapse, Sokurov has been "aboveground," but he goes his own way, and his films continue to stand apart. Sokurov's gifts for the unexpected are on view in dozens of fiction films and documentaries, mostly shown on the festival circuit, with an occasional theatrical opening in the U.S. (most successfully of *Russian Ark* in 2002, now probably his most widely known work). Distribution of his vast output has been limited, but Facets Video has released a batch of Sokurov documentaries on DVD. Watching wall-to-wall Sokurov is not always an easy experience, though worth the effort for the subjects he helps us probe, and for the craft he unfolds. His thematic range is so diverse, and his productivity so great in a variety of ever changing styles, that there are bound to be ups and downs. Often the sheer length of the films, the slow pacing, the *ostinato* musical fragments, Sokurov's own *sotto voce* minimalist narration, and the long, l-o-n-g, lingering takes can induce reactions that range from mesmerizing fascination to narcolepsy and back. But allowing for a certain artiness in his strategies (what the Soviets used to denounce as "formalism"), Sokurov is always meeting his subjects from a deeply humanist perspective. Moreover, in their quirky way, his studies are always educational. Embedded in his singular camera and sound techniques is the documentarist's pedagogy, whether it's understanding Soviet collective farming, as in *Elegy of the Land* (1988), or the experience of combat and what it means to be a recruit aboard a ship in the White Sea, as in *Spiritual Voices* (1995) and *Confession* (1998).

Sokurov's use of the title "Elegy" for many of his films — the term generally means a lament for someone dead — also conveys something of his melancholic view of human affairs. *Maria*, the first part of his *Elegy of the Land*, focuses on a collective farmer, a familiar and appealing Russian woman who can handle a tractor and work a harvester. Some beautiful photography — one panoramic, painterly shot pictures horses, haystacks, and women threshing — frames several chapters of Maria's short life: she weeps for her dead son, killed by a drunken truck driver; recalls a brief holiday at a Black Sea resort; and works hard in the summer sun. After Maria's death, Sokurov took what he had filmed back to the collective farm, and screened it for its members, who included Maria's daughter, and her remarried husband. And he filmed the screening, too. The effect is stunningly sad. (The disc also contains Sokurov's *The Last Day of a Rainy Summer*, certainly of interest to students of Soviet agriculture, but he makes a dull subject come to life through some energetic editing and the very tight close-ups of concerned faces as collective farmers of the "Red Lighthouse" discuss matters at a meeting — the result sometimes resembles a Depression-era film of poor farmers in the U.S.)

The comparison of Sokurov to Tarkovsky, who championed his early work, is inevitable. Both had a profoundly serious attitude about the place of film in the world of art (a film was never "just a movie"), and both had what might be loosely described as "spiritual" concerns. Humor never enters their realm. There are other, technical similarities, pacing and long takes among them.

But Tarkovsky never made documentaries; he died (in exile) after making only a handful of films; and he never had the benefit of working in his own land in the permissive conditions of *perestroika*, or in a de-Sovietized Russia. All of which is to say, we don't know what genres and experimentations in style Tarkovsky might have practiced had he lived. Put another way, we do know that Sokurov has investigated territories that Tarkovsky never did.

Sokurov's tribute to Tarkovsky forms one of his "elegies"—*Moscow Elegy* (1987), another sorrowful work that alternates between some straight documentary bio-pic narrative and numerous illuminating clips drawn from Tarkovsky films and home movies made in Russia, Italy, Sweden, and France. Sokurov is fond of slow pans around homes where Tarkovsky and his family lived, as if these pensive interior shots might convey something of the interior life of its occupants.

By training his camera on a subject—a face, a sleeping head, a painting—and staying there for an unusually long time, Sokurov's intention might be to rivet the gaze so as to escort the viewer into the subject's interiority or hidden character. In an informative interview, a special feature accompanying *Elegy of a Voyage* (2001), Sokurov relates cinema to painting in that both exist in flat imagery, without three-dimensionality, and consequently there's a "mystery" for the viewer behind the surface.

This brings to mind a recent exhibit of photos by Chris Marker, another by-now-legendary documentarist who matches Sokurov for productivity and innovation, although his emphasis is always political. The exhibit, called "Staring Back," is a collection of photographed faces from around the world, and one critic has written that "in Marker's work, the face as irreducible mystery has been a gravitational force." Photography, like painting, is also one-dimensional.

Tarkovsky also liked reproductions of classic paintings, especially portraits. In his *The Mirror*, he settles on Leonardo's "Ginevra de' Benci," with its enchanting face of a young woman. By staring long enough, you are compelled to explore and come up with solutions to the "mystery.", or as someone says in Orhan Pamuk's dazzling novel, *My Name Is Red*, "If you stare long enough [at a beautiful picture] your mind enters the time of the painting."

That seems to apply to the last part of Sokurov's *Elegy of a Voyage*, a strange, many layered, dreamlike journey that takes the director out of Russia across time and many spaces, and culminates in Rotterdam, at its Boijmans Van Beuningen Museum, where he is seen from behind wandering before different canvases, staring at them, almost conversing with them, almost as if he had lived in the eighteenth-century town pictured in one of them. Later, at another museum, Petersburg's Hermitage, Sokurov fused art with recreations from Russian history in his astonishing *Russian Ark*.

The same *Voyage* disc also has Sokurov turning to art again, and his preference for the eighteenth century, in his *Hubert Robert: A Happy Life*, a kind of art-appreciation instructional film about the French painter, but with lots of oblique (and often mystifying) touches—an opening montage has an outdoor kabuki-like performance, plus a lyrical passage from Dostoevsky read in Sokurov's whispering voice, and the film ends with the Neva River and the Hermitage in shimmering sepia.

Sokurov's two long, ambitious studies of military life take us to diagonally opposite ends of the Russian plain—*Confession (From the Commander's Diary: A Cinema Narrative in Five Parts)* pictures young recruits aboard and off a ship up north in the White Sea, while *Spiritual Voices: From the Military Diaries* (also in five parts) is set among young soldiers in the mountainous terrain of the Tadjik-Afghan border. The physical contrasts couldn't be greater: the claustrophobic ship and icy, churning waters of the first, the spectacular, high and wide, dusty open spaces of the second. But both share Sokurov's very personal way of capturing lives in challenging conditions; both might have been titled "elegies," though death is only hinted at.

The translation, "Confession," might be misleading; the original Russian title, *Povinnost'*, usually means an obligation, as in compulsory military service. The film's subject is partly the recruits going about their duties, and partly the ship's commander (a character invented by the director), who "confesses" his innermost thoughts. The documentary and fictional forms alternate seamlessly: Sokurov has here given us a film facsimile of the nonfiction novel. If it weren't for the long takes, the muffled repetitions of a haunting motif by the composer Toru Takemitsu, the sounds of ship and wind, and the sensuous shots of water and fog, much of the film could be a training manual for conscripted life aboard a vessel. The camera pokes everywhere and watches the men swabbing decks, undressing for a medical inspection, at mess, getting a haircut, washing their garments, in random conversation, at a first-aid exercise. Then there is the brooding captain—Sokurov's alter ego?—offering his extended pessimistic musings on existence and the senseless sea.

A Chekhov story is mentioned, as is Dante's Charon (who conveyed the souls of the dead across the river Styx—is that a metaphor for the captain and his men?). Enough; the commander goes topside and hears a sentry compose a letter, starting "Dear Mama... ." A nice ending, and not an accidental touch. In *Dialogues with Solzhenitsyn* Sokurov tells the author that he is interested in the spiritual relationship between mothers and sons, a theme he elaborated with great feeling in his feature *Mother and Son* (1997). A similar concern informs his later feature, *Alexandra* (2007), only this time it is set between grandmother and grandson.

Confession is not judgmental or politically aimed, although there is a comment on military life as cruel, and only as cruel as the nation of its origin. If Sokurov's sentiments are pacifist, as they surely are, they are not loudly broadcast. Paradoxically, the same applies to *Spiritual Voices*, which is directly about war, outwardly, at least. (Sokurov's father was a Soviet officer with World War II experience.) Since there is no definite or indefinite article in Russian, the subtitle of the film could be translated as *From the Diaries of War*, or *From the Diaries of a War*, or *From the Diaries of the War*. There's not a clue in the film which of those might be best; all might be OK. There are no helpful title cards or narration explaining the politics of the situation; all we know is that there is some fighting by Russian border units in Tadjikistan with some unnamed insurgents (from Afghanistan? involved in the drug trade?). The filmmaker and his crew are there recording the action (mostly inaction), and the filmmaker contributes an occasional observation or comment; this forms the "diaries." It seems more like a universal statement about young men in a combat zone, not a specific geopolitical document or polemic. But it is, in Sokurov's unprecedented style, another fine addition to the hallowed Russian war-film genre.

The film opens poetically, contrasting with the prose of daily military life that will follow. A handsome snow-covered Russian landscape and some exquisite photography at nightfall share the opening with, oddly, music and commentary about Mozart and the French composer and organist, Olivier Messiaen. Let's get our priorities straight, Sokurov seems to be saying in his always surprising fashion—before we enter the combat zone, remember the homeland, and don't forget that nature and art and music should preoccupy us, not war. These are the "spiritual voices" of eternity.

After a daybreak shot in Russia dissolves into a mountainous landscape in Tadjikistan, Sokurov, often shown riding and flying with the men, chronicles their missions and daily activities. At moments here and there, we hear his brief, commonplace, soft-voiced comments: "Goodness, its hot here." "The day is over. No fighting. Thank God." "War is hideous." "It's sultry." No sermons; no political statements. Soldiers eat, lay mines, sleep, muster, smoke, lie in the sun, celebrate New Year, stare impassively at the camera (which likes to find an interesting face and hold it there). There is no fictitious commander here, as in *Confession*, and we don't get to know anyone. But we get to understand, via Sokurov's simple direct cinema and hand-held camera, what being a soldier in a combat region is like. Again, this could be a kind of training manual perhaps, but some gorgeous photography of the imposing scenery, sometimes rendered in sepia (although the prevailing dust makes everything look brown, even without any mono-tinting), gives a wider scope to the film. And, once again, there is Takemitsu's *ostinato* (Sokurov is enamored of Japanese esthetics). A mountain scene fades to black, and we are back in cold and snowy Russia.

Back in the Russian countryside during a cool end-of-summer season, Sokurov brings his crew to Solzhenitsyn's dacha to record his conversations with the author, a film tribute in honor of his eightieth birthday. Both iconoclastic filmmaker and iconoclastic politico/literary giant are in fine form. This is no simple Q&A session. Think two acute minds obsessed with philosophical, existential issues meeting head to head. (Often quite literally; throughout, there are striking head shots of Solzhenitsyn, with his biblical prophetic appearance, and, in one long section, he keeps turning to his left to reply face to face to the partially seen Sokurov.) There are no major conflicts of opinion between them, although

Sokurov turns repeatedly to the presence of *cruelty* in human behavior, and asks for an explanation. But Solzhenitsyn demurs. The author of *One Day in the Life of Ivan Denisovich* and *The Gulag Archipelago* certainly knows about cruelty, firsthand. He allows that cruelty defined the Soviet order; his own character, he says, was "affected by the severity of the Soviet regime." But his rejoinder to Sokurov emphasizes *greed* as a cardinal human failing. (Earlier, his wife and help-meet, Natalia, speaks of lies and violence. She too is photographed full face, up close, bringing out her handsomely wide and open, very Slavic visage.) At one point Sokurov mentions that winter is so peacefully pleasant (such imagery recurs in his films). To which, Solzhenitsyn: not if you're breaking ice with a pickax in below-zero weather. *Touché.*

And so they talk and talk, on great matters and small (how do you determine a tree's age from its trunk rings? They agree Petrograd is better than the Dutch/German sound of Petersburg). Solzhenitsyn looks surprisingly fit and vigorous. The only time he displays his celebrated fiery convictions is when a discussion on present-day Russia and the primitive capitalist accumulation of the new oligarchs gets him going. Sometimes the camera, as if bored by all the talk, wanders away from the dialoging couple and takes long pans around the room, a familiar Sokurov habit. (Another familiar one is the curious intercut. For a discussion of Chekhov he inserts a shot of the ghost of the dead author as played by an actor from his film, *Stone*, 1992.) This, and the other lengthy films discussed above, may have their *longueurs* and what in other hands might be self-indulgent experimentalism. But under Sokurov's direction, the skill of a master filmmaker shows through, and it is imbued with a merciful humane outlook that yields some remarkable achievements in the documentary form.

[*Cineaste*, XXXIII, 1, 2007]

SHORT TAKES

Wings and *The Ascent*

This double release by Criterion/Eclipse reminds us how Larisa Shepitko's early death deprived Soviet and world cinema of an acute talent. (She was only 41 when she was killed in a car crash with crew members in 1979 preparing her film *Farewell*, later completed by her husband Elem Klimov.) *Wings* (1966) was her first work after film school, where she studied with the Ukrainian silents master, Alexander Dovzhenko. The Dovzhenko influence shows in her pictorial style, but she also contributed sophisticated psychological dimensions, very evident in these two brilliant offerings. *Wings* has outwardly a Soviet feel, with its slow pacing, the high-contrast black-and-white photography of its very Soviet themes—the conflicts at a vocational school and in her personal life of a seemingly "positive heroine," the headmistress Petrukhina (Maya Bulgakova), once a decorated wartime pilot. Severe and sure of herself, her daydreams give her away as yearning and dissatisfied, ready to break loose. I won't tell you how Shepitko resolves her anguish, except to note that it plays on an expected Soviet "kheppy ending." *The Ascent* (1977), Shepitko's last film, though set on a snow covered Byelorussian front in 1942, is very distant from classic Soviet war epics like *The Cranes are Flying* and *Ballad of a Soldier*. In its pitiless depiction of brutality it is closest to Klimov's *Come and See*, but outdoes it for exposing dramatic moral tensions: conscience or survival? The Christian overtones are hard to miss in the sacrificial behavior of the central figure Sotnikov (Boris Plotnikov), as are the extraordinary head shots that seem to spring from medieval paintings. The outstanding Anatoly Solonitsyn, a Tarkovsky favorite, has a turn as a cunningly cruel inquisitor.

[*Cineaste*, XXXIV, 1, 2008]

7. The Program cover for the *Glasnost Film Festival* which toured the U.S. in 1989. The design highlights stills (top to bottom) from three of the *Festival*'s documentary films: Joseph Pasternak's *Black Square*, Hertz Frank's *Final Verdict*, and Sergei Miroshnichenko's *And The Past Seems But A Dream*.

CHAPTER IV

Glasnost Galore: Cinema in the Soviet Twilight

To the array of historical signifiers cited in the Chapter III Introduction, above, we now should add glasnost, perestroika, Gorbachev, Yeltsin, *and (unfortunately)* Chernobyl. *Those Russian words and names became part of the global vocabulary during what one scholar has called "Seven Years that Changed the World."*[1] *The quixotic attempt to reform the Soviet system started with Mikhail Gorbachev as new General Secretary of the Communist Party of the Soviet Union in 1985, and ended with the destruction of that system by former Politburo member, later ex-Communist Boris Yeltsin in 1991. Both figures came out of the culture and structures of the Party, but they personified markedly divergent currents within it and, more significantly, outside of it. Gorbachev represented the reformist wave that aimed for within-system modifications steering the USSR away from its authoritarian moorings and from its "stagnant" socio-economic patterns. But as Alexis de Tocqueville, the wise observer and analyst of French and American societies, pointed out, there is no more dangerous moment for a bad government than when it begins to reform itself. In the USSR, the reform attempts, genuine enough, only widened existing cracks in the system that allowed destabilizing forces to break through, from reactionaries alarmed by the reforms—and who staged a maladroit* coup *attempt in August, 1991—to those, like Yeltsin, who abandoned any hope of a reformed Communist Party administering a reformed Soviet Union. Their solution: destroy both. In one of the most dramatic and ironic historical denouements of modern times,* restructuring *the Soviet party-state system* (perestroika!) *led to its* destruction. *And, contrary to many fears at the time, it happened with a whimper, not a bang. There was no Armageddon.*²

Soviet filmmakers were immediate, natural beneficiaries of what became collectively known as glasnost—*transparency or openness is the best translation, but the overtones connoted liberalization and freedom of expression. The "seven years" also "shook" the film world, but the expected burst of high-quality creativity never really took shape even as the volume of production ballooned. The short life of* glasnost *in Soviet cinema footnotes the Soviet collapse itself.*

---

¹ Archie Brown *Seven Years that Changed the World: Perestroika in Perspective* (New York: Oxford University Press, 2007)

² See Stephen Kotkin *Armageddon Averted: The Soviet Collapse 1970-2000* (New York: Oxford University Press, 2001). Civil wars broke out in several former Soviet republics, but Russia was spared major conflict after the collapse. Later exceptions are the brief but violent encounter between the Yeltsin government and opponents in 1993, and the savage campaigns in Chechnya over its quest for independence from the Russian Federation.

From Stagnation, *Perestroika: The Mirror, Oblomov, Autumn Marathon, Scarecrow, Little Vera*

Quite a few superb films were crafted by Soviet directors during what was generally referred to in official circles, rather self-servingly, as the period of "stagnation"—broadly speaking, the twenty years of Brezhnev and his successors, especially the decade or so before Gorbachev's advent in 1985. Certain conventions had to be observed, certain taboos respected, both in political and esthetic senses. Still, Soviet studios turned out a variety of subjects and genres, and directors left highly individual imprints. Everyone agrees that no group of *glasnost* films—works, that is, *made* in the Gorbachev period, as opposed to those that were *released* then—can measure up to the best of the "stagnation" era pictures created by such talent as Andrei Tarkovsky, Nikita Mikhalkov, Andrei Konchalovsky, Kira Muratova, Alexei Gherman, Gleb Panfilov, and Larisa Shepitko.

At long last, posthumously, as was too often the case with twentieth-century Russian genius, Tarkovsky was rewarded with official adulation. The Communist Party's Central Committee and the Soviet Government's Council of Ministers graced his memory with the Lenin Prize "for his outstanding contribution to the development of cinematic art and his innovative works that promote the affirmation of universal human values and humanistic ideas." Affirming universal values in place of class or Soviet socialist principles was a recurring Gorbachev theme. This, plus the freer reign for the Orthodox faith and the resurrection of old Russian culture, including the church restoration movement, would have gladdened the spirit-intoxicated Tarkovsky. *The Mirror* (1974) is Tarkovsky's most personal, most autobiographical film, and also perhaps the most difficult of the only five features he was allowed to make in the USSR. (And all of them are more or less difficult.) It begins with a documentary-like sequence of a speech therapist treating a young stammerer successfully (the tongue set free) and ends with the unseen hero of the film expiring (the soul set free). Between the two scenes Tarkovsky tells the story of his life, as only Tarkovsky can, as a series of memory fragments delivered with uncued flashbacks, intercut documentary footage, alterations in color, a dream within a dream, buckets of rain and crackling fire. To confuse matters, Tarkovsky casts the luminous Margarita Terekhova as both his young mother and his wife. His old mother is played by his real-life mother, while the soundtrack has his father Arseny reading his own lovely lyrical verse. This homage to the Tarkovsky family is all quite beautiful and oddly powerful, and worth the confusion. It may also be seen as a series of violent images of Soviet and world history, as scenes of the Spanish Civil War, World War II (with pre-war Stalin Terror), and the Chinese Cultural revolution are woven into the biographical nonnarrative.

More conventional in its beauty is a film by Nikita Mikhalkov, *Oblomov* (1979), in which he does what Soviet directors did best, bring to life the great literary classics of pre-Revolutionary Russia. I've always wondered why Woody Allen chose Tolstoy's *War and Peace* (i.e., *Love and Death*) over Goncharov's magnificent novel as his tribute to the Russian masters. After all, Oblomov is a Woody Allen character—timid, self-doubting, neurasthenic, and anhedonic, but entirely decent and lovable. With gorgeous photography by Pavel Lebeshev—lots of chiaroscuro and pastels and long shots of snowy landscape—Mikhalkov has enveloped Oblomov's sad incapacity to act in a benign, soulful aura of Old Russia. It is an idealized, romanticized portrait, of course; some might even condemn it as overly Slavophilic-nationalist. But it has it merits as an elegy to those, like Oblomov, who opt out of the rat race and stay out of step with progress.

Mikhalkov's (or Goncharov's) program aside, the film's greatest virtue is the ensemble of impeccable performances by Oleg Tabakov as the gentle Oblomov, Elena Solovei as the playful young aristocrat who captures his heart and momentarily stirs him into action, Yuri Bogatyrev as Oblomov's bosom buddy and foil, the stout-hearted Stolz, and a sparkling array of players in supporting parts. Many of them appear as well in Mikhalkov's two other melancholy songs of Old Russia, *Unfinished Piece for Player Piano* (1977) and *Dark Eyes* (1987), both derived from Chekhov.

Oblomov has often been taken to be a national type of that time, but his descendants can be spotted in contemporary Soviet, as indeed any other, society. A distant relative is the weak-willed intellectual who thinks one thing, says a second, and does a third, someone like the unhappy Leningrad teacher and translator at the center of Georgy Danelia's "sad comedy," *Autumn Marathon* (1979).

Unlike Oblomov, Buzykin is constantly in motion—lectures, family obligations, meeting publishers' deadlines, early-morning jogs, helping friends in need, and trying to handle an extramarital affair. It's a modern urban tale that could be set in Boston. It sounds like Buzykin is living life to the brim, but he is disaffected, miserably so. As with Oblomov, it's not that Buzykin is morally corrupt, unless we judge him by the strictest standards. His problem is that everyone is always making demands on him and he just can't say no—to his wife, to his girlfriend, to his jogging friend, to his colleagues, to his students. He never wants to offend; unfortunately, it's the kind of goodness that only leads to complications and more unhappiness to himself and sometimes to others.

Danelia keeps the story moving with just the right balance of the comic and the touching, and just the right emotional distance; it never cloys. The mood and colors are autumnal. There is a climax when it appears that Buzykin is going to break loose from his self-imposed traps. A lesser film would have had him shutting the door in everyone's face and the audience would have cheered. Buzykin does set himself free, momentarily; then the webs close in on him again. This is among the best of pre-*glasnost* Soviet filmmaking; solid, nothing flashy.

Rather more dramatic in conveying the textures of late Soviet life, but no less surefooted in execution, is one of the most popular and talked-about works of the Russian screen, Rolan Bykov's *Scarecrow* (1985). Bykov is perhaps best known in the U.S. as the accomplished actor who was perfect as the pathetic Akaky Akakyevich in Alexei Batalov's adaptation of Gogol's masterpiece, *The Overcoat* (1962), and as the Jewish tinker who takes the pregnant commissar into his crowded home in Askoldov's *Commissar*. (Bykov makes brief appearances in his *Scarecrow* as the brass band conductor at the start and end of the film.)

"Scarecrow" is what the sixth-graders in a provincial town call Lena, the new girl in class, who is a bit awkward and has long, straw-colored hair. She lives with her grandfather, a left-over from old Russian culture who collects local art and is known as "Patch-pockets," the town eccentric. Bykov uses a standard device to unfold the story, a series of flashbacks as Lena tells Grandpa a horrible tale of youthful cruelty, ostracism, and a sweetheart's betrayal. That familiar device keeps you at the edge of your seat as you learn how Lena's classmates decide on the silent treatment toward her when they mistakenly take her for the class snitch, and then turn nastier and nastier. The emotional high point of the film, as the realist style turns powerfully fantastic, is a public burning of Lena in effigy.

The cruelty of the young is of course one of those universal themes, but in Bykov's hands it sounds a particularly Soviet pitch with its overtones of the tyranny of the collective over the individual, the denunciation and purging of the falsely accused, and the general climate of terror that forces those who know the truth into silence. In a larger arena, this was the political culture of Stalinism. In Bykov's town the truth comes out in the end, but no one celebrates. Scarecrow and Patchpockets leave town in despair.

Despair, raging despair is the keynote of Pichul's smash box office hit, *Little Vera* (1989). Whatever its reasons for success in the U.S. (not quite on the scale of its triumph in the USSR), the sexual *glasnost* that eventually brought its star, Natalya Negoda, onto the pages of *Playboy*, does not entirely explain the popularity of the film among Soviet viewers. Of the dozens of people I asked about the film in the USSR, only two responded negatively. An old woman selling tickets at a movie theater in Stavropol thought it was "disgusting," while a young Leningrad cab driver told me, "Who wants to see such ugliness on the screen, we have enough of it in real life." Both responses, of course, help explain its popularity.

Pichul was an angry young man, and his film is an angry study in contemporary urban sociology replete with alcoholism, broken families, teen promiscuity, brawling, bleak intellectual, cultural, and career horizons: Welcome to Pichul's home town, Mariupol, on the Black Sea (formerly Zhdanov, named after Stalin's notorious culture boss). There is no subtlety here, not in the story (which ends up with attempted manslaughter, attempted suicide, and a fatal heart attack), not in the characterizations (though the acting, as usual, is first rate), not in Pichul's style and techniques. An hysterical energy carries it along to the point of numbness. Yet it was a breakthrough film in the new Soviet cinema of candidness, and deserved its huge success.

[*Cineaste*, XVIII, 1, 1990]

Discovering the "Unknown Cinema"

This is my Introduction to the Program for the Glasnost Film Festival, *of which I was an organizer and Publications Editor. The festival, a Project of Citizen Exchange Council, consisted of "A National Tour of Twenty-Two Recent Documentary Films from the Soviet Union," Spring 1989.*

I have left the introduction reprinted here unaltered from the original in order to convey the sense of exhilaration we felt at the time about developments in Soviet cinema and society. Historians might call this a "primary document" in the record of U.S. reactions to perestroika.

There are few better ways to understand the remarkable transformations shaking up the USSR today than through film. Soviet film, especially the documentary, has now become a self-conscious instrument of *glasnost* and *perestroika*—the terms no longer need translation—much as early Soviet filmmakers pioneered the cinema of revolutionary engagement.

Soviet cinema has always shaped our images of Russia in revolution, civil war, World War II, and after. It is hard to think of the Revolution of 1905 without recalling Eisenstein's Odessa steps massacre in *Potemkin*. Powerful images of the Soviet ordeal in World War II come from such films as Kalatozov's *The Cranes are Flying* or Chukhrai's *Ballad of A Soldier*. More recently, audiences were stunned by the lurid pictures of Stalinist cult and tyranny in Abuladze's metaphoric *Repentance*.

But these are images from feature films, not the documentary. It is a sad paradox that a genre pioneered by early filmmakers in the USSR as a way of recording Soviet actuality became a way of hiding it, bypassing it, or dressing it up. The Soviet documentary, born with the Revolution, became a victim of the same political forces that despoiled the ideals of the Revolution. Now, thanks to changes set in motion by the Gorbachev regime since 1985, Soviet documentary filmmakers are recovering long silenced voices, and Western audiences may now get an unprecedented glimpse of unadorned Soviet actuality. The Soviet documentary film is now a strategic window on all corners of Soviet society, past and present.

The documentary impulse was there at the beginning of the Soviet regime. "Agitation trains" sent far and wide to spread the news and ideals of revolutionary Soviet power to largely illiterate peasant masses carried with them newsreels and "agitation films" (*agitki*), or "living posters" of the Revolution. One of the men working on the *agitki* was Dziga Vertov (1896-1954), whose theories and practice of *Kino-Glaz* (*The Film Eye*) and *Kino-Pravda* (*Film Truth*) established principles of documentary cinema that shaped the art beyond Soviet borders, and far into the future. (The term *cinéma-vérité* is a direct translation of *Kino-Pravda*.) Though Vertov and many other Soviet documentary filmmakers were active throughout the 1920s and 1930s, their work was increasingly constrained by the rigid cultural politics of Stalinism, affecting both form and content.

The Soviet documentary impulse was flattened into dull propaganda. Triumphalist, one-dimensional positive glosses on Soviet life accorded with the doctrines of "socialist realism," which in practice was neither realist nor particularly socialist.

World War II brought a revival of the Soviet documentary, mainly in the form of compilation films from the battlefield, as documentary and feature filmmakers alike trained their talents on the common enterprise of expelling the German invader. But the post-war Stalin years were as ferocious toward the arts, and cinema in particular, as anything in the pre-war period. Post-Stalin thaws produced some notable advances for feature films, but no major breakthroughs for the documentary. By the late 1970s some two dozen documentary studios turned out about 40 full-length films annually, and over a thousand shorts. But the political bosses defined a whole range of subjects as unacceptable, effectively muting the potential power of the documentary as a vehicle of social concern. Anyone who has seen documentaries in the USSR from this period—television being the most accessible source—would agree there was great competence and always a certain high-mindedness about many of them, as they portrayed educational, scientific, historical and cultural themes. But something was missing; important things were left unsaid—and both public and filmmaker knew it. What was missing constitutes the "Unknown Cinema" discussed in Sergei Muratov's essay [in the printed Program]. New documentary cinema is now a fact of public life in the USSR. The new films attract large audiences, they generate wide controversy in the Soviet media, and they have become a major force for social and political renewal.

The Glasnost Film Festival is a way of discovering for ourselves this "unknown cinema." In so doing we not only see new developments in the Soviet documentary, but we get at the new views of Soviet politics, the revisionist history, and the new social concerns as well. In the film world, the Soviets use the term *kinopublitsistika*. Any simple translation is bound to be awkward, but it has the sense of cinema-advocacy, cinema-*engagé*, or cinema-critique.

No selection of films, even one as large as the 22 films that comprise the five programs of the Festival, can do justice to the full range of recent Soviet documentaries. We have tried to gather a representative sample of genres, of films reflecting fallen taboos, and of themes that highlight current Soviet preoccupations—re-investigating the Stalinist past; looking anew at the Orthodox Church; the Afghanistan war; alienated youth and the disenchanted old; squalor, poverty, and vice in Soviet life; Chernobyl and other industrial and environmental disasters. The work of smaller studios in Irkutsk and Sverdlovsk, and in the non-Russian national regions of Armenia, Latvia, and elsewhere are represented here, as are the larger studios in Moscow, Leningrad and Kiev.

Twenty of the Festival films were made in the last three years, mostly in 1987 and 1988. Two films, Sokurov's *Evening Sacrifice* and Sadykov's *Adonis XIV*, were made earlier, but only recently brought off the shelves thanks to *glasnost*. Sometimes certain films were dropped, with great regret, for technical reasons (the difficulty of transferring video to film), or owing to the pressures of scheduling—some films were too long and would have crowded out several shorter ones. Special mention must be made here of valuable films that could not be included in Festival programs: Marina Goldovskaya's *Solovetsky Power*, about the notorious prison camp established in 1923 at the site of the monastery complex on the Solovki Islands; Andrei Khrzhanovsky's *Landscape with Juniper*, an unusual portrait, using animation techniques, of the Estonian artist Julo Sooster, who suffered imprisonment and Siberian exile; and Arkady Ruderman's *Theatre in the Time of Perestroika and Glasnost*, an ironically titled investigation of a controversy at the Byelorussian Encyclopedia involving an article about a world-famous *émigré* from Vitebsk, Marc Chagall. (This film has faced release problems in the USSR, a sign that *glasnost* has not yet meant complete freedom for cinema.)

Landscape with Juniper is, like *Black Square* (a Festival film), more open in form than most of the documentaries presented here. (Sokurov's *Evening Sacrifice* is perhaps the Festival's most difficult, most "experimental" film.) But it should be kept in mind that the power of these films derives much more from subject matter than from stylistic risks. Another caveat: the subject matter itself is far more likely to impress a Soviet audience than a Western one; we have to accept these things relatively. Seeing former unpersons such as Bukharin or Khrushchev on screen has little punch for an American audience, but it packs a comparative wallop for Soviet viewers. The West is familiar with and almost jaded by the record of Stalinist horrors, but Soviet audiences weep at the documentarist's revelations.

Viewing these films in full historical and political context is a way of fulfilling a Festival goal, better understanding of the USSR through the pioneering efforts of its contemporary documentary filmmakers. Similarly, we hope that an intended reciprocal festival of American documentary film in the USSR will help achieve a better understanding of us.[1] *[Leonid Gurevich offers a fond account of Soviet documentaries of the '60s, in the interview, Chapter VII, 3.]*

[1] A reciprocal festival of U.S. documentaries was in fact organized, and toured the USSR the following year.

Some Perspectives on Soviet Cinema in the *Glasnost* Era

The pleasures of *glasnost* came to Soviet cinema for the same reasons that animated reforms in other sectors of the USSR. Layers of bureaucracy, over-centralization, waste, censorship, arbitrariness, indifference to the public, inability to compete in world markets, protecting the mediocre and knocking down the innovative: these were ailments that afflicted Soviet cinema as much as they hurt the economy or scientific research.

In part, the *glasnost* program was just a way of juicing things up through virtuous rhetoric, exhortation, and glossy public relations—just take a look at a Soviet film catalogue of this period and compare it to the stodgy stuff Moscow's marketing agencies used to turn out. In part, in more substantial part, *glasnost* overhauled institutions, goals, and leading personnel. The consequences for Soviet cinema were immediately apparent—there were new heads of both the Filmmakers Union and Goskino, the State Cinema Committee; a Conflicts Board was created to review dozens of suppressed films; and other projected reforms would affect the entire industry, from production to domestic distribution and foreign marketing, from film magazines and criticism to film schools.

But in the arts, cinema among them, no amount of indignation or self-criticism, no matter how righteous and eloquent, and no structural rearrangements or personnel shuffling, especially when generated from above (and which just as easily might be withdrawn from above), could by themselves guarantee quality or soul or whatever it is in art that has the power to move us.

That the *glasnost* campaign was no simple panacea for Soviet filmmaking was one cautionary observation that needed mentioning amid all the welcoming hoopla. Much of the hoopla was justified; it was certainly good to be able to see Elem Klimov's *Agoniya/Rasputin* (and to know that the creative and energetic Klimov was the new head of the Filmmakers Union), or to see Alex Gherman's *My Friend Ivan Lapshin* and Gleb Panfilov's *The Theme*—to cite just three of the many fine films previously suppressed and later released. (I'll return to these films below.) But this leads us to a second cautionary observation about the new look in the Soviet cinema industry, a paradoxical one: for all of the palpable problems besetting Soviet filmmakers, they managed over the post-Stalin years to create works of enduring beauty and significance.

Soviet cinema before *glasnost* was not a wasteland. Though suppressed under the old system, the three examples I cited were also made under the old system (in 1975, 1984, and 1979 respectively; some of the banned films go back to the 1960s). I realize we all have differing lists of our favorites, but who would not at the very least consider Sergei Paradzhanov's *Shadows of Forgotten Ancestors* (1964), Andrei Tarkovsky's *Andrei Rublev* (1966), and Georgy Shengelaya's *Pirosmani* (1969) for their preferred masterpieces of world cinema? (Of the three directors, alas, only Shengelaya has operated more or less normally in the usually less restrictive environment of the

Georgian film industry, Gruziafilm in Tbilisi being located far from Moscow, figuratively and geographically. Paradzhanov's career was twice interrupted by jailings, on charges unrelated to his films, while Tarkovsky's was cruelly terminated by exile and death. One of the great commendable features of *glasnost* and *perestroika* was Tarkovsky's rehabilitation in the USSR, albeit posthumously.) There are other, superb pictures that were produced and distributed earlier without the aura of struggle and controversy that surrounded, say, *Andrei Rublev*. Panfilov's powerful *Vassa* (1983) comes to mind, based on a Gorky play about lust and greed in a rich pre-Revolutionary business family. Another is Georgy Danelia's *Autumn Marathon* (1980), a "sad comedy" about a middle-aged translator in contemporary Leningrad trying to juggle work, friends, family, and an extra-marital affair. If there was considerable disaffection within the Soviet cinema industry prior to *glasnost*, there was also considerable vitality.

With these qualifications noted, we are better positioned to survey some of the reform developments and place them in a wider context. If by *glasnost* was meant a general loosening of controls over expression in general, then Soviet cinema witnessed two important relaxations prior to the *perestroika* period. In each case, as with *perestroika*, artistic dividends came as an offshoot of state policy in matters of, say, the economy, or political reform. The young Soviet film industry was given a tremendous lift by the atmosphere of "NEP" Russia for most of the 1920s. The New Economic Policy introduced by Lenin's government in 1921 centered on promoting private farming and private trade, but the spirit of toleration also extended elsewhere. It was a long way from genuine freedoms; the ethos of the "proletarian dictatorship", permeating the structures of the single-party state, still prevailed. But within these confines a relatively relaxed press, literature, history-writing, and theater flourished. For cinema, the NEP years were a golden age, an unparalleled effusion of talent that brought global acclaim. The young directors Sergei Eisenstein, Vsevolod Pudovkin, Alexander Dovzhenko, Dziga Vertov, Grigory Kozintsev and Leonid Trauberg fashioned a new film idiom unmistakably Soviet in its attention to revolution and the masses, its novel politics and lyrical propaganda propelled by exuberant technical experiments. (Speaking of lists, who can leave out Eisenstein's *Potemkin* or Pudovkin's *Mother* or Dovzhenko's *Earth* from enumerations of classic silent films?)

By the end of the 1920s the Stalin government began to snap cinema into the conformities of what would be known as "socialist realism"—broadly, the state's credo of an uplifting art that was accessible to the masses. Cinema was called on to arouse and entertain the nation as it underwent the travails of industrialization, peasant collectivization, and, later, war against the Nazi invaders. Political authorities kept a close watch on arousing and entertaining. For two and a half decades the Soviet screen reflected their tastes and taboos. (Unfortunately for Soviet cinema, Stalin loved films.) The results imparted new meaning to the designation "Soviet movies"—ponderousness of style, mawkish melodrama, a studied, sentimental folksiness, overblown heroes, and quite a bit of historical falsification. Sometimes these elements worked well enough—Eisenstein's *Alexander Nevsky* (1938), the Vasiliev Brothers' *Chapayev* (1934), Mark Donskoy's *Gorky's Childhood* (1938) and his *The Rainbow* (1944), for example. But the overall output was dully conformist; by Stalin's death in 1953 Soviet cinema had nearly been wrecked.

The trademark of Khrushchev's successor regime was de-Stalinization, a personal attack on the dead ruler's memory, a dismantling of the enormous "personality cult" that had grown up around him, and a substantial—though not nearly complete—undoing of his legacy of political terror with its stranglehold on the arts and media. To augment these efforts, Khrushchev approved greater permissiveness for the creative intelligentsia, especially if anti-Stalinism was a motif. In this regard, the quintessential work of the period was Solzhenitsyn's *One Day in the Life of Ivan Denisovich*, about the grim, hushed-up subject of prison-camp life, published through Khrushchev's personal intervention in 1962. Cinema benefited from the liberalization as well, although Soviet screens during this period never achieved anything comparable to the power of Solzhenitsyn's slim volume. Indeed, no Soviet film even confronted the subjects of Stalin or Stalinism, as writers, historians, and journalists were doing. Filmmakers simply unpersoned Stalin, as they had earlier glorified him. I remember at least one exception—in Grigory Chukhrai's *Clear Skies* (1961), a family crisis is resolved when a son enters breathlessly to announce "Stalin is dead!" —cut to a river where massive blocks of winter ice break up under the warming sun. The most prominent signals of de-Stalinization in cinema were the same Chukhrai's *The Forty-First* (1956) and *Ballad of a Soldier* (1959), and especially Mikhail Kalatozov's *The Cranes Are Flying* (1957)—films of the Civil War and World War II that reintroduced human beings to epic subjects, made them emotionally credible, and touched on unpleasant themes like draft-dodging or marital infidelity. They also brought the camera back to life again, although even the best of the Soviet films of this period were still rather clunky by Western technical standards. Perhaps the most striking release of the time—another emblem of de-Stalinization—was Part II of Eisenstein's *Ivan the Terrible* in 1957, a decade after it was made.

There were always limits to what was possible under Khrushchev. His fall in 1964 came from excessive experimentation in the Party and in the economy, not from excess of liberalism in general, or in the arts particularly. His cultural views were quite traditional and dogmatic. He once denounced Soviet avant-garde artists as "pederasts" and their work as "dogshit". Still, the Khrushchev program had electrified the Soviet film world. Among other things, incidentally, new diplomatic initiatives lessened Cold War tensions and ushered in cultural exchanges with the West; more and more Western films appeared on Soviet screens. A new generation was at the film schools in those years and their work over two and a half decades, from the early 1960s to the mid-1980s, changed the face of Soviet cinema.

We come to a group of very talented filmmakers united as a generation but who did not comprise a school or subscribed to a common manifesto or gathered around a single figure. Their styles were eclectic, though commonplaces crept in—black and white sequences alternated with color or monochrome tinting; the synthesizer was heard more and more on sound tracks; narrative lines dissolved in favor of unidentified flashbacks and successions of tableaux; the pictorial possibilities of the folkloric were exploited. The Soviet film industry is a tight community; family lines can be traced in these commonplaces. Andrei Konchalovsky co-scripted *Rublev* with Tarkovsky, and later went on to direct his own epic of the 20th century, *Siberiade* (1979); Yury Ilyenko's *White Bird With*

Black Markings (1971) owes much to Paradzhanov's *Shadows*, for which he served as cameraman; Konchalovsky's younger brother, the actor turned director, Nikita Mikhalkov, employs the color-alternation scheme in his stylish handling of the Russian Civil War theme, *"A Slave of Love"* (1975). Fresh approaches to literary classics were introduced with almost a loving sympathy for the melancholia of the 19th-century gentry and intelligentsia. (An indirect commentary on the frustration of the *Soviet* intelligentsia?) Konchalovsky directed Chekhov's *Uncle Vanya* (1971) and Turgenev's *A Nest of Gentry* (1969); Mikhalkov made a slavophilic *Oblomov* based on Goncharov's novel, and a tender *Unfinished Piece for Player Piano* after Chekhov (1980 and 1977 respectively; his *Dark Eyes*, 1987, an Italian co-production, is based principally on Chekhov's *The Lady With a Dog*, and featured Marcello Mastroianni). Even war films took on a new look, from Tarkovsky's often surrealistic *Ivan's Childhood* (1962), to the religious intonations of the late Larisa Shepitko's *The Ascent* (1977), to Klimov's hyperrealistic *Come and See* (1985). World cinema was treated to a vigorous new ensemble of Soviet productions; there was more than just *Alexander Nevsky* and *Ballad of a Soldier* when one thought of Soviet films.

What, then, accounted for the compelling need for a radical housecleaning of the Soviet film industry? Here again, for this third period of liberalization, the nod came from above. The Gorbachev regime, especially in the wake of the 27th Party Congress in 1986, was determined to energize Soviet society in all walks of life out of the Brezhnevian torpor that had settled in over two decades. Compared to other liberalizations, a key difference was that from the beginning, freer creative expression in the media and the arts was at the top of the reform program. Gorbachev himself is perhaps the first Soviet leader since Lenin to qualify as an intellectual (like Lenin he was trained in law), and to move in intelligentsia circles. (Klimov told me that Gorbachev enjoyed his film *Farewell*, and that he was familiar with the works of Valentin Rasputin, on whose novel the work was based. The film was consigned to only limited circulation when originally released in 1982.) Soon after the 27th Party Congress, the filmmakers met for their 5th Congress and used the occasion to infuse Soviet cinema with the spirit of *glasnost*.

It was the right moment. The contemporary USSR was now a

mature urban society with more comprehensive contacts with the rest of the world than ever before. For all of the achievements of Soviet cinema during the last couple of decades, the film mainstream was insipid and unsatisfying. An output of some 130 feature films annually was playing to declining audiences. Soviet cinema reflected the immobilism of the Brezhnev age. Daring films—daring by Soviet standards—were quashed by Goskino, the ministerial-level committee bossing the Soviet film industry. Before 1979 they were generally banned outright; after that date they were effectively killed through limited circulation, or withdrawn after release. Authorities favored the standard war epics and the historical mammoths (e.g., Yuri Ozerov's series, *Liberation*, 1968-1971, or Sergei Bondarchuk's *Boris Godunov*, 1986); treatments of contemporary life or historical subjects had to dodge long lists of politically or sociologically delicate topics—Stalinism, say, or Jewish emigration. The bureaucratic labyrinths that filmmakers had to traverse to get projects approved were bad enough, especially when decisions at all levels might be incoherent, petty, contradictory, and arbitrary. (Reasons for certain decisions often remain mystifying. What prevented the release of Panfilov's *The Theme*, the explosive scene with a Jewish "refusnik" writer, or the frank portrait of a successful establishment writer without talent? The former head of Goskino, Filip Yermash, approved Tengiz Abuladze's powerful indictment of Stalinism, *Repentance*, provided a slang term for "prostitute" was cut. What shelved Klimov's *Agoniya/Rasputin*? Its eroticism? The unflattering portrait of Old Russia?) Worse than the external censorship were the inner compromises, the self-censorship that came from years of frustration and learning how the system worked. The stronger personalities fought on; some managed the compromises with esthetic grace; others sought foreign shores to breath more freely—Konchalovsky, Tarkovsky, Otar Ioseliani, the cameraman Yasha Sklansky (who worked on Guerman's long-banned, later released *Checkpoint/Trial on the Road*, 1971), for example.

The 5th Congress resolved to alter this state of affairs. Some results were registered already, but the real pay-off, ongoing production of films that reflect genuine creative autonomy in style and subject matter, lay in the future. Several figures in the Soviet cinema world insisted that the process would take about three years before the impact of the reforms could be felt. One film that worked *glasnost* and *perestroika* into the screenplay itself was the work of, predictably, the satirist, Eldar Ryazanov. His *Forgotten Melody for Flute*, about the inevitable conflicts between new and old ways in the *glasnost* era, debuted at the Moscow Film Festival in 1987. (Ryazanov's magnificent *Garage*, a biting masterpiece that crosses anti-bureaucratic comedy with a situation reminiscent of Buñuel's *The Exterminating Angel*—personnel at an institute are confined until they can figure out who gets the recently vacated garage spaces—ran into trouble when first released in 1980.) Among the most immediately gratifying results of *glasnost* in cinema were, of course, the cluster of previously banned or tokenly released films that appeared on Soviet and international screens, and at film festivals everywhere. Notable among these features were two films by Alexei Gherman, *My Friend Ivan Lapshin* and *Checkpoint/Trial On the Road*; Abuladze's *Repentance*; Panfilov's *The Theme*; Alexander Askoldov's *Commissar* (1967); Kira Muratova's *Brief Encounters* (1968); Konchalovsky's *Asya's Happiness* (1966); Klimov's *Agoniya/Rasputin* and *Farewell*; and Alexander Alov's and Vladimir Naumov's *A Disgusting Anecdote* (1977).

Checkpoint is a war film unusual for its exploring the embarrassing subject of Soviet soldiers deserting to the Nazis, while *Lapshin* sets its detective story in the crowded apartments and grimy streets of a provincial town in the mid-1930s, in the shadow of Stalin's Great Purges. *Repentance*, one of the greatest box-office grossers in the USSR, is a stylistically bold treatment, the third in a trilogy, of Stalinism, or more broadly, totalitarian dictatorship. *The Theme*, shot beautifully against the backdrop of the medieval town of Vladimir, probes the attempts of a successful writer to overcome a crisis of self-doubt. (As usual, Panfilov's wife, Inna Churikova, contributes a stunning performance as a local museum guide who tells the writer the truth about his mediocrity, and, in a memorable scene, pleads with a Jewish refusenik not to leave her and Russia.) *Commissar*, which had an unscheduled screening at the Moscow Film Festival, is a Civil War tale with several interesting twists: a poor Jewish family takes in a pregnant Bolshevik commissar who then leaves after turning over her baby to the family. In a flash-forward, the family is heading for the gas chambers. *Brief Encounters* features the director herself as part of a love triangle which also includes the late legendary bard Vladimir Vysotsky. Some critics consider Konchalovsky's *Asya's Happiness*, his best film (it was his second feature, after *First Teacher*, 1965), an unresolved love story involving a non-conformist, crippled village girl. Klimov's *Agoniya* is not so much, as he put it, about Rasputin as "rasputinism," that is, the climate of decay enveloping the court and government of the last Tsar, Nicholas II—a figure presented by Klimov as a troubled family man, not a pasteboard villain. *Farewell*, begun by Klimov's wife Larisa Shepitko, who was killed in a motoring accident early in film production, is based on the popular novel *Farewell to Matyora* by the Siberian writer Valentin Rasputin. In common with the concerns of a large number of the Soviet intelligentsia, the Rasputin/Shepitko/Klimov film dwells on the poignant contemporary—not just Soviet—tragedy of people, nature, and folkways overwhelmed by the inexorable march of industrial progress. The Alov-Naumov film is a provocatively expressionist handling of a Dostoevsky story.

These and other films created a stir at home and captured prizes at film festivals abroad—in 1986 *Lapshin* earned the critics prize at Locarno, as did *Farewell* at Tenerife (for ecological films); *Repentance* won the special jury prize at Cannes in 1987, while *The Theme* got the Golden Bear (over *Platoon*) at the Berlin Festival. Did they deserve those accolades? It's not an ordinary question nor are there easy answers. Somehow, we view Soviet films differently; there was an enormous amount of ideological and political baggage brought to a Soviet film that is rarely ever carried to Western productions. Our criteria for judgment shift into different gears. We might, for example, hail a Soviet film for its courageousness even as we made little of it esthetically. I walked away from *Checkpoint* impressed by a certain gritty black-and-white, war-film tonality but was otherwise disappointed by much stagey dialogue and a conventional Hollywood shoot-out ending. Yet this film—because of its controversial theme in the Soviet context—prompts a suspension of normal critical measures, especially when we know that Soviet audiences wept openly at screenings. The same might be said of the same director's *Lapshin*. The main character is brilliantly played, as is the ensemble work (often the best part of even the most ordinary Soviet films; this perhaps has something to do with the great theatrical traditions that Soviet actors come out of). But what's all the fuss about? The film travels at a self-consciously hectic and confusing pace, and the situations are contrived and melodramatic. But again, Soviet audiences were moved by the dialogue and the setting; they knew the fearful period in which the story takes place, and they see on screen what memories of the older generation remember: the raw and troubled business of survival amid shortages and organized crime (not only the political sort) during a period of national upheaval. At a screening I attended, Gherman commented that the film could not be understood in the West. (Who, save for us historians, knows that the film takes place "on the horrible eve," as Gherman put it, of the year 1937, the acme of the Great Terror?) Finally, especially when we are considering films made a decade or two ago, but later released, charity demands that we allow for the passage of time. It's not the fault of the filmmakers when a dated and imitative Fellini or Truffaut look pervades some of these features (*Lapshin*, for example). They may have looked a lot fresher when they were made.

In short, *glasnost* gave us an array of films off the shelves, on a great range of subjects and of variable quality, though all were distinctive for one censored reason or another. Only good films were banned, said Yasha Sklansky. A Soviet film critic lamented, "our best films are the old ones." One can see their point, although you may not agree that all the films are good. All of this has some bearing on the matter of Soviet films in the world arena. According to Chris Wood, Executive Vice President at International Film Exchange, defunct now, but long a distributor of Soviet films in the U.S., the Soviets were eager to plunge more aggressively into the world market because they sensed a sag in the output of quality films from European producers. They boasted a certain amount of success in promoting formerly forbidden treasures. But this was a kind of *succès de scandale*, or the curiosity factor at work. To generate genuine esteem and enthusiasm among film critics and film-goers in the West, and not just among Soviet experts, Russian language specialists, Tarkovsky cultists, the large *émigré* populations, and the still loyal and ever congratulatory remnants of the old pro-Soviet Left, the Soviet film industry had obviously to—I use the term as a form of shorthand, not of derogation—commercialize its offerings, to fashion a livelier, more universally appealing body of films.

The success of Vladimir Menshov's *Moscow Does Not Believe in Tears* in the U.S., where it won an Academy Award in 1981, is instructive here, though one hopes that popularity need not always equal hackneyed superficiality. (There is a story at Mosfilm Studios that a Hungarian film delegation walked out on the film.)

It was a tall order: to create an attractive new corpus within the framework of the lofty traditions of Soviet cinema: *glasnost* plus the motto of the Moscow Film Festival—"For Humanism in Cinema Art, For Peace and Friendship Among Nations." This high mindedness in Soviet cinema art was a worthy ideal; it had some noble embodiments, but also many staid exercises, particularly when political bosses and timorous bureaucrats decided what was acceptable. Too often, the result was neither good art nor good propaganda.

Enter Klimov and company to rectify the scene, thanks to the imperatives of the Gorbachev program. Klimov spoke of an "urgent call... to normalize the moral atmosphere in filmdom, to establish valid artistic criteria and ensure openness as a natural principle of art." Toward these ends, the Filmmakers Union would, if current plans were institutionalized, assume full parity with Goskino; in all important matters, Klimov said, the Union would be a co-signer with the State agency. Ultimately, the intention was to turn full artistic control over to the individual studios, which would eventually operate on a self-financing basis. (Observe how the reforms parallel Gorbachev proposals for restructuring the economy.) Goskino might still have to clear individual projects, but only, according to Union representatives, to avoid duplication. The system would operate on market, rather than bureaucratic principles in order, said Klimov, "to provide cultural services to the broad masses." The assumption was, rightly, that filmmakers and audiences, and not the political appointees knew best what those cultural needs were; in any event, the box office would be the best arbiter: in order to survive, the autonomous studios would have to finance themselves primarily through brisk trade at the movie houses.

Was all of this a recipe for the Hollywoodization of the Soviet film industry, if by the term we mean sensationalism and happy endings for commercial purposes? I doubt it, if the dynamics of *glasnost* were to be played out. Those old traditions against mindless vulgarity and cheap formulas—violence, flesh, car chases— were still too sturdy among the Soviet intelligentsia, filmmakers included. Their quest was still for art, and not as Mel Brooks put it in *Spaceballs*, for more money. In the Soviet instance, there was reason to hope that "market principles" were genuine passports to creative flexibility and freedom, rather than to corruption of artistic standards. The real dangers lay deep within the Russian tradition and came from the structures of Soviet political organization and culture management: what do they consider publicly acceptable? The old idea of censorship exercised as a moral/educational, not just political function by governing elites may clash with the principles of *glasnost*, in cinema as elsewhere. What some might consider liberty, others might take as license. There was no way to predict the shape and direction of this conflict; such things depended on the Kremlin, not just the Filmmakers Union. Yet Soviet cinema had always played an important socio-political role. Abuladze's *Repentance* was not just a movie; it was an Event, a participant in the ardent political debates that pit old and new ways of thinking and behaving against one another. When Rolan Bykov's *Scarecrow* was released in 1984, its treatment of the victimization of an odd-ball student by her fellow classmates (the "collective") triggered an outpouring of articles and letters in the press—not about the film's esthetic merits, but about the pointed questions it posed about the individual and the group, the nature of Soviet school kids and schooling, the responsibilities of teachers and parents, and so on. Cinema, the best Soviet cinema, played a role in the moral and even political life of the nation. The filmmakers got the three years indulgence they asked for to realize the promise of *glasnost*, but just then the Soviet screen faded to black. A title card said *Finis*.

[*Cineaste*, XVI, 1-2, 1987-1988]

Sideburns

No one who has seen Yury Mamin's *Neptune's Feast* will ever be able to watch the battle on the ice section of *Alexander Nevsky* with a straight face again. In *Neptune's Feast*, a short satirical gem filmed in 1986, Russian villagers prepare a faux folkloric ritual ordered by Moscow to impress visiting Swedish tourists. To the accompaniment of Prokofiev's classic score, the anxious villagers gaze at the horizon awaiting their confrontation with the Swedish invaders. What a moment! All at once Mamin updates Potemkin's villages, recalls Gogol's *Inspector General*, and manages to send up Eisenstein as well. This is Soviet film satire of the *glasnost* epoch at its most Soviet-tweaking best.

Mamin's next film, *The Fountain* (1988), was his first full-length feature. Here the milieu shifts wildly from Central Asia to a contemporary urban apartment house in Leningrad, so shoddily built, in the Soviet manner, that it is literally collapsing. A parade of colorful characters and absurd situations (Soviet reality was absurd) career to a whacky denouement in which an elevator rockets a Kazakh back to Central Asia, and placards with Party slogans prop up the buckling roof. "My goal," Mamin has said, "is to make people laugh at reality before they die of horror."

Mamin (b. 1946) is a Leningrad director who studied with the celebrated film satirist Eldar Ryazanov after some years in the theater. Mamin's experience with variety stagings shows up in his taste for clowning and the grotesque. Add his serious concern with public issues and you have *Sideburns* (1990), a three-ringed circus with deadly overtones that charts the factionalized political landscape of Soviet Russia before its collapse. This is satire, but it can give you the creeps.

The film was shot when Gorbachev and the reforming Party were trying to hold to an even centrist keel as all hell was beginning to break loose in politics, the economy, and in the national borderlands. (Mamin has said that one of the shadows affecting the making of the film was the massacre of peaceful demonstrators in Tbilisi in April, 1989.) The new freedoms had allowed for cultural experimentation, in the film represented by "Cappella," a tribe of rockers given to street theater and orgies and anything that thumbed its nose at Soviet convention.

The new freedom also brought forth the sword bearers of Russian cultural nationalism horrified by the westernizing decadence of the young. A sidewhiskered Führer, absurd and chilling at the same time, affecting 19th-century clothes, language, and attitudes, with Pushkin as his idol, organizes the local skinheads to give battle to the new trends. The Party and State authorities, anxious above all to maintain stability, and concerned about rival centers of mobilization (Pushkin busts replace Lenin's; Pushkin slogans replace the Party's), try their best to cool things off and co-opt factions. But in the end, they have to resort to force to stop the challenge to the existing order: in a mock massacre complete with attack dogs, special detachments assault the Pushkinites and.... shave off their whiskers.

Sideburns goes over the top, and lacks the light-hearted satirical charms of both *Neptune's Feast* and *The Fountain*. The film carries a whole lot of freight in its Soviet political and Russian literary references, too much, I'm afraid, for the ordinary Western viewer, though often delicious for its intended audience. There are wonderful thrusts at Communist-speak and Communist-kitsch, as well as amusing literary asides, as when a group of Lermontovites tries karate against the cane-wielding Pushkin gang. But Mamin, who appears in the film as a roving reporter, has an overall message that should get through to everyone. His mocking laughter is directed at dogmas, political idols, and mass movements mindlessly obeying charismatic and violence-prone leaders. The film is a satire-parable of the late Soviet scene, but the attitudes and conflicts it evokes resonate into the future.

[*Cineaste*, XX, 1, 1993]

Woman with a Movie Camera: The Films of Marina Goldovskaya

The *glasnost* policies of the late Soviet period, the last Soviet period, 1985-1991, liberated Russian documentarists. With a burst of candid, exposure films they showed the public contemporary and historical themes once forbidden by the cinema bosses, and their collective work is among the most valuable sources we have for understanding Soviet times, the dark earlier periods as well as those intoxicating *glasnost* days associated with Mikhail Gorbachev. Just as they were stretching their legs, enjoying the peculiar circumstance of making anti-Soviet films with Soviet state monies, filmmakers were confronted by an unforeseen, epochal development, the collapse of the USSR itself (and their regular funding sources)—not with a bang but with a whimper. Plenty of fireworks would follow, especially in the non-Russian borderlands of the once Soviet realm. As for Russia itself, things still weren't, to put it delicately, sorted out until stabilization *à la* Putin; there was much economic pain, much political confusion, and a terrible sense of disorder and disorientation hanging over the land, punctuated by the occasional assassination of a Petersburg democrat or a Moscow businessman. A good window of understanding on the Soviet experience before the collapse comes from the 22 films comprising the "Glasnost Film Festival" which toured the U.S. in 1989, and assembled on video by the California-based distributor, The Video Project [see Discovering the "Unknown Cinema" above]. The Video Project has since made available the vivid documentary work of Marina Goldovskaya in a series of five films, "Revealing Russia," that covers Soviet and post-Soviet themes, usually in her distinctively moving, personal ways.

Goldovskaya describes herself as an authentic "Homo Sovieticus" who grew up in the Soviet film environment. A neighbor was Alexander Medvedkin, the off-beat Soviet director, "The Last Bolshevik" of Chris Marker's documentary of that name. Her father, Yevsei Goldovsky, who devised standard Soviet systems for wide-screen, panoramic, and close-up filming, was for a time Deputy Minister of Cinematography, and headed the department of film technology at Moscow's famed State Cinema School (VGIK), from which Goldovskaya graduated. (Also part of the Soviet film environment: Yevsei Goldovsky spent five months in a Stalin prison in 1938.) Goldovskaya remembers she was always bored with the details of feature film production and preferred instead getting into the field, filming "real people, real stories." She found a niche in news documentaries at Gosteleradio, the State Television Agency, this "citadel of ideology," as she called it, where she often had to fight Party-hack philistines and sometimes make her way "through the forest of anti-Semites." Never, she reports, was her gender a problem; in filming, rather an asset, she thinks—being personable and attractive helped, but she also believes a woman documentarist is more easily received into the personal lives of filmed subjects.

Her specialty at Gosteleradio was crafting film portraits of individuals, past and present. One of those film portraits (unfinished), was a group study of provincial weavers in 1968 which Goldovskaya claims as the first use of the 16mm *cinéma vérité* style in Soviet documentary film making, something she came to independently of like developments in the West. She was astonished and proud when she discovered that Leacock, Pennebaker, *et al.* had been working along similar lines. Later, as in some of the films described below, and also blazing her own trail, she practiced the very subjective "video diary" style favored by many U.S. documentarists. (Once, meeting Jonas Mekas, she asked him, was he working on something? "I'm always shooting," he replied. To which, Goldovskaya: "Oh, me too!") To these stylistic characteristics, add Goldovskaya's historicist sensibilities and social concerns—she is a born historian—and you have a premier chronicler of Soviet and post-Soviet life and times.

Two works of the *glasnost* period brought Goldovskaya Western attention. *The Peasant from Arkhangel* (1987) centered on the barriers faced by a *muzhik* determined to realize what *perestroika* half-heartedly promised in Soviet agriculture: private farming and the market. *Solovky Power* (1988), one of the five in The Video Project's "Revealing Russia" Goldovskaya package, is an historical dissection with contemporary commentaries of the notorious prison camp in the White Sea that served as an early laboratory for the Gulag (Solzhenitsyn devotes a chapter to it in his *Gulag Archipelago*). *Solovky Power* had an added punch for Soviet television viewers at the time for its clear message that the camp system originated in the early years of the Bolshevik state—in Lenin's day—and was not Stalin's invention. Goldovskaya not only located an old propaganda film showcasing the camp and its happy campers, but tracked down survivors (and even a couple of their jailers), then screened the film for them and filmed their reactions and comments, in one case bringing tears of recollected pain to one survivor. *Solovky Power* begins with an epigraph taken from a 1918 poster, "We shall drive mankind to happiness with an iron hand," and ends with the admonition, "We have no right to forget!" (The title comes from a play on "Soviet power"; the camp was located on the site of the Solovetsky Monastery on a White Sea island.)

Goldovskaya's next three films were realized with the help of major Western funding, ranging from Ted Turner's TBS in the U.S. to Canal+ in France. She was anxious, she says, "to explain my people to the world," but she did impose the condition that her films be shown in Russia. One of those films, *The House With Knights*, (1993) is a kind of social-history essay, very human in the telling, covering many decades and conveyed through old photographs and the reminiscences of those who once inhabited a fine old apartment building for the well-to-do on Moscow's Arbat Street. (The title refers to the sculpture adorning the pre-Soviet architecture.) Old-timers recall that the dwelling housed some 200 tenants before the Revolution, then saw it converted into a communal-apartment complex for 3000 after the Civil War. Goldovskaya inserts recurring aerial and other shots of the building into the stories her subjects tell, and these personal tales illuminate some of the major stages of Soviet history, the purges of the 1930s most dramatically.

If *Solovky Power* and *The House With Knights* effectively offer some standard history in more-or-less standard documentary style, the other three films in the series are pictures of a later period with a very active pulse, captured by Goldovskaya's restless and ever-present camera on the streets, during demonstrations, in trains, at workplaces, and in the homes of her subjects during the tumultuous times before and after the Soviet collapse. Goldovskaya blurs the distinction between the filmmaker and the filmed; she and her first-person narration become part of the subject. (Like Ross McElwee minus the puckishness and self-deprecation.) Aside from the common "self-referential" device of catching herself in mirrors or windows, she dialogues with her subjects on camera, and in *The Shattered Mirror* (1992) she even cries on camera. (Only a woman filmmaker could do this?) But her personal video diaries have a larger purpose, too. Training her camera in *The Shattered Mirror* on someone waiting to tank up at a Moscow gas station, she is asked, "Who are you filming for?" "For history!" she replies.

This *troika* of films might take as a collective name the subtitle of *The Shattered Mirror—A Journal of a Time of Trouble*. They comprise some of the best documentary pictures we have of the jagged period, 1990-1993, from just before the USSR breaks apart, to the post-Soviet disequilibrium, including the attempted putsch that led

Boris Yeltsin to bring out the guns to bombard the sitting legislature in the White House (see *Lucky to Be Born in Russia: The Shattered Mirror*, Part 2). There are no high politics in Goldovskaya's films, no politico talking heads expatiating on policy. Personal stories reveal the general atmosphere and the political crosscurrents that envelop Goldovskaya and her friends. They are all for the new freedoms, for Yeltsin (at least for what he was supposed to stand for), and for the new economic opportunities of Russian capitalism. But there is joy mixed with anxiety, optimism tempered by fear, an overall uncertainty. Goldovskaya can't sleep; others confess the same. For many outside of Goldovskaya's circle, there is much anger. Goldovskaya's point of view, and those of her friends, professionals and the creative intelligentsia for the most part, is anti-Soviet and democratic and generally optimistic; witness the title of the last in the series, *Lucky to Be Born in Russia* (1994)—a phrase uttered in deliberate mockery of slogans of the Soviet period by a cheerful young woman whose freeze frame ends the film. In this sense, Goldovskaya's collective portrait is skewed, and doesn't offer a comprehensive look at all strata in Russian society, and their reactions, in town and country. (And certainly, the general later moods might be far from the "Lucky...." optimism expressed in the films.) The point of view of the distressed other side, the assorted communists, neo-fascists, and nationalists also gets some air time in the films, even if only in the form of banners and shouted curses during demonstrations: "Down with Zionism!" (*A Taste of Freedom*, 1991); "the Americans and the CIA are to blame!" "Yeltsin, traitor!" (*The Shattered Mirror*); "We'll Drive the Yids to America!" (*Lucky to Be Born in Russia*). Fortunately, not all those who were uncomfortable with the new Russia shared those thuggish sentiments.

Goldovskaya married an American engineer/businessman in 1992. (*The Shattered Mirror* begins with her marriage. A day later her mother died; there was, she narrates, "trouble in my heart, trouble in my country.") She settled in California and now spends much of her time teaching film at U.C.L.A., and serving on the Board of the International Documentary Association, but her mission of helping us "understand Russia" and using history to shed light on the present continues. Anthology Film Archives in New York has featured Goldovskaya retrospectives, including the films discussed above, as well as two "reverse angle" video diaries, i.e., shot in the U.S. and best suited for foreign audiences (one on Allen Ginsberg, 1997; another, *This Shaking World*, 1995, on her personal encounter with a Los Angeles rocked by an earthquake and by O.J.) Also screened was *Children of Ivan Kuzmich* (1997), an engrossing report, with archival footage, on the graduates in 1941 of a Moscow school where the eponymous principal touched their lives. Goldovskaya got on-camera interviews with some of the remarkable alumni: the daughter of the executed Bolshevik, Nikolai Bukharin; the son of the *God that Failed* communist, Louis Fisher; and none other than Markus Wolf, once head of the *Stasi*, the notorious East German secret service. Fascinating stuff. Her two most recent films continue her emphasis on individuals in post-Soviet Russia, and the challenges they face, or the hopes they share. *The Prince is Back* (1999/2003) chronicles the efforts of a contemporary "Prince" from an old aristocratic family to restore and live in what was once the ancestral estate. In the short film, *Three Songs About Motherland* (2008), Goldovskaya's inquiring camera crosses Russia from east to west, visiting three very different cities exposing the different understandings of past and present voiced by some of their inhabitants.

Collectively, Goldovskaya's documentary films offer us a singular portrait, with feeling, of a society whose members are searching for new bearings after the old ones, like her "mirror," have been shattered.

[*Cineaste*, XXIV, 2-3, 1999]

Adam's Rib

There were many Russian films portraying what turned out to be the last days of Soviet society, but none so bittersweetly, and so in control of its material as this small testament to survival. *Adam's Rib* (1990) is a film about four Soviet women—three generations, with a fourth possibly on the way—trying hard to make the best of things in straitened circumstances, and it's not just that they are crowded together in the usual tiny Soviet urban apartment. There are men problems. There are financial problems. There is a teen pregnancy. And the matriarch of the group lies mute and paralyzed in her bed.

Vyacheslav Krishtofovich, a director from Ukraine, takes a loving look at these women and conveys, with warmth, humor, and some snappy dialogue, the spirit of their survival. He seems particularly fond of women's themes. His *Lonely Woman Seeks Life Companion* (1986) had a brief theatrical showing in the U.S. It was one of those familiar Soviet "sad-comedies" starring the talented Irina Kupchenko as a middle-aged lovelorn driven to tacking up man-wanted notices around town. In 1977 Krishtofovich directed *Before Exams*, a television film about a young woman in high school considering an affair with one of her teachers. Viewed as unacceptably racy by the stodgy standards of the Brezhnev era, it was shelved. No such inhibitions operated during the Gorbachev years, when *glasnost* mandated candor about daily life. "Many films," Krishtofovich is quoted as having said of *Adam's Rib*, "showed how we lived. This film shows how we survived." How, exactly? In this case, through sisterly solidarity and love for one another, come what may. And, odd as it may sound, what with two broken marriages, no men in the house, and an out-of-wedlock pregnancy, through something resembling family values.

Economically speaking, Russians have been known to survive not just by tightening their belts, but by eating them if necessary. Emotionally speaking, they have survived through enormous patience and great globs of sentiment and mutual sympathy. With humor, too. In this family they may complain, but everyone takes a turn at emptying grandma's bed pan, and turning the TV around so she can watch her favorite program. When grandma's daughter, played by the incomparable Inna Churikova, can't contain an outburst blaming the now helpless old woman for wrecking her life, the scene ends with Churikova in tears herself telling her mama, "Don't cry... I'm sorry. Forgive me."

Churikova plays Nina, a museum guide, just shy of 50, still open to a new relationship, still vibrant and capable of having a meek dispatcher swoon over her. (Churikova as guide: a reference here perhaps to her role as museum guide in the controversial 1979 film, *The Theme*, in which she attracts the attention of a jaded writer.) Nina has two daughters, "by two very different husbands." Lida (Svetlana Ryabova) and Nastya (Masha Golubkina) are very different themselves. Lida is a beautiful and naive office worker having a liaison with, and then betrayed by, her married boss. Her younger and plainer sister Nastya is a street-smarts teenager who incidentally shows us another set of buffers in the Soviet repertory of survival against a harsh reality—sharp wits, cynicism, and good connections. When she wants easy access to a seat on a bus, she affects a serious limp and boards away from the crowd. She amazes her mother by locating some meat for a dinner party. "Communism," Nastya explains to her, "is being friendly with your local butcher." (Nastya also has most of the funny lines.) The complication in Nastya's life is that she is pregnant, and is resolved to have the baby. The problem is the father is a good-hearted, not very bright young man for whom Nastya hasn't the slightest regard.

Krishtofovich sets these contemporary stories into motion after a prologue in monotint recalls grandma's lyrical youth in less complicated times. The stories keep touching base back in the tiny apartment with its frenetic mornings and tearful afternoons. But unlike so many slice-of-life film reports from the late USSR, in documentaries and features, there is no morbidity here. The mood is sweetened not only by the characters and their redeeming high spirits, but by Pavel Lebeshev's quiet and often soft-focused camera, and by a production design bathing the apartment in soothing pastels—lavender, blue, and pink. One might call all of this Chekhovian-contemporary, except that the dominant tone in Chekhov, as Nabokov pointed out, was a peculiar kind of grey.

Also rather Chekhovian is the film-ending dinner party, which offers the cast something Soviet actors on stage and screen have always excelled in, the kind of tight ensemble performing that just carries you along through laughter and tears. For the party the two very different ex-husbands join the women, as does Nina's suitor. Nastya's ex-boyfriend tries to crash but she won't let him in. The party, which begins merrily, but soon gets to the shouting stage, also allows Krishtofovich to make some additional wry glosses on Soviet life. The name is Goldberg, Nina's first husband announces to her current suitor, "any objections?". Goldberg also brings sneakers from relatives in Israel, and some medicine that, as Nastya puts it, "the whole world has except us."

Through all of this, grandma, whose birthday it is, lies silent and apart in her bed, as usual. But she has a big part to play in the surprise ending. As the screen fades to black, we know these women will make it.

Adam's Rib, shown originally in the U.S. at the 29th New York Film Festival in 1991, and then enjoying a comparatively successful commercial run in New York, is another film from the former Soviet Union that throws a frank, unflattering light on Soviet men. While not exactly a Soviet *Thelma and Louise*—it's too sweet-natured for that—it does highlight the social relations in a society purportedly honoring and liberating its women, but consigning them in daily life to old-fashioned drudgery and, in the battle of the sexes, great emotional pain. Maybe Russian women are stronger as a result, or just stronger, period. Certainly they are, as shown in this film. If liberation for post-Soviet society is to have any meaning, its Eves must be as free as its Adams.

[*Cineaste*, XIX, 2-3, 1992]

Historians of the USSR Cross Over into Filmmaking

At a meeting of the American Association for the Advancement of Slavic Studies (AAASS) in Philadelphia, 1994, historians of what used to be called the Soviet Union gathered to share ideas and compare experiences on a theme of mutual interest: how to convey aspects of the singular, complex, and volatile epoch of Gorbachev's *perestroika* in documentary film.

Rendering history through film generally needed no special pleading in those days. The subject turned up in diverse quarters, from academic journals to panel discussions at the Sundance Film Festival, where a session in 1994 subtitled "Animating the Past" centered on such films as *JFK* and *Quiz Show*. The Philadelphia session, however, had a certain distinction for reasons of both milieu and participants. The setting was the annual AAASS conference. The sponsor for the session was the "Working Group on Cinema and TV, the Soviet Union, and Eastern Europe", formed several years earlier by a group of scholars, Russian/Soviet specialists particularly, who sought to elevate film studies alongside traditional disciplines like literature and language, or who used film in their classes to illuminate politics and society. Isn't it natural to connect film to the history of the Soviet Union, where the founding father anointed the new medium "the most important art" and where artists devised images that continue to flood our ideas of the Soviet past? When we think of the Russian Revolution, we see Eisenstein's Odessa steps from *Potemkin* or the storming of the Winter Palace from *October (Ten Days That Shook the World)*. Never mind that Eisenstein invented such scenes; they have assumed a near-documentary reality. Haven't we all seen such shots treated as found footage for documentaries?

The Working Group was eventually accredited by the AAASS, but not without first overcoming mainstream doubts regarding the legitimacy of its work as a properly scholarly enterprise. Film just didn't have the right credentials. It was always a struggle, for example, to get the association to provide and pay for projection equipment for sessions where films or clips were to be shown. Not so in Philadelphia, and, it is safe to say, not anymore. Recognition of the Working Group is also palpable in its growth, as more and more academics, especially historians, rely on film and familiarize themselves with film language for their teaching and research. (See, for example, the essays in the collection *Revisioning History: Film and the Construction of a New Past*, edited by Robert A. Rosenstone, who was writer for the documentary *The Good Fight* and consultant for Warren Beatty's *Reds*, a historical melodrama of the Bolshevik Revolution and American socialism, based on the life of John Reed.)

Another distinction of the Philadelphia session was that four of the six historian panelists spoke on the subject from the inside—not as consultants, translators, or fact checkers, but as *makers*, with varying degrees of control, of documentary films about the Gorbachev period. From the written word or the classroom lecture, they had crossed over into image land to tell students and the public the story.

Outwardly, there are some obvious similarities between the historian's craft and the documentary filmmaker's. Each strives for a truthful, fact-based rendition of contemporary or historical actuality. Parallel "production stages" are involved, from conceptualization to research (archives, secondary sources, interviews) to writing and editing. And, as we all know, the most objective historian and the most detached *vérité* documentarist share an agenda, latent or acknowledged, that shapes the raw material into a coherent, subjective whole. Ultimately, what we get in text or film is an imaginative re-creation, a kind of deception, you might even say. But of course: History, said Voltaire, is a joke we play on the dead or, as the great historian of Soviet Russia, E.H. Carr, put it in a more empirically English way, history is a hard core of interpretation surrounded by a soft periphery of facts.

There is another subtle and rarely confessed dimension uniting documentarist and historian, something noted by historian Susan Heuman of Manhattanville College in New York, who worked for NBC's *Today* series on life in Gorbachev's Russia in 1987. Likening her presence in central Moscow to a camera operator's in a war zone, she reported filming a demonstration by Soviet Jews that was assaulted by the police. She found herself shouting at the police on behalf of the demonstrators and experienced the exquisite feeling of not just filming a bit of history but participating in it. Scratch a historian or a documentarist and you might find a historical actor *manqué*. (Those who can, do; those who can't, teach... or make a film about it?) Heuman also alluded to a related truism of our image- and media-driven world: the demonstrators' conviction that being filmed helped their cause, that the camera was itself a political instrument with enormous powers to reach mass audiences and policymakers. "The whole world is watching," shouted the demonstrators at the Democratic presidential convention as they were beaten by the Chicago police in 1968. Two decades later that convergence of media and politics had materialized in the Soviet section of the global village. Some analysts argue that not only had this convergence prepared the way for Gorbachev's *perestroika* and *glasnost*, but that it was pivotal in shattering the Soviet structure itself. Television and film, especially documentary film on formerly repressed aspects of Soviet history and contemporary life, played an incalculable part in the ferment of the Gorbachev years.

Anyone with any experience of the pre-Gorbachev period was immediately struck by this. I certainly felt it, as did the correspondent I worked with, Hedrick Smith. I was Associate Producer for two sections of the four-part PBS documentary *Inside Gorbachev's USSR*, researched and shot in 1988-1990 (Martin Smith was executive producer). Hedrick Smith, the Pulitzer Prize-winning Moscow correspondent of the *New York Times* in the early 1970s, returned to the Soviet Union after a decade and a half's absence to make the series. I remember how dumbfounded and delighted he was to see people in Moscow, near the Kremlin, race toward the camera and jostle each other to make their voices heard, a phenomenon unthinkable earlier.

The power of the medium should also bring its practitioners an acute sense of responsibility; I know I felt it. An article I or any historian might publish reaches a comparative handful of people; only the rare historical monograph or biography becomes a best seller with an impact. The PBS documentary, by contrast, reached an estimated 10 million people, making it a powerful instrument affecting U.S. public attitudes about the Gorbachev reforms at a time when many still doubted their substance.

Perhaps it was this sense of responsibility, or maybe it was my training about getting details right and being able to, as we say, "document" any assertion, that often led to differences with my film colleagues. There were many instances of divergence between narration and image that made me uncomfortable, as did several dramatic reenactments in another film I worked on as Associate Producer, Sherry Jones's *In the Shadow of Sakharov*, for PBS's *Frontline* (1991). In the end, I was won over to the idea that the story (the best history is a at bottom a good story) is most effectively advanced in film through images, not narration. Jones was always critical of correspondents she had to work with who were "text driven, not film driven." And Nancy Schoss, one of the Associate Producers I worked with, was fond of boasting that a good script for a documentary should be *incoherent*; the film's coherence and emotional power comes from what is on screen or from an effective synergy of image and text, with the latter serving the former. (All of these discussions, incidentally, illustrate another difference between writing history and filmmaking: The latter is a collective endeavor, involving many, many people, and inherently collaborative even under the most forceful and authoritarian producers/directors.)

The need to de-emphasize the historian's "fact driven" compulsions was a film theme argued by the New York University labor historian Daniel J. Walkowitz, coproducer with Barbara Abrash of *Perestroika from Below* for England's Channel 4, about the miners' strike in southern Russia in 1989. Walkowitz called upon fellow historians to begin serving their students with combinations of film and book, and he favored obliterating the pedagogical—or epistemological—distinction between documentary and fiction film in historical use. He also leaned to postmodern, nonlinear narrative strategies for documentary and fiction film alike, and he saw part of the historian's task as teaching film literacy in general.

These issues of modality are related to another, somewhat more historic graphic question: What constitutes the proper subject for historical inquiry and documentary presentation? Historian Lewis H. Siegelbaum of Michigan State University, who worked with Walkowitz on a follow-up project, a video-oral history of the Donetsk miners in 1991-1992 stressed the "history-from-below" approaches cultivated by younger historians. Transferred to film, this "new history" envisions the *auteur* as only one among many "multiple subjectivities," with the most important being the subjects themselves. For the large Gorbachev story, Walkowitz and Siegelbaum chose miners and the many issues churning through their public as well as personal, and even intimate, lives in order to illuminate the epoch.

I remember constantly confronting such choices in making *Inside Gorbachev's USSR*. Do we aim for the Kremlin interview with Gorbachev and his associates, or do we root around ordinary lives in Yaroslavl and Ivanovo to highlight those extraordinary times? Interestingly, academics involved in the project, the advisors and consultants, usually favored the first approach; film people—from camera and sound operators to producers—were inclined to the second, and usually they were right, if simple visual or human interest is the test. Perhaps both are essential, but note how the dilemma of choice commonly confronts historian and documentarist alike.

I can't help noticing another functional similarity in writing and filming history, especially contemporary history, what might be called the serendipity factor, when the unplanned and spontaneous come into play. Walkowitz and Siegelbaum intended a general documentary portrait of the miners when they began their project, but the whole effort was transformed when a massive strike erupted. I remember how on the way to filming an election campaign in rural Russia we stumbled on a women's hunger strike on the steps of a local church in Ivanovo. It's that strike that stayed in our film, not the election campaign. Sometimes the serendipitous can alter one's whole paradigm. In our case, what we were witnessing was the rebirth of civil society through the spontaneous and undirected self-organization and activity of the Russian masses, actions duplicating the women's hunger strike in innumerable forms. Understanding this eroded our original conception of what was going on; before shooting, we had assumed that a dynamic Gorbachev leadership was having a hard time moving an inert population into democratization. In some fundamental way, it turned out the opposite was true.

In commenting on our presentations, Andrew Horton, a screenwriter, film scholar, and historian of Russian cinema, applauded the unique contribution that documentarians make to future generations and to their understanding of the past. The images preserved on tape or celluloid become the raw data or primary sources for future historical investigation. But he also chided academics who still refused to accept filmic legitimacy. He told of a colleague who was denied tenure because he had not published a book—he had only produced three prize-winning films. Siegelbaum confessed that in writing funding proposals for their film, they often resorted to the ruse that the film was only a means for collecting testimonies and that the end result would be a written text. Horton called on us to "educate university committees" in these matters.

Denise J. Youngblood, a historian of Russian film and society at the University of Vermont, chaired the session and warned in her summation that historians who ignore film do so at their own peril as teachers and communicators in our age of visual information. Young people learn of the Holocaust through Steven Spielberg, she noted. To which we might add, not every historian can be Spielberg, but all historians should be as conversant in filmographies on their specialty as they are in bibliographies. They might even consider making a film themselves. Documentarists—look out!

[This article originally appeared in the May-June 1995 issue of *International Documentary* (now called *Documentary*), a publication of the International Documentary Association.]

Requiem for Soviet Cinema 1917-1991

The first time I saw Eisenstein's *Potemkin* was in Havana, in revolutionary Cuba, many years ago. At the climax, the audience itself provided the soundtrack of cheers for the victorious, insurgent sailors as their battleship sailed, unchallenged, through the Tsar's Black Sea Fleet. I cheered, too.

It was a thrilling moment for me. So much seemed to come together in that Havana theater—a film work of genius, acknowledged as such *even* by bourgeois critics, made in the service of the revolutionary Soviet state to inspire the Soviet masses, was now inspiring a fraternal revolutionary people at the doorstep of Yankee imperialism. How fortunate were the Soviet people, I thought, to have Art and Revolutionary Ideology so perfectly fused in their movies, the medium for the masses. Later, when I got to know more about the history of Soviet cinema (and much else about the Soviet Union), I learned that *Potemkin* was a box office flop at home, though hailed by the Western intelligentsia. The Soviet masses preferred Douglas Fairbanks, Mary Pickford, and Hollywood's adventure, melodrama, and the "kheppyend" to Eisenstein's rebels and innovative montage.

How disappointing. No matter, Eisenstein's *Potemkin* is still a great film. Or is it? Let's leave that question aside except to point out that it has always been difficult to judge Soviet cinema by ordinary and universal standards. We always looked at Soviet movies through unusual filters, with complex sensations of political sympathy (as in my case) or antipathy, or out of simple curiosity about an exotic, experimental society that for much of its history remained inaccessible to outsiders. Now that the Soviet Union has imploded, its films are more exotic still, for they are among the remaining artifacts of a vanished civilization, its themes and icons preserved in celluloid.

Those films reveal and, being Soviet, made under the censor's eye, they also conceal; thus we have to watch them cautiously, alert to omission or hidden meaning. Judgments about their cinematic worth always have to factor in political context and the painful conditions in which Soviet filmmakers labored. And, inevitably, any consideration of Soviet cinema takes us to such large timeless issues as the relations among art, the artist, and the state; between cinema and the masses; about the moral and social function of films; and about the filmmaker as enchanter, entertainer, teacher, or propagandist. In one form or another, these issues surface in all societies, but is there any doubt that their collective story is more tortured and more poignant, and considerably more absurd, in the history of Soviet cinema than anywhere else? And where else was the state so determined a *cinéaste?*

A series of books published during, and just after *glasnost* indicated a renewed fascination with that remarkable story. In part, the great burst of film activity during the Gorbachev period inspired attention. Another reason, I'm happy to say, is that film study became an increasingly acceptable methodology among historians and other analysts of Soviet culture and society. (The Soviet collapse showed, after all, that Kremlinologists and other social scientists had not done too well in their assessments and predictions.) Much work focused on the beginnings and on the end stages of Soviet cinema; later, studies appeared on the post-Stalin period associated with Khrushchev's cultural thaw, and on what followed, the period known derisively by the post-Brezhnev generation as *zastoi* ("stagnation"). Oddly, some of the finest creations of modern Soviet cinema belong to the stagnation period, easily outshining the works freely crafted during the brief Gorbachev period, when the old restraints finally came down. Unintentionally, those *glasnost*-era books form a collective *Requiem* for Soviet cinema.

The young Soviet state enthusiastically embraced the young film medium, and government patronage was responsible for the parade of silent film classics wrought by a brilliant group of directors (also young) that included Sergei Eisenstein, Vsevolod Pudovkin, Alexander Dovzhenko, Lev Kuleshov, and Dziga Vertov. But as the historian Denise Youngblood makes clear in her superb study of the "unknown cinema," *Movies for the Masses* (1992), the Golden Age of Soviet cinema glittered more abroad than at home, where "the unvarnished truth is that Soviet audiences... did not like the pictures that made film history, finding them dull and difficult to understand.", or as Peter Kenez, another historian, puts it in his skeptical survey, *Cinema and Soviet Society* (1992), "The films of... [Konstantin] Eggert, [Iakov] Protazanov, and [Fridrich] Ermler, who aimed to entertain audiences, were seen by many more people than the works of Vertov or Eisenstein." And, as both authors point out, Soviet audiences, given a choice, would readily take a foreign over a Soviet film.

In other words, even though the Soviet film industry was nationalized in 1919, the authorities were continually more tantalized by their political expectations for the new medium than satisfied by its achievements. They hoped for a cinema that would teach and arouse the masses. This "ecclesiastical" understanding of the function of art, as the historian Richard Stites calls it, was traditional among the Russian intelligentsia, and inherited by the Bolsheviks. To it they added their authoritarianism, not to mention their deadly factional battles. There was never any doubt that film, like other arts, would be subject to state and party control. "Our standard" in art, noted Trotsky, "is, clearly, political, imperative, and intolerant." Of cinema, he wrote in 1923, "Here is an instrument which we must secure at all costs!"

During the 1920s, "securing" the medium did not yet mean the complete subservience of the film industry that the next decade would bring. The Bolsheviks were certainly not "pluralists," yet a diversity of film studios and directorial styles, as well as contrasting opinions in film criticism, characterized the pre-Stalin epoch of "The New Economic Policy." (The NEP allowed for limited private enterprise in town and country.) Youngblood gives us a fine picture of the rich and inevitably acrid debates carried on by critics, ideologues, filmmakers, and film distributors during this period as to what was a proper socialist art for proletarians and peasants. The success of certain films, Eggert's fantastic *The Bear's Wedding* (1925) or Abram Room's wry *Third Meshchanskaya Street* (known to us as *Bed and Sofa*, 1927), for example, or of foreign films in general, infuriated those critics committed to "enlightenment." They saw such films as "commercial deviations" that made money at the box office but subverted the aims of political pedagogy. The great innovators, Eisenstein, *et al.*, whose political allegiances were wholeheartedly with the Great October Socialist Revolution, could carry on their distinctive work (within certain limits, of course) thanks in part to the money coming in from "the commercial deviations," but they were to be branded with the cardinal sin of "formalism." Later, they were alternately silenced or forced into pathetic compromises.

One of the few films, notes Youngblood, that won popular favor as well as critical acclaim, at home and abroad, was Pudovkin's *Mother* (1926). Couldn't the studios turn out more of the same? That is the question that hovered over Soviet filmmaking throughout its life, and perplexed the culture bosses. But legislated art is invariably mediocre. Worse, as Anatolii Lunacharskii, the first Commissar of Enlightenment and a screenwriter himself, complained, "boring agitation is counter-agitation." Attempts to codify "proletarian" cinema yielded prattle like the following from a critic in 1924: *the worker... demands intelligibility, simplicity, logic, orderliness, everyday life. The worker does not suffer... affectations, idiosyncrasy, mysticism. The world view of the working class, Marxism, is the most well defined and harmonious of existing world views. Only one style, realism, corresponds... to this world view.*

Youngblood poses a question even more fundamental than what constitutes proper proletarian cinema: Is there such a thing as "class culture" at all? Her answer is a tactfully framed negative; she is inclined to believe that such an idea is a "Marxian pipe-dream." When it comes to films, Kenez is even more skeptical. He argues, much as Hollywood bosses have learned (or never learned), that no one can know how any film might be received by the public, and what values or inspiration they might draw from it. William Goldman's famous dictum, "Nobody Knows Anything," could apply to Soviet filmmaking as well. Hence, a "proletarian film" might sound fine on paper, but draw yawns from proletarians. Kenez is also skeptical about the designation "revolutionary cinema" for the films of the 1920s: since they upheld the values of the existing Soviet state, they were complicitous, not revolutionary. The truly revolutionary film, he argues, distantly echoing Amos Vogel, subverts existing values. Altogether, Kenez is rather unforgiving of the compromises Soviet filmmakers had to make. This is, I think, an overly unsympathetic and coldblooded judgment about many individuals whose lives were wrecked, and not only creatively.

The "bourgeois" solution governing production is, ultimately, Let the Market Decide. That was never a real option in Soviet Russia, least of all in Stalin's Russia beginning in the 1930s. Yet, not so surprisingly, a big nod to the need for entertainment, that is, satisfying one of the market's demands, marked the Stalin period once the strait-laced calls for a strict proletarian cinema during the "cultural revolution" (1928-1932) were set aside. Even the canonized doctrine of "socialist realism," enunciated in 1934, was partly a warrant for the mythic and romantic. What else could it mean since the realism it called for could not possibly be *realized* in any ordinary sense of the term? Andrei Zhdanov's defining pronouncement about combining "the most matter-of-fact, everyday reality with the most heroic prospects" in literature was, as applied to film as well, also an appeal for accessibility, seconded in film boss Boris Shumiatsky's demand for a Soviet "Cinema for the Millions" (the title of both his decree and book).

The bosses got that kind of successful cinema in the 1930s with a series of films unabashedly designed for entertainment, but also approved politically by the censors. (Foreign imports, meanwhile, were denied to the public.) One of the emblematic films of the epoch, popular even today, though largely for campy reasons, was the Vasilyev Brothers' *Chapayev* (1934), which delivered humor, heroism, and sentiment with a near Hollywoodian mastery of pacing and characterization. It was the closest thing to a Western, set in the Russian Civil War, pitting wicked Whites against resourceful Reds. Grigori Alexandrov's string of musical comedies and melodramatic musicals, *Happy Guys* (1934), *Circus* (1936), *Volga, Volga* (1938), and *The Shining Path* (some-times known as *Tanya*, 1940), were all "massive successes," as Moira Ratchford points out in the anthology edited by Andrew Horton, *Inside Soviet Film Satire*.

Such films, with their handsome heroes and beautiful heroines, their sight gags and slapstick and hummable songs were a welcome, entertaining distraction from reality, much as screwball comedies and musicals distracted Americans from the Great Depression. But the analogy mustn't be taken too far. Soviet reality was murderous. Those films came right after the horrors of forced collectivization, and squarely in the midst of the Great Terror, when millions were executed, sent to the camps, or exiled. Yet Stalin had told the nation at the time, "Life has become better, life has become more joyful," and Soviet filmmakers were charged, in effect, with constructing a feel-good counter-reality. This combination of the terroristic and the absurd surfaced in the process of film production itself, where Stalin served as Supreme Censor and Ur-Production Manager, with full rights over the final cut. (Stalin's love of films forms the take-off idea for Andrei Konchalovsky's melodrama, *The Inner Circle*, 1991, based on the career of one of the private Kremlin projectionists, played by Tom Hulce.) Alexandrov picked the title for *The Shining Path* from a suggested list prepared by Stalin. *Volga, Volga* was produced on Stalin's command, and is said to have been his favorite Soviet film. Stalin's shadow affected the film in other ways: in *Inside Soviet Film Satire*, the Soviet critic Maya Turovskaya tells us its production manager disappeared into exile during preproduction, while its director of photography was exiled during shooting. The Great Critic could also be vindictively petulant. Just as film awards were to be distributed in 1940, Stalin saw *The Great Waltz* and is said to have crossed out the list of nominees with the snarl, "When they learn to work like the Americans, then they'll get their medals."

This story is related by Konchalovsky and Alexander Lipkov in their companion volume to *The Inner Circle*. Kenez reports similar tales of Stalin's obsessive involvement in films, as do Dmitry and Vladimir Shlapentokh in their survey, *Soviet Cinematography 1918-1991* (1993). Such reports are based on the many new revelations of the Gorbachev *glasnost* period, when older Soviet filmmakers published candid reminiscences, and film production notes and other related materials surfaced from formerly restricted archives. Incidentally, the Shlapentokhs, or their translator, meant cinema, not cinematography, in their title. They allowed this and far too many other simple errors of fact to crop up in their book to make it a reliable survey although it has good intentions, using cinema for evidence about Soviet life. But, as in Kenez's work, the analysis centers on film in relation to official ideology and policy issues, and little or not at all in relation to society. One interesting aspect of the Shlapentokhs' study, however, is the way films and filmmakers are slotted, particularly during the later periods, according to certain categories—bureaucratic, antibureaucratic, liberal, Russophilic, neo-Leninist, etc. These may seem arcane to Western viewers, but very apparent to Soviet filmgoers, especially intellectuals. This reflects the very Soviet habit of filmgoing, or media consumption in general, as special exercises in decoding.

Was Stalinist film art a contradiction in terms? Would film propaganda more aptly describe what went on? Paradoxes abound. As a student at Moscow State University in the early 1950s, Mikhail Gorbachev saw Ivan Pyriev's *Cossacks of the Kuban* (1949), a glowing musical of merry and bountiful life on the collective farm. Gorbachev, a product of a collective farm himself, is said to have muttered privately, "That's not the way it is at all." Yet surveys of peasant reactions to the film suggested they were pleased at the idealized portrayals of themselves. Propaganda? Of course, but also a testament to the power of film, even Stalinist film, to enchant, to transcend reality, in this case, the hard life of collective farmers in a land just ravaged by war.

That war, "The Great Patriotic War of the Soviet Union," also generated a range of films, inevitably propagandistic, but varying in quality within the Stalinist confines. Among them were several stodgy invocations to patriotic heroes of the Russian past. Such specious and mannered films as Vladimir Petrov's *Kutuzov* (1944) had a purpose then, but are today, as Kenez notes rightfully, "almost unwatchable." At the other end, there were the devastating evocations of suffering under Nazi brutality that so moved Western audiences then and remain powerful even now. Among them was Mark Donskoy's *The Rainbow* of 1944 which won a special award in Hollywood. Then there was Eisenstein, who weighed in with his own unique contributions to patriotism in the form of two masterpieces, also propaganda, that bracketed the war period, his *Alexander Nevsky* (1938) and *Ivan the Terrible* (Parts I and II, 1944 and 1946).

So we have propaganda and paradox: the State with its chokehold on art vs. filmmakers gasping for air, occasionally managing something standing the test of time. This counterpoint ran through the Stalin years and beyond. The "film hunger" of the final Stalin period was certainly the bleakest time. The Soviet cinema industry was so throttled by pettiness and paranoia as to be virtually wrecked; from 1946 to 1953 Soviet studios averaged about fifteen features a year. After the death of the tyrant the choke-hold remained, though the grip was loosened.

Soviet cinema survived. In fact, though no one has ever described them that way, the three decades after Stalin's death perhaps comprise the true "golden years" of Soviet cinema. The development and growing sophistication of Soviet society brought a thematic variety and emotional richness not seen in earlier Soviet cinema. I'm not speaking here only of the break-through films about the Second World War much adored in the West for their antiwar messages, Mikhail Kalatozov's *The Cranes Are Flying* (1957), Grigori Chukhrai's *Ballad of a Soldier* (1959), Sergei Bondarchuk's *Fate of a Man* (1959), among them. These were justly admired for their portrayals of Soviet suffering and Soviet endurance during the war. They were also rightful reminders, amid Cold War stereotypes about the Soviets, that humanistic impulses throbbed beneath the political dictates of the Politburo. (Never mind that such films were also dictated by the Politburo.) Such films may still be viewed with approval today, but they do not rank with the startling ensemble of films by Andrei Tarkovsky of the 1960s and 1970s, or the primitive surrealism of Sergei Paradzhanov's *Shadows of Forgotten Ancestors* (1964) and Georgy Shengelaya's *Pirosmani* (1971). Again the paradox: working within a perimeter of the permissible only slightly relaxed by Khrushchev's thaw and its aftermath, such directors produced films of (often overtly) religious intensity in a language far removed from clichéd socialist realism. Others such as Alexander Sokurov, Konchalovsky, Elem Klimov, Kira Muratova, and Alexei Gherman wrestled with the censors and struggled to convey everyday or historical subjects from new angles. Often they both won and lost. Their works got produced, but for arbitrary bureaucratic reasons weren't released and distributed; they were deposited on the shelves and freed only during the *glasnost* years.

But there were others that made it to the screens. These were films of wit and insight, and not just officially acceptable pap. The two-decade Brezhnev period, including the rule of his successors Andropov and Chernenko, was dismissed during the Gorbachev years as the era of "stagnation." But, as the British journalist Martin Walker put it, while Brezhnev slept, a social revolution was going on. This transformation was reflected in cinema, in the shelved films and the unshelved. In fact, as Anna Lawton points out, cinema was "the least stagnating" of all the arts in the era of so-called stagnation. One thinks of enduring satires on Soviet mores such as Eldar Ryazanov's *Garage* (1980); or Eldar Shengelaya's *Blue Mountains* (1985); the creepy world of teenage vengeance in Rolan Bykov's *Scarecrow* (1984); the *dolce vita* of the old Russia gentry portrayed by Nikita Mikhalkov in his *Oblomov* (1980); or the same director's brilliant dramatization of early Russian filmmakers caught between Whites and Reds in the Crimean theater of the Civil War, *"A Slave of Love"* (1976). The complexities and griefs of everyday life in different Soviet settings was captured with loving, if sometimes sardonic care and sympathy by Georgy Danelia in his *Autumn Marathon* (1980), or by Yuli Raizman, a filmmaker of the older generation, in his *Private Life* (1983). Danelia's subtitle for his *Autumn Marathon*, "A Sad Comedy," could apply to many Soviet films of the "stagnation" period. It could apply to modern Soviet life itself.

This whole intriguing period awaits its film historians. Meanwhile, historians and critics have been pulled into the glamorous *glasnost* epoch, for obvious reasons. They were anxious to record the on-screen explosions marking the tumultuous changes in Soviet society and politics. At last! No censors! No political, ethical, or sexual taboos! No restrictions on form! Full frontal *glasnost!* The return of the Un-Persons and the Demolition of the Idols! *Glasnost* galore! Yet, the last great paradox of Soviet cinema also came with its final years. The full freedom bestowed on creative artists by the Gorbachev regime, or wrested by them from the regime, did not live up to its promise. Certain films, most notably Tengiz Abuladze's *Repentance* (1984/released 1986), or Vasily Pichul's *Little Vera* (1988), and Pavel Lungin's *Taxi Blues* (1990), even earned comparatively successful commercial runs in the West. But it was clear then, and not just in retrospect, that the reasons for success had more to do with how and what the films were saying, with the once forbidden fruits they were offering, than for their genuine creative merit. Abuladze took on Stalinist tyranny in densely metaphoric images, while Pichul and Lungin raged at the indignities of ordinary Soviet life, especially among the young, in their sociologically candid melodramas.

Yet the promise of great things to come was there in the air at the time, and it was in that spirit that three *glasnost* books by Nicholas Galichenko, Anna Lawton, and Andrew Horton and Michael Brashinsky were conceived and written. That spirit is both their merit and their blemish. But who could know that the Soviet Union itself would evaporate, and with it *glasnost* cinema and its promise? Hence reading through volumes that in some sense were invalid almost with publication has a slightly unreal quality and is also very sad. These books (and so many others on other Soviet *glasnost*-era themes) stand now as history, rather than as the breathlessly exciting current unfolding story they thought they were chronicling.

Change the present tense to the past, and the books gain some perspective. What had happened, and what had been expected? Lawton's *Kinoglasnost* (1992) tells the story best. [See my review of her book, below, at the end of this chapter.] (Galichenko's *Glasnost: Soviet Cinema Responds*, 1991, was the first on the subject; it is a short collection, enlightening in an introductory way, of diverse materials, including the author's essays and criticism, and a guide to *glasnost* directors and their films.) The major organizational shifts creating "a new model" for Soviet cinema in the aftermath of the celebrated Fifth Congress of the Filmmakers Union in 1986 generated high hopes—and disarray. Creative control was ostensibly in the bands of the studios now; state funding continued, although accounting systems stressed "self-financing," meaning market success as the chief mechanism for accumulating funds. Ultimately, the studios were to be self-supporting. The doors were now thrown open to private film enterprise; new, independent production companies emerged, often with foreign money and with access to much needed foreign technology. "Co-productions" flourished. The possibilities, given all that talent, were immense. But the results return us full-circle to the beginnings of Soviet cinema. *Glasnost* also meant openness to cultural imports, and foreign films flooded Soviet screens. The public, and, consequently, distributors, preferred them. "There are entire cities where for many years Soviet movies have not been shown at all," complained the director Andrei Smirnov in 1990. Soviet films, even the new breed, could not compete with high-tech cheap thrills coming from the West. (Always the complaint of the European, especially the French, film industry against Hollywood.)

But it wasn't simply a case of the bad driving out the good; that is itself a cheap, simplistic argument. In the Soviet case, the causes of failure went deeper. Some directors were badly disoriented by the new freedoms. The old habits of fighting for creative self-expression in an environment of repression were of no use in the new atmosphere. A director of enormous talent, Alexei Gherman—

whose *My Friend Ivan Lapshin* (1983/released 1985), is acclaimed by critics as among the finest Soviet films of all time, long remained mute. The Soviet comic genius Mikhail Zhvanetsky put the matter well and saucily when he described the difference between old and new times: "Everything in those days could bring happiness. A little sausage, you're happy. A little toilet paper, you're happy. The greatest disillusionment has come now that nothing is forbidden."

Others, however, reacted with great eagerness, and little restraint. For many Soviet directors the once forbidden fruits were fetishized, and the Russian love of the carnivalesque and the grotesque, a way of thumbing the nose at the official and the conventional, became the salient, but not so attractive film esthetic. A more positive assessment is found in Horton and Brashinsky's idiosyncratic survey *The Zero Hour* (1992), itself very *glasnost*-cinematic. It bristles with ideas and insights, often framed in a world-cinema context, it is free-form in organization, and it throbs with excitement over the novelties and breakthroughs of new Soviet films. One of the characteristic films of the new epoch was Karen Shakhnazarov's *Zero City* (1989), its title perhaps not unconsciously paralleled in the title of the Horton-Brashinsky book. (Horton also explains that, recalling Godard, filmmaking is "an effort to get back to zero, back to the basics of film language," i.e., where Soviet cinema was at during the *glasnost* period.) The film *Zero City* represents everything the old canon was not. It takes a bureaucrat through a series of incoherent, absurd, plotless episodes, some funny, most of them, to my taste, weighing a ton. Other films in this vein were Kira Muratova's *The Aesthenic Syndrome* (1990), and Sergei Soloviev's *Black Rose is a Symbol of Sorrow, Red Rose a Symbol of Love* (1989). Absurdity is the most difficult of styles, the one, ironically, demanding the greatest restraint and discipline. Unfortunately, there wasn't a Buñuel among the liberated Soviet directors. The point, however, was that these directors were enjoying themselves, gleefully smashing the old canons, recklessly and uncontrollably.

Horton and Brashinsky may be over-indulgent in their treatment of this new genre, what Russians often refer to as "kitsch." They write of *Zero City* as "a significant contribution to the evolving *glasnost* canon," and suggest Soviet audiences were not ready for "such honest experimentation." But who can refrain from a little sympathy for a long-suffering muse trying to find a voice? Brashinsky's overall assessment, in a concluding dialog, is sober and fair enough: "[T]o be honest," even films successful abroad like *Little Vera* and others, "have been recognized not so much for their development of a new universal film language, but in terms of the freedom of subject matter, the creation or representation of new truths about the Soviet Union, and a freer use of film language in a Soviet context. We are still waiting to see what contribution the new Soviet cinema will make as a worldwide art."

We didn't have to wait much longer. There is no "Soviet context" anymore, and "Soviet cinema" and its "contribution" are history. The new scene was marked by a divided legacy; the Soviet imprint was a contradictory one, with considerable idealism beneath the terrible burdens. The old burdens were gone, but so was the old idealism. The sound studios at Mosfilm were still there, and the Soviet film people were still around, struggling in terrible economic circumstances to eke out their work in the aftermath of the collapse. But in some sense the slate had been wiped clean, and a new subject, requiring fresh consideration, confronted us: post-Soviet cinema, divided along national lines, from Russian to Uzbek.

I don't cheer anymore when Eisenstein's ship sails into the open sea, but *Potemkin* is still a great film.

[*Cineaste*, XXI, 1-2, 1995]

Anna Lawton Trailer, 1:
Kinoglasnost: Soviet Cinema in Our Time

Anna Lawton's long essay on cinema of the late Soviet period for the volume edited by Daniel J. Goulding, *Post New Wave Cinema in the Soviet Union and Eastern Europe* (1989), was a model of good sense and clarity, and showed a mastery of the Soviet film scene, its aesthetics as well as its politics and personalities. Her book, *Kinoglasnost* (1992), has germinated from that essay (which constitutes its first chapter), and to it she has brought the same good sense, clarity and mastery. It is easily the best of a large crop of articles and books triggered by the remarkable transformations in Soviet cinema during the Gorbachev period. (See, for example, Nicholas Galichenko's medley of materials, *Glasnost: Soviet Cinema Responds*, the first book on the subject to appear [1991], and *The Zero Hour: Glasnost and Soviet Cinema in Transition* by Andrew Horton and Michael Brashinsky [1992], an idiosyncratic interpretive survey; Richard Stites has some good pages on *glasnost* cinema in the concluding chapter to his *Russian Popular Culture* [1992].)

Written as a work of contemporary reportage on what seemed like a cluster of ongoing, liberating developments, Lawton's book now stands as a valuable work of *history* on one aspect of a collapsed system. There is an amusing/pathetic ring to phrases such as, the "recent artistic renaissance has been planned and sustained by the Party, under the leadership of Gorbachev." True enough then, but how could she know—how could anyone know—that the renaissance was a last cultural flickering of a society about to implode? Lawton wisely finesses the problem in her Preface when she admits that "some of the commentary needs revisions in light of the latest developments [that is, the August putsch, and its aftermath]. Nevertheless, this remains as a testimony of a fateful moment that has changed the course of history."

With this disclaimer, Lawton's study stands as a solid historical reference work. She touches all the bases, sketching in the background from the 1970s, identifying the major organizational shifts in the system of production leading to the "new model" developed by the Fifth Congress of the Filmmakers Union in 1986, explaining the problems thereafter, and offering concise summaries of major films to roughly 1990—all placed within the wider context of societal and political change, and the furious debates, reminiscent of the 1920s, over the meaning and purpose of film art. The emphasis is on Russian and feature cinema, although there are good brief sections on documentary films, with their *publitsistika* edge and revisionist-history focus.

Throughout, Lawton eschews grand aesthetic theory and sweeping interpretive synthesis in favor of summary and chronicle. But she also takes note of a central paradox of the *glasnost* renaissance: For all the liberating organizational reforms and emancipation from taboos, Soviet cinema in its final free phase failed to produce anything comparable to the masterpieces of its captive periods. During the *zastoi*, Lawton rightly points out, cinema was the most lively of the arts, and such directors as Tarkovsky, Konchalovsky, Mikhalkov and Panfilov, among others, managed to create works of enduring beauty and insight. (Others working during the same period, such as Gherman, Sokurov and Muratova had to wait until *perestroika* for their films to be released.) Intoxicated by the new freedoms, many directors exalted the absurd, or gave the public "a long-overdue repertoire of naked truth, naked bodies, and naked violence." Only, Lawton notes, "the Muse has been silent."

All bets are off now that *glasnost*, *perestroika* and "new models" belong to the quaint lexicon of the past. As Russia and the other republics undertake their arduous journey on the path of privatization and freedom, a new cinema Muse, one hopes, will help guide and ease the passage.

[*Russian Review*, Vol. 53, No. 4, October, 1994]

CHAPTER V

Transitions

If perestroika *raised high hopes of a Soviet socialism "with a human face," its aftermath, an independent Russia detached from the other former Union republics and free of Communist Party hegemony, lifted expectations of a capitalist prosperity and a stable democratic political order. The hopes were dashed, as were the expectations. The Yeltsin leadership squandered the historical opportunity to remake Russia and take her in a healthy direction. Instead, among other features, political deals were made in exchange for state properties bought at fire-sale prices, creating a new class of mega-wealthy tycoons (oligarchs—add that to the Russian vocabulary), while the "shock therapy" economic reforms sank millions of Russians below the poverty line. Yeltsin himself, not in the best of health and very fond of the bottle, was not the able transformer the new Russia needed at the helm. His regime survived two very severe political (1993) and economic (1998) crises before turning over the reins of leadership in 2000 to Vladimir Putin, a former KGB agent who went up the ladder of the new politics, from municipal affairs in his native St. Petersburg to Moscow central at the Kremlin.*

As for others in post-Soviet life, this "transitional" period ushered in confusion and disarray among filmmakers who now confronted a dramatically altered environment inside and outside of the studios. The political stability and relative economic gains achieved by the Putin regime, though at a cost to areas of free expression in the media, among other signs of its authoritarian bent, helped put the Russian film establishment on a more even keel. For Russia, for Russian film—new perils, new challenges.

Out of the Present

One of the quirkiest episodes connected with the implosion of the USSR (the implosion itself was the strangest thing of all), came when the once proud Soviet space program sent the cosmonaut Sergei Krikalev rocketing to the Mir station in May 1991. While Krikalev was up there, his country was, you might say, pulled out from under him. This cosmonaut Hero of the Soviet Union would experience the collapse of the Soviet Union from outer space. What an entry for the mission log! He left from the USSR, and returned to the Russian Federation; Boris Yeltsin, not Mikhail Gorbachev, was now in charge; Leningrad had become St. Petersburg; and.....you get the idea. Andrei Ujica captures well this whole strange business in his frequently handsome, often amusing (how could it not be?), very appealing and revealing 1996 documentary from Facets Video.

With Harun Farocki, Ujica had earlier chronicled another communist demise, the overthrow of the hated Ceaucescu regime in the director's native Romania, by assembling found video footage and newsreels. The result was their riveting *Videograms of a Revolution* (1992 also from Facets), an extraordinary documentary portrait of the mass movement that brought down the Ceaucescu dictatorship in a matter of days at the end of 1989. Someone's camera was always present as Ceaucescu attempted to address an unruly crowd, or tried to flee by helicopter, or faced a hastily arranged court accusing him of numerous crimes. Finally, his corpse and that of his wife were shown on liberated Romanian television. Several sequences pictured weary activists trying to pull together the forms and personnel of post-Ceaucescu political structures. These dramatic "Videograms" offered a kind of ground-zero perspective on an important, tumultuous political event.

Out of the Present captures the Soviet collapse from a very different, more ingeniously contrived perspective, far above any ground zero. The film starts out as a conventional space documentary, recording the docking of the capsule at the station—crackling voices over intercoms, unearthly sounds of silence and synthesizer, roars and whooshes, striking panoramas, welcoming the travelers aboard, and so on. There is much of this throughout the film, which should make it attractive to any space junkie. (For another, more conventional film concentrating on the Soviet space program, with revealing personal testimonies of several cosmonauts, see Maciej J. Drygas's 1994 documentary, *State of Weightlessness* from First Run/Icarus Films.) Krikalev's mission also included the Russian Anatoly Artsebarski, and Helen Sharman from England. We see them at the training center, "Star City," outside of Moscow, then at the Soviet equivalent of Cape Kennedy in the Baikonur region of Kazakhstan, at the time a Soviet republic, where they are feted and well-wished before blasting off. A ritual there: sprigs of wormwood are presented to the cosmonauts for a safe journey. This journey was successful, as was the docking. Another Russian habit: the travelers are welcomed aboard the Mir with bread and salt. These are fascinating, odd juxtapositions of pre-modern tradition with the mores and technology of the space age.

We then see, of course, the now familiar scenes of members of the crew floating gravity-free inside the space station, exercising, doing research tasks, and horsing around (Artsebarski, who contributes occasional explanatory narration, comments abashedly on their "childishness"). The inside of the space station, by the way, is far from the hi-tech interiors that gleam in sci-fi space films; there is not a straight line anywhere, and it's cramped and very cluttered. But the crew works well, the mood is good, so is the camaraderie. Gorbachev puts in a call of congratulations. Some will leave, others arrive to take their place. Days and months go by. Krikalev stays on; his mission calls for a tour of 160 days. A 'freighter' brings the crew some equipment, letters from home, sweets.

Suddenly, Ujica jump-cuts us back to earth, to Moscow near the White House, where tanks and armored personnel carriers mingle with Volgas and Zhigulis and pedestrian crowds, and unidentified voices from inside a traffic jam wonder what it's all about. The soft coup of August 1991 is in progress, and Gorbachev is under unofficial house arrest at his vacation dacha down south. Some of the most engrossing footage of this space-odyssey film is intercut here—very earthy newsreel material that highlights the barricades, the mass anger, and the fraternization between the crowds and soldiers that undid the reactionary coup. At the Mir, "we continued our work," even as the crew knew what was going on down below—the "unsettled" situation in Moscow, they called it—and they listened to Boris Yeltsin's defiant speech on their radios. A new crew arrives, an Austrian and a Kazakh. The presence of the Austrian prompts Ujica to lay some Strauss waltzes on the soundtrack, one of his sly references to classic films of the space genre, in this case Kubrick's *2001*. Later, he will use a shot from Tarkovsky's *Solaris*, inserted seamlessly.

But what of Krikalev? It is natural to assume that his mission was extended because of the "unsettled" conditions below, and as a consequence of the subsequent break-up of the USSR in December. This is how some commentators have explained it, and promotional material for the film implies the same. In fact, as Artsebarski points out, almost as an embarrassed aside, there were very Soviet reasons for the extended tour. For political purposes—honoring one of the fraternal national minorities of the Soviet motherland, as Moscow official-speak might have put it—a Kazakh cosmonaut came on board, but he was not a flight engineer. A flight engineer is always a must for the station, and that was Krikalev. So Krikalev had to stay on…. and on…. and on—a total of 310 days in space, 150 more than his original mission called for. At one point, ground control tells him that maps have been altered; the Baltic republics (the first to break away) are a "different color." When he touched down in March 1992, the Soviet Union had already ceased to exist. The media quickly dubbed Krikalev "the last Soviet citizen."

Krikalev may have been a terrific cosmonaut. He had earned many honors before this mission, and earned many more thereafter, including NASA's Space Flight Medal in 1994; later, he was part of the three-member crew for the International Space Station. But he was a man of few words, and in *Out of the Present* there is a sequence that exposed what I think was his very Soviet breeding. Naturally, media people down below were intrigued by the tale of the cosmonaut who left the Soviet Union and was still in space as the Soviet Union disappeared. What did he think? Artsebarski, whose narration cites Hemingway and French poetry, might have offered some appropriate eloquence when that query was posed from earth, but he had left the Mir earlier. A female voice asks Krikalev about his reaction to all those remarkable, surprising changes—Leningrad was now St. Petersburg; Yeltsin, not Gorbachev; etc. "I didn't hear the question," he replies, stalling, no doubt. She repeats it. Then comes what I take to be the very Soviet non-answer: What is most impressive and surprising, he says, is the passing of day into night, and the changing of the seasons. The rigorously nonpolitical cosmonaut shied away from any politically inflected commentary; besides, one should hedge one's bets—who knows?, Gorbachev or the old regime might stage a comeback. When a Reuters correspondent asked him the same kind of question, Krikalev didn't respond at all. Well, maybe it was all too disorienting and rather embarrassing.

Ujica's synthesis of music, some breathtaking photography, plus pictures of the daily life of the cosmonauts aboard the Mir station make *Out of the Present* a major contribution to the space-film genre. But it is more than that; the documentary is an intelligent, artful gloss on a hugely significant political development of the late twentieth century. Surely Krikalev understood that, even though he wasn't saying.

[*Cineaste*, XXVIII, 1, 2002]

What is There to Celebrate? The Russian Documentary and the Petersburg Festival, "Message to Man"

It's not a pretty picture, this present condition of the Russian film world [in 1996]. "We are," says Naum Kleiman, curator of the Eisenstein Archive in Moscow, "in a fog with the magnetic needle fluctuating wildly." Switching metaphors, he adds that "we don't know how to move from the kolkhoz to the farm". I paraphrase what he said and what others and we all know: Surviving in the market requires attitudes, structures, institutions that are still woefully underdeveloped. There are no funds for renewing film technology; a protective system of law is not in place; managerial and

8. The Program cover for the 1st International Documentary Film Festival, "Message to Man," Leningrad, 1989.

organizational know-how is missing; the distributing infrastructure has broken down for Russian films—why should anyone market a Russian film when cheap foreign films are available?; and the links have been severed between producers (filmmakers) and consumers (viewers; the audience).

In New York a few weeks ago the director Elem Klimov, who once led the transition to "new models" as Filmmakers' Union chief during the heady days of *glasnost* and *perestroika*, lamented the condition of Mosfilm Studios, reduced to renting space for banking and industrial enterprises. And with great bitterness he complained that neither his nor Larisa Shepitko's films were earning a cent from screenings abroad or on television. The film world was populated now by thieves and the half-dead.

All this as it applies to the state of Russian feature cinema is familiar. But for the condition of documentary film today in Russia you have to zoom the magnitude of the problems manyfold to get an accurate picture. Documentary film—funding, production, distribution, venues for viewing—is an orphan everywhere, not just in Russia, but the vast *perelom* there of the last five years has, to put it gently, complicated matters to a degree unknown elsewhere.

And yet, and yet.... What is Russia—its past, its people, its very identity—if not the national personification of survival? "It's a catastrophe," said the Ukrainian director Mikhail Ilyenko, "but we're not finished yet." *That's the spirit.* We can't help holding back a tear or two, but let us not weep; we have a thing or two to celebrate. Beyond the *fog*, the *perelom*, the *smutnoe vremya* there are signs of promise and hope. Normal life in the film world won't be easily attained: the realm of art, as of politics, is not as smooth and straight as the Nevsky Prospekt. One should note that not everyone shares the sour evaluations of Kleiman, Klimov, and so many others. I hesitate to be sociologically simplistic by way of explaining the optimism, but there does seem to be a clean discernible divide between the gloomy and the enthusiastic along rather generational lines.

Above all, we should all celebrate the passing of the USSR. *No nostalgia, please.* The state subsidies are gone, but so are the state shackles and bureaucratic absurdities. Soviet state paternalism encouraged a comfortable mediocrity, and devalued—prohibited— the stylistic risks or thematic innovations that have enriched the documentary in the West. Out the land of the early Dziga Vertov came the land of the bland. But from the proto-*perestroika* generation who are now maturing in the post-*perestroika*, post-Soviet epoch, there is a stratum of filmmakers anxious to keep the door tightly shut on the past, and energized, challenged by the new conditions of work. Although in Petersburg, among young and old, I always detect a certain "Leningrad-Petersburg Identity", there is no center to this group, geographic or otherwise, it is not a circle revolving around a revered figure and teacher, there is no "school". They want very much to break the ties that bind to the state, and chart their courses based on independence in funding, independence in their creative work. They want the creative freedom of the Western documentarians, and are not petrified nor even disoriented by the funding hazards that go with it. Among feature filmmakers there are people like Sergei Livnev who would like to restructure Gorky studios in Moscow on market foundations, and his associate the Peterburzhets Alexei Balabanov, who decries the old dependence on the state. They have their counterparts among young documentarians like the Kiev filmmaker Alexander Rodnyansky, who opts for Western funding for his recent work on primarily Jewish themes, and the outspoken Vitaly Mansky who juggles various funding sources, foreign and domestic, for his eclectic body of work—everything from the irreverent *Lenin's Body* (1992) to decaying village life (*Blagodat/Bliss*, 1995).

Not all are as carefree in their attitudes as Mansky, who poohpoohs lamentations over funding and told me it shouldn't constrain the committed filmmaker—even when money is scarce, all he needs is a camcorder. In this regard of course the documentarian has the edge over the fiction auteur whose resource needs are typically much greater, what with casts, special effects, sets, stagehands, and so on. Yes, the documentarian, if he or she is to develop something more than a film with some talking heads, also needs to support researchers, locate archival footage, and must attend to the care and feeding and travel of a crew. But necessity is the mother of funding, we might say, and it is attitudes such as Mansky's, grateful for the new freedoms and accepting the reality of the market, that will find a way among today's misfortunes.

There are amusing, ironic overtones on these matters whenever

Western documentarians get together with their Russian counterparts. Betsy McLane, Executive Director of the International Documentary Association based in Los Angeles, speaking last year in St. Petersburg, summed up the problems of American documentarians as "money, money, money." "Ah, just like us now," said many in the audience, but others rejected the idea that funding is the core of the challenge. Rather, it is cinematic artistry, inspiration, and commitment to one's vision that counts.

Which brings us to the rather more weighty issue before Russian filmmakers, more important than mere rubles or francs or Deutsche Marks for funding—namely, to get out from under the old rubble, to devise a new set of visions to replace the old, officially sanctioned ones, and even to get beyond the intoxicating *kinopublitsistika*, the *chernukha* and historical revisionism that dominated documentary work in the recent past. Such documentaries constituted a collective political intervention affecting public attitudes during the Gorbachev years. They exposed much about the past that was once consigned to the memory hole, and held up as to a harshly lit mirror the seamy sides of what everyone knew to be life in the present. The Latvian Juris Podnieks' film *Is It Easy to Be Young?* (1986) led the way in breaking taboos about the present, in developing the I can't take it anymore trend in filmmaking, exemplified by Stanislav Govorukhin's *You Cannot Live Like This* (1990), or *Stalin is With Us* by Tofik Shakhverdiev (1989). Marina Goldovskaya's *Solovetsky Power* (1988) was among the first to sound the historical motif—remembering the repressed—that was picked up in documentary after documentary. Semyon Aranovich's cycle of films conveying facets of Stalinism and its victims stands out here—*The Akhmatova File, I Served in Stalin's Guard, The Great Concert of the People*.

This orgy of exposure has I think run its course, in part because its purpose has been served; it helped shatter the Soviet Union, not a small thing. Yes, *He* was right: it *was* the most important art...And still is: Interestingly, the Yeltsin-dominated television media highlighted films like these during the campaign before the first round of presidential elections in June. Vitaly Mansky also produced a whole new series for national television featuring home movies he solicited from people all over the former USSR, constituting their own informal testimony and reminder about life as it used to be.

Pro-Yeltsin infomercials were made by documentarians. (Everyone in the film world I met or read about backed Yeltsin.) The Moscow filmmaker, Alexei Khaniutin, whose documentary, *DMB-91* (1990), chronicled the depressing boot-camp experience of Soviet military recruits, made one such 40-second slot that I saw. He filmed a Stalinist demonstration and then challenged the viewer. "They are voting—What About You?"

On the eve of the elections Nikita Mikhalkov's glossy, *Burnt by the Sun*, really a fictionalized variation on some of the themes in those historical documentaries, was broadcast. Also consider Mikhalkov's *Anna*, now opening in New York, a longitudinal home movie (sort of) centering on his daughter as she grew up. He shot an episode and asked her the same questions every year from 1980, when she was six, for the next twelve years. It is purportedly about the developing Anna, but really it is about Mikhalkov himself—no surprise—and his views of the Russian past and present, augmented by some rich documentary footage, especially of the *zastoi* and *perestroika* periods. (See my "Kinojournal" comments, Chapter I).

So even a talented and successful fiction filmmaker couldn't resist the pull of the documentary impulse to record and indict. That impulse will always be there among the Russians; it should be there. The de-sacralization of Lenin, of Stalin, of all the old myths, together with the recovery of historical memory is not only part of a curative national catharsis, but a continuing political necessity so long as the totalitarian temptation, the temptation to favor those who would return to the communist past, exists. Also, there are still so many compelling themes, so many uncovered layers in the archaeology of Stalinism that Russian documentary filmmakers will always have a nearly inexhaustible supply of subjects on hand. Just to take a recent example—Oksana Dvornitchenko, who worked in the documentary section at Ostankino for many years, produced two films, based on newly released materials, about Russian POWs, some of whom escaped German captivity, or were released after the war, and whose fate on return was the Gulag or the executioner's bullet: *Why Are You Alive?* (1995), and *Why Am I Alive?* (1996). As for the current political scene and the ever-present menace of the foes of democracy, video diarists like Marina Goldovskaya in her *Lucky to be Born in Russia* (1994), and Felix Yakubson in his *Overture* (1994) chronicled, each differently, the bloody September "White House" days. Then of course there is Chechnya. Witness, for example, the same Yakubson's *Grozny. May 95*, shot on location.

Still, the volume of political documentaries or politically-minded historical documentaries is certainly down, and not just for scarce-funding reasons. (On that score, the volume of documentaries is down in general.) It may be time to turn a new leaf to freshen or discard old genres, discover new voices, and craft new languages for Russian documentary film. Are we witnessing this process? To be sure, in the interstices of producing the standard documentary form there was always Sokurov and his very personal, idiomatic, often enigmatic but ever visually striking body of documentary work on subjects and figures ranging from Tarkovsky and the Lithuanian musicologist and political activist Vytautas Landsbergis in his "Elegy" series, to a surreally shot May Day demonstration (*Evening Sacrifice*, 1984-1987), and his most unusual commemoration of the Great Patriotic War (*And Nothing More*, 1982-1987). Some of these were not released when made, and had to wait for *perestroika*. His most recent effort in the "Elegy" series is what one critic described as a "prayer"—*Eastern Elegy* (1995).

Perestroika uncorked the freedom to construct new forms, bust the old genres, find new heroes, or anti-heroes, thumb some noses, flash a little whimsy, break the pattern of: narration-talking head-archival or live footage-talking head-narration. If we look at the repertory screened at the Leningrad, later St. Petersburg, International Documentary Film Festival, "Message to Man," from 1989 to 1996, we see that some of these novelties began to surface. The Petersburg Festival is an excellent subject for study, for its problems as well as achievements are paradigmatic of the Russian documentary scene. The Festival began with official, central funding and then was reduced to scrambling for money wherever it could be found, locally or privately. It scheduled the event bi-annually on the off years of the big Moscow Festival, then convened annually so that its identity and presence would not be overlooked in the difficult post-Soviet period. It took place originally in January-February, then switched to the more congenial White Nights period of June. It was designed to showcase the best international documentary work alongside the best Russian (or Soviet) counterpart, then expanded to include short fiction and animation because Russian documentary production shrank. I attended the Festival in the years 1993-1996, and in my reports a recurring major theme was the life-threatening financial condition. Last year that condition brought it to the edge of extinction. On the eve of the Festival, mayoral elections resulted in the culture-patron Sobchak being displaced by the economy-minded Yakovlev. With that displacement essential municipal funding disappeared, and days before the Festival was to commence emergency faxes were sent out by organizers telling invited participants from abroad that their room and partial board could not be covered by the Festival. Really, they were about to cancel. But thanks to the chutzpah, last minute financial efforts, and the love of cinema and its powers of humanism and enchantment on the part of the chief organizers, men like Misha Litvyakov and Viktor Semeniuk, documentarists themselves, and their tirelessly devoted, mainly young, mainly poorly paid staff, the Sixth Festival materialized, if in a no-frills incarnation.[1] (In Sverdlovsk/Ekaterinburg, the Seventh Annual Festival of Soviet/Russian Documentary Film, called "Rossiya," and favored by Moscow, was held in October.)

A review of the main prize, The Golden Centaur ($5,000), awarded at each Petersburg Festival is suggestive. In 1989 and 1991 it went to Arkady Ruderman's *Countersuit* (an imaginative treatment of Stalinism in contemporary Byelorussia), and Alexei Khaniutin's *DMB-91*, mentioned above. Both exemplified the political, exposure preoccupations of the *glasnost* wave. At the Third festival in 1993, the Golden Centaur went to the acclaimed young Petersburg director Viktor Kossakovsky, for his brilliantly shot black and white—actually Chekhovian gray—portrait of country folk, *The Belovs*. Stylistically, it could be pegged somewhere between the *vérité* or direct, and catalytic cinema forms, and in substance offered a detached view—and the more powerful for it—of laughter and tears in the life of rural Russia. The same could be said of Sokurov's earlier, haunting *Maria* (1988); or Murat Mamedov's *Early on Sunday* (1987), which eavesdrops on a group of village women gathering wood and chatting—"the way we live now, what's the use," says one of them; or Mansky's recent *Bliss*, tracking an elderly woman in a dying village as she cares for her deformed sister. Here we have a major new genre, carried over from *perestroika*—the focus on village Russia, with its squalor, sacrifice, and soul.

The main prize at the Fourth Petersburg Festival was awarded to Rodnyansky's *March of the Living*, a simple rendition of reactions to Auschwitz and other death camps by young people from all over the world: a Russian-Ukrainian-Jewish documentarist amplifying a universalist theme. At the last two Festivals, no Russian documentary won the main prize, a telling symptom perhaps, although last summer the Golden Centaur went to the Moscow director Andrei Khrzhanovsky's touching animation study of the relationship between a circus lion and his master, *The Grey-Bearded Lion*.

Not always main prize winners, but indicative of other new genres favored by contemporary Russian documentarists, are films honoring individuals, sometimes oddballs, living private lives away from grand historical or political arenas, but heroic in their own way. Kossakovsky's profile of the philosopher *Losev* (1989) is an example, as are Sergei Miroshnichenko's *The Marriage Sacrament* (1993), in which a young provincial woman talks to the camera of her loving union with a famous, much older actor; and Pavel Pechonkin's *The Story of Turin, A Painter and a Victim* (1994), about a provincial radiologist who paints in his spare time and suffers a serious physical assault.

Other developing genres are the unsentimental ethnographic portraits, splendidly exemplified by a winner for best debut documentary at the Petersburg Festival in 1995, Sergei Dvortsevoy's *Happiness* (or *Paradise*), a narration-free, unadorned assembly of daily-life pictures of a family on the Kazakhstan steppe. Then there is something I would love to see more of from the Russians, the wry and the humorous, though there is not too much these days to evoke laughter. Bravo to Sergei Loznitsa and Marat Magambetov for their gibe at the Russian work ethic, *Today We Are Going to Build a House* (1996), which won a debut-film prize in Petersburg last summer. The film was shot at a construction site. There is much hanging about, conversation, smoking; nothing seems to be getting done. Then, in the final frames, *voilà*, an apartment building is up!

These films are all proof of new departures in Russian documentary cinema, for subject matter, certainly. Perhaps we might even say, in comparison with the past, "fewer, but better." But breakthroughs involving real stylistic risks are much less in evidence. Or even not at all, Sokurov excepted, if I'm to judge. Naum Kleiman grieves that the young have no models, that they don't know anything, not even their own cinema past; that they are so angry at the past that they sneer even at Dziga Vertov. Maybe this is a good thing; starting fresh and not bowing to older models, either out of anger or ignorance, is not a bad spur for innovation. Haven't they had enough of "The Russian Idea," the didactic or ecclesiastical principle in art? I use the title not only of Berdaiev's meditation but of the beautiful compilation film recently produced in St. Petersburg by Sergei Selianov and Oleg Kovalov to commemorate the centennial of film, a project commissioned by the British Film Institute. (Directors were asked to survey or profile their national cinema history. The Russians did it in a novel way, and there has been considerable controversy over it.)

Secondly, the Russians are now positioned to join the currents of international culture, to contribute to, and draw from, its plural patterns. That is why the Petersburg Festival bears such singular importance, for it brings together documentarists and their films from an international repertory. Where else, to cite only some recent examples of innovative documentary filmmaking, could the Russians see Jan Oxenberg's personal, multi-form chronicle of her dying grandmother, *Thank You and Good Night*; or Marlon E. Fuentes' *Bontoc Eulogy*, an experiment in the developing genre of the "fake documentary"; or Barbara Politsch's ingeniously titled and crafted *The 28th Instance of June 1914, 10:50 A.M.*, which blurs the line between documentary and fiction; or Vincent Monnikendam's compelling *Mother Dao, the Turtlelike*, which assembles clips from old films shot by the Dutch in the East Indies (Indonesia)? Exposure to experiments like these can only help fertilize the still parched Russian documentary field. Then, maybe, we'll see cross-fertilization as well.

This was originally presented as an invited paper, AAASS Convention, Boston, November 15, 1996. Opinions and attitudes expressed here come from conversations and interviews with Kleiman, Mansky, and Balabanov in Moscow and St. Petersburg, June-July, 1996; with Klimov, New York, October, 1996; and with Rodnyansky, St. Petersburg, February, 1994. Ilyenko is quoted in Variety, *October 28-November 5, 1996. My reports on the Petersburg Festival appeared in the* Soviet *and* Post-Soviet

Review, 20, Nos. 2-3 (1993); International Documentary, 13, No. 10 (December 1994/January 1995); and 14, No. 6 (September 1995).

Some of the older documentarists constantly stress the need for "compassion" in filmmaking now. Compare Leonid Gurevich, a seasoned documentary scenarist, on Kossakovsky: "...over the last two years, I've been trying to promote films about love, about charity, about compassion. ...we don't always have the resources to realize our ideas. But I know that, beginning with Kossakovsky, who tries to comment on the good by showing us evil, who calls for greater compassion by drawing attention to the lack of it in our lives. Well, that's an artist's approach. But alongside this, there's a film that defends compassion, compassion with a capital "C." That's what our viewer's need." (Interview, Moscow, July, 1994.) And here is Litvyakov: "Russia is filthy only on the outside right now—inside she's quite rich, and she has much greater spiritual wealth than in the West. ...there are films in the festival that portray human beings with concern, compassion, love. I think that without love, you can neither organize a festival nor make a movie." (Interview, St. Petersburg, June, 1994.) See Chapter VII for the full Gurevich and Litvyakov interviews.

My gratitude to Anne Borin, New York, ever generous with her knowledge and insights, who is indispensable for information, contacts, and films from the Russian cinema world. Thanks too, to Bart Teusch for back-up support.

[1] See my interview with Litvyakov in Chapter VII, 3.

Moscow Believes in Tears: Problems (and Promise?) of Russian Cinema in the Transition Period: A View at the Turn of the Century

It is conventional, and certainly legitimate to think of Russia, since the Soviet collapse in 1991, as "in transition". There is a post-Soviet joke: "What is communism? Answer: The longest distance between capitalism and capitalism." One hopes there will be no *post*-post-Soviet joke about the current "transitional" period as the shortest distance between communism and communism. I hope, that is, we can safely say that the Soviet past is really past. But how painful for

Russia is the present transition period? How long will it last? Any direction known?

Russian cinema is also suffering from the aches, pains, and angst prevailing in other sectors of post-Soviet society, whether culture, politics, the economy, or psyche. Are there only more problems ahead, or is there a glimmer of promise already evident?; or inescapably in transition periods, will both problems and promise co-exist? In cinema, where art intersects with commerce, some clues appear at the points of production (the studios), and the points of consumption (the kinotheaters). These areas are not entirely depressed, at least not as much as they were only a few years ago, even when we take the financial crash of August 1998 into consideration.

I. THE PAINS OF TRANSITION

What do we mean by Soviet cinema, and are we witnessing a contrasting, "New Russian Cinema" in development? Really, we should refer to *several* Soviet cinema periods and personalities, because beneath the generalization—the Party-State controlled industry subject to the enforced official ideology of socialist realism—there was great diversity, from Eisenstein to Bondarchuk, from Pyriev to Panfilov, not to mention the aberrant Tarkovsky, or the even more aberrant, consequently shelved Sokurov and Muratova, or the occasional hapless figure like Askoldov. And there were periods ranging from the "film hunger" of the late Stalin years when only a handful of films were produced, to the late Soviet epoch before the fall, when studios in 1991 turned out 375 features (and when films were used to launder money). The years 1986-1991, the period of *perestroika-glasnost* constitutes a film mini-epoch in its own right. The benchmark film production figure for the modern Soviet period, from the stable times of Brezhnev—later dubbed self-servingly as *zastoi* ("stagnation")—through the tumult of *perestroika*, was about 150 films per annum.[1]

In those days, say the late 1980s, the average Russian went to see films 14 times a year, the world's highest movie-going figure. Film receipts were a major part of the Soviet state budget. "Doctors and teachers," notes the director Sergei Livnev archly, "were financed by the love of Soviet citizens for alcohol and cinema."[2]

The free fall in production and attendance appears in the mid-1990's, coinciding with similar trajectories in the post-Soviet economy. Only some 30 films were produced in 1996; about the same figure applies to 1997. That year some 49 films were in production, but 23 were suspended because of insufficient funding. Fifty-one films were completed in 1998, 30 in 1999, as of October of that year, with an additional 38 planned or in production. Similar, low double-digits film production continues today. The average Russian went to see a film less than once a year in 1996. Economic and structural factors colluded with alterations in mass culture consumption to account for precipitous drops. State funding shrank for cinema, as did family budgets. Another major development: Television and the home video market displaced the film distribution and theatrical network. And if Russians went to the theater, it was for a foreign, probably an American film, a pattern that continues today. Foreign films, mostly American, were on 54 screens of Moscow's 79 theaters in November, 1999. As for video sales and rentals, foreign films outpaced Russian films; the ten top videos in October, 1997 (for example) were all foreign. American films filled the top-ten video sales list for 1999 at Moscow's largest outlet. [3]

The once proud flagship studios at Lenfilm and Mosfilm, until this year still state-owned, are badly funded and poorly equipped, turning out since the mid-'90s only tens of films annually. A Russian reporter offered these gloomy tidings in the spring of 1997: "More than anything, Mosfilm today reminds one of a cemetery. Echoing corridors, desolation, silence. There are no people around because no films are being shot. To shoot films you need money. No money; no people. The till is empty, the pavilions are empty. It is the dead season." (Those were my impressions as well during visits to Lenfilm in 1996. One of the sets there for Alexei Gherman's much delayed *Khrustalyov, My Car!* was gathering dust.) Small wonder that Russian filmdom's "fine actors," as a Russian critic put it, "with a melancholy look in their eyes, are doing commercials for bad laxatives and the dubious ruble devaluation; and viewers are certain that our film-industry workers are a bunch of do-nothings and are flocking to *Men in Black*."[4]

Money slated for the film industry continues to fund festivals—a "waste," says director Yuri Mamin, especially for "the stupid

Moscow Festival." Yes, the festivals circuit in Russia, especially the 10 international events, with their screenings, prizes, seminars, foreign luminaries, media attention, and celebrations have become, as someone put it, the nation's "virtual cinema," although I think such showcases are still essential for preserving the self-respect of Russian film culture, such as it is, and its connections to the wider world. Outside of Russia, too, there is always enough interest in Russian film to support periodic festivals, even if Mosfilm and Lenfilm aren't exporting box-office winners. In New York, for example, two festivals ran simultaneously and successfully in December 1999, one sponsored by the Museum of Modern Art, the other by an ad hoc *émigré* group, with funding from mainly local, American sources.[5]

New conditions have also altered patterns of programming and attendance at Cinema Clubs, which played such an important role in bringing the forbidden-fruit of the West to Soviet audiences from the '60s through the '70s, especially in the provinces. Local clubs now can't afford the high prices charged by Moscow distributors for film leasing, and screenings are necessarily via videocassette. Meanwhile, attendance has dropped since popular American fare is available theatrically, and especially on television and video. "Only true enthusiasts stayed in the cinema clubs," says one film scholar, and the provincial clubs are contemporary "islands of culture in the ocean of screen pop-commerce," for they are the only venues outside of Moscow and St. Petersburg where quality films are shown.[6]

Problems of infrastructure and finances aside, how can Russian cinema compete for the affections of its natural audience when it has Hollywood's technothrills and sheer all-round entertainment appeal to contend with? Russia is not alone in experiencing American domination of its film markets; the French are perennial complainers about this. But somehow, the present Russian submission to U.S. cinema hegemony is particularly poignant and ironic in our post-Cold War world.

Polls show that Russian film-goers express a preference for domestic over foreign films, but when they vote with their feet the results are otherwise. The film critic Daniel Dondurei summed up the general inclinations of the Russian viewer this way: "Russian films shot before Chernenko [i.e., before 1984] always win over films from late Gorbachev times. All the old Soviet films compete remarkably with the freshest American crop. But new Russian cinema loses to both." Television data bears him out: in 1999, of total films shown, 35% were from the Soviet-era; 34% were from the U.S.; 20% from Europe; only 8% were new, post-Soviet productions.[7] The consensus among certain critics, studio heads, and filmmakers is that Russian directors lost touch with, or were indifferent to, the film consumer. One corollary is that only the market and market production norms, i.e., satisfying consumer demand, can return the filmgoer to the theaters for Russian films. This direction clashes with the high-minded Russian Idea, traditionally expressed by filmmakers as much as any other stratum of the Russian intelligentsia, that Art and Principles and Ideals, not the Market, should govern culture production. From this lofty height, cinema is perceived as an intellectual, not an entertainment medium. (For Russia we might reverse what Dickens admonished Americans: "It would be well [if they] loved the Real less, and the Ideal somewhat more.")

That high-mindedness plus nostalgia for bountiful government funding generates a certain yearning for the past among many in the Russian film world. When Vladimir Gusinsky, the head tycoon of the Media-Most empire proposed in 1997 to infuse Mosfilm with capital in return for 49% stock ownership, there was predictable horror at the notion. What?!—convert the venerable studio into "*Most*-Film"? Entrust a national treasure, the Mosfilm back catalog, to entrepreneurial hands? Fill Mosfilm's ample acreage with restaurants, hotels, and swimming pools? And, as has happened to other media in print and television, see the studio turn out films favoring the business or political interests of the owners? These are understandable critiques and fears, but the prevailing despair led to other conclusions: Better to shoot with Gusinsky than not to shoot at all. The director Georgi Danelia commented: "I am not for Gusinsky particularly....But he did buy and refurbish four film theaters, he is prepared to offer interest-free credit for production at Mosfilm for ten films—this at a time when all of only one film has been completed at the studio! I voted for [the proposal] because ten films means work for more than 400 people!"[8] (The flight of personnel from the film industry, from directors on down, especially on the part of the young, is an alarming fact.)

Danelia represents a sign of despair—any port in a storm. But others look to the market from a hopeful perspective, and have been trying to embrace the new opportunities. They are developing a different outlook on the character of film itself, and on viewer-filmmaker relations. Sergei Lavrentiev laments present conditions: "We're a great country; the absence of Russian film is abnormal". People, he adds, pay money for films, and expect something they value in return, but directors "forget about the audience!" In 1993 Dondurei warned that "Well-educated, artistically sophisticated and middle-aged people are driven out of theaters" and that not "a single film...has captured the public's attention" since *Little Vera* [directed by Vasily Pichul, 1988]. "We have to realize," he warned, "that both the socialist and *perestroika* eras of filming are over. The customary sources of energy—opposition to the authorities—are dried up (creativity without censorship is a colossal test for Russia). No matter how hard it is, [film-school] graduates must stop being insensitive to the public and putting the *auteur* above all the other participants in the filmmaking process; the director-centered model will have to give way to a producer-centered model..." Sergei Livnev argues that directors started playing at Tarkovsky, but unfortunately, "the majority are not Tarkovsky". Directors neglected viewers, and "in reply, viewers forgot about film". Four years later the same Dondurei was insisting that "you can't survive without market relations" and decried the constant appeals to the state for more money.[9] Besides, the state, which has had trouble enough paying everyone from pensioners to miners and the military, has not been keen on disbursing its own scarce funds to the film world. In 1998 Goskino, the state film unit, budgeted $30 million for the industry, about the cost of a single average Hollywood production, and less than the reported cost of Nikita Mikhalkov's *The Barber of Siberia*—$45 million, $10 million of which came from the state. State funding for film in 2000 was about $15 million.

Concretely, "market relations" and "concern for the public" also requires a consideration for that point of consumption mentioned above, the theaters themselves. Everyone alludes to their horrible condition, with perhaps a dozen decent places up to global standards of comfort, sound, and projection in the whole country. All of 46, out of about 1,000 theaters throughout the country, have Dolby sound systems. Even Mikhalkov, the Slavophilic critic of Western consumerism, weighs in here: "What's the sense of creating great films if people have to watch them on tattered screens, in the cold, seated on rock-hard chairs and catching a whiff of the theater's ancient toilet?"[10] Or putting up with the clothing, cosmetics, and furniture bazaars that some theaters have leased their lobbies to?

Before the economic meltdown of August, 1998, Moscow's modernized Khudozhestvenny and the new Kodak-Kinomir (financed by Eastman Kodak and Golden Ring Entertainment based in Los Angeles) were drawing capacity audiences, even with tickets priced as high as about $12. In St. Petersburg, the comfortable, improved Crystal Palace charges about $4 for foreign attractions. (Average monthly wages are now about $60, higher in Moscow and St. Petersburg.) Figures for 1997 suggested that Russians—the emerging "middle class"?—were returning to the theaters, possibly because they had more disposable income (after having bought color TVs and VCRs), and/or they wanted more than videocassettes or made-for-TV movies. Expectations of an expanding filmgoing population prompted diverse efforts to upgrade theaters, and not just in Moscow and St. Petersburg. Igor Tolstunov, the General Director of NTV-Profit (part of the Media-Most empire), saw a "kinoboom" across the country and described plans to establish a network of reconstructed theaters, including multiplexes, in some 80 cities. Livnev envisioned a touring film festival to spur local investment in modern, profitable theater refurbishings. The first Russian drive-in, a "Kinodrom," opened in an upscale Moscow neighborhood the summer of 1999, with per-person admission at about $8. And this was a nice touch: James Cameron donated three tons of new sound equipment to the "Darya" theater in Kaliningrad. Evidently he was grateful for the diving equipment developed for underwater filming there, and he wanted his *Titanic* to debut in a proper venue.[11]

Many of the ambitious ideas above were rocked by the financial dive of 1998, and the deep-pocketed magnates were no longer so forthcoming. By 1999, Gusinsky's Media-Most, burdened with debt, was offering stock to foreign investors. Gusinsky himself is now under house arrest in Spain, awaiting extradition to Russia on charges of fraud, and his media enterprises are endangered, or face transfer to other hands. Hypothetically, a successful, widespread upgrading of kinotheaters could have positive ripple effects on the studios themselves—the point of production. And vice-versa, of course. Absent major state subsidies and bailouts, the studios have to think of financing and supporting themselves not by renting space out for producing TV commercials (or other enterprises), but by putting together films of quality attractive to the public and up to competing with Western imports. This was Livnev's goal as head of Gorky Studios in Moscow, and privatization seemed the only solution, there as elsewhere. Livnev also suggested that state subsidies, on the European model, could support the equivalent of low-budget, "independent" films in the $300,000 range.

Livnev's Gorky Studio turned out a dozen such films in his two-year tenure there. Though he managed to keep the studio from bankruptcy, and introduced the idea of a "vertically integrated" operation where production, distribution and sales would be studio-controlled, the financial crisis torpedoed his (and others') plans. The state did not then permit the privatization of the studios, and monies from private sources dwindled: a double bind. Under the circumstances, Livnev resigned as head in October 1998.[12]

The "European," especially the "French model," by which is meant state largesse for cinema, has also been invoked by Nikita Mikhalkov as newly elected head of the Filmmakers Union (the organization includes all those working in film) in his proposals for revitalizing Russian film. The core of his program was creating a federal-level government agency with its own budget for producing and distributing Russian films. Mikhalkov and the Union is a story in itself, and in a way mimics Russian political life, with its new, messy freedoms that unsettle the proponents of order and the firm hand. His critics argued that Mikhalkov wanted to turn the Union into a "ministry" run dictatorially. But the majority that elected him wants a strong leader with plenty of power. Mikhalkov has played on the theme of restoring Russian national pride, and sees film as an essential sparkplug. At the special Congress of the Union in 1998 he screened a montage of clips from current Russian films that trafficked in sex and violence—the *"chernukha"* and *"pornukha"* that deflates, not uplifts the Russian national spirit. "Filmmakers have betrayed their audience," he said. They have "rejected its love—and at the very time when they could have helped people get through difficult times...when they could have instilled hope. Russian films today are vacuous, rootless and pointless. They are not born of pain, of love, or of an artist's compassion. The vast bulk of them are irresponsible experiments at government expense."

He also blamed the celebrated 5th Congress of the Union during the heady days of *glasnost* for its "new model" that de-centralized the film distribution network, and opened the country to the American deluge. Mikhalkov's appeals and critiques may have touched many hearts, but others were wary of such zealous simplifications. "The miners didn't have any Fifth Congress," countered the late actor and director Rolan Bykov, "and the collapse of the film industry is not the result of the Congress. That Congress took place in a different country and dealt with relations between the artist and totalitarianism."[13]

Recent developments since those debates point to unpredictable, arguable outcomes. The new government of Vladimir Putin has placed Goskino under the Ministry of Culture, which many see as downgrading cinema, while others are amused by film people defending an institution left over from Soviet times. When it was rumored that the Putin government wanted to end the ban on privatizing the studios, alarms were raised similar to those expressed earlier when Gusinsky sought to buy into Mosfilm. Karen Shakhnazarov, present head of Mosfilm, expressed those fears in his defense of keeping the studio beyond the reach of the private, profit-minded sector: New owners "will be tempted to restructure Mosfilm to earn them money. We suspect that any private investor will be tempted to develop the valuable land on which we are based and we'll have casinos, hotels and flats here instead of film studios. This will have a catastrophic effect on Russian culture.... Mosfilm made a massive contribution to the development of cinema in the last century. It isn't simply a business. It is a cultural institution, no less important than the Hermitage or the Bolshoi Theater. It has to be preserved." The Putin government was not moved by such pleas: Mosfilm, or at least some of its 40 component studios will be put up for joint-stock ownership, while the state will retain its hold over the lucrative back-film catalogue. At the same time, according to Minister of Culture Mikhail Shvydkoi, the government will pump funds into modernizing a state-owned film distribution network ("*Rossisky Prokat*") and building and improving theaters. It is hard to anticipate where this novel combination of state ownership (the spectre of the old bureaucratized Soviet model?) plus privatization will lead the film world, except to note that it mirrors other patterns in the post-Soviet economy. Around Mosfilm, some have been heard to mutter, we should have let Gusinsky in on ownership in 1997....

II. THE ESTHETICS OF THE UGLY

Russian cinema can be proud of a rich tradition, and has had—still has—enormous talent at all levels of the craft. What's holding it back today? Where are the creative breakthroughs that would return the Russian public to their (improved) theaters to enjoy popular Russian films not made yesteryear—films, moreover, that might command global respect? Finances and the structure of the industry are obviously a problem, a terrific problem, but they are not the whole story. Judging by the films that overcome financial hurdles and do get made—often with foreign co-production assistance—Russian cinema is still in a transitional mode where gloom is, perhaps inevitably, the esthetic order of the day. And shoddy production values don't help.

The film curator and historian Naum Kleiman a few years ago called for imitating what he called "the healthiest reaction by a national film industry to a crisis situation." He meant Hollywood during the Depression years, and he identified three genres for emulation—the socially critical films of Frank Capra, John Ford, and Mervyn LeRoy; comedies and musicals "which reminded people that life could also be funny and enjoyable, that they could pull through"; and historical films that described the past, instead of "consistently settling scores with it." Mikhalkov, who stands with those pleading for patriotic (*otechestvenny*) cinema, had his own spin on the Hollywood model: "America walked out of its crisis thanks to its cinema," which created a national myth people could identify with and strive toward. Soviet cinema did something like that, he said: "You may or may not like the ideology, but we created the image of a Soviet man and stuck to it." Others have called for more *dobroe kino*, ("feel-good" film), more *svetlukha* instead of *chernukha* (a play on the Russian terms light and dark), while Dondurei deplored the collapse of film "as an instrument of social influence. The country is undertaking modernization and reform, yet not a single film has 'voted' in favor of reform..." A political party, the liberal Union of Right Forces, even put up $120,000 in prize money for film and television scripts that would avoid *chernukha* and portray the country in a positive light.[14]

These are sound enough admonitions, but of what value are such shoulds and woulds and simple prescriptions? The Russians have had enough of external, top-down tutelage. No *ukazes*, from critics or other sources, guarantees good movies. Besides, I don't think there are any Russian Frank Capras or Howard Hawkses or Busby Berkeleys ready to hand (not even a Grigori Alexandrov). The Russian film ethos is an unavoidable, maybe necessary, reflection of the mood and condition of the country at large, and its disorientation. This also meshes with and reinforces what is perhaps an ingrained national disposition to the morose in art. Russian lightheartedness in film is, presently, at least, almost an oxymoron. There are attempts to replicate American commercial cinema, but even the best efforts only fall flat. Just compare Alexei Balabanov's recent *The Brother* (1997), or Alexander Zeldovich's *Moscow* (2000), Tarantino wanna-be's both, to the real things. In the hands of lesser directors than Balabanov or Zeldovich, the results are even more embarrassing. Grigory Konstantinopolsky's *$8½* (1999) is a garish example. *The Check*, directed by Boris Giller and Alexander Borodyansky (2000) is another failure in the same mode. More successful, but still clumsy and earthbound, is Vasily Pichul's latest effort, *Sky Studded with Diamonds* (1999). I'm afraid we have been witnessing the emergence of an unfortunate new genre, the Russian crime or the crime-cum-comedy film, with contorted plotlines, where the special effects are tinny, the humor crude, very broad at best, and the constant resort to magic realist devices a sign of creative insolvency. Also unfortunate is the all-too-frequent attempt on the Russian side to explain away poor reception in the West as a cultural problem, as cognitive dissonance. "There are a lot of things that the Western viewer won't understand," said the "necro-realist" filmmaker Yevgeny Yufit in a recent interview. "He has different social stereotypes, for one thing. And he doesn't react well to the elements of black humor—that's something Russians find easier to swallow."[15] That's very debatable. Admittedly, there is much a Western viewer might not understand about a Russian film (or any foreign film), but good films, including black humorous ones, share universal values that overcome local references.

The recent work of three of Russian filmdom's greatest figures are more successful than those lame imitative efforts I have mentioned, but they also illustrate what might alienate film-going publics in Russia and abroad. Kira Muratova's *Three Stories* (1997) is a grim, very grim triad, three chilling chronicles of murderous crimes that go unpunished. Her recent *Second Class Citizens* (2000) is in the dark-comedy mode. Alexander Sokurov's *Mother and Son* (1997) is an achingly melancholy elegy on nature and dying, rather distant and surreal.[16] These are powerful films; we know that whatever the epoch or its conditions Muratova and Sokurov will go their own very personal way, but here the personal tonality coincides with the somber hues of the land. Maybe catharsis first, then laughter.

Alexei Gherman's long awaited *Khrustalyov, My Car!* (1998), almost ten years in the making, is certainly no laughing matter, and offers plenty of material for historical mourning and catharsis. In a chaotic, often incoherent cascade of cluttered scenes shot in high-contrast black-and-white, and delivered with high-octane editing, Gherman assaults the audience with his bleak vision of a horribly bleak Soviet period, the last days of Stalin. Included in Gherman's portrait of the death rattle is an agonizing rape sequence (of the male hero), and the very squalid end of the tyrant himself. Provincial life just after Stalin's death is conveyed from the laughter (some) and tears (mostly) of Valery Ogorodnikov's odd gallery of characters in his powerful *Barak* (1999; "Dedicated to Our Parents"). Contemporary provincial life is not much happier despite the director's more tender-hearted and lyrical ministrations in Lydia Bobrova's *In That Land* (1997). The talented Balabanov showed his taste for the grotesque—one might say the Russian taste for the grotesque—in his very gothic *Of Freaks and Men* (1998), a kind of Slavic *Boogie Nights* minus the humor. Balabanov's sepia-toned and genteel St. Petersburg early in the century is the milieu for lust, voyeurism, pornography, and murder: highly stylized pre-Soviet *chernukha*, in idiosyncratic minimalist form suggestive of silent film. The illogic of nightmares, the experience of frustration and powerlessness—what we think of as Kafkaesque—is a natural subject for filmmakers in the arduous ambience of today's Russia, and Balabanov went into such territory with his evocative rendition of *The Castle* (1994).

No, such cinema is not likely to attract mass audiences, though they may garner cultish followings. But even recent films that have won domestic popularity and international recognition, Academy Award nominations no less, and one winner among them—Mikhalkov's *Burnt by the Sun* (1994, the Oscar recipient), Sergei Bodrov's *Prisoner of the Mountains* (1996), and Pavel Chukhrai's *The Thief* (1997)—even such films are not exactly cheerful romps. *Burnt* is a treatment of High Stalinism; *Prisoner* captures the passions and violence of the Chechen war; and *The Thief* is a well crafted retro melodrama that highlights the destructive and self-destructive exploits of a very smooth con-man of the 1950s (played by Vladimir Mashkov)—a film which concludes, incidentally, with the war in Chechnya. It's perhaps emblematic that the kids in all three films—Nadia in *Burnt*, Nina in *Prisoner*, and Sanka in *The Thief* all have more-or-less bad ends, unlike the finally happy Kolya of the Czech film of the same name that beat out *Prisoner* for the 1996 Oscar in the foreign language category.[17] All three directors also displayed that other recent and regular affectation of Russian cinema, daubs of magic realism, something that turns up too in Vladimir Khotinenko's sprawling indictment of the brutalities of (once again) contemporary village life, *The Muslim* (1995).

It's hard to find a solid comedy offering from the Russians, though we know they have had the gift. Presently, when directors try their hand at comedy, there is always a dark underside, or the laughter is awash in tears. The sardonic and satirical seems the comfortable habitat of contemporary Russian directors, not the simply comical. Their intent is not to make us laugh, but to make us wince, whether they're kicking around old Soviet mores or jabbing at current realities. Alexander Rogozhkin's *Particulars of the National Hunt* (1995) comes to mind, a film that incidentally demonstrates the director's versatility, a welcome satirical contrast to two of his other recent works, *The Chekist* (1991) and *Living with an Idiot* (1993), both violent and ugly enough to make you turn your head away or close your eyes in some parts. The critic Oleg Kovalov's "optical poem," *The Gardens of Scorpio* (1991) is an ingenious compilation that weaves found footage into an old Soviet potboiler, yielding a cerebrally satisfying, if not a side-splitting put-on. Livnev's *Hammer and Sickle* (1994) is a brilliant parody of Stalinist culture and politics, very acerbic and clever, but also terribly gloomy. The present (post-Soviet, hence also anti-Soviet) Russian fascination with absurdist esthetics can be self-defeating; comedy will surrender to intellect. Buñuel could bring it off, so might a new cinema-Gogol—Eldar Ryazanov came closest in the past—but there are none around. Farce and fantasy are also alluring for cinema, but hard to realize successfully. Labored situations and unfunny slapstick spoil Yuri Mamin's *Window to Paris* (1994)—too bad, for his earlier tweak at Eisenstein's *Alexander Nevsky*, among other targets, in his *Neptune's Holiday* (1986), showed real comedic flair—and they spoil Sergei Ovcharov's *Drumroll* (1993), for all of its Buster Keaton antics and enchantments. Otar Ioseliani's *Brigands, Chapter VII* (1996), is overly long, frequently tiresome, but interestingly contoured, an angry and mocking epic of human folly and violence from medieval times through Soviet *vlast*, and on to the sordid Uzi-and mafiosi-ridden present. There is material for laughter here, but the laughter wears a straight face and comes through clenched teeth, which is the way I imagine Ioseliani looks when he ponders the human condition. (Forgive me for using a Georgian, and one in Parisian emigration at that, not a Russian, to make my point.)[18] Too often, solid efforts at comedy or melodrama are subverted by over-long descents into farce, as if directors took to heart Oscar Wilde's maxim that nothing succeeds like *excess*. Several recent examples come to mind, all well-made but over-doing it—*The Wedding* (2000) directed by Pavel Lungin, whose gritty-sad *Taxi Blues* (1990) enjoyed a theatrical run in the West; Vladimir Menshov's *Envy of the Gods* (2000; his popular *Moscow Does Not Believe in Tears* won an Oscar for best foreign film in 1980); and Vladimir Fokin's *House of the Rich* (2000). *The Wedding* is a dizzying portrait of good and bad folks in a mining town; ultimately, a simple Russian humanism triumphs over violence, corruption, and alcoholism—the stuff of most films about contemporary Russian life, for obvious reasons. *Envy* is set in the

Moscow of 1983, when a Soviet fighter plane brought down a Korean passenger airliner, and brings out well some of the imagery of the period, from Ronald Reagan's "Evil Empire" speech to the repressive official attitudes that force people to watch *Last Tango in Paris* with conspiratorial secrecy. A brilliant performance by Vera Alentova (of *Moscow Does not Believe in Tears*) and a comical cameo by Gerard Depardieu are overwhelmed by banal scripting and contrived plot turns (a visiting Frenchman—played, unfortunately, by a Russian—unlocks the heroine's sexuality). *House of the Rich*, a longitudinal melodrama—different generations occupy a house from Tsarist through Soviet times, down to the present—has some engrossing historical sections, but also fritters away its substance, at great length, in farce. (Fellini has always been a powerful influence on the Russian film world.)

The Russians are presently doing best, it seems to me, in recovering their past. Not only are they good at getting details of costume and historical dramas down right, but there is the added *frisson* of taking old themes and giving them an anti-Soviet complexion, of telling the history as it could not be written or filmed in Soviet times. Such is the case with Alexander Proshkin's colorful epic *The Captain's Daughter* (2000; based on Pushkin), about the violent (and violently crushed) Pugachev peasant rising of the 18th century, a painful reminder, the director has said, of the regular cruelties in the Russian experience. Add to this category Vitaly Melnikov's *Tsarevich Alexei* (1997), focusing on the tortured relationship between Peter the Great and his son, Alexei, conveyed with sympathy not for the tyrannical state-builder, but for his sensitive son. (For a comparison with a Soviet treatment of the same subject, see Vladimir Petrov's bloated, two part *Peter the First*, 1937-38.) I have not yet seen the most recent work of Gleb Panfilov, one of the most capable of Soviet-era directors, on the last Tsar and his family (*The Romanovs*, 2000), but he likely re-tells the story of Nicholas II from an anti-Bolshevik perspective, which may recall a standard Western treatment of the subject, Franklin J. Schaffner's *Nicholas and Alexandra* (1971), although I suspect Panfilov's is less hackneyed and more accurate. Also departing from Soviet conventions is Alexei Uchitel's *His Wife's Diary* (2000), a handsome and honestly told, Merchant-Ivory sort of rendition of pages in the life of Ivan Bunin, the first Russian writer to win the Nobel Prize. Bunin detested the new Soviet regime and ended his days in emigration. *His Wife's Diary* dwells on the *ménage à trois,* and other erotic complications, that developed in the author's circle while living in southern France. (Old Soviet-style attitudes die hard. Members of the state financing commission were reluctant to grant Uchitel funds on the grounds that a great writer's love life is not an appropriate film subject. From another universe came a different kind of obstacle: the French withheld co-financing because Uchitel didn't agree to their demand to star Omar Sharif as Bunin. The film was the official Russian entry for the foreign-language Oscar, but was not nominated.)

Sometimes I think that extra-esthetic considerations explain some of the unappealing mannerisms of recent films. They are overpopulated, for example—is it because directors want to write in parts for unemployed actors? They are also claustrophobic—is it because outdoor shooting on location or constructing elaborate sets is so much more expensive than grouping your cast around a kitchen table? Some extended research might clear this up, but the sense of overpopulation or confining spaces comes across in Vadim Abdrashitov and Alexander Mindadze's rambling *Time of the Dancer* (1997), Natalya Piankova's *Happy New Year, Moscow!* (1993), Sergei Ursulyak's *Russian Ragtime* (1993), and Boris Frumin's *Viva Castro!* (1993). The last is nevertheless a very vibrant (and sad) study counterpointing adolescents and adults in a provincial town of the 1960s.

There is something else about so many of the films I have mentioned, both the better and the worse—an absence of strong narrative. The films unfold not around a narrative axis or clear story line, or within a well-defined plot, but as a collage of scenes, as a series of situations with indeterminate resolutions at the end. At times, especially in those crime-comedy works described above, you get the feeling that scenes and situations are improvised from day to day during production. Does this denote a certain indifference to scripting and structure in the strapped film industry of today, or does it flow from some mildly post-modernist impulse, augmented by a strong reaction-formation against the conventions of Soviet socialist realist esthetics? Or is it that, as the critic Mikhail Brashinsky has explained, storytelling in the usual sense is not in the Russian tradition; a story might be used for some ideological or moral purpose, but is not valued as such.[19] This is not necessarily a bad thing. Visuals and characters in film can very well carry their own story and bring it to life without, as it were, narrative help, whether revealing past horrors (*Khrustalyov*), or exposing villagers drinking themselves to death (*In That Land*). Besides, the (many) characters that (over) populate these situations are often vivid, colorful, striking, sometimes even memorable, thanks in great part to the still superb acting talents of Russian screen performers, especially in ensemble work.

But overpopulation, even with talented actors and their vivid characters; claustrophobia; leaky plots and structures; and visual ugliness are not the stuff of an appealing, popular cinema, at home or abroad. "There is such a thing," said Yuri Mamin, "as the esthetics of the ugly. Life is not all about beauty. Vulgarity, chaos, and paradox are all part of our social life, and they prompt the visual solution." Similarly, to his critics who fault *Khrustalyov* for being "complex and frightening," Gherman answers, "no more than life itself."[20] Do Russian directors fetishize the ugly for their own expressive purposes, and as therapeutic mirrors held up to the ugly past and the ugly present?; or as I speculated above, are there less weighty reasons: They settle for ratty *mise-en-scène* to cut down on production costs?

Whichever, maybe both, Russian cinema is no dream factory today, or Republic of Entertainment. Not surprising: Remember, Russian filmmakers are in the Transition Period, not on *The Shining Path*.

Originally, a paper presented at the Conference, "Reimaging Russia: Cultural Transformations in Post-Soviet Russia," College of William and Mary, Williamsburg, Virginia, April 4, 1998. Revised and published, Cineaste, Vol. XXVI, No. 3, Summer 2001. Special thanks to Maria Solovieva for research assistance in St. Petersburg. Jytte Jensen, Assistant Curator, The Museum of Modern Art Department of Film, Boris Frumin, and Anne Borin, Director, New York Expo of Short Films, shared their views on the current Russian film scene with me: Thank you.

¹ Ironically, some of the best Soviet films from a cohort of talented directors—Tarkovsky, Konchalovsky, Mikhalkov, Panfilov, G. Shengelaya, Klimov, and many others—were turned out during the Brezhnev years. The best survey of *glasnost* cinema and backgrounds is Anna Lawton *Kinoglasnost: Soviet Cinema in Our Time* (Cambridge, 1992). The 1960s are covered by Josephine Woll in *Real Images: Soviet Cinema and the Thaw* (London, New York, 2000), while Vida Johnson surveys the films of "Russia After the Thaw" in *The Oxford History of World Cinema*, edited by Geoffrey Nowell-Smith. (New York, 1996). Other Soviet periods are covered in the same collection by other authors. For a brief general overview, see my review-essay, "Requiem for Soviet Cinema 1917-1991," Cineaste, XXI, Nos. 1-2, 1995, 23-27, reprinted above in Chapter IV.

² Quoted in *Ekspert*, No. 43, 10 November 1997. Film receipts followed income from petroleum, alcohol and tobacco.

³ Figures given here on film production, theater attendance, video sales, etc. come from diverse sources, including *Seans*, No. 12, 1998; *SK Novosti* (Newspaper of the Union of Filmmakers of the Russian Federation), 26 November 1999; *Kino Park*, No. 12, December 1999; the publicity brochure, Filmmakers Union of Russia (in English), 1999. Carol J. Williams's "Russia's Film Czars Revive Sad Cinemas," *Los Angeles Times*, February 15, 1998 is an informative report with data and commentary by film-world figures.

⁴ Yekaterina Barabash in *Nezavisimaya gazeta*, 26 December 1997; at Mosfilm, Yulya Polyakova, "Kinosvadba s pridanym," *Ogonyek*, Spring 1997.

⁵ Mamin in *Moskovskie novosti*, No. 51, December 29-January 4, 1995. Alexander Zhurbin, Chairman of the Organizing Committee of the "New York Festival of Russian Films" (December 10-12, 1999) told me he was pleased with attendance at the Festival, and that it "covered its costs". The screenings I was at were, understandably, heavily attended by *émigrés*. The same may be said of the 2nd Festival, October, 2000. Zhurbin is planning the Festival as an annual event, hoping to attract the American public in several cities. A group of Russian-film scholars has organized an annual symposium with screenings at the University of Pittsburgh.

Aside from the regular staging of festivals that feature Russian-made films, Russia as an ever-exotic film subject continues to attract producers and audiences in the West. In the last few years we have seen productions of *Anna Karenina* and *Eugene Onegin* (titled as *Onegin*), neither very successful despite filming on Russian location. More satisfying was the French entry for 1999 Academy Award consideration in the foreign-film category, Regis Wargnier's *East-West*, a French-Russian co-production starring Sandrine Bonnaire, Catherine Deneuve, Oleg Menshikov, and Sergei Bodrov, Jr., in an engrossing political thriller about Russian *émigrés* enticed from abroad by the Stalin regime to return home after World War II. The screenplay has a more historically authentic flavor than is commonly found in Western productions, perhaps because Rustam Ibragimbekov and Sergei Bodrov (Senior) were part of the scripting team. See my review above, Chapter II, 1. Jean-Jacques Ammaud's *Enemy at the Gates* (2000) is set at the battle of Stalingrad.

[6] Alexander Fedorov, "Cinema Art in the Structure of Russian Modern Media Education," Report to UNESCO Media Education Conference, Vienna, 1999.

[7] *Ekspert*, No. 43, 10 November 1997; Peter Rutland, "Russian Film and Television: Making a Slow Comeback," in Johnson's Russia List (Online), No. 4422, July 25, 2000. According to Minister of Culture Mikhail Shvydkoi, Russian films capture only 7% of the national market, 3% in Moscow. Report by Agence France Press in Johnson's Russia List, #5197, 11 April 2001.

[8] *Ogonyok*, Spring, 1997. Media-Most accounts for about half of all present television and theatrical film production.

[9] Dondurei, *Nezavisimaya gazeta*, 10 April 1993; Dondurei and Livnev, *Ekspert*, No. 43, 10 November 1997. See also Dondurei in *Iskusstvo kino*, No. 10, 1996.

Interview with Sergei Lavrentiev, November, 1999; Lavrentiev is Program Director of the Sochi International Film Festival.

[10] Quoted in Carol J. Williams, "Film Czars Review Sad Cinema," *Los Angeles Times*, February 15, 1998.

[11] Williams, "Film Czars...," ibid; Tolstunov, *Ekspert*, No. 43, 10 November 1997; on Kinodrom, *Ekspert*, No. 24, 21 June 1999.

[12] Interview with Livnev, January, 2000; Gusinsky and Media-Most, *Variety*, December 6-12, 1999.

[13] The old Union's celebrated Fifth Congress, representing all the constituent Soviet republics, took place in May, 1986. The Third Congress of the post-Soviet Russian Union elected Mikhalkov as Chairman, December, 1997. For Mikhalkov and the Union (and its special Congress, May-June, 1998, held at the Kremlin and not in its usual venue at Moscow's Dom Kino) see *Trud*, 25 December 1997 and 2 June 1998; *Rossiiskaya gazeta*, 4 June 1998; *Kommersant Daily*, 30 May and 2 June 1998; *Izvestiya*, 2 June 1998. Translations are in *Current Digest of the Post-Soviet Press*, Vol. 49, No. 52, and Vol. 50, No. 23, 1998. See also *Russia on Reels: The Russian Idea in Post-Soviet Cinema*, edited by Birgit Beumers (London and New York, 1999), for the views of Dondurei and Mikhalkov.

[14] Dondurei would head the selection committee: *Variety*, February 1, 2001. Dondurei, *Ekspert*, No. 43, 10 November 1997; Mikhalkov in his

inaugural address, quoted in *Russian Life*, February, 1998; Kleiman interviewed by Jean-Michel Frodon in *Le Monde*, July 29, 1993. Mikhalkov's grand *epopeya*, his patriotic *The Barber of Siberia*—dedicated to the Russian army—had a festive Kremlin opening complete with an orchestra in Imperial dress uniform playing "God Save the Tsar," on February 20, 1999. Most Russian critics were hostile, while the public went for it. Much of the dialogue is in English, a decision, according to some, aimed at the American market and at an Oscar nomination outside the category of foreign films. "He made it for the Americans," several Russians have commented to me, but so far it hasn't found an American distributor, much less an Oscar nomination. The film has high energy and its virtuoso cinematography and editing weaves the U.S. and Russian story lines in and out of flashbacks with great polish. But its farcical elements are hyperbolic, and it suffers from some terrible casting strategies—Julia Ormond and Richard Harris as Americans, Mikhalkov himself, in an unintentionally (?) comical cameo as Tsar Alexander III, and the usually brilliant Oleg Menshikov playing a *Junker* as a kind of wide-eyed *ingenu*. See the amusing report by Stephen Kotkin, "A Tsar is Born," *The New Republic*, April, 1999. Michael R. Gordon profiles Mikhalkov's attempt to "conjure up an ideal of Russia that its people can live by: a world of pageantry in which honor endures, love is pure and a noble czar rules with a firm but benevolent hand" in *The New York Times*, February 21, 1999. Mikhalkov is reportedly planning another patriotic epic set in World War II, along the lines of a Russian *Saving Private Ryan*.

[15] *Pulse* (St. Petersburg), June, 1999.

[16] Sokurov's later *Molokh* is no less odd, an eerie portrait of the banality of Nazi life at the top—Hitler and his entourage, Eva Braun especially—during a retreat at Berchtesgaden. The dying Lenin is the subject of his last film, *Taurus*. See the interview with Sokurov and the Filmography by Kirill Galetsky in *Cineaste*, Vol. XXVI, No. 3, Summer 2001.

[17] Bad ends also cap Rogozhkin's *Outpost* (*Blokpost*, 1998), a *Platoon*-like treatment of Russian army buddies facing the hostile Chechens.

[18] Boris Frumin, mentioned below for his compelling *Viva Castro!*, also filmed while in emigration; he taught at New York University. Ioseliani's *Brigands* was made in 1995-96; his last film, *Farewell, Home Sweet Home* (*Adieu, plancher des vaches*, 1999), set in contemporary Paris, is considerably lighter of heart, but with—of course—some dark edges.

[19] Interview with Brashinsky, St. Petersburg, June, 1999.

[20] In planning his New York Festival Alexander Zhurbin (see Note 5) was warned by fellow *émigrés*, "Russian films are complicated, slow, dirty, and dark. Nobody is going to like them." "The most discouraging thing about [low-budget films] is that they show backyards, refuse dumps,

squalid apartments ...The directors seem to flaunt their lack of funds." S. Kalvarsky, a Petersburg filmmaker, from a roundtable discussion, *Seans*, No. 16, 1997. A Russian film-goer complained after a screening of Stanislav Govorukhin's violent film of rape and vigilante justice, *The Voroshilov Marksman* (1999), "How long can you make such sad films? We encounter injustice everyday without them...You don't have to show it." *Argumenty i Fakty*, No. 25, 1999. I remember hearing similar sentiments from Russians about *Little Vera*. Mamin is quoted in J. Hoberman's review of *Window to Paris*, *The Village Voice*, February 21, 1995. Gherman's rejoinder to his critics is from his message to the audience at the Museum of Modern Art screening of *Khrustalyov*, December 6, 1999.

Border Crossings in the Baltic: The "Transit Zero" Film Conference

Sweden and Latvia are two small nations, neighbors across the Baltic Sea, but worlds apart in modern historical development. The Swedes entered the 21st century enjoying the comforts of an advanced welfare capitalism, while the Latvians are scraping their way out from under the ruins of Soviet socialism. But both share affection for film, and boast some strong film traditions. We associate Sweden with Bergman, and his massive influence on world cinema, but Latvians will remind you that Eisenstein was born in their capital, Riga, and that Eisenstein's cinematographer, Eduard Tisse, the son of a Swedish father and Russian mother, studied art and photography in Liepaja, on the Latvian coast, which is where half of an unusual film conference, "Transit Zero," took place the summer of 2000.

The other half was held on the gorgeous island of Oland, off the southeastern Swedish coast. Contrasts between East and West, making contact across borders, and navigating the transit into the new century were the central themes of the Conference, organized by film communities in both nations, primarily The Swedish Institute, Sweden's Eureka Film, and the National Film Center of Latvia, with support from the Sundance Institute. The Soros Foundation provided additional funding. Those prevailing themes were evident in the locations of the Conference itself, in many of the films shown, and in the topics under discussion, especially that of co-production.

One of the chief figures in pulling the Conference together, Carl Bjorsmark, is a border-crosser himself, in more ways than one. A Swede now living in Latvia, and a founder of the multi-media arts group, "Locomotive International," Bjorsmark is director of *Checking Out* (1998), an unconventional documentary that folds fiction film episodes into a non-fiction format in order to dramatize the problems of Russian nationals in post-Soviet Latvia. (When Bjorsmark's film was shown at the Museum of Modern Art, I asked him how he would categorize it, and he replied in that wry, best post-modern style, that he checks off both "fiction" and "non-fiction" on festival applications.) The young Latvian director, Laila Pakalninja was also fascinated by borders/non-borders in her film, *The Ferry* (1999), a stark, narration-free documentary that tracks crossing after crossing of a simple passenger craft from river bank to river bank, ignoring the new borders that divide post-Soviet Latvia from post-Soviet Belarus.

In the old Soviet Union, the Latvians occupied a special place in documentary cinema, especially in the final, *glasnost* period when once forbidden themes and forms began appearing regularly on television and theater screens. The late Latvian director, Juris Podnieks, is credited with the most important break-through documentary, *Is It Easy to Be Young?* (1988), a graphic portrait of disaffected Soviet youth in changing times. Hertz Franks, the respected documentarian of an older generation, and a prominent member of the Soviet Latvian *glasnost* film movement, attended "Transit Zero," and introduced some of his films. (He now lives in Israel.) Interestingly, those films, too, revolved around the border-crossings motif, one subliminally, the other directly. Franks collaborated with the Latvian Uldis Brauns in 1967 to (outwardly) honor the 50th anniversary of the Bolshevik Revolution and the birth of the Soviet state with the documentary *235,000,000*. The "tribute"—really to the Soviet people, its makers insisted—is a wonderfully edited montage of scenes from Soviet life. No blemishes are shown, but the final shots feature a young couple standing on a bridge looking into the distance, then a big plane soaring away, i.e., crossing the border to liberty, away from the Soviet Union. Or so one is free to interpret.

A fine example of how Soviet filmmakers often used conventional means to smuggle taboo ideas into their work. Twenty-one years later Franks chronicled the sad real tale of a real attempted escape from the Soviet Union in his documentary, *The Seven Semyons*, also shown at the Conference. The Semyons of the title were the talented young brothers of a musical family who decided their jazz repertory needed a Western stage beyond Soviet borders, and that the only way to get there was by hijacking a Soviet airliner. The plan failed badly, in violence, with several dead and imprisoned as a result. A discussion after the screening raised the questions of guilt—the Soviet system for erecting barriers to the elementary human freedom to travel, or the hijackers for endangering lives, theirs and others?—and of the stance of the documentarian in relation to that issue. Franks made it clear that, whatever he thought of the Soviet system, guilt lay with the hijackers, and that his film made personal responsibility the focus.

The Franks-Brauns film, *235,000,000*, was shown in a very exotic setting, on a big screen, under a full moon, in the "Alvar," a vast barren, one of Oland's raw natural beauties. Conference organizers thoughtfully provided participants with woolen blankets to cope with the chill night air. Perhaps the most exotic setting of all, certainly a very dramatic border-crossing, came with our sleeping and dining quarters, as provided by the Latvians in Karosta, on the outskirts of Liepaja, at a former Soviet naval base on the coast— originally established in Imperial Russian times, and it looked it. The Russians, as was their custom throughout Eastern Europe and the Baltic after the Soviet collapse, left the place a shambles, and the Latvians are doing their best to convert the base, now housing some military detachments, into a seaside resort. Many in the Conference took one glance at the place and decided to reside at a local hotel instead. I stayed. I shared a barracks room with some young Swedes ("Our basic training was palatial compared to this," they told me) and Latvians, and slept on a simple iron-framed cot that a Soviet sailor, or maybe even a pre-Soviet Russian mariner, once crawled into. Courtesy of the Swedish Air Force, we were flown into Liepaja on a Lockheed C-130 cargo plane. The whole experience felt like something out of a Hollywood war film. All that was missing were parachutes, and I thought I saw the ghosts of William Bendix and

Richard Conte sitting alongside us on the bare canvas straps. At our first mess—boiled chicken, rice and tea—Hertz Franks offered me a seat at his rickety table and asked with a grin, "Well, how do your American comrades like the Soviet Union?"

This vivid border-crossing of course pointed up the contrast between the wealthy Swedes and the indigent Latvians, and symbolized the serious fiscal divide separating Western and East European film establishments. The days of ample state funding were gone, and film production had dwindled to a trickle in all of the former Soviet republics, Russia included, and in the former socialist countries. Is co-production the answer to the financing problems faced by the East Europeans? In one form or other, this was a constant question posed at the Conference. There were no conclusive answers, but much was revealed—or dispelled—in the many formal and informal exchanges that marked the event. Laila Pakalninja was probably expressing the anxieties of many filmmakers from the East when she confessed to total naiveté about making deals with Western producers. She recounted her dispiriting experience of unknowingly giving away the distribution rights to one of her films when she secured some German funding. Tom Garvin, a sophisticated attorney from Beverly Hills with a wide international co-production background, distributed reams of helpful resource materials at the Conference—"Finding a Distributor in the US"; "Co-Finance and Co-Production Checklists"; "Production Loan Checklist"; etc.—but, given how green the Easterners are in these matters, the manuals may have looked like so much hieroglyphics to them. Their Rosetta Stone can only come with more and more experience. But even if co-financing is secured, there is no guarantee of quality and success. Co-productions often yield "Europuddings," with different accents and different sensibilities muddling the product. Reaching for "a world market," directors often lose their national bearings, succumbing to a kind of cognitive dissonance. The same Pakalninja made the sensible comment that successful co-productions may be those that have an appeal to common cultures—in other words, a Latvian director's film is inherently more likely to be appreciated in Minsk than in Sacramento. Another myth shared by so many filmmakers from the East that I hope was dispelled at the Conference was the perception that U.S. film means Hollywood. Several of us emphasized that the U.S. film world is a house of many mansions with diverse funding sources, different distribution agencies, large and small, a variety of independent producers, and a kaleidoscopic festival scene.

I don't think any major "deals" were concluded at the Conference, but one serendipitous happening materialized at one of the sessions. One of the Swedish organizers proposed a role-playing meeting where directors and scripters would pitch a proposal to producers—among the latter were Lisa Heller of HBO and Alan Hayling of England's Channel 4. Playing his part, Mark Saunders, an independent English director specializing in films with a social-political emphasis, suggested a work based on a famous 1910 incident in London, the Sidney Street Siege, when immigrant anarchist revolutionaries—from Latvia, no less—bungled a fund-raising burglary and were assaulted by a security force led by Winston Churchill. Bruno Ascuks, the Managing Director of the National Film Center of Latvia, and a Conference organizer, was at the session and—Eureka!—at once announced he knew a Latvian producer interested in the very same idea. Saunders and Ascuks subsequently followed up on the proposal and were negotiating a co-production. For the record: Hayling thought it interesting but backed out of any Channel 4 support for the project, while Heller agreed it had merit, but not necessarily for an American audience.

[*Cineaste*, XXVI, 3, 2001]

The Return

A stage actor by training and career, Andrei Zvyagintsev (b.1964) hits an emotional bull's-eye with his first film. (His slim directing experience included only three episodes for a television series, plus several TV commercials). And he does it with an economy that is rare for so much of post-Soviet Russian cinema. The film has just the right, taut balance between spare story telling and psychic shock.

The Return (2003) blends a chronicle of a week's journey—marked by intertitles for each of the days, undertaken by a father and his

9. The enigmatic "Father" (Konstantin Lavronenko) in Andrei Zvyagintsev's *The Return* (2004).

two young sons—with the ambience of a thriller. The tension between father and sons builds continually throughout the journey and its way stations, augmented eerily by musical pedal points on the sound track and the dirge-like drone of reeds. Zvyagintsev's interest in film was awakened by a chance viewing of Antonioni's 1960 masterpiece, *L'Avventura* ("absolutely amazed" by it, he told me), and *The Return* has some superficial stylistic similarities—the long shots, some beautiful photography capturing the lyricism and menace of sea and sky (Antonioni filmed the waters off Sicily; Zvyagintsev chose Lake Ladoga in the Russian north), and, especially, the unresolved mysteries. There is common, universal human significance in both stories, but Zvyagintsev's *alienazione* operates on the father and his sons, not among adult lovers.

We meet the brothers Andrei and Vanya, ages 15 and 13, at a diving tower with some friends. They all jump, except the suddenly fearful Vanya, who remains squatting alone and shivering until he is comforted and taken home by his sympathetic mother (Natalia Vdovina), or since the film unfolds as a kind of fable, and as Zvyagintsev in interviews insists on the mythic, as against the personal dimensions of the tale, he is comforted by the Mother, or metaphysically speaking, the Feminine Principle. Vanya, brilliantly realized by Ivan Dobronravov, is the moody core of the story. In appearance he is reminiscent of another tortured young character in another harrowing Russian film from Soviet times, the boy-partisan Flyora (Alexei Kravchenko) in *Come and See*, Elem Klimov's chilling recreation of a German massacre of Byelorussian villagers in WW II. Flyora is shook up by the violence and atrocities he witnesses, while Vanya is victimized by a dispassionate, demanding father—or Father.

The un-named Father (Konstantin Lavronenko) appears out of nowhere after an absence of twelve years. The brothers are shocked, delighted, baffled. They race up to the attic to locate an old photograph—is it really him? Yes, yes! In this wonderful episode the elements of psychological realism (for me the essence of the film) are set against mythic intimations (Zvyagintsev's essence)—the photograph they seek was hidden in an old, illustrated book of bible stories; the page where they find the photo has a drawing of Abraham about to slay Isaac. Uh-oh … is that where the tale of the mysteriously reappearing father will take us? What follows, a journey that father announces the three of them will make, seems to point in that direction. Or to its Oedipal opposite? Shadowing scene after scene is an atmosphere heavy with sinister possibilities. Head games between father and the sons, especially between him and Vanya, occasionally get physical. Father doesn't hesitate to use force and humiliation to get his way. Is he determined to teach the boys some life lessons and survival tools to make up for all the time he's been away? That would be a fairly benign paternal motive, except that his boot-camp style is terribly misguided. It might work up to a point for the needy and all too accommodating Andrei (Vladimir Garin), but not for Vanya, who is at once sensitive and headstrong.

The boys are burning with curiosity about the suddenly

materialized father they never knew, but he never tells them (or us) where he's been or who he is. They are prepared to adore him, but are troubled by his peremptory pedagogy and abrupt, upsetting shifts in itinerary—wasn't this supposed to be a fun fishing trip? Several times father stops to make calls at pay phones: Why? To whom? The boys don't know, and neither do we. Is it important? Out on a boat with an outboard motor, Vanya points out something to Andrei; they both stare at it and smile. We never see what it was and what amused them. Is Zvyagintsev teasing (and vexing) viewers with these enigmatic moments and especially by wrapping father up in a riddle? (See the *Coda* below for the mystery of the strongbox.) Zvyagintsev's explanation to me was that, on the contrary, he was showing respect for the audience, and for their ability to imagine and invent for themselves. (My biography of Father would make him a navy man, what with his terse commands and his ease with fog, sea swells, and sheets of rain when the outboard sputters to a stop. There is also more to him than meets the eye; for all his off-putting frigidity, there are gloomy depths in him, one can't help thinking.) This tantalizing strategy has a way of drawing you into the story, but it also has a distancing effect, making Father and Sons (and earlier, when we meet them briefly, Mother and Grandmother) rather abstract; mythic.

Yet there is so much in the film that is solid flesh. The portrait of Vanya, in particular, is authentic, filled with psychological insight; he is a very real kid, alternatively high-spirited and introspective. Father—he has his real moments, too—stares through his rear-and side-view mirrors at a curvaceous young woman walking past their station wagon. From the back seat Vanya catches him in the act, and his face expresses disdain. Any man who has had the experience of fatherhood would recognize the frictions over the simplest things that develop between Vanya and his father, and the anguish and tears they lead to. The more Father insists and the more he punishes, the more Vanya reacts with opposition and defiance. Near the film's end, raging with frustration and the injustice of it all, he threatens to use the big knife he swiped from Father. (Zvyagintsev did not draw on his own background—his son was born after he separated from his first wife, and he had no part in raising him—but Alexander Novototsky, one of the co-scripters, had a similar experience with a knife as a boy.)

The Return in its formal contours will immediately bring to mind the work and film esthetics of Andrei Tarkovsky. Zvyagintsev shares the late Russian master's hydrophilia; their films are waterlogged; rain is almost a member of the cast. There are long unbroken silences. The images are strong and framed gorgeously, but they always suggest something—what is it?—beyond their beauty. There is in *The Return* some of Tarkovsky's regular vocabulary—a German Shepherd wanders about; embers glow in a fireplace (even though it is summer). Zvyagintsev is flattered by comparisons to Tarkovsky, but, he says, any similarities are accidental. The fireplace into which grandma stares in a brief opening scene?—ash-covered embers, Zvyagintsev points out, are traditional symbols of femininity. (They are?) He admits to one unconscious echo of a Tarkovsky moment in *The Return*. Mother is smoking on the porch when Andrei and Vanya first learn of Father's appearance, very like the expectant mother sitting on the fence, smoking, in the opening sequence of *The Mirror*.

Zvyagintsev's explosive denouement involves another tower, a kind of bookend to the tower we watched the boys jump off at the beginning of *The Return*, the one that gave Vanya such a fright. What happens here to conclude what started out for the boys as a joyous family fishing trip will make you jump out of your seat. Two end pieces follow, the second a striking montage of black and white photos taken by the boys on the journey. They add up to a satisfying, albeit very melancholy touch.

There have been too many tawdry imitations of Western action films, clumsily trafficking in car chases, shoot-out violence and sex in post-Soviet cinema. *The Return* is different, and a worthy part of the attempt to find an authentic voice in Russian filmmaking.

Coda: Zvyagintsev's McGuffin

In a central sequence of **The Return***, Father, without explanation, takes the boys to an uninhabited island. He leaves them and heads for a site he's obviously familiar with; there he begins digging and uncovers what he is looking for, a rusting strongbox. What's in it? We don't know, and won't know. We can speculate, but was this the point of the journey, for the Father at least? Again, Zvyagintsev leaves it there, to the viewer's imagi-*

nation. *I interviewed Zvyagintsev for Cineaste magazine in New York in January, 2004, the day before he left for the Sundance festival, where* The Return *would be shown. (The film was Russia's official entry for the Oscar in the foreign-language category.)*

Menashe: You are fond of leaving things unexplained, most notably in regard to the strongbox father digs up.

Zvyagintsev: I realize many viewers are irritated by not knowing what's in the box, but I respect the audience's intelligence, and their own creative potential.

Are you familiar with Hitchcock's idea of the McGuffin?

McGuffin, McGuffin!, Yes, I've often heard the word in connection with that unopened box, but I have to admit I don't know what the word means. What is this McGuffin?

Well, Hitchcock says the word comes from some Scottish anecdote, and he uses it to identify something that simply puts the plot into motion. It's not important in itself.

I understand, but is the McGuffin a person or an object?

That's irrelevant. For example, we can interpret The Return *as a tale of father's journey to retrieve this box—the McGuffin—but that's not really important; what really matters is the interaction between father and sons.*

Ah, so the McGuffin, the box here, is a pseudo-objective.

Exactly!

[*Cineaste*, XXIX, 2, 2004]

Last Resort

If they are less than A-list features, few Russian films get to Western screens, so there is little reason why we should be acquainted with Dina Korzun, a popular Russian actress who is the greatest asset of *Last Resort* (2000), a low-budget English film that is stunning in its simplicity, and in which everyone and mostly everything is superb, and superbly understated.

Korzun brings pathos and a quiet dignity to a film that could easily have been a documentary. Its Polish-born director, Pawel

Pawlikowski, in fact started in documentary cinema before turning to fiction, and some of *Last Resort* has the feel and look of a good, arty news documentary—what with its very tight close-ups, and the cool, unadorned naturalism of its hand-held camera, not to mention the important issues addressed. Or it could easily have been a powerful, politically weighted protest film highlighting the indignities experienced by aliens applying for refugee status in England (or, say, Belgium, as in the Dardennes brothers' *La promesse*, 1996). But Pawlikowski is not the Dardennes or Ken Loach. In his film matters of the heart concern him more than exposing the cruelties of bureaucratic rigidity—although, Pawlikowski's expressed disclaimers aside, we can't help noticing the cruelty and rigidity.

Two people looking for love come together accidentally in the seedy terrain of a "designated holding area" by the sea for political asylum seekers. Graham Greene meets Russian desperation. The setting is not Brighton, but "Stonehaven" (the film was shot in Margate on the Kentish coast), and "Tanya" (Korzun) is no criminal or spy or courier, but a single, twice-divorced mother from Moscow coming to London with her feisty ten-year-old son to meet "Mark"—the Englishman who promised marriage—her "fiancé," she explains confidently at passport control. In the Russian film, *Land of the Deaf* (1998, directed by Valery Todorovsky), Korzun is a deaf nightclub stripper who reveals her fantasy of a utopian realm for only the deaf, where harmony and sisterhood prevail. In *Last Resort*, Utopia is the idealized West, and a Mark, unlike the chauvinist, alcoholic boors back home, will transport a Russian woman there. In this case, Tanya seems really to have fallen for Mark; he wasn't just her ticket to Utopia. In the Russian film, Korzun, loose-limbed and leggy, is animated, loud, aggressive. But a transformed Korzun shows her acting versatility in *Last Resort*, where she is contained, still, withdrawn, and willing to endure pain. She wears her hair in a Garbo cut, and with her thin, arched eyebrows over expressive, suspicious eyes, she even resembles Garbo. Lucky guy, Mark. But of course—whether cad or fool—he never materializes, and Tanya, along with her savvy preadolescent "Artyom" (Artyom Strelnikov), is beached; the two are refugees thrown together in a global ethnic and national mix at a desolate seaside.

Here is another 'documentary' theme—the plight of Russian

women, or others from Eastern Europe, hungry to escape the degraded and disoriented post-Soviet scene, enticed by 'employment agents' to the alluring West, only to be coerced into prostitution or lap dancing. Pawlikowski echoes that theme in one of the film's wonderfully realized sequences. Tanya is spotted by an online porn producer who notices her "gorgeous cheekbones" and tries to recruit her to perform for his web-cam. She rebuffs him at first, but later, anxious to earn some money, she agrees to give it a try. ("Les," the producer, is well played with smarmy realism by the real-life porn impresario, Lindsey Honey.) When it comes time to perform—with a lollipop and a teddy bear—Tanya breaks down in tears. But Les comes around again to pay her for the incomplete stint, especially since the live, interactive cyberaudience "loved you, the crying schoolgirl act." (That audience, Les has told her, is global—everywhere from "Saudi Arabia to Pakistan"—thus adding several more nice documentary-like contemporary references, globalization and the Internet, to the film.)

Tanya tries to keep Les out of view, but the scene is witnessed by her embarrassed son, and by an angry "Alfie" (Paddy Considine), another kind of marginal person, a loser populating this dispirited Greeneland, who befriends the desperate Tanya, tries to show her the ropes and is drawn to her romantically. Considine plays him perfectly as a sensitive ex-con on the mend who runs the local bingo evenings and manages a cheap-thrills game arcade, called—what else?—"The Dreamland Fun Park." In one of the two misfiring indulgences of the film—an unnecessary, borrowed genre convention—Alfie attacks the porn king and wrecks his studio in wrath over his attempted corruption of Tanya. The other: Artyom falls among some young drifters; he steals, smokes, and drinks himself sick. (Still, another good subject for a documentary—the unfortunate effects of culture shock on the immigrant young.)

The painful moodiness of the film hangs over the tender liaison unfolding between Tanya and Alfie like a fog rolling in from the sea. Pawlikowski and his cinematographer Ryszard Lenczewski make the most of the dreary land- and seascapes with long shots, often from high overhead, emphasizing the loneliness of those below, seen from a distance. They use color subtly, as well—a deep blue tint at sea, a glowing red beside a campfire. Then there is the depressing local architecture. Several times we see a horizon disfigured by ugly, massive cooling towers (another subject for the "documentary").

The bare apartment Tanya and Artyom are housed in is on the upper floor of a grim, high-rise building that dominates the region, and could just as well be one of those ungainly tenement-like specimens hastily thrown up in Moscow and other Soviet cities to ease the housing shortage, especially during the Khrushchev years. Maybe that is precisely what Tanya is thinking as she confronts her unsought lodgings with that beautiful, impassive face on which the camera lingers. The irony is apparent here: Surprise! Welcome to the affluent West of your dreams, Tanya! (More material for that documentary.)

Tanya, like most Russians, is used to adversity. But "Stonehaven," where she is told she will be consigned for a year and a half while her application is processed, is too much for her to handle. Pawlikowski augments the natural bleakness of the place with some fictionalized, Orwellian features. Barbed wire, guard dogs, police patrols, and surveillance-video cameras ring the area; phone calls are not easy to make, and there is no train service at the station. Dead End. No Exit. (Or, Last Resort). But thanks to the resourcefulness and loving attention of Alfie, Tanya and her son manage to escape. Russian endurance and the kindness of a stranger, in a way, triumph over Oceana and Greeneland.

But the sad, existential character of the film—and it all seems so real—would be violated by a formulaic happy ending, and there is none here. I won't reveal what the ending is, except to note that Pawlikowski is a master of the understatement. One sequence in particular is striking for his (and his editor's) talent, and could serve as a good example for film students wishing to work emotional distress into a story without melodramatic excess or swelling music; almost off camera, in fact. (Pop tunes, the mega-hit "Downtown" among them, are heard on the soundtrack, but the original music by Max de Wardener with Rowan Oliver is a minimalist, recurring syncopation nicely complementing the edginess of the action.) Tanya, struggling with the only working phone around, makes several attempts to reach Mark with her pleas for deliverance, but only speaks to his answering machine. When she finally makes contact, her eyes light up and, then, a jump cut to Tanya in her grubby apartment sobbing, her son trying to console her; he never believed in her English Romeo, anyway. We know, without hearing or seeing Mark, what brutal news he has delivered.

Some serious, large themes refracted through a simple, straightforward tale of personal disappointment and frustration—or is it the other way around?—are the stuff of this enormously appealing, very moving film.

[*Cineaste*, XXVI, 3, 2001]

Buttons, Buttons, Who's got the Workers?
A Note on the (Missing) Working Class in Late- and Post-Soviet Russian Cinema

"Farewell to the Working Class?" was the title of a scholarly controversy in an issue of the journal ILWCH (International and Working-Class History). The title could also serve to introduce an aspect of modern Russian cinema, in both its Soviet and post-Soviet forms—the disappearance of the working class and working-class heroes from their once prominent place on Soviet screens. This is an impression gleaned from a sampling of many films, probably the best and most important ones by any measure, and not from an exhaustive survey based on a statistical and content analysis of the whole Russian film corpus turned out over the last decades. (Soviet film production was substantial during the first part of that period, peaking at over three hundred titles in 1991, but then plummeted to double digits in the immediate post-Soviet years.) Would such a survey confirm or disprove the impression? This "Note" stresses the disappearing act and offers some possible explanations. When workers reappear, they are far from heroic. In some sense, Russian cinema paralleled the course of Soviet life and society, from beginning to end, and after.

A strange thing happened when I took up the subject of workers in recent Russian cinema. I couldn't find them, or if I found them, their representation was not especially positive. What happened to the workers in the films of the workers' state, or the once workers' state?

What happened to those heroic figures—faces shining, the future in their eyes, spotlighted in mass array or individualized—that we all know from the classics of old Soviet cinema, from the great silent films of Sergei Eisenstein (*Strike*) and Vsevolod Pudovkin, (*The End of St. Petersburg* and *Mother*) to the Grigori Alexandrov musicals of the 1930s (*Volga, Volga* and *The Shining Path*, sometimes known as *Tanya*), with much in between and later? There were times when the worker-hero theme was overshadowed by or coexisted with other state-mandated genres. Patriotic-historical subjects gained prominence in the late 1930s with the gathering of European war clouds (*Alexander Nevsky, Peter I, Minin and Pozharsky*) and later (most notably, *Ivan the Terrible*, but also *Suvorov* and *Kutuzov*). The Great Patriotic War (as World War Two is known) also generated at the time memorable battlefield films like *Zoya* and *The Rainbow*. The figure of Josef Stalin himself monopolized all heroism, leaving little room for others in the sparse film output after the war (*The Fall of Berlin, The Unforgettable Year 1919, The Battle of Stalingrad*).

Ordinary folk, not necessarily workers, were the heroes of films from the de-Stalinizing period of "The Thaw," which also saw the revival of the war genre in rather different, more human form in such films as *The Cranes Are Flying* and *Ballad of a Soldier*. Ideologically correct directors like Alexander Zarkhi could still evoke the "beauty of the workers' world" in his *Heights* (1957), but such films are not the ones we remember.[1]

None of the great directors and their great films of the 1960s through the mid-1980s, the truly Golden Age of Soviet cinema—Andrei Tarkovsky, Andrei Konchalovsky, Nikita Mikhalkov, Alexei Guerman, Gleb Panfilov, Sergei Paradzhanov, Georgi Shengelaya—were particularly concerned with worker themes and characters as such, and certainly not disposed to treat the problem of workers as a class in the manner of contemporary British, Italian, and French cinema, or even of Hollywood, for that matter. (Compare *Matewan, Hoffa, Norma Rae*, and the independent documentaries *Harlan County USA* and *Roger and Me*, to name only a few of many US productions on worker themes.) Of course, these "class conscious" films of the class struggle are set in the capitalist West, but I can think of no Soviet film that broaches worker themes on the level of, say, Andrzej Wajda's *Man of Marble* from Poland, or Pal Gabor's *Angi Vera* from

Hungary, films that raise the problems and contradictions of workers in purportedly socialist societies with dramatic eloquence.

Andrei Tarkovsky's student film, *The Steamroller and the Violin* (1960), has a worker-driver as a main character, but the director's purposes here are lyrical and humane, foreshadowing his later work with decidedly nonworker themes. Andrei Konchalovsky's epic *Siberiade* (1979) concludes with an oil-field adventure centering on some roustabouts (one of them played brilliantly by his brother Nikita Mikhalkov), but the film is devoted primarily to the ideas of respect for nature's beauty and the preservation of old Russian culture. Significantly, a tractor, once the proud symbol of Soviet agricultural and industrial modernization, here knocks down a beautifully crafted ancient village gate. In Elem Klimov's similarly themed *Farewell* (1982), based on the angry novella by Valentin Rasputin about the drowning of an old Siberian island-village in the name of progress—a hydroelectric station—a bulldozer unsuccessfully rams a wonderfully grand and ageless tree marked for razing. Gleb Panfilov did offer another version of Maxim Gorky's *Mother* (as had Mark Donskoy earlier), but, interestingly, he chose another Gorky novel for a fine but little known film, *Vassa* (1983), a melodrama set among the prerevolutionary Russian bourgeoisie (*kupechestvo*). His most recent effort is a saga of the last Romanovs, just as Elem Klimov's shelved *Agoniya* (1975, released in 1985, known abroad as *Rasputin*) pictured Nicholas and Alexandra in a sympathetic, tragic light—a common evaluation among Russians today, offsetting old official Soviet views ("Nicholas the Bloody"). Alexei Gherman's masterpiece, *My Friend Ivan Lapshin* (1983, released 1985) has a provincial policeman as its likable, pathetic hero, while his last film, the nightmarish, phantasmagorical *Khrustalyov, My Car!*, throws a blinding light on the last days of Stalin, as experienced by a highly placed surgeon. Nikita Mikhalkov's recent work includes the Oscar-winning *Burnt by the Sun*, an evocation of the Great Terror of the 1930s in a Chekhovian-cum-Soviet setting as it affected a Russian Civil War hero of plebeian origins and his gentry family by marriage. A comical, luckless truck driver shows up repeatedly in the film, literally riding around in circles only to be liquidated by an NKVD bullet. The same director's lavish *Barber of Siberia*—the most expensive Russian film ever, and as yet unreleased in the United

States—is a paean to Imperial Russia in the time of Alexander III (played with—unintended?—comic flair by Mikhalkov himself).

Village themes, folkloric epics, screen renditions of Russian classics, and diverse portraits of contemporary or historical figures (or of the spiritual and the self: Tarkovsky), or the undefinable, deeply personal visions of Alexander Sokurov and Kira Muratova characterize the work of the great directors as well as the work of many lesser ones. But there are no major worker themes, nor a solid, identifiable working-class genre. One thinks of Sherlock Holmes and his sagacious observation that what was significant about the dog is that it did not bark; in late Soviet film, what is striking about Soviet workers is their absence—as workers, members of a real class with real, acute problems under Soviet socialism.

Sometimes, when we see a worker on the screen, the picture is not altogether flattering, particularly when we enter the *glasnost* period of late Soviet times. Earlier, to take a couple of examples from notable films, what do we learn about the Soviet worker—once the hero, now the fall guy? In Vladimir Menshov's very popular *Moscow Does Not Believe in Tears* (1979, another Oscar-winner), one of the three provincial women, Tonia (Raisa Riazanova), who come to Moscow to better their lives settles for a modest happiness by marrying a fellow construction worker, a reliable, good-natured, and friendly sort. The couple bears several children and tends to the vegetable and fruit patch of the husband's parents' small *dacha*: This is a quiet Soviet life over a period of twenty years, roughly the late 1950s to the late 1970s; there is nothing either negative or heroic here.

The real heroine of *Moscow Does Not Believe in Tears* is upwardly mobile and transcends her working-class life. Katya (Vera Alentova) works in a metals plant; a funny scene there parodies the canned Soviet TV profile of a model worker, but she speaks out on camera about low wages for fitters. Despite an unsatisfactory affair that left her an unmarried mother—her lover's mother dismissed her as lower class—she studies hard at a chemistry institute and moves up an enterprise ladder to a directorship, which brings with it those Soviet luxuries (wow!), a car and a nice apartment, very different from the workers' dorm she lived in when she first came to Moscow. What's more, the man of her dreams is a special kind of worker, no ordinary worker for her; the unorthodox Gosha (Alexei Batalov), a laboratory mechanic beloved by the scientists he works for, affects a gruff working-class style, but can cite Diocletian. He may don an apron to fix dinner—greeted with jaw-dropping amazement in the Soviet household—but he also insists on traditional, male-dominant values to govern his relationship with Katya. He is mortified to learn that she is an executive and earns more than he does, becoming so upset that it prompts a drinking binge. Executive or not, the seemingly liberated Katya accepts Gosha's rules of the game in order to keep him.

Alcohol figures in—and ruins—the marriage of the third girlfriend in the film. The high-spirited Ludmila (Irina Muravieva), who has her eyes set on anyone of high social standing, be he an officer or a professor, succeeds in a glamorous enough catch—he is working-class in origin, but he is also a famous hockey star. Sadly, he descends into alcoholism, presented here as a consequence of his fame, but it is also one of the unfortunate and enduring features of Soviet (and post-Soviet) working-class mores. All in all, *Moscow Does Not Believe in Tears* offers a generally appealing view of Soviet urban life in the Leonid Brezhnev years, complete with a happy ending for the central couple, Katya and Gosha. However, the darker side is also revealed, and in the course of the narrative one is left with the impression, so different from earlier Soviet idealizations, that the working-class life is something to escape *from*.

The milieus of Georgi Danelia's lesser-known but superior film, *Autumn Marathon* (1979), are different from Menshov's. The story takes place in Leningrad, and its main character is the harried and hapless Buzykin (Oleg Basilashvili), a translator and university lecturer who is carrying on, with very painful contortions, an extra-marital affair with a younger woman (Marina Neyelova) who works as a typist (the office worker as home wrecker?). Two vignettes bring us face-to-face with workers outside of the intelligentsia orbit: one, a brief episode on a thoroughfare Buzykin is crossing, the other, in his apartment. In the first, Buzykin is almost run down by a van, whose boorish driver blames him for the mishap and even accuses him of denting his vehicle. In the other, a working-class neighbor, played with pungent comic brilliance by the late Evgeny Leonov, barges in on Buzykin and a colleague at work at home, and insists on fueling the encounter with toasts of vodka. He then persuades them to go mushroom picking, an expedition that ends with Buzykin's trusting colleague, a foreign scholar hungry for the Russian experience, winding up in an overnight lock-up for intoxication. The office-worker girlfriend aside, does *Autumn Marathon* present emblematic miniatures—through the eyes of the intelligentsia to be sure—of the Soviet worker as either surly lout or amusing goof-off?

Of course, the intelligentsia are the filmmakers, and whether we perceive them as artists who are conscious or unconscious conveyers of societal moods, or as a caste with their own independent point of view and prejudices, their resulting work certainly doesn't idealize the worker—fair enough—but neither does it take up his cause. As a state enterprise, Soviet cinema would hardly be permitted to produce film polemics about worker exploitation in the Soviet Union, or polemics about the real meaning of the so-called social contract, best expressed in the folk formula, "We pretend to work, and they pretend to pay us." But instead of a little sympathy, within permissible boundaries, filmmakers extended to workers an indifference at best, or an attitude toward them as the "dark people" of a modernized Russia, replacing the peasantry of the old society in that role.[2]

The coarse realities of Soviet life, belying the ever-growing triumphalist official rhetoric, constituted one of the main preoccupations of *glasnost* cinema in the Mikhail Gorbachev years and after the collapse of the Soviet Union itself.[3] These *"chernukha"* films (daily life painted in black), as the genre was dubbed, was a mark of emancipation from state-regulated norms that always insisted on positive portraits of "Soviet reality." (Certain foreign films were often banned because they showed ordinary workers in capitalist societies abroad living in what were, by Soviet standards, enviable material conditions.) Vasily Pichul's *Little Vera* (1988), the most popular film of the epoch—and not because of its explicit sex scene, a first for Soviet cinema—is perhaps the best example of this neorealist genre. But rather than sympathize with the working class and call attention to the victimization of the class in the class-ridden, exploitative, elitist, and authoritarian ensemble of political and economic institutions that structured Soviet society, this film, like many others, positions workers as part of the general Soviet problem, a degraded social order without culture, without soul, whose most prominent outward features are alcohol and violence.

At the center of *Little Vera* is a dysfunctional working-class family in the grimy southern port city of Mariupol (once called Zhdanov) and its disconsolate eponymous heroine (Natalya Negoda). Alienated from her family, drifting into promiscuous sex, accustomed to watching the working-class guys brawling at gatherings of the young, without clear career directions, Vera is a stand-in for the Soviet provincial teens living out harsh, barren, dead-end lives. Significantly, the young man (Andrei Sokolov) she casually marries is from a professional intelligentsia family (or so he implies, perhaps as a put-on), and has nothing but contempt for Vera's working-class household. He and her hard-drinking father (a truck-driver, Yuri Nazarov) fail to hit it off from the start, and their relationship ends with violence: In humiliated rage, Vera's father drives a kitchen knife into his son-in-law, nearly killing him. Vera's response to all the misfortune is attempted suicide. This is not a very pretty picture, but it is a realistic one, not just metaphoric, according to the many people I asked about it when I traveled in the Soviet Union in 1988–1989. (A young Communist Party official in Yaroslavl exclaimed to me: "110 percent true!")

If Pichul is brutally frank in his portrait and not particularly sympathetic to his working-class characters—they are simply part of the bleak Soviet scenery—an extraordinary post-Soviet film by Sergei Livnev, *Hammer and Sickle* (1994), offers more insight into the nature of rulers and ruled in Soviet life. The setting is historical (Moscow in the late 1930s) and the director's general aim is to lampoon Soviet political culture, and much else, the working class included. The subject is Stalinism, manifested through some unusual goings-on revolving around a sex-change operation ordered by the tyrant—Evdokia becomes Evdokim (Aleksei Serebryakov). Stalin and his Beria-like sidekick reverse their support of the experiment, and leave Evdokim to fend for himself in a Moscow where the metro is being built, soon to be one of the proud, gleaming products of Soviet industrialization during the Five-Year Plans. Reconciling *herself* to his new *himself*, Evdokim works hard as a Stakhanovite groundhog, attends evening classes, and is celebrated as a worker-hero among whose prizes are a peasant-hero wife (a tractor driver, naturally; played by Alla Kliuka) and—the ultimate Soviet reward—a handsome roadster, a convertible no less. He and his wife even become the real-life models for Mukhina's famous monumental steel couple, the collective-farm peasant and the worker, their arms holding aloft the sickle and the hammer. (The world-famous statue is also the logo of Mosfilm Studio: a sly dig by the director?)

This worker-saga is recounted by Livnev in a brilliant, mimetically accurate parody of the Soviet documentary in all its kitschy, hortatory, and mendacious glory. But the totalitarian state, and Stalin himself, have claims on Evdokim, and permit him no real private life, and certainly not one deviating from the Party-State agenda scripted for him. Stalin denies Evdokim's assertion to be himself, a man of free will, and refuses his request to leave his official post and leave his loveless marriage. In a violent confrontation with the tyrant, Evdokim is shot and paralyzed, suffering even further frustration as a now speechless, bedridden propaganda icon of a new type shown off to foreign communist and fellow-traveling dignitaries. Livnev's knowing, dark satire is a magnificent, idiosyncratic portrait of the real power relationships between workers and the state in the Soviet workers' state. And in Livnev's bureaucratically "deformed workers' state," to use Trotskyist analytic lingo, where some workers are privileged, especially in the sphere of material consumption, so long as they abide by the rules of the system, there is actually a worker rebellion (the Trotskyist will-o-the-wisp) in Evdokim's symbolic assertion of manhood, futile, of course.[4]

Ultimately, the Soviet system was overthrown not by the exploited workers, but by a section of the ruling elite who embarked on a reform program that led—can one say, *inevitably?*—to the implosion of the system. I know of no Russian films, documentaries or features that take up these issues within this framework. The *glasnost* and post-*glasnost* fiction films, i.e., late and post-Soviet cinema, portray workers according to *chernukha* norms, or in the fantasy genre. Filmmakers had abided by official ideology in different ways, according to the epoch, in their treatment of workers on screen. The pre-Stalinist classic silent films were made when the embers of revolutionary fervor were still warm, not long after Great October; we see the worker as revolutionary. Later, Stalinist film necessarily idealized the worker, builder of socialism, in Soviet society. In the considerably more relaxed ideological atmosphere of post-Stalinism through the Brezhnevian era (the period later self-servingly characterized as "*zastoi*," or stagnation), the studios and their leading filmmakers no longer went in for idealization, but still could not tell it as it is, and more or less ignored workers or worker themes.

When the censorious chains were finally broken, the resulting film portraits of the worker's personality and working-class life in contemporary Russia or in the Soviet past were colored in very dark (because very real) hues. Some of the better known films in this vein came from the directors Pavel Lungin, Yuri Mamin, and Valery Ogorodnikov. Ogorodnikov's powerful *Barak* (the basic one-story wooden structure housing workers in communal conditions) is set in postwar Central Asia, where exiles mingle with ordinary workers.[5] There are some light moments in the episodic film, but crime and violence seem to be the depressing norm. Ogorodnikov's 1999 film recalls another, earlier work set in a *barak*, this time in the Soviet Far East in a labor-camp zone that included Japanese prisoners of war—Vitaly Kanevsky's gut-wrenching *Freeze, Die, Come to Life* (1989). Yuri Mamin's burlesque, *Sideburns* (1990), pokes fun at political reactionaries who seek to revive a style of life modeled on Alexander Pushkin's time; naturally, they recruit working-class skinheads to their cause.

Working-class skinheads—violence-prone, xenophobic, and anti-Semitic—populate Pavel Lungin's *Luna Park* (1992), his follow-up film to his successful *Taxi Blues* (1990). The latter was something of a hit in the West as well, not simply, I think, because of its sex and violence, but from Lungin's layered portrait of a Soviet working-class character, the taxi driver (Peter Zaichenko) figuring in the title, a strong presence whose alternately brutal and sensitive disposition both attracts and repels his accidental buddy, a Jewish jazz musician (Peter Mamonov)—the feelings are mutual. Lungin describes his last film, *The Wedding* (of a coal miner), a Golden Palm entry at Cannes, 2000, as somehow "joyous," and disavows any "coded social or political message," but, once again, the dreary environment of a small town not far from Moscow is marked by crime, alcoholism, police corruption, and out of wedlock births. We are in the post-Soviet time of free markets and new class structures and disparities here, but the tableau might just as well represent provincial working-class life before 1991. Such is the portrait offered by Tomasz Tot in his *Children of the Iron Gods* (1993), set in Soviet times at a big metallurgical plant in the Urals (Magnitogorsk?). Tot mixes the inevitable brawls and boozing with some high adventures on the steppe, but, sadly, all roads lead up blind alleys.

Afterword

Yes, Soviet socialism led workers up a blind alley, not onto the promised *Shining Path*. At first, and for a long time, Soviet filmmakers did their best to bend their art to revolutionary goals, to build socialism, advance industrialization, hail collectivization, and bless the existing sociopolitical order, its leaders not least. Workers had starring roles in such cinema. When ideological vigilance weakened, or ideology failed altogether, workers fell off the stage. Directors lost interest in them, or even showed them up with a veiled contempt. The best of them turned to the high-minded themes that normally inhabited the mental world of the Russian intelligentsia, where mere issues of working-class life had little place. The old elitism dividing *us*, the intelligentsia, from *them*, the dark people below, reasserted itself in a new way. But there was always another side to that elitism, a kind of *intelligence oblige*—many intellectuals, filmmakers among them, needed to be engaged and speak for the voiceless. The *glasnost* and post-*glasnost* cinema of exposure did just that. On screens playing to millions, such cinema showed what working-class life was really like, then and now. It also made for better films.[6]

Did Russian audiences, workers among them, appreciate that? A middle-aged woman selling tickets at a theater in Stavropol, where *Little Vera* was playing in 1988, told me she thought the film was "disgusting." The following year a Leningrad taxi cab driver opined, "Who wants to see such ugliness on the screen? We have enough of it in real life!" Perhaps, as with film audiences everywhere, the masses want the Hollywood dream factory, not the Magnitogorsk steel-works. A mirror to working-class life is not necessarily what the working class wants to see. Russian viewer surveys and opinion polls seem to suggest the truth of this seeming paradox. When the formerly state-subsidized Russian film industry nearly collapsed after 1991 and the new free market conditions for film distribution beckoned films from abroad, Russians, when they went to the movies at all, showed a preference for Western, and especially American, films. This was a natural, understandable reaction to decades of state-mandated restrictions on foreign imports. At the risk of sounding like some culture commissar myself, I would hope Russian filmmakers turn to serious consideration of working-class life, not for the cheap thrills of *chernukha*, but for analysis and enlightenment. Is that asking for too much of a medium that has always valued entertainment over sociology? But where else can we pose that ideal if not in Russia, where the social purposes of art have always been enshrined?

---

[1] Josephine Woll, *Real Images: Soviet Cinema and The Thaw* (London, 2000), 67–70.

[2] Dmitry Shlapentokh expresses this point another way: "While the Soviet regime maintained the notion that it represented the masses, in its providing film producers with a sense of economic freedom from market forces, it was actually providing them with an independence from the masses. This helped instill in Soviet intellectuals, including film producers, a sense of elitism, which in many ways was responsible for the creation of movies (e.g., Tarkovskii's) that became real masterpieces." Dmitry Shlapentokh, "Soviet Union/Russia," in the *International Movie Industry*, ed. Gorham Kindem (Carbondale, IL, 2000), 183–84.

[3] The best examination of *glasnost* cinema is Anna Lawton, *Kinoglasnost: Soviet Cinema in Our Time* (Cambridge, 1992).

[4] Unfortunately, Livnev's *Hammer and Sickle* has never been released in the United States.

[5] Boris Yeltsin spent his boyhood in these *baraks*. His biographer offers this description: "The most common variety of communal lodgings in urban Russia at the time, *baraks* were a veritable institution that shaped two generations of Russians. As much a fixture of 'socialist industrialization' as the gulag, these structures became an indelible part of Soviet popular culture. Like hundreds of thousands of other *baraks* throughout Russia, Yeltsin's consisted of a long corridor, into which opened twenty rooms—one per family. Behind the *barak* were a wooden privy and the well from which the tenants drew water." In one of the *baraks* four Yeltsins and a she-goat "slept together on the floor, pressed close to one another." Leon Aron, *Yeltsin: A Revolutionary Life* (New York, 2000), 6.

⁶ Soviet and post-Soviet documentaries are another subject, and deserve separate attention, but the generalizations offered above about feature film patterns serve as well for the documentaries. *Glasnost* documentaries, for example, opened up a whole range of previously taboo themes—the poverty of village life; prostitution; drug addiction; pollution of land, air, and water; frankness about the Afghanistan war; and the "blank spots" of Soviet history—but no special attention settled on the industrial process, workers, or the working class. Younger notable Russian documentarists—Viktor Kossakovsky, Vitaly Mansky, Sergei Dvortsevoy, among them—have set their talented sights on villagers, Central Asian nomads, and diverse biographical subjects, but not on workers. Contemporary worker themes are often found in the work of some Western documentarists. See, for example, *Perestroika from Below* by Daniel J. Walkowitz and Barbara Abrash, about the striking coal miners of Donetsk in 1989; and *Magnitogorsk—Forging the New Man* by Pieter Jan Smit (1996), which looks at Magnitogorsk today, and traces the fate of some of the worker-heroes once hailed in *Song of the Heroes* (1932) by the celebrated Dutch director Joris Ivens. (Both are available from First Run/Icarus Films, New York).

[*International Labor and Working-Class History*, No. 59, Spring 2001, pp. 52-59 © 2001 International Labor and Working-Class History, Inc. Reprinted with permission.]

SHORT TAKES

4

More *chernukha* from the Russians. The term derives from the Russian for "black," but shouldn't be confused with *film noir*. *Chernukha* applies to the late-Soviet and post-Soviet film genre dwelling on the really dismal sides of daily life. And things can't get much bleaker than in this first feature (2005) by director Ilya Khrzhanovsky (son of the celebrated animation filmmaker), with a script by the notorious Vladimir Sorokin, lately hounded by Putin's young moral vigilantes for his purportedly pornographic fiction. The time is roughly the present, highlighting all the familiar troubles besetting the disjointed life of post-Soviet Russia—alcoholism, prostitution, poverty, the archaic village in its death throes, suicide, the wealthy "New Russian" entrepreneur. Into the mix, Khrzhanovsky adds strong doses of the absurd, beginning with the film's title. For fun, try spotting all the things adding up to the number four, starting with the four stray dogs at the jarring and disorienting opening. The film relies on the hand-held camera, very tight close-ups and long tracking shots for its visuals, and grating industrial sounds at very high volume on the audio side. After a fascinating after-hours exchange of made-up stories by three strangers at a chance encounter in a bar (the most agreeable part of the film), the focus shifts to one of them, a hooker whose sister has choked to death in a freak accident involving dolls made from masticated bread. Her journey to her native village for the funeral is capped by a long grief-filled episode including graveside keening and orgiastic drinking and scarfing with village crones who bare and flaunt their overripe bosoms, and a pagan-tinged ritual by fire. We meet the two other barroom strangers again, and their fates are equally bizarre. Ironic, bizarre, entirely consistent with the shock strategies of the *chernukha* mode, and—here's the sad rub—very believable, too.

[*Cineaste*, XXXI, 4, 2006]

Anna Lawton Trailer, 2:
Imaging Russia 2000: Film and Facts

Don't let the bland title mislead you. Anna Lawton's latest book is not some kind of almanac of cinematic and other information for Russia in 2000. It is, rather, an imaginative amalgam of autobiography with film analysis that incidentally offers a way to understand an important transitional period in post-Soviet life and times.

The author was on hand during that period, 1991-1996, and strategically placed. She was already an established scholar and teacher with a long *résumé* covering Russian cultural themes—cinema, most notably. (Hers is the definitive English-language study of *glasnost* film, *Kinoglasnost: Soviet Cinema in Our Time*, 1992, revised and updated as *Before the Fall: Soviet Cinema in the Gorbachev Years*, 2004.) For *Imaging Russia*, she drew on her experience living and working in Moscow, with a position at the Press and Culture section of the American Embassy, and as film columnist for *The Moscow Times*. She has always worn her well researched scholarship lightly, with crisp and clear writing, but never more so, nor more engagingly, than in this study.

Presented here is the fate of the Russian film industry after the Soviet collapse, together with an insightful survey of some 80 films belonging to that period (virtually all from the '90s; chronologically, the last is Alexander Sokurov's *Russian Ark*, 2002). The films are arranged in several clusters that parallel particular developments and moods in the new Russia. For example, in a process that began with the Gorbachev years, and took on steam thereafter, the past was liberated from Party dogmas, and books, periodicals, the media and grass-roots organizations subjected historical themes and personalities to revisionist interpretations. Cinema was an important voice both echoing and amplifying that endeavor. Lawton shows how films like Nikita Mikhalkov's *Burnt by the Sun* (which won a best foreign-film Oscar in 1994), or Gleb Panfilov's *The Romanovs: The Crowned Family* (2001) explored old topics like Stalinist terror and the last days of the last tsar from novel angles. Cinema was also central, she notes, in the effort to re-establish pride in the Russian, pre-Soviet past, with Mikhalkov's *Barber of Siberia*

(1998) heading the list, though not very successfully crafted or well received by critics.

Other "film and facts" correlations cover such issues as the wealth and glitz of the "New Russians" of Moscow in the Chapter, "New Babylon" (e.g., Alexander Zeldovich's *Moskva*, 1999); the search for new identities and new environments, whether at home or abroad, in the Chapter, "Faraway in Space and Time" (e.g., Lidya Bobrova's *In That Land*, 1997); the confrontation with an often grotesque, rather Gogolesque reality in "Laughter through Tears" (e.g., Eldar Ryazanov's *Old Nags*, 1999). What enriches these surveys is Lawton's own encounter with history-making events, or her own confrontations with Moscow reality, whether it was witnessing the attempted *coup* of August, 1991, or hunting for an apartment. Her writing here is just as appealing as her film analysis and criticism, and just as informative.

Of her film criticism, aside from minor differences about an interpretation here or there, I would say she, in common with other scholars and critics who specialize in Russian cinema, is over-generous with praise for what the studios have been turning out. This is an act of mercy for, let's face it, some Sokurov excepted, those films have on the whole failed with good reason to revive Russia's reputation in world cinema. But, what with abundant young talent in a dynamic society, that day is sure to come. One hopes the Putin regime or its successor does not try imposing political and ideological barriers to that development. Whatever the course of Russian cinema, one also hopes Lawton will continue publishing her valuable chronicles.

[*Slavonica* Vol. XIII, 1, 2007]

CHAPTER VI

A Concluding Montage Across Time and Borders

A genuine reckoning with the Soviet past never took place. The period of "disgraced monuments" (see below) gave way to a renewed sense of official and popular confidence throughout the Russian Federation, thanks in great part to oil revenues in the economic sphere, and from the very firm, quasi-authoritarian style of the Putin leadership in the political realm. Neither sector rests on sure foundations; that confidence and Russian national pride and patriotism could suffer as well. Meanwhile, a certain security has developed in the film world now backed by the reliable source of state funding, and co-production support from abroad, mainly from Europe. The two decades since the Soviet collapse have not seen any grand directorial debuts, nor have any Russian films made a truly global impact. Closest, in both senses, were Timur Bekmambetov and his sci-fi thrillers, Night Watch *and* Day Watch, *each, in my view, of dubious quality. Established filmmakers continue to produce, dwelling on new and old themes. The general mood leans to the gloomy side. Sokurov addressed the Chechen war in his unique way (*Alexandra*), and continued his projected tetralogy on men of power with* The Sun *(Emperor Hirohito in 1945); Balabanov resorted to the bleakest of the* chernukha *mode for his pitch-black evocation of life in late Soviet times as war raged in Afghanistan (*Cargo 200*); Lungin reinterpreted, rather lamely, when measured against Eisenstein's version, the reign of Ivan the Terrible in* Tsar; *Soloviev turned to Tolstoy for a very vapid rendition of* Anna Karenina—*Russian literary* classics have always been a familiar source for Russian filmmakers, and more successful in this vein was Shakhnazarov's **Ward No. 6**, *a modernized variation on the great Chekhov tale; and Mikhalkov offered a self-centered replay of Sidney Lumet's* Twelve Angry Men *in his* 12. *New figures have appeared, among them Fyodor Bondarchuk, with his smash hit on the Afghanistan war,* Ninth Company *(which converted the Soviet defeat into a source of Russian honor). The respected animation specialist, Andrei Khrzhanovsky, directed one of the most imaginative films to emerge from post-Soviet Russia,* A Room and a Half, *an ambitious biographical portrait of the Nobel Laureate poet, Joseph Brodsky.*

As those few examples show, Russian cinema continues, commendably, if not always with winning results, to stretch wide across time and borders—like the films discussed in the Chapter that follows.

Monuments and Musicals as Mementoes of Communism
Disgraced Monuments and East Side Story

The battle of the monuments raged in Moscow in the early '90s. A year-old statue of the last Tsar, Nicholas II, was blown up. Later, explosives at the base of the massive new memorial to Tsar Peter the Great were deactivated before they could send the monument into the Moscow River. (Not a bad idea, according to many Muscovites, for esthetic if not political reasons.) A Romanov Dynasty monument in a Moscow cemetery was also attacked. Neo-communist grouplets took responsibility for these actions, in two of the cases in reaction to all the talk, including hints from the Yeltsin government, about taking Lenin's corpse out of the Mausoleum and giving it a normal "Christian burial." Mainline Communists have called such a thought "blasphemous." The campaign over Lenin's body promises to be the mother of all battles of the monuments.

A perfect introduction to these passionate issues, with intelligent commentary about how Russians remember and un-remember their past, is *Disgraced Monuments*, a documentary film produced by Mark Lewis and Laura Mulvey in 1991-1993, when widespread anti-communist iconoclasm destroyed or removed, among others,

50 of the 60 Lenin memorials in Moscow. As the film shows, there were ample precedents in the other direction. Under the Soviets, when public art—when all art—had a political purpose, monuments of the Old Regime were pulled down or altered in favor of memorializing Red heroes. An obelisk at the Kremlin wall, for example, once listed the names of the Romanov Tsars; in 1918 they were replaced with names of revolutionary thinkers, from Campanella to Plekhanov. The biggest, most notorious case of official vandalism came when Stalin decided to blow up Moscow's imposing Christ the Savior church in 1931 and replace it with a Palace of Soviets skyscraper topped with a gigantic statue of Lenin. The church was blown up—the film includes old footage of the event—although construction problems prevented the skyscraper from going up. But history's cunning cycles are now at work again. To the delight of the Orthodox Church and its believers, and thanks to the efforts of Moscow's energetic mayor, Yuri Luzhkov, Christ the Savior has now been reconstructed and finished in time to celebrate the capital's 850th anniversary. (With uncanny cinematic insight, Eisenstein captured the spirit of such ups and downs in his *October*, aka *Ten Days That Shook The World*, when he has a revolutionary crowd tearing apart the statue of Tsar Alexander III; then in a later sequence he ran the film backwards to reconstruct the statue and mark a reversal in the revolution.)

In *Disgraced Monuments*, there are effective montages of old clips showing the unveiling of countless memorials to Lenin, and of statues of Stalin, who, as someone says, had a "Medusa complex"—he liked turning figures into stone. These sequences are complemented with contemporary scenes of statue-bashing, or of workshops where rows and rows of busts and statuettes gather dust, or of fallen idols lying in the grass of a "Temporary Museum of Totalitarian Art".

Intercut among such images are interviews with curators, critics, and sculptors who decry these post-Soviet festivals of destruction or consignments to the rubbish heap. They are disturbed not necessarily out of political nostalgia for the old regime and its heroes. Sculptors who specialized in Lenin no longer have government commissions, and now have to bid for work in a competitive free market. Naturally, they are upset. And no sculptors, their politics aside, can be happy to see their work wrecked. But there is a deeper criticism, voiced by several figures in the film. How, they ask, is this populist rage against old memorials different from what the Soviets used to do? A healthy national consciousness calls for an honest confrontation with its past, not its obliteration. There is a wonderful episode in the film, drawing on clips shot at the time, of pulling down the monument of Dzerzhinsky, first head of the Cheka, antecedent of the KGB, opposite the fearsome Lubyanka. Crowds gathered round the monument in August, 1991, desecrating it in an atmosphere of carnival. The free-wheeling spirit of 1968 had finally come to the Soviet Union at its deathbed. The critic Viktor Misiano, who was there, rues what followed: the anti-communist Moscow municipal authorities had the monument dismantled. "So removing Dzerzhinsky," he comments, "was a key moment which marked the end of the 'performance' and the start of the new ideology when the mechanism of history began to work again." (On the pedestal where Dzerzhinsky stood lay a stone from the Gulag "as a memorial to the millions of victims of the totalitarian regime.")

This post-ideological, post-modern political critique by Misiano and others has its merits. The crowd, says Misiano, "would have been content to paint [Dzerzhinsky] blue with polka dots... or just putting a Fool's cap on his head or giving him a false nose." Yet from the angle of an ordinary Muscovite, one, say, who had the Gulag or worse in his family biography, wouldn't that have been trivializing the monstrosities of the Soviet regime and one of its notorious representatives? There is no entirely satisfactory answer: leave the monuments where they are? disgrace them with graffiti? tear them down? cart them off to a museum? I'm inclined to at least summarize the issue as Yeltsin did in calling for a referendum on what to do with Lenin's body. "On the one hand," he said of Lenin, "we know that he brought Russia many woes, but on the other hand, this is our history and we can't hide from it."

Cinema forms another kind of monument of the Communist past, one providing a treasure of intact material for understanding popular culture and the state-directed attempts (failures?) to manipulate it. We don't often think of musicals in this regard, but, as the cleverly titled and archly narrated documentary, *East Side Story* (1996), shows, they played an important part in the film histories of the USSR and its fraternal regimes in Eastern Europe. Some forty musicals were produced in Eastern Europe over four decades, and were rarely seen in the West, if at all. Judging from the many clips assembled here, they ranged from the campy agit-prop ("We sing the song of the coal press....") to the slightly more sophisticated fare of beach and rock musicals with Doris Day look-alikes and glamorous dance ensembles. Soviet musicals are really another story; they were not, as the film implies, unknown in the West, especially in the 1930s when audiences everywhere were treated to such endearing pictures of Soviet life as in *Volga, Volga* (1938; Stalin's favorite film), even as the Great Terror tormented the nation. As the fine Russian critic, Maya Turovskaya, points out in one of her many appearances in the documentary, people needed untruths to survive; escapist entertainment was a balm for the wounds of Stalinism.

The excerpts from Eastern European musicals shown here, mainly from East Germany, are often charming enough, though I doubt anyone could sit through the whole films now, save in the interests of research, or for those who saw them originally, for nostalgic reasons. (The East German *Hot Summer of 1968*, featuring Frank Schobel, "the Elvis of the East," was "like a cult film for us kids," comments someone.) The travails of filmmakers and official ideologists to bring out appealing musicals that upheld socialist values are well represented in surveying the work of East Germany's DEFA studios. Dana Ranga, the director and narrator of *East Side Story*, tells us East Germany was "least likely" to host musical film fare, not because the public didn't care for it—far from it; before the Wall went up in 1962, East Germans flocked to Western musicals screened in West Berlin—but because of the hard-line outlook of the leadership. Musicals were a prime example of an unwanted invasion of American pop influences, and "the most flagrant offspring of the capitalist pleasure industry". (*East Side Story* could have done without several staged scenes of grim-faced female commissars mouthing official directives; we get the point without them.)

East German filmmakers, like their earlier Soviet counterparts Grigori Alexandrov and Ivan Pyriev, were asked to entertain, but were boxed in by the imperatives of "education"—read: propaganda. They came up with often resourceful ways out of the dilemma, with results well received by the public. In *My Wife Wants to Sing*

(1958), the musical numbers embroidered the acceptable theme of women's liberation under socialism. No matter that the film was initially attacked for its *"Amerikanismus"*: it went on to become one of the biggest hits of the Eastern Bloc, including in the USSR. Alexandrov had done the same kind of thing in *The Shining Path* (1940), when he cast his wife, the ever idolized singer Lyubov Orlova, as a heroic Stakhanovite textile worker. DEFA's *Midnight Review* (1962) neatly engaged the entertainment-education problem by making that issue the subject of the film. Directors, writers, musicians are shown sweating the problem tunefully:

It's enough to make you tear your hair out
It's easier to wait 10 years for a car
It's simpler to go ice-skating in the desert
Than to make a socialist musical!

"Too hot, too hot to handle," they chant, but all is well at the finale. Not very different, change a venue and a "problem" or two, from what a triumphant Donald O'Connor or Mickey Rooney and Peggy Ryan used to accomplish in the old days of the classic Hollywood musicals. And the East Germans did it with painfully little of the Hollywood technology. A few excerpts from musicals from Poland, Romania, Bulgaria, and Czechoslovakia round out the documentary, with the Czech *Woman on the Rails* (1965) offering the raciest scene of the lot.

Ranga and the film's producer, Andrew Horn, deserve credit not only for looking for and retrieving these musicals, but for crafting *East Side Story* from them into an entertaining film in itself.

[*Cineaste*, XXIII, 2, 1997]

From the Caucasus 1: *Vodka Lemon*

Why do you call it "Vodka Lemon" if it tastes like almonds?, asks a character at the roadside stand that gives the 2003 film its title. Because this is Armenia, replies the vendor in this minimalist village fable by the Kurdish filmmaker Hiner Saleem. Absurdity abounds in the Kurdish community dwelling in woebegone, post-Soviet Armenia, where everyone and everything is shabby, and everyone's relatives and friends are off anywhere—Kazakhstan, Samarkand, Novosibirsk, America—to make ends meet. As in Julie Bertuccelli's *Since Otar Left* (also 2003), set in neighboring post-Soviet Georgia, to which *Vodka Lemon* bears some resemblance, though it is not as subtly crafted, a key figure whom we never see has gone to Paris. The money he is expected to send his ever hopeful father Hamo (Romen Avinian) never arrives; in fact, in keeping with the film's pathetic-amusing twists, it is the son who finally asks papa for money. Like his characters, whose survival skills rely on an abundance of patience, Saleem takes his time in unfolding the narrative, really a succession of short sketches, too often repetitiously, against an always snow covered landscape. (A local bus driver is fond of crooning the French *Tombe la Neige*.) The temperature is icy but much warmth is generated by the characters' good humor and wry acceptance of what fate has thrown their way. None is more endearing than the widower Hamo, with his twinkling eyes and mop of white hair, a shy courtier of the handsome widow (Lala Sarkissian) who sells the Vodka Lemon—and, no surprise, he gets her in the end. Not all is serendipitous, however, in this harsh, economically deprived environment. Saleem's picturesque episodes have an ugly side. As in post-Soviet Russia itself, alcoholism and violence punctuate everyday life. And recourse to prostitution is for some women one avenue for material improvement. It was better in Soviet times, says Hamo; we had everything. Except freedom, counters his friend.

[*Cineaste*, XXX, 2, 2005]

From the Caucasus 2: *Pirosmani*

Bernstein of *Citizen Kane* saw a girl in a white dress only once and never forgot her. I saw Georgi Shengelaya's magical *Pirosmani* (1969) only once many years ago; it made a powerful impression on me, and I never forgot it. Unlike Bernstein, for whom not a month went by without thinking of that girl, I recalled the film only now and

10. *A Family Celebration* by Niko Pirosmani. The director Georgi Shengelaya recreated scenes derived from similar paintings by the artist in the film, *Pirosmani* (1969).

then, promising myself to catch it again at some festival, or at some indie theater or art house that risked some imaginative programming. And surely I could always locate it on video or DVD. None of that ever happened. But thanks to Cineaste's 40th anniversary and the Editors' asking for a special contribution, I made an effort to find it, got hold of a video copy, and watched it again. I was not disappointed.

There have been many bio-pics based on celebrated artists, but Shengelaya's life of the Georgian self-taught painter Niko Pirosmanishvili (1862-1918) is like no other. The same might be said of another Soviet filmmaker's rendition of an artist's life—Andrei Tarkovsky's magnificent *Andrei Rublev* (1966). Both are unconventional portraits, brilliantly designed, but if Tarkovsky gets it across with a kind of complex and feverish, hypnotic realism, Shengelaya recreates a life by appropriating the paintings themselves, inserting them into the minimalist drama or duplicating them or their likenesses as a series of *tableaux vivants*. Art (film) imitating art (paintings). Leafing through a volume of Pirosmani reproductions, one sees how closely Shengelaya followed the paintings themselves.

The result is a film of breathtaking beauty. I can think of only Sergei Paradzhanov's *The Color of Pomegranates* (1970), also based on the life of a creative artist, the medieval Armenian poet, Sayat-Nova, as comparable.

Pirosmani painted in the flat, primitive style, with odd, subdued coloring, and stylized portraiture of people and animals. Shengelaya transfers that style to the film: Characters appear in carefully composed and lit interiors or wide-angle exterior landscapes as if they stepped out of the paintings. They move slowly, sit stolidly at tables for drinking feasts, and speak little. Wandering in and out of the *tableaux* is the artist himself, a lonely, aloof, often homeless alcoholic figure painting sign boards and canvasses in exchange for food and drink at the *dukhans* (taverns) he frequented in the turn-of-century Tiflis of his native Georgia. Stylized though the plotless inactivity may be, we do get some sense of the artist's biography. Shengelaya has used the scanty available documentation to record episodes of his life—withdrawing from a celebration introducing him to a possible bride; gazing longingly at a music-hall performer, immortalized in his painting of "Margarita"; failing at running a produce shop because he gave goods away to the poor; his discomfort at a salon meeting of artists who had discovered his work a few years before his death—when asked to say a few words, he proposes constructing a space with a large samovar where artists can gather, drink tea, and converse about art.

From the doleful organ melody played during the opening credits against a dull-green landscape painting on the screen, we know this film and the artist's existence will be sad. "Stuck," he says, "in the throat of this cursed life." In what may or may not be a bow to prevailing Soviet tenets of the time, Shengelaya has Pirosmani express resentment of the rich and well born. At his shop, he charges the wealthy higher prices than for the indigent. Someone toasts all the unfortunate who suffer in life. Yet there is a religious undercurrent to the film, which opens with a reading from the New Testament. The closing has a now grey and dying Pirosmani taken to the hospital from his mean shed on Easter Sunday, as townsmen greet and kiss each other. That doleful organ melody sounds again.

[*Cineaste* (Web Exclusive), XXXII, 4, 2007]

Poisoned by Polonium: The Litvinenko File

Political poisonings, some imagined, others quite real, have often turned up in Russian and East European history. Some were dramatically recreated in Russian film. Eisenstein pictured the young Tsar Ivan flashbacking to his mother's anguish, having been poisoned by the Boyars. Later, Ivan, now the Terrible, realized it was his own aunt who poisoned Anastasia, his beloved wife. Rasputin's deadly encounter with the aristocrats who plied him with sweets and wine laced with potassium cyanide has been portrayed in many films, East and West, but none so powerfully as in Elem Klimov's *Agoniya* (1974). In 1978, the Bulgarian anti-communist Georgi Markov was fatally poisoned in London by a ricin-laced pellet from an umbrella. The Ukrainian opposition leader, later President, Viktor Yushchenko dined with security agents in 2004, and soon after suffered a disfiguring illness from what was diagnosed as dioxin poisoning. (Both of those poisonings present ample material for films, but I don't know of any.)

In 2006 in London there occurred the most exotic poisoning of all, by the rare radioactive isotope Polonium-210, of the anti-Putin exile, Alexander Litvinenko, the main subject of Andrei Nekrasov's disquieting documentary (2007). The circumstances surrounding Litvinenko's death and questions about responsibility for it are the stuff of fiction thrillers—or films. (According to Marina Litvinenko, the victim's widow, talks have already begun with Johnny Depp mentioned in the leading role.)

Nekrasov knew of Litvinenko well before the lethal dose killed him. Litvinenko and other members of the FSB: (né KGB) had gone public in Russia in 1998 with accusations of corruption in the security agency. Their whistle blowing only brought them serious trouble, and Litvinenko sought and received political asylum in the United Kingdom in 2000 (reportedly after being turned down by the U.S.; Washington evidently didn't want to complicate relations between President Bush and ex-KGB agent and newly installed President Putin). Litvinenko had also co-authored a book, *Blowing up Russia*, charging the FSB with setting off deadly explosions in 1999 and pinning the blame on Chechen terrorists as a means to justify renewing Russia's anti-separatist assault on Chechnya. (Nekrasov's earlier film, *Disbelief: A Documentary Composition in 12 Parts*, examines the bombings through the eyes of two sisters whose mother was one of hundreds killed in the blast at a Moscow apartment building.)[1] Nekrasov eventually tracked Litvinenko down in London, filmed several conversations with him and the results were cut into the documentary at various intervals. After some opening fright music we hear Litvinenko's chilling plea that the film be shown to the world "if anything happens to me."

The focus is naturally on Litvinenko, but since he practices a highly subjective, self-referential style for his film, Nekrasov himself is another important subject. His narrative is in the first person, and he appears throughout the documentary, affecting the role of a roving inquirer who seeks answers from others, not so much about *Who Killed Litvinenko?*, as about *How to Understand Contemporary Russia*. As such, if one watches its rather jagged construction carefully—it swings back and forth in time, and sometimes a scorecard is needed to keep track of who's who—the film is a valuable document highlighting some of the personalities and issues in post-Soviet Russia these last two decades. The picture is depressing. Continuities in Russian history is one theme stressed by several of the figures he interviewed, Litvinenko included. If the KGB was the repressive security organ for maintaining Communist Party power in Soviet times, he says, the FSB's major function is protecting the interests of a new ruling class today.

Nekrasov also offers pages from his own biography. As a youngster in Leningrad he heard elders speak about the "Big House," i.e., KGB headquarters, and as a student, was invited to become an informant for the KGB, a role that Litvinenko tells him was gladly undertaken by Vladimir Putin when the latter was a student. Nekrasov interviewed the courageous reporter, Anna Politkovskaya, before she was gunned down in her apartment building elevator (earlier, she was a victim of a suspected poisoning attempt), about the suffocating hold the Putin regime has on the media, and the methods, including deadly force—"wet operations" in KGB lingo—that are used to intimidate print and television journalists. Another interview has the oligarch Boris Berezovsky, once a Putin supporter, now in British exile a fierce opponent, expatiating on how the collapse of the totalitarian system freed the Russian people, but only temporarily, from their traditional "slave mentality." Putin's crushing of individual liberty, Berezovsky says, is why he fights him. (He commands many resources for the fight from the vast wealth he accumulated during the wild get-rich opportunities after the Soviet collapse, when former state properties and enterprises were looted.) Nekrasov includes a press-conference clip of a churlish Putin remarking after Litvinenko's death that he "was no Lazarus," and that the whole affair has been converted into a "political provocation." Marina Litvinenko offers some tearful comments about her late husband's obsessive commitment to what he felt was right, something that led him to rebel against his own government and the FSB. (Nekrasov's original title for the film was *Rebellion*.) In what feels like extraneous filler, Nekrasov also interviews the French pundit, André Glucksmann, who reviews the persistence of authoritarianism in Russian life, and cites "the crime of indifference" that permits it.

Possibly the oddest interview, edged with dark humor, is with Andrei Lugovoi, widely suspected of slipping the Polonium in Litvinenko's tea at a meeting in London's Millennium Hotel. That meeting took place on November 1, 2006 and the hospitalized Litvinenko died three weeks later, after an agonizing illness that was correctly diagnosed only days before his death. (The film includes somber scenes from the hospital.) At what looks like his *dacha* Lugovoi delivers a mini-lecture on the properties of Polonium (it gives off Alpha particles, etc., etc.), then offers his guest some (*gulp*) tea.

Litvinenko pointed to Putin's responsibility for his poisoning in a deathbed statement drafted by a figure heading a Foundation financed by Berezovsky. Nekrasov doesn't address the issue head-on, although the general drift of the film leads in the same direction. British prosecutors, however, "are 100 percent sure who administered the poison, where and how." The "who" is Lugovoi, a former KGB man himself, and a sometimes business colleague of Litvinenko's. (Many former members of the agency are in the lucrative field of private security services.) The Brits have demanded Lugovoi's extradition but the Russians have rejected the request, citing their constitution's prohibition on the extradition of Russian citizens (the Russians are of course strict constructionists, don't you know). Lugovoi denies responsibility, and the Russians have said there are no grounds for bringing charges against him on the basis of their own investigation, nor from evidence supplied by British authorities. All of this has led to gestures on both sides reminiscent of tit-for-tat Cold War practices—mutual expulsions of diplomats, most notably.

None of this appears in Nekrasov's film, nor is the subject broached of other possible sources of Litvinenko's poisoning, and the reasons behind it, speculation that others, not just the Russians, have fueled, including the author Edward Jay Epstein, known especially for his writing on the John Kennedy assassination. For Polonium-210, a substance produced only in sophisticated state-run nuclear facilities, and potentially a trigger for a crude nuclear weapon, to appear in London is a serious matter in and of itself, Litvinenko's sad fate aside. Was his death indeed a crime exposing the long vengeful arm of the FSB? Was it evidence of some illegal operation gone wrong, by design or inadvertently? Whatever the explanation, Litvinenko's death had very alarming overtones. It's hard to say where any future investigation that is comprehensive and impartial would lead. Nekrasov's film, meanwhile, remains a compelling collection of testimonies and a riveting excursion into some of the ugly terrain of post-Soviet Russia.

[*Cineaste*, XXXIII, 3, 2008]

[1] Another engrossing documentary, more a tribute than an investigation, was released by The Cinema Guild: *In Memoriam Alexander Litvinenko* (2007) directed by Jos de Putter and Masha Novikova.

Nostalghia

Tarkovsky reminded interviewers that the word nostalgia in Russian is pronounced with a hard g, as if to convey the hard pain of loneliness and longing that comes from distance or exile from one's homeland. G as in *gloom*, as in the gloom that envelops the Andrei of the film (Oleg Yankovsky), wandering through Italian interiors and landscapes or drifting into Russian reveries and dreamscapes.

Nostalghia is Tarkovsky's penultimate work, the first of the two films he made abroad before his death in 1986. (The other is *The Sacrifice*, 1985, shot in Sweden.) It is also the most subjective of his always subjective films, in a double sense here. Its main character is named Andrei, and like his creator is a Russian working in Italy tortured by *hard-g* nostalgia. (For cruel Soviet bureaucratic reasons Tarkovsky was forced to leave his family behind while working abroad, as was, we assume, his Andrei in the film.) There is a peculiar Russian nesting-doll (*matryoshka*) character to the whole enterprise: a Russian director in Italy makes a film about a Russian poet in Italy researching the work of an 18th-century Russian composer living in Italy. Tarkovsky's own condition is mirrored in that of his character Andrei, who in turn reflects the longing of his antecedent, the subject of his research. (Elsewhere, in an illuminating documentary film brought out by Kino Video, *Directed by Andrei Tarkovsky*—about the making of *The Sacrifice*—Tarkovsky declares there are no boundaries between his life and his films.)

This personal dimension of the relatively plotless *Nostalghia* (co-written by Tarkovsky with Tonino Guerra) is really the less important of the two subjectivities we encounter in the film. The other is formal, the reconstruction of the inner consciousness and mood of its main character through virtuoso cinematic devices—flash-cut reveries; disorienting tracking shots; un-cued dream sequences and memories that glide seamlessly in and out of present reality; shots of long, long duration of slow action in real time, or of no action at all in the conventional sense. Vintage Tarkovsky, and no more so than in the final shot—gorgeous and spine-chilling—in which the camera pulls back slowly to reveal a Russian pastoral tableau within the high ruined walls of an Italian abbey.

With that final hallucinatory shot, stunning both in its oddity and its radiance of color, sound, and texture, Tarkovsky obliterates distinctions of time and space in a vision of unity—of past and present, of Russia and Italy, even of life and death. (The release, by Fox Lorber Home Video, is a digitally remastered widescreen version which brings out much of the burnished tones of the original.)

In a formal exercise that seeks to translate an emotional state—disassociation, even a borderline clinical depression—into cinematic language with minimalist dialogue and action, Tarkovsky has succeeded brilliantly, I think. (Any character that is indifferent to the sexual allure of the gorgeous Domiziana Giordano, who plays Andrei's Italian interpreter, Eugenia, has got to be very depressed.)

Less successful, or at least, very debatable, is Tarkovsky's way with Russophilic attitudes and state-of-the-world apocalyptic philosophizing. (Add his seeming anti-feminism. Women's role, he has a sacristan tell Eugenia, is to bear children and to exhibit patience and self-sacrifice.) Italy is caught up in Western materialism and has lost its faith; cataclysmic war is at hand. Only a Russian style "holy fool" in the person of Domenico—a haunted Erland Josephson, prefiguring a similar role in *The Sacrifice*—understands this. Instinctively, Andrei sympathizes with him, though others consider him mad, and both perish in suicidal acts of faith. The two-part denouement has Domenico immolating himself in a Roman piazza, a scene staged with immense pathos, and Andrei literally walking himself to death in a weird ritual that was shot in a single take lasting almost 9 minutes.

Tarkovsky, ever puzzling, with a prophetic bent, was an always compelling filmmaker. He was cut down by lung cancer, in exile. One watches *Nostalghia* with great grief.

[*Cineaste*, XXIII, 3, 1998]

SHORT TAKES

Animated Soviet Propaganda

Animated Soviet Propaganda (2006) offers a superb, wide-ranging introduction to the politically charged animation films of the USSR, from the 1920s to 1984. (The subtitle of the six-hour assembly from Films By Jove and Kino International is *From the Revolution to Perestroika*, but the latter period—the Gorbachev years, 1985-1991—is not represented.) The set is an invaluable historical pageant of Soviet art in service to ideology, replete with the music, graphics, outlook and slogans of the epoch as a whole, and of its individual parts, starting from the Revolution and Civil War. The producers, Joan Borsten and Oleg Vidov, tapped the archives of the USSR's main animation studio, Moscow's Soyuzmultfilm, for 38 titles, and divided them topically into "American Imperialists," "Fascist Barbarians," "Capitalist Sharks," and "Onward to the Shining Future: Communism"—that should give you some idea of content. There are influences throughout from Soviet constructivist and poster art; from 1920s expressionism; and especially from the Russian storytelling *lubok* style (originally from woodblock prints). The films vary from the entertaining to the boringly didactic. All deliver messages. Fat capitalists smoking fat cigars are recurring images, while vultures and wolves stand in for militarists, particularly the Fascist species. The U.S. in Vietnam and the 1973 military coup in Chile are slipped into critiques of Nazi violence. My favorites: V. Tarasov's *Shooting Range* (1979)—a despairing, unemployed young man finds a job, but he discovers he's the living target in a for-profit reality show; Tarasov's free-form history lesson as fantasy, using the poetry of Vladimir Mayakovsky, *Forward March Time* (1977), with the title song by the Soviet rock band, The Tin Soldiers; and *Soviet Toys* (1924), a quirky parable of workers, peasants and the Red Army chasing out the old order in line-drawing animation by none other than Dziga Vertov. Commentary by several Russian animators and historians supplement this unique collection.

[*Cineaste*, XXXII, 3, 2007]

Theremin: An Electronic Odyssey

What stands out chillingly on such disparate soundtracks as *Spellbound*, *The Day the Earth Stood Still*, and even the Beach Boys' hit, "Good Vibrations," is the theremin, a remarkable electronic contraption developed long before modern synthesizers and named for its remarkable inventor, born Lev Sergeyevich Termin, in old St. Petersburg, Russia. Plaudits go to Steven M. Martin, who did considerable detective work for this fascinating documentary (1993) about the man and the instrument, and the improbable tale therein. Termin/Theremin emigrated to the U.S., had some fleeting fame, and then disappeared. Either he was working for, or was abducted by, the KGB. From 1942 to 1967, he tells Martin, who tracked down the nonagenarian in Moscow, he "worked on bad things," i.e., for Stalin and successors. He probably invented the electronic 'bug' in his capacity as the caged 'Soviet Edison.' Martin even brought him back to New York, and we witness his wide-eyed encounters with Times Square and people from his past, especially Clara Rockmore, the foremost theremin performer. Watching a performance is almost as spooky as the sound. The performer doesn't touch anything; she just waves her hands as in some mysterious incantation, manipulating sound waves. Martin showed his film in St. Petersburg at the 1994 International Documentary Festival and discovered that Russians knew the instrument as the 'Terminvox,' but knew nothing of its inventor. For them, as for us, Martin's film is a revelation.

[*Cineaste*, XXI, 4, 1995]

Kolya

A randy, 55-year old cellist expelled from the Czech Philharmonic by the Communist authorities for some minor political indiscretion, becomes, reluctantly, the guardian of a 5-year old Russian boy in Prague, on the eve of the "Velvet Revolution." This implausible situation from a scriptwriter's imagination has predictable consequences: We know the two will love each other at film's end.

But the scriptwriter is Zdenek Sverak, who also plays the bachelor-cellist with equal measures of wry and rue, looking like a grizzled Central European Sean Connery; the director is Jan Sverak (father and son teamed up for *Elementary School* in 1991); and Andrei Chalimon plays the eponymous young hero with a rare unaffected artfulness. The result is a film of exceptional charm. The occasional dollop of schmalz never overcomes the subtle flavors the Sveraks concoct thanks in part to arresting close-up camera work, the music of Dvorak, and the very crisp editing. The film is as strong and knowing in politics as in human relationships. There is much to learn here about Czechs and Russians, about the Soviet occupation, and about how the Czechs endured the large and petty insults imposed by their own Communists. In a couple of final episodes Sverak skillfully weaves his story into some documentary footage shot in the rapturous time of liberation, 1989-1990. *Kolya* captured an Oscar for Best Foreign Language Film of 1996.

[*Cineaste*, XXII, 4, 1997]

Transsiberian

Embedded in this mostly conventional train thriller (from Beijing to Moscow, with unexpected stops along the way) are several compelling character studies performed by a superb elite cast. Another benefit therein: Emily Mortimer and Ben Kingsley confront each other in a virtuoso cat-and-mouse encounter. Brad Anderson wrote and directed a film (2008) that deserved wider circulation and success than it got. Never mind a plot that hinges on drugs, smuggling, a narcotics gang, corrupt police officials, and violence, with a gruesome torture scene thrown in (administered by a thuggish, very Russian looking Thomas Kretschmann)—this is post-Soviet Russia, and the atmospherics are about right. Woody Harrelson's Roy and Mortimer's Jessie are an unlikely American couple; he's a simple guy in hardware supplies, and has a sweet, accepting disposition, she's a troubled former bad girl who can quote Tennessee Williams. They cross paths with a seductive Spanish rogue (Eduardo Noriega) and his girlfriend, an American drifter (Kate Mara). Mortimer is not ordinarily attractive; she's thin, with kind of squashed down facial features, but she has real talent for emotional range, and in a fateful scene with Noriega's Carlos—he challenges her as a *"mala chica"* —she generates plenty of heat. Kingsley plays a police inspector—his Russian accent is better than Viggo Mortensen's in *Eastern Promises* (2007), and his few phrases in Russian are not bad either. Sir Ben can do anything. He appears in an opening establishing scene, then disappears for most of the film; when he reappears, he and Mortimer take over the screen. He is the suspicious and relentless interrogator; she is the cornered woman desperate to maintain self-control in order to cover up a terrible crime. Dostoevsky's Porfiry and Raskolnikov, anyone?

[*Cineaste*, XXXIV, 2, 2009]

Letter to Anna

According to the International Federation of Journalists, 152 journalists were murdered in Russia between 1994 and 2008. Courageous investigative reporters are an especially endangered species in Putin's Russia, where Anna Politkovskaya, the subject of Eric Bergkraut's fine, elegiac documentary, was gunned down in 2006. Bergkraut's *Letter*, subtitled *The story of journalist Politkovskaya's death* (2008) is "written" with great affection and feeling for the striking woman he came to know several years before her assassination while he gathered material for a film on Chechnya. We get to know her as well, thanks to interviews with her, her family, co-workers, and a roll-call of prominent critics of the Putin regime. (Moscow officials declined to be interviewed for the film.) As with the radioactive poisoning of Alexander Litvinenko in London, responsibility for the crime, if not Putin's personally, was, as someone put it in the film, enabled by Putin's style of rule, which throttles all independent, critical voices. Politkovskaya was not easily throttled. Her instinctive sympathy for the powerless was stiffened by a stubborn and fearless temperament; she refused to give up her investigations, even after surviving a poisoning attempt as well as a gruesome captivity in Chechnya for her reporting there. She had blunt words about Russian actions against the local population in the 2nd Chechen war; in the film she describes them as *genocide*. She calls her survival a "miracle," though her international reputation helped protect her—all too briefly. Narration by Susan Sarandon and Bergkraut threads background information into the story, although the film loops back and forth in time and place, and the many political and personal strands are not always woven seamlessly. But Bergkraut succeeds in conveying Politikovskaya's special radiance, and her martyrdom for truth.

[*Cineaste*, XXXIV, 1, 2008]

The Lady with The Dog

This Facets Video release of Iosif Heifitz's 1960 film, based on one of Chekhov's—and world literature's—greatest short stories, had me nostalgic. No, I never had a holiday affair with a young married woman in Yalta, but I do remember welcoming the cluster of films of the post-Stalinist cultural "Thaw" that brought humanism to Soviet screens. Heifitz (1905-1995) didn't belong to the younger pioneering generation (Chukhrai, Konchalovsky, Tarkovsky, *et al.*), but his old-fashioned, straight and unadorned adaptation of Chekhov's tale is one of the standouts of the period, with its pitch-perfect gray "Chekhovian" tonality enveloping a sad love story that has no resolution. (For a later souped-up version, see Nikita Mikhalkov's *Dark Eyes*, 1987.) The irresolute lovers are perfectly played by the always reliable Alexei Batalov and the young Iya Savvina in her first film role. Neither "Gurov" nor "Anna Sergeyevna" has the strength to break from their married moorings, but Chekhov and Heifitz cast them in a sympathetic, understanding light. Heifitz's conventional tools capture the melancholy mood and its quietly desperate characters—a slow narrative pace, a soft, melodic score, and, except for one episode, an unhurried camera. The beautiful Crimean sea- and mountain-scapes of the opening scenes in which the vacationing lady and her spitz meet the charming vacationing banker, give way to vivid alternating portraits of Moscow and provincial Saratov. Best take: Gurov surprises her at the opera, and the camera follows the startled Anna Sergeyevna as her conflicted emotions drive her mindlessly, breathlessly up and down stairways and through hallways, with Gurov giving chase. The race ends. Reunited at last? Not really, this is Chekhov; a difficult path lies ahead.

[*Cineaste*, XXXIV, 3, 2009]

CHAPTER VII

Soundtracks: Interviewing the Filmmakers

I interviewed these directors, well known and lesser known (and one— very special—actress) during **perestroika***, 1986-1991, and in two years of post-Soviet Russia, 1993-1994. Konchalovsky is an exception; we met for an interview in 1982, when he was in the U.S. promoting* Siberiade, *plus drumming up interest for his ambitious Hollywood proposals, and I was beginning to study Soviet cinema more closely.*

Naturally, each period is reflected in the kinds of questions I asked, and in the general themes that came up—creative freedom under **perestroika** *and* **glasnost***, or its absence earlier; financing problems; the prevalence of co-productions; Jewish subjects finally appearing on screen; how women are treated on and off screen; personal biographies in the context of Soviet society and film culture. The interviews with Gurevich, Litvyakov, Khashchavatsky, and Rodnyansky (who went on to a very successful post-Soviet career as television head and film producer) are particularly rich and revealing on that last theme. Gurevich (1932-2001), a prominent figure and tireless promoter of Russian documentary film, was most outspoken about the Soviet experience, offering candid assessments of certain personalities in the kino world, and commentary on the bold but ill-fated Experimental Studio at Mosfilm in the 1960s. I usually identified myself as an historian to start things off, and for the most part I stepped aside after a question to let filmmakers speak; occasionally I engaged in give-and-take dialogue and conversation, though never with any confrontational rancor.*

Often the idea for an interview arose when the filmmaker was accessible at a festival, or in connection with his or her new, or recently released film. In latter cases, the interviews are generally clear about the film triggering the session—e.g., Klimov's Rasputin (Agoniya), Askoldov's Commissar, Djordjadze's Robinsonada, *etc. The sessions took place in New York, Moscow and St. Petersburg, and were conducted in Russian, unless there was fluency in English on the part of the interviewee (Konchalovsky, Rodnyansky, Tsabadze), then later transcribed by Moira Ratchford, whose superb translation skills are augmented by her fine knowledge of Russian cinema.*

1 Andrei Konchalovsky and *Siberiade*, 1982

"I can tell you that the talented person here, in the U.S., and the talented person in Russia, can have the same kind of confrontation between power and the individual, because power does the paying, and in both senses, power is concerned about the masses."

Menashe: *I'm speaking to Soviet director Andrei Mikhalkov-Konchalovsky.*

Konchalovsky: Just say Andrei Konchalovsky, because it's too complicated.

We don't want to mix you up with your brother?

So as not to mix us up. In fact, I took the name because there are too many Mikhalkovs in Russian culture. My father is a writer and my brother is an actor and director. I go by Konchalovsky because my mother was Konchalovsky. Konchalovsky is the name of a famous Russian painter, who's my grandfather. I can even show him. As a historian you must appreciate it. [Shows a painting by Pyotr Konchalovsky].

He's from Moscow?

Yes. This is a self-portrait.

I did my doctoral dissertation on the Muscovite Alexander Guchkov and his family. Do you know anything about Guchkov?

He was a Minister?

Yes, he was a Minister in the Provisional Government, but there's a lesser known, fascinating history to the family. His great-grandfather was a serf and an Old Believer.

He was a Kadet?[1]

No, an Octobrist. And I always thought that here was a wonderful subject for a film.

An industrialist?

He himself, no. He was beyond that, he was a rentier. *But the family was industrial, in textiles, and I always thought it would be the perfect story for a film, you know, chronicling the history of the Moscow merchant class, or bourgeoisie.*

Who would subsidize it?

Why, it's not acceptable?

The Soviet government, to glorify... ?

To glorify?

For them to make a movie is to glorify because they invest money in that.

Well, last night I went to the United Nations Russian Book Club, and they showed a film based on a play by Ostrovsky, called Easy Money, *directed by Yevgeny Matveyev. So that's about a merchant and the different values he has...*

But this merchant was lucky he wasn't in the Provisional Government. That's the problem.

That is a problem. Well, how do you overcome that problem? When and how?

I don't have any answer. I think that we have reality and we have to do our best applying to that reality, pray a lot: "grant me the courage to change what I can, the serenity to accept what I can't, and the wisdom to know the difference." What I feel I can change, I try to, and I've worked, for example, on *Siberiade*, but I don't believe that a movie about Guchkov would be possible to do.

Regarding Siberiade, *in what way do you think you were reflecting change?*

Siberiade is not a movie about the progressive role of progress, which is the official standpoint. So this is the main thing. For me this movie was about the conflict between civilization and culture, when civilization develops at the expense of culture. [*See my review, above, in Chapter III.*]

You're covering several generations of Russian and Soviet history and yet the subject of Stalinism is dealt with in a very indirect way, a very oblique way; the scene in the forest, in the hut, and the picture of Stalin, and so on. Now, wouldn't you have wanted some greater confrontation with that whole subject?

Maybe I would, but it's impossible. Let's face it. The problem of Stalin and the role of Stalin in history is a very sensitive subject even for Russian historians, because it's linked to the policy of the time. So it's a kind of sensitive item because of the shifting inner policy at the higher levels. So when you touch this subject, you might spark reactions and it could be judged completely unacceptable. So what I have to do—but I'm not a politician. I'm an artist. I'd like to express more important things than that. More important things because I think that the conflict between civilization and culture is more important than the conflict between liberals and conservatives on any level. And second, it's very difficult to make a real statement about Stalinism, not because it's difficult from the political point of view, but because it's very difficult to say what is good and what is bad in the long term.

You're speaking personally about your own examination of the subject?

Yes. And as I said, I'm not a politician. But I think that we still don't know how to deal with nature. We still don't know how to deal with the forest, the swamp. We still think that if we go and make something.... We still think that we can make nature work better than nature works itself, without realizing that all we can do is just destroy. So I think that human society is a part of the same ecological structure. It's like a kind of technogenesis. There's biogenesis and ethnogenesis, and every nation has its own ecological formation. You can't apply the same rules to every nation and expect the response to be the same. No, the response will be different. So from that standpoint the relationship between power and the individual is sort of individual too.

Varying from nation to nation.

So from that standpoint, I don't know what is good and bad. I lived only forty-four years...

It's maybe that impenetrable complexity that's interesting, that you have to sort out good and bad.

Yes, but you know that when you have to show, you have to be clear. Otherwise you don't know what you're saying. If you say, "I am lost," if your premise is, "I am lost," why the hell do you have to make a movie? Nobody will help you if you'll be this way. I think a person has to talk about his point of view. Because I think with a person who is lost, it's a tragedy for this person. Not his judgment of history, but his own personal judgment. Only because art is a subject of concrete human character. Only on the level of a concrete human character can you make declarations and become infectious, captivating.

You can reach out and communicate.

Yes. It's just interesting. I can tell you, I don't know what I'm going to say next. I'm interested in our conversations, because while discussing things, I find interesting conclusions.

Unfortunately, that raises all sorts of very concrete problems for you as an artist in the USSR. Take the case of Andrei Rublev; *as you were talking, I could see the film as expressive of a lot of the things you were saying, but it's bound to run into trouble, no?*

Yes. What is it, trouble?

Trouble means we can't see the whole film.

I think you can see the whole film, by the way. But not the absolute whole—about twenty minutes are cut out. I don't want to complain to anybody about any of this. I'm here trying to make a movie. I haven't succeeded. I have, I think, fantastic ideas. Nobody wants me because I have no credits.

Here?

I don't want to complain about it. I don't want to say, "how difficult it is to work in a capitalist society." I can do that very easily now, because I know a little bit about the subject. But the same thing about Russia. It's the same, but different. It's a different side of the coin. In Russia you have the state—with structure, with censorship—which pays for the movie. So if you can't do something, you have to deal with it, and you have to do your best. If you're unable to, you're an unhappy person. You just have to deal with it. Anyway, *Rublev* got beaten down. Tarkovsky is a much more impulsive person, much more nervous, he is much more of an artist, maybe. I'm maybe more of a philosopher, in the sense that I know how to do my best. Maybe not. But I can tell you, *Rublev* was done in Russia. Here, you wouldn't be able to do that film. It wouldn't be possible to find money. It's very interesting. On the other hand, here you can do *Apocalypse Now*. But it would be impossible to make a movie about Russian tanks in Afghanistan, even claiming that it's a very progressive part of the historical process. Everybody has his own certain freedom and limitations.

If Charlton Heston were to act in Rublev, *then I think it would work.*

Yeah, and he would have a lover, a young monk...or some kind of very nice relationship in the community of the monastery.

Touché. Nicely put.

Yeah it's difficult sometimes, and sometimes it's *very* difficult. But on the other hand, I was never paranoid that I'd be doing a movie and my movie wouldn't get money or that I wouldn't get my next job. Just the opposite. Only five copies of my second movie were released. It was almost banned—it was banned for a year and a half. Even longer. It was a movie about peasants. It was a movie called *Asya's Happiness*. Some of the critics said, "Konchalovsky's best movie is banned." How is it possible that the best movie is banned? It's very clichéd thinking, and the movie was banned. I did my next movie, nonetheless. In three weeks, immediately, they said, "you want to make a movie?" Right away. And I was ready. Movies aren't always banned completely, to avoid this kind of precedent, that the movie was "banned." Goskino releases the movie in very small venues, like universities, five copies, limited run, and that's all.

Yes, different structures here can do similar things.

I can tell you that the talented person here, in the U.S., and the talented person in Russia, can have the same kind of confrontation between power and the individual, because power does the paying, and in both senses, power is concerned about the masses. Here, the power is concerned about masses because of money. There, power is concerned about the masses to get the right ideological message. Because of guarantees, because in [our] society you are guaranteed, there are maximum guarantees and there are minimum. You are not paranoid. Not paranoid as I feel how I become here paranoid, because I have to film my first movie. Otherwise I won't be able to do my next project, which I'd like to do. It's very interesting. In one sense it's very good if you're free to express yourself, in the sense of art in Russia, or in Poland, or in Hungary, but in the other sense it's bad because you don't have any kind of competition, and you become less demanding.

That's the critique of socialism.

Sure. The absence of competition. So now to have somehow

both the eagerness of directors to get to the masses and be successful commercially, the Soviet film industry tried to create a kind of competition. They tried to make a link between the commercial success of the movie and your profit, your personal income.

That's being done experimentally?

No, it's the law. It's an experiment anyway. It's been in effect for about a year and a half. But I've been out of the country for a year and a half now.

So where do you think you could fit into filmmaking here? What do you have to offer?

I'm very interested in being in America, for different reasons. First of all, it's a great experience. Second, I have something to say.

Do you care to tell us what, exactly?

No, some things, I mean I know I like to—it isn't important what the story will be. What's important is my attitude towards people. And I like people. I don't like to make movies about people I don't like. Some say there is only one course—in a sense, this is bad, this is good, this is wrong, this is right. And I think that if art is part of world consciousness and part of the learning process about ourselves in the world, we have to give the audience the right to decide who is good and who is bad. The best movies, as a matter of fact, from my point of view, talk about complexity, and the personal right to be wrong. Like *Raging Bull*, like *The Great Santini*, like *The Godfather*, *Taxidriver*. I mean, life is not one way or the other. It's much more ambiguous, in the sense that I think people have to learn something from every movie. It doesn't mean that this lesson has to be boring and didactic. It could be very entertaining and at the same time, have socially redeeming quality.

It has to be a challenge, a challenge for the audience.... But, American pragmatism gives you the recipe how to achieve, how to succeed. So it's like a vicious circle when you've got the recipe for how to make several millions making movies without knowing how to make a good movie. It's no longer expressing yourself like Stevens, or John Ford, or even Griffith, or Charlie Chaplin. Now young people don't want to make good movies. They want to make movies which are successful. So it's like legal drug-dealing. Because you go to a movie, for two hours you're conked out, then you go out and forget about it. It's a great movie. It's a fantastic—what is fantastic? Maybe you loved it. Maybe some of the movies are a little more... I was told that Scorsese wanted to make *Raging Bull* as an independent movie and that the budget was five million or so. When a major company took on the project, they doubled it immediately, to pay themselves. To pay themselves. In order to pay themselves, they doubled the project, and in order to get the money for the project, they asked Scorsese how to get this money to pay themselves. So it's completely self-pigging-out. It's absurd.

What's also absurd is that a lot of bucks doesn't ensure quality. Take Warren Beatty's Reds, *for example. I don't know how you feel about that. But for $34 million something of better quality could have been produced. And maybe it's the fact of its having such a huge budget that destroyed it. Have you seen the film?*

Yeah.

It just destroyed whatever simple line there may have been for the film.

Yeah, but I don't think it's the director's or the producer's mistake. I think that if someone gets hurt by this situation, it's the director and the producer. Of course, because his name allows a major company to double the budget. They pay themselves. It's the same thing. They use a big star to get an enormous budget. They use a big star because they know the bank will go along. But all that is to pay the overhead. Of course they'll give more bonuses and more advantages and more facilities to the director, but this director will be told, "once we cover the overhead, just make the movie, and the rest is yours."

What did you think of Reds, *by the way?*

I think it's very decent attempt.

Decent? Attempt at what?

It's a decent attempt to talk about the roots of socialism in the United States. For me, I have kind of blisters on my brain from talking about socialism.

A Balkan proverb: "every man desires what he doesn't have."

I can tell you that I was amazed and pleased to sit in the Chinese Theater in Hollywood, with popcorn and ice cream cones, and people who filled the hall and filled the projection room, and from the screen there's a discussion about socialism and the working class, and these people are watching it. It wasn't even important whether it was good or bad. I was amazed...

I still think it was a bad film, but I agree that it was an extraordinary undertaking.

I can't say it was a bad film. The film suffers from the same shortcomings as major Hollywood productions about history. The figures are up front, like the foreground, and the history is in the background. Instead of being melded together, there's a wall between the character and history. And to put it together, I think it's the mistake of the script.

I think you're right. I'm considered heretical for saying this in my circles, but I think Dr. Zhivago *was a much better film, and it integrated precisely those two dimensions.*

Because the literary basis was there.

Exactly. How do you think Bondarchuk will do with his version of John Reed's diary?

I can't say anything until I see it. Bondarchuk has incredible power, not as a big Soviet official director but as an artist. I think he has incredible clout. But his problem is almost the same. He thinks that he can write the scripts himself. And he never succeeds. I had a lot of confrontations with him. We'd fight each other. He called me an asshole and I called him an asshole. He was playing in my movie, *Uncle Vanya*. But he, in his eagerness to transmit literature on the screen, he sometimes perceives it literally. Literally. And it never can be literal. It has to be melted into another genre. You can make *Romeo and Juliet* as a drama, you can make it as a ballet, you can make it as music, but the means will be completely different.

That's exactly the criticism of Easy Money, *the film I saw last night. Somehow, it was an exact replication of the drama itself and there was no filmmaking quality to it. You know what I mean? I mean, all the performances were beautiful. Solovei was wonderful and everything about it was correct, but you might just as well have been watching something on the stage. It wasn't a movie. It's sort of puzzling why a filmmaker would go to the trouble of assembling all this talent simply to convey what is ordinarily conveyed on the stage by Ostrovsky. I don't know, did you see it?*

No, I haven't seen it. I know very well the director. It's an interesting problem in and of itself, what is theatrical and what is not theatrical. Because sometimes the theatrical approach to filmmaking could be very, very fruitful and can feed back. It's up to the filmmaker. But I don't know. Sometimes it seems theatrical, but it never seems that it's theater. So it's a question of how you operate, what your language is. Language is important.

It's so interesting, you know, everything is possible. Everything has the possibility of being good and everything has the possibility of being awful. And it's so difficult to find out why. Sometimes you say it's bad because it's theatrical. But you see [Bergman's] *The Magic Flute*—it's total opera theater but it's incredible cinema. He makes opera, makes artificial light that everyone admires because it's neither cinema nor theater.

Your brother's "A Slave of Love" was very theatrical, and I thought very successful. I must tell you that I give a course, basically a history course but through films. I use a whole series of films, beginning with some Eisenstein and Pudovkin, coming right up to the present.

You could use *Siberiade* very well.

I will be able to use it excellently. It's a perfect historical film. And "A Slave of Love" was very successful, I think, among students. These are American students, and they were very pleased to see that kind of film. The tendency among Americans is to see anything that's Soviet as propaganda, by definition.

It's very interesting.

I'm sure you're aware of that.

Yes. It's a very complicated problem, because the image of the scarecrow of socialism is so deep-rooted in this country, that it's very difficult to break through and to say to their amazement that there are some old-world processes, culturally, quite rich cultural processes in theater, even in literature. I'm sure Soviet literature is extremely interesting—the best, I'm talking about the best—not only because it criticizes the system, because sometimes you can criticize the system and have no talent at all.

---

[1] Konchalovsky knows his pre-revolutionary history. The "Kadets"—Constitutional Democrats—were a liberal party. To their right were the monarchist "Octobrists."

2 *Perestroika*, 1986-1991

Alexander Askoldov

"Many of our filmmakers shout *"perestroika, perestroika!!!"* until their throats are sore. But we must bring back some moral values that have been lost."

Menashe: *I'm an historian, and your film interests me in a variety of ways. It's about the Civil War; about the problem, let us say, of the nationalities in the Soviet Union; and finally, as a film in its own right, especially since the film was not shown for twenty years. I notice the film was made at Gorky Studios in Moscow. Why there?*

Askoldov: The choice was very limited. There are only two studios in Moscow. The Gorky Studios are better equipped. To a certain extent the Leningrad Studio is more or less well-equipped. Other studios differ from the Moscow studios in terms of the facilities they offer.

And also in their artistic profiles? For example, we speak of a Leningrad school or a Ukrainian school. Would you type yourself in this way?

These are unsubstantiated theories. I think that both Mosfilm and Lenfilm have lost their traditions over the years. The concept of a Moscow and a Leningrad school only exists in papers written by film critics.

You don't think they have a basis in reality?

I think that almost all such traditions have faded.

When did they fade?

I think that it was sometime during the mid-fifties that this process of deformation began, when the people who had carried on the traditions of classic Soviet cinema passed away.

On the other hand, the late fifties and early sixties were periods of great creativity and certainly potential creativity.

I think that this explosion in film—and it wasn't just in film, but in other spheres of art—was not motivated as it usually is, by artistic forces, but rather by political forces. But this explosion, like any explosion, couldn't last long.

Did you study at VGIK [the Moscow film school]?

No, I graduated from the Graduate Program for Directors and Screenwriters. It's a two-year program.

Did you study formally under someone—under the influence of one person or several directors at the time?

No, they didn't have workshops run by particular directors. It was more like self-directed studies. And I think this was a more successful approach to mastering the profession of being a director. Now we've been discussing whether to make these two-year courses the only form of education in this area. Despite the shortcomings of these two-year courses, they had obvious merits. They would admit only people who were at a certain level of maturity. They were either actors or writers and had already done some work in their field. That's why they didn't waste any time in general education, and could concentrate on professional issues.

You say that this is being debated now, and is it a possibility?

I myself don't take part in the decision-making on this issue. But I know that in the Filmmakers' Union there is great dissatisfaction with the state of affairs at VGIK. And as far as I know, it's justified. VGIK provides almost no practical experience. You can't train a swimmer without a swimming pool. But the students spend five years without any practical experience. But it's also important to mention who teaches them. It's important not only to have a very experienced professional teaching, but to have someone with a broad education, an intellectually-oriented person. But you can imagine how their instructors are simply churned out on conveyor belts. They treat it like a commodity. I don't know how things are in American cinema, but when Eisenstein died, and Pudovkin, Kuleshov, and Kozintsev, when Trauberg was very old and stopped teaching, when Zarkhi and Kheifitz ended their careers, when Mikhail Romm died—the thread was broken. Moreover, how many films in Soviet cinema in your opinion have carried on and developed the traditions of Russian revolutionary cinema of the twenties?

I see your point.

How many films by their character can be called Russian films? I mean this in the positive sense of the term, I don't mean any chauvinistic trends. Many very interesting trends have developed in the national cinemas of the Soviet Union, but, for example, I can't consider Georgian cinema to reflect a Georgian school.

Why not?

I see a lot of things borrowed—it's not that they're foreign themes—but it reminds me very much of Italian cinema.

And you're saying it's imitative.

It's an imitation. But all the same, you must respect that too. Something similar is happening with Lithuanian cinema. It is also imitative, but it has a certain professionalism. Mosfilm Studios, and Gorky Studios in particular, have lost their understanding of professionalism in many of their films. It's obvious when you see these films. They lack even a basic level of film culture. The level of cinematic ideas, and ideas in general, is very primitive.

Do you attribute this to this break in the continuity of Soviet cinema? Or are we talking about organizational, political and technical problems?

Well, cinema as a component of spiritual life does not exist as an independent entity in society. In our society there have been heavy layers of stagnation that have influenced culture. But these overflowing swamps have wiped out the giants of our cinema. Eisenstein long resisted the ideology of Stalinism. He was not simply a great filmmaker in my view, but a Leonardo Da Vinci of the twentieth century. He was a great philosopher.

Ah, I see who the influences on you were. Eisenstein, Leonardo. In other words, your vision is very high...

Marx and Lenin also.

So there you were in the 1960s. You felt that there's been a break in the older tradition. And in a sense you're in an interesting situation where as a young director you can explore new ground and new traditions. What happened?

You know, it seems to me that when someone begins a project, like producing a film, and thinks he'll create something new, then usually nothing new comes of it. At best he'll create some kind of forced innovation.

Can you give me an example of this forced innovation in Soviet cinema of this period?

There's a huge number of examples. Unfortunately, they gave rise to disappointment among our generation. It's easier to name the few, maybe the few dozen or so good films. But the general stream of bad movies isn't even an attempt at innovation. They proved incapable of any kind of thought—and not just they, but the whole country. They couldn't make decisions. They couldn't take responsibility. And what about an artist? He's a part of society. I can compare a true artist to a snowplow. When the snow hits the ground he's the first to plow it. To return to what we were talking about, I recall that two months ago was Eisenstein's 90th anniversary. Normally I don't go to "Dom Kino" [the Moscow Film Center] even to screen American movies. That's not good, I know. I just have a lot of daily responsibilities. But they sent me a brochure, and I said that by all means I would go. Because this was an evening commemorating Eisenstein. So I went and saw that in this huge hall with over 8,000 seats, there were only a few dozen people. But when they show American films, even very bad ones, the house is full. And I didn't see a single person that night from the Secretariat of the new Filmmakers' Union. I was very upset.

I can understand that. How do you interpret this?

We've already spoken about the decline in intellectual and social activity. One of our very famous theater directors, Georgi Tovstonogov from the Leningrad Theater, the best in the country, once told me at a rehearsal that his actors were over-playing their roles. You shouldn't do that. In art it's easier to shout a lie than to whisper it. I think this is true not only in art but in the sociopolitical sphere as well. Many of our filmmakers shout *"perestroika, perestroika!!!"* until their throats are sore. But we must bring back some moral values that have been lost.

And that can't be brought back by simple restructuring?

There are many ways of interpreting *perestroika*. Some people see it in a very mechanical way. We'll make pants a thousand times faster than we did before. And they call that *perestroika*. Aeroflot planes will fly on schedule. But so far they're just as late as Pan Am—in fact I prefer Aeroflot. But *perestroika* is also the revival of the human soul. It's the return of a lost sense of moral values. Even if the Roman Pope has a special mass and Gorbachev joins him, morality won't return tomorrow. It's a very complicated process. We need to revive our lost religion—the religion of the revolution, I'm not afraid to say it. I think that in the history of different nations, revolutions start out wonderfully. The revolution imparted a lot to Russia, and the great American Revolution gave you a constitution. But it's another thing when you look at these two ships—that are in some ways very similar, the American and Russian ships—and barnacles have grown on their hulls.

Which slowed down the revolutionary process? What are some of those "barnacles"?

There is a serious perversion of the relationship among different nationalities in our country. And as members of this society, we have always known about these problems. But the political analysts always said they didn't exist. It's absurd. Society is like a living organism. Maybe this is a bit simplified, a bit primitive, but I'll allow myself to use this comparison to make things clearer. A living organism gives off "dross" [waste], the name we intellectuals give to what the human body gets rid of. And society also gives off waste. Drug addiction is a waste, prostitution is a waste, corruption is a terrible waste, anti-semitism, chauvinism in any form is waste. But our society developed according to some incredible laws. We had no corruption, and so on. Thank God we are beginning to look at ourselves in a realistic light. And human society is grateful to us if only for that.

Commisar is a rather simple story based on a short story by Vasily Grossman. What you're saying, however, seems to be a rather grandiose, moral, political statement. What's the relationship between the simple story and your vision?

Your definition of its relationship with the Grossman story is absolutely correct. But people who don't like my movie—and there are many in our country—more than you would like—years ago when they struck down the film, one of the charges against me was that I destroyed Grossman's story. Now that this film has become reality, they don't want to acknowledge it as a cinematic, artistic work in its own right. These people say, "what a successful guy Grossman is for coming up with the film, *Commissar*." This doesn't create a conflict between me and Grossman, because I have always considered him to be a great writer, a very original writer, with a very keen understanding of human nature. And now they've already published his novel, *Life and Fate*.

Is there any plan to film Grossman's novel?

You know, you can't cross a river in the same spot twice. Now Grossman has unfortunately become a fashionable writer and everybody will be trying to make screen adaptations of his works. I don't want to become a fashionable interpreter of a fashionable Grossman. Moreover, Grossman's prose is very dangerous for film.

Why?

Because it's a mistake to think that an accurate portrayal of Grossman's themes on the screen would be a simple matter. In general, the true plot of a film—I'm speaking in the broad, philosophical sense of the term—can only be found between the lines of great literary works. Because you can't produce a successful screen adaptation of Tolstoy—you end up with a literal interpretation. Grossman's short story, which takes place in the town of Berdichev, is just a small part of my film's plot. It's just a short story. And if you go sequence by sequence, ninety percent of it was never written by Grossman. For example, Grossman states simply: "she was in labor for several hours." In the film, this sentence takes up thirty minutes. Moreover, it's not a depiction of the physical suffering of childbirth. Probably I was influenced by Russian cinema of the 1920s. It's the birth of the revolution. The birth of a new morality. Grossman wrote this story in 1934—there were certain issues that troubled me in the 1960s, but that neither Grossman nor society had faced. In Russia of 1934 the Jewish question didn't exist. It seemed that this question had been solved once and for all. But Stalin—Stalinism—solved this problem in its own manner. I've always reflected upon that and have devoted my life experience to that period in history. This is one of the many layers in the film.

In the sense that you were trying to place yourself in the context of an earlier time?

The story, which takes place in 1920, is the story of a Jewish family, the story of a tragedy connected to the history of *pogroms*, of discrimination against Jews. I tried to portray the relationship of a Jewish family with a Russian woman. There is a certain balance between the Russian and Jewish characters in the film. These characters acted in the tradition of Russian realistic art. The film was structured so that these characters could serve simultaneously as metaphors, not simply individuals. The relationships among these characters is a metaphor of the relationship between Russians and Jews. Furthermore, Grossman was a product of his time. He had a very narrow understanding of the class-based problems of the revolution. I'm not trying to put him down for that. He couldn't help it—he was a product of his time and of his generation. He then underwent a tremendous evolution.

So I took a rather simple story by Grossman, and along with this short story, brought about an evolution in the understanding of these issues. So the film stands on its own in a philosophical sense. And now on the surface it seems very banal, but it's interesting, this tragedy of Grossman, of this film based on Grossman's work. I repeat that I have the greatest respect for Grossman—he is a great writer in my eyes—but this film stands entirely on its own merits.

I'm trying to uphold certain universal values, a universal understanding of morality, of duty, of life and death. For me, universal values take precedence over class values. So when people ask me why my film was banned, I answer—"because the system of moral and political principles that this film depicts went against the system of morals and political principles that prevailed for seventy years in the USSR." Our compass had gone awry and our ship was heading for the cliffs. But in my view I steered my boat in the right direction. The pirates who steered that big ship couldn't admit that I was right and they were wrong. Now they say—though not all of them, only certain ones—that this film represents "new thinking." That *perestroika* produced this film. I don't want to object to this flattering characteristic. Especially since it has brought me to America. But if we want to speak seriously and soberly about it, I think that this is fair. That's why I've worked out certain lines to tell audiences—and the poor translator has been translating the same one over and over.

Can you give me an example?

When I speak before an audience, I say that this old movie seems to embody new ideas. I think that these ideas are as important to our society as oxygen. These ideas are proof of the new openness in our society. They reveal the hidden kindness within us. This film will revive in people a sense of their own value. It calls on people to respect their neighbors and to respect themselves. This film in my view seeks to unite people.

Are you planning to make more films now?

In Moscow the production process is very complicated. We already talked about the fact that *perestroika* isn't a mechanical process. All the radio stations shout out the word *"perestroika."* But the chemical industry produces film stock that's unusable. You have to do 20 takes, because you never know which one will come out. It doesn't matter how loudly you say *"perestroika."* Our film equipment is from the Stone Age. But that's still not the most important thing. Because for me it's even better to use this outdated equipment. I'd probably be lost in Hollywood. I've never held a videocamera in my hands. It's easier for me to work with one lens. Coppola could never shoot a film with one lens. I think he's a great director. Fellini couldn't stand working even half a day at Mosfilm. He couldn't stand it. But in Russia people are trained in tough circumstances, and sometimes they even make good movies.

You're very politically committed and socially concerned and morally concerned and it sounds like you feel you have some kind of mission to wake people up. How will you do this?

Everyone has to be patient but at some point I want to make my own *Amarcord*. But what I'm trying to tell you about is a crazy movie. It's practically impossible to make these kinds of movies in the USSR. Because everyone, from a janitor at the studio up to a minister will ask me "what does this episode mean?" "Why is he upside down?" The actors will say they don't understand how to act this out. And I'll tell them that when the film is ready they'll understand everything. But everyone is against having this film produced. That's how *Commissar* was made. Actors were saying I was nuts, and they were right. But then they were amazed that I finished it despite everything. They couldn't understand how I could have completed it. Each day was a struggle. I was not fighting for my film, I was fighting for each frame. At home I have an amazing document signed by the former head of Goskino. He was reproached by the Council of Ministers for allowing this film to be made.

Who was it?

Alexei Romanov. He sent this document to his superiors and in it, he totally denounced the film. He had to explain why he had disbursed the funds for this film. And he explained—I don't remember it word for word—today it's very funny to read it. It went like this: "Askoldov consciously and insidiously concealed the true meaning of this film, and to the very last day of shooting, it wasn't clear what kind of movie he was shooting. But when we saw what he had done, we took appropriate measures." And they did indeed take action. I was barred from making movies, fired from the studio, they discussed my work at various conferences, I was expelled from the Communist Party. But I spoke before them and explained that I had made a film about the international solidarity of people of all nationalities, and I naively said that I was convinced that over time the ban would be lifted. But it took a long time.

Well your faith was justified.

I'm convinced that faith is a material force.

Maybe we should end on that note. I just have one question. Who among Soviet filmmakers today shares your general Weltanschauung?

I'm sure there are people who share my point of view, but I don't have any friends among filmmakers. My friends are theater actors, directors, writers, many of them of the older generation. And among them, despite all the perversities that have happened around them, many have held firm to their moral values. That's why today's movement forward is in fact a return to the morality of the past. Because it would be difficult to find greater moral values anywhere in the world than in Russian art and the Russian people.

Dmitry Astrakhan

"I never want to make a movie that only Jewish people are going to watch. I want to make a movie that everyone will watch, that will be of interest to anyone. I want to make people think about their own national backgrounds as well."

Menashe: *Tell us a bit about yourself, please.*

Astrakhan: I graduated from the Leningrad Theater Institute, in 1982. I majored in Theater Direction. After graduation, I traveled to Sverdlovsk to work.

Why?

Because I couldn't find work in Leningrad. It was a time when the zones of influences were already carved up. And even though I had terrific grades in theater, I still couldn't find any work in Leningrad and left for Sverdlovsk.

Was it because of difficult political circumstances or because you are Jewish?

No, I wouldn't say that it had anything to do with politics or with me being Jewish. It's just that a certain clique of people was already working in the theater and they didn't let outsiders in. They weren't interested in bringing in new people and new ideas. So I traveled to the Sverdlovsk Young People's Theater. I worked there for six years and directed many plays. For example, Ostrovsky's *Dokhodnoe Mesto (A Profitable Post)*, a classic, and Fonvizin, Vampilov, a Soviet classic. I also directed plays by contemporary Soviet and Western playwrights. For example, Steven Polikov, a well-known British author. He's famous in England, one of the main people at the Shakespeare Theater there. I also taught at the Theater Institute, training actors. After that I returned to Leningrad.

How did you end up in film?

I returned to Leningrad because the biggest theater in the country hired me: The Bolshoi Drama Theater, where Tostonogov was working. I directed plays there. Then I wanted to make a change, to shoot a film. I felt that I wanted to have full control over my production. I wanted to make a movie because it's a very independent kind of art. It's the kind of art in which the director has the best role. And at that time my plays were already departing quite a bit from their scripts. I started changing the playwright's ideas. I already had experience writing screenplays with my friend, Oleg Danilov. We produced a play at the Leningrad Young People's Theater. Oleg Danilov is a pseudonym—his real name is Oleg Alshchitz. He's Jewish too. He had to have a pseudonym because it's difficult for a Jewish author to get published.

And Astrakhan is not your real name?

I chose Astrakhan so that people can't figure out what I am.

They think I'm a Tatar or something. It's Jewish but not a typical Jewish name. So nobody knows exactly what my nationality is.

So you and Danilov...

We wrote this play and gained experience in this area. Danilov is a professional playwright. We worked together and with that experience under our belt, I felt we could write a pretty good screenplay for film.

Danilov is also from Leningrad?

Yes. And at that time, Lenfilm asked me to direct a film. Alexei Guerman asked me to work with him. He had seen my plays and felt that I could do something unlike any other Soviet filmmakers.

But it was your idea to produce a film?

Guerman simply made it possible. His name could guarantee that I could get through the *nomenklatura* at Lenfilm. At that time, the state funded all films.

That was of course even during glasnost.

Glasnost had already started. We started thinking about the kind of movie we should make. We had different ideas, but it soon became clear that we should make our first film about something very important to us. I wanted to do something very important because this was my first film. This would be the first word that I hoped would be heard not only in our country, but maybe throughout the world. And in general, film becomes a part of history. A play was performed and then over with. The art of theater is live, instantaneous. Movies should also be alive, but if you watch them years from now they should have meaning as well.

What themes did you think of?

We had many different ideas. They were quite disparate. But it became clear that we had to focus on the most important things. For us this was the national question. Because we're both Jewish, we realized that the Jewish question was closer to us and we knew more about it. We could take it as an example of the larger national issues in our country. After that we began thinking of how we would do this. We thought for a long time, about thirty minutes. We came up with a fantastic idea.

It's an interesting story. But I had heard that it was based on Sholom Aleikhem and Alexander Kuprin and Vasily Grossman.

Not Grossman, but Kuprin, yes. Sholom Aleichem, Isaak

Babel and Kuprin. You see, we came up with a situation. After that we started thinking—what do we know about this issue? We remembered that there was a chapter in one of Sholom Aleikhem's works, in his story, "Tevye the Dairyman." The last chapter of this story is called *Izydi!* (*Go Away!*).[1] And this chapter recounted how some Russian villagers created a fake *pogrom*. It was a fake *pogrom*. That's the only thing we borrowed. From Kuprin we borrowed the character of the village constable. We borrowed not so much the actual person but Kuprin himself. Kuprin was a famous writer. He liked to drink. He was also a Russian aristocrat. He was very much against Jewish *pogroms* and spoke out against them. His personality was for us the bright spot in our film. He was closer to us as a person. Characters like the constable are quite common in his stories. They don't do anything, but just create a certain atmosphere. From Babel we borrowed a sequence in which a Jew visits a brothel. But all together it created just a general atmosphere. We were reading these authors, not specifically for this purpose. We'd read them when we were kids.

Well, congratulations.

And we were thinking of what this film would be like. After that we kind of blended it all together. Because they were a great help to us with the kind of atmosphere and literature they created. We had certain literary criteria for our script, some literary standards we held to. Then we wrote for a very long time, for an entire year. We had many different versions. We finally completed the script and it was accepted by Lenfilm. Though the money for the film came from an independent organization, a private group. I then began working on the film and realized we had to do more work on the script. So we rewrote it again. We came up with a lot of new material. But when we had chosen the actor who would play the main role and had filmed half of the movie, I realized that we again had to rewrite the script. So we rewrote it once again. We had to reshoot almost everything that was shot before. Because the actor playing the main role was so unique that we had to change the movie because of his character. He was very good at acting scenes of high drama.

A Georgian actor, yes?

Yes. Otar Megvinetukhutsesi.

He's not Jewish.

No, he's Georgian. And we rewrote the first half of the script. Because we wanted to put some humor into it, to make him a funny person. I feel that if we're not going to laugh with the hero, we won't cry with him. Because laughter brings the audience closer to the hero. When were laughing either with the hero or at him, or at the situations he ends up in, it brings us closer to him. And we also feel sorry for him. So when we rewrote the script we specifically put in some situations that were created especially for him. There are different scenes, with his wife, when she beats him up.

Did Guerman give you advice?

He didn't interfere. Guerman didn't interfere and it was great. He read the script. I don't know how much he got into it, but he felt it was a very good idea and he supported us. His support was quite valuable, because he's a very well-known director.

Was it a co-production — between Lenfilm and a private organization? Did you have freedom to do what you wanted?

It was interesting. On the one hand I had total freedom to do what I wanted, because I brought in people who provided funding from the outside. On the other side, I was producing this film under Guerman's studio, "First Film." There Guerman had to look over the rushes. Naturally, I didn't want anyone to control my work. So when I left for our shoot in Ukraine, someone demanded that he see the rushes. I told him I don't have time for that. We had only forty days. I had to shoot a major film. If I'm going to have to pass some kind of exam, I won't have time to make this movie. So if you don't like it you can expel me from school. I'm going to make my movie. At that point I left Guerman's studio and shot the rest of the film on a different arrangement with Lenfilm. They didn't have any control over what I was doing.

This is an example of the new type of filmmaking that emerged under Gorbachev and glasnost.

Of course. Ostensibly the people who gave me money were the ones who were supposed to have control. But they didn't understand anything. They didn't have any idea what I wanted to do.

They were simply generous or...

No, they just were involved in another business. They simply gave me the money and didn't quite understand why and where it was going. They just wanted to see the completed film. And they liked it and everything was fine.

Were they also Jewish?

No. In the beginning, it's a funny story how I got the money to make this film. When it became clear that Lenfilm had no money, but I had my completed script, I asked Guerman whether I could shoot the film if I got the money from some other source. He said sure. So I went to a Jewish organization in Leningrad. It was a new organization. Jewish people were there and I told them I was a famous theater director, that I wanted to make a movie about Jewish people and that I needed money. One of them asked me how much I needed. I thought a bit and said one million rubles. At that time this was a lot of money in Russia. Films were being shot for 800,000 rubles. That was for a major movie. He said, "well, what's the film about?" I told him the story. His name was Slava Kamyshev. He was a journalist. And I discovered he was a real good man. He understood everything right away. And I'd only told him my general idea. He said he liked it very much and would give me the money.

The next day he came and signed a contract with Lenfilm in the name of the Nevsky Prospect Association. He gave me a small advance. And we started working. After that, I worked very quickly. He then advanced me a bit more. Then I had to shoot the film in Ukraine. So he told me, "I'm leaving for Israel." And I said, "how can you do that? I'm about to shoot my movie!" He said, "You know what? You're going to make your movie, because I already signed this contract and already gave you a part of the money. I'm a hundred percent sure that they'll give you the rest. But nonetheless, shoot it as fast as you can." So he left. And after that I realized I should shoot it as quickly as possible. I didn't tell anyone about this conversation. I just shot this really fast. And at a certain point it became clear that there was no more money for the film. And while the owners of the Nevsky Prospect Association tried to figure out what kind of contract had been signed, I just shot my movie as fast as I could. Because Lenfilm was basically giving me the money I needed as a loan. This happened over one month. A huge controversy erupted at Lenfilm. Guerman got scared. He didn't know who would end up paying for all this. He was worried the film would be terrible.

So he couldn't understand this new market, this new way of doing things?

He understood everything. He just didn't want to be responsible for this. And I can understand that. But I spoke with the head of Lenfilm, and he allowed me to shoot on credit. Afterwards he was actually sorry that he didn't purchase the film outright. Though I told him to do so.

So this film belongs to the Nevsky Prospect Association.

Yes.

And is it still available?

Yes, but in the U.S., thanks to Anne Borin, she loved this movie even on videotape. And she made it possible for this film to break into the New York film market, not at a festival.

All this is a very interesting commentary on the new state of affairs in Russian film. Another question. Do you consider yourself to be a "Jewish director?"

I think of myself as a director first and foremost. But I'm also Jewish. So I'm a director and I'm Jewish. I understand the question. Probably in considering Jewish issues, I approach them as a Jew. But when I direct a Russian classic, that's what I do. But at the same time I'm also Jewish. This is the kind of head I have, this is how I think, that's how I feel. My parents are Jewish, my whole family is Jewish. I have four older brothers who all live in the U.S. And probably I was raised in a certain environment. It's unavoidable. But I don't feel that it was a particularly religious environment. Yet all my life I've known that I was Jewish.

I've noticed that there are many new films on Jewish themes, both documentaries and features.

I never want to make a movie that only Jewish people are going to watch. I want to make a movie that everyone will watch, that will be of interest to anyone. I want to make people think about their own national backgrounds as well.

Yes, that's clear. But what's interesting for me as an historian is this birth or rebirth of Jewish themes in film. For example, the documentary film, The Great Concert of the Peoples *by Semyom Aranovich. Alexander Zeldovich also had a film,* Sunset. *And of course the first film of this type, released under glasnost was Askoldov's* Commissar. *So this is a phenomenon. Filmmakers couldn't touch this topic at all before. Will this trend continue?*

You see, in principle people can talk about anything in Russia.

You just need the money to produce whatever you want. And no one can prevent you from doing it. It's another question that maybe some people aren't going to like what you do. You see, you don't know where the brick is going to fall.

Yes. During the time of the film there were the "Black Hundreds," and now there's "Pamiat." Some of today's events have an historical resonance.

Of course. There's "Pamiat'," there's "Sobor," a very strong political organization—have you seen how they dress? In fascist uniforms.

If you don't consider yourself to be a Jewish director, do you feel yourself to be a Leningrad director, and what does Leningrad-style cinema mean?

You know. I consider myself to be neither a Jewish nor a Leningrad director. I'm a director above all.

But isn't there a Leningrad style—Guerman's, for example?

There is a Guerman style, but it's not the Leningrad style. And unfortunately a lot of people copy him. That's their problem. That means that there aren't a lot of talented people in this world.

Maybe I shouldn't talk specifically about the cinema, but consider the Leningraders Akhmatova, Shostakovich, Brodsky.

Leningrad is of course a specific region. I would say that in a good sense this area has preserved a traditional approach to art. I always felt that people in Leningrad don't give in to what is fashionable, but rather hold to certain basic laws of professionalism in their art.

To a classical style?

I consider myself a very traditional director. In theater as well. Because a theater like Tostonogov's is an example of classical, traditional theater. The high traditionalism of this theater lies in the fact that every play is aimed at a contemporary audience but at the same time strives to bring out the original intent of the author as much as possible. The actors have always had a very high level of professionalism. The theater doesn't get involved in political grandstanding. It always addresses deeper, more serious issues. But at the same time these are modern-day issues as well.

As I already told you, I liked your film very much. I only have one little criticism. It was with Yefrosinia—Belka. She was too modern.

She seemed to me to be very touching. I personally really liked that part, even though I feel uncomfortable speaking about it, when she shouts "Grandmother, they're going to kill us, why are you silent? They're killers!" And when at the end, she screams, and when her mother and father try to hold onto her. I'll tell you something: at that point, I think, "now that's a good director, and a good actress."

You have to take into consideration that her sense of modernity comes from her relationship with Petya. But you need to take into account the fact that they've known each other since childhood. They have a different relationship. It's a different kind of love, springing from friendship. If they had just met, and just begun their relationship, she would have acted entirely differently. Because she would have had to act embarrassed and ashamed in front of him. They went swimming naked together when they were little. They live in the same little village. Kids go running along the shores of the river. She'd already seen Petya. Then they started feeling ashamed around each other. Their relationship was different. Later things became more complex.

I invented this backstory just now. Because you asked this question. But now I have to prove that I'm right. So I was thinking, why did I do it this way? And I realized that this must be why. They had a very simple relationship. I don't know how they could be any different if they grew up together.

But Petya was a Russian peasant and she was like a hippy.

My mother lived in a Ukrainian village as a little girl. She told me stories of how they lived, how she performed in this village in 1925. She told me how her older sister lived as well. We often think that things were somehow so special, so different. But often kids and young girls acted like hippies, as you say. Because Jewish girls were very active—they put on plays, played tricks on people. All this happened.

OK, thank you—that's a fascinating explanation.

I won't insist upon it, but that's just my vision.

She also touched me, but...

I understand what you're talking about, but it was done that way, it wasn't by chance. We decided to do it that way.

At the end of the film, there's a freeze-frame, fade to white, so we're left wondering what will happen.

You realize that of course these four or five people died. But I hope that maybe they killed some other people, twice as many as were killed on their side. Because I want to see evil punished. Those people set out to kill them, so someone should take revenge. But in fact, in the places where people resisted the *pogroms*, the *pogroms* were stopped. With no resistance, you have the old Russian game of Jew-killing. This wasn't just murder, it was entertainment. That's what's so horrifying. The murderers organized a festival around it. That's why we set this scene to such cheerful music, a waltz, which makes it like a festival, and makes it all the more horrifying.

Yes, I noticed that. There was that expression, "Beat the Jews and save Russia."

You see, I'm Jewish. I grew up among Russians. I have a lot of Russian friends. I know what anti-semitism means. But I also know what friendship means. I know when Russian people have acted in a very principled way, when my Russian friends have acted on a very high level. Some *émigrés* who left Russia want things to be terrible there. Because that would justify their departure. They want everything to be terrible there. They lie to themselves. Maybe they had a bad experience. Maybe they really had a bad experience. But I don't believe that anyone who has lived in Russia never had any Russian friends. You see, then I'd ask what kind of person is this? If he never had a single Russian friend. I know too many Russian people, and they're all very different. And there are bad ones and good ones. But as a whole, they're people with a positive outlook on life, people with a heart. It wouldn't be the truth if we denied that.

OK, a last general question. What do you think of the situation in Russian film today, and what of the future?

I think it's a difficult situation, because the internal market is very difficult for the distribution of Russian films. There aren't any rules that operate in that market yet. But on the other hand, I think these are natural processes. Everything is possible right now. Anyone who has money can shoot a film. Everyone should have a chance to make a movie. There needs to be some kind of standard which the viewer will have a hand in determining. And through this process things will settle down. And only then can we talk about some new trends. So far there's a huge disparity in quality. You see some unbelievable trash being produced right now. But sometimes some very interesting work appears. New people and new names surface.

Like you! I gather you're an optimist.

Yes.

---

[1] The film is reviewed in Chapter I.

Mikhail Belikov

"Over the last ten years, bureaucrats have been in charge of the film industry. Bureaucrats who had no connection to the creative process, and they had no right to have such authority."

Menashe: *I want to congratulate you on your film,* The Night Is Short, *which I had the pleasure of seeing this week. My interest in it is in part from my interest in Soviet films in general. But also because I'm roughly of your generation—I'm a little older than you, but I too remember the war. And secondly, I'm interested as an historian in the presentation of historical material. So my first questions to you will be of a precise historical nature. For example, where does the film take place?*

Belikov: It was filmed in the places where I grew up, where I spent my childhood—in Ukraine, which was occupied at the time.

In the Crimea?

No, I was born in Kharkov. It was very important to me to shoot the film in the places where I grew up. Because I wanted to convey the proper atmosphere, with the right cast, the right costumes, and in particular, the characters had to have a real setting in which to play out this drama. In another place this story could not have happened.

And the body of water that's shown in the film—that's why I thought perhaps it was the Crimea. What was that?

In principle it could have been the Crimea, because the Crimea was also under occupation. It's a typical Ukrainian setting. But the place where we shot was Taganrog. Near the shores of the Sea of Azov. The Germans occupied that area too. I spent my childhood on the seashore. The seashore was a very important backdrop to the film. It has always been connected to my dreams, and it was very important in helping develop the characters.

That came through in the film very significantly. So we've established the place, I would like to establish the time. I believe it begins in 1944, correct?

Just about. If we want to be more specific, this story could have started in 1944, but...

There was a reference to the liberation of Minsk in the beginning.

Perhaps it was 1944. Although in the beginning of the film, someone's talking about the end of the war, so it could have taken place early in 1945. But a difference of two years isn't of great importance, and I'm pleased that you could sense the time period in which it was taking place.

And at the other end as well, my calculations tell me that the film ends in 1955.

That's very right. Near the end of the film we referred to the events of 1953. And after that two more years passed. So it could well be that the film ends in 1955.

Let me just say that I think I understand why there's constant attention to the theme of the Great Patriotic War. But often Americans are constantly asking—those of them who see Soviet films—why do they make so many films about the war?

I don't think that this film is literally a war film. There isn't a single gunshot in the whole film, no tank attacks, no bombings. But the consequences of the war were of course very important to me personally.

So it's essentially a film about growing up, rather than a film about the war.

The problem is that the people of my generation—a generation that has a tremendous influence on the social and cultural life of our society—in one way or another have linked all their creative work to that period of time, because that's when we were kids. It was an extremely difficult time, very complex, a time of poverty, and nonetheless, it was at that time that our generation experienced extraordinary spiritual and moral growth.

Is that what you meant, even though you were saying it was a very difficult time, a poor time, you still say that that time was richer for the young than today's young?

Yes, I think that's true. In any case, my contemporaries and I are all witness to the growing predominance of materialism over spiritual and moral principles.

So what has been the reaction to the film on the part of contemporary Soviet youth?

I think that it has been very successful with younger viewers.

Is it in part because of what we're talking about, that there is a generation gap?

I think that first of all there is a problem of genre. My film has no real plot. There is no strong story line. It doesn't have the features that young people like in a film.

Nostalgic, lyrical, melancholic.

Yes. To a certain extent I didn't try to make a commercially successful film. It was more a declaration of love for my childhood. Love for my childhood and for the coming of age, which, no matter how difficult it was, will always be the happiest period of any person's life.

Good or bad.

It represents truth, which is the greatest value.

*I've noticed that you did another film, which I have not seen, and I don't think it has appeared here—*How Young We Were.

I'm very sorry that we didn't bring both the films together, because How Young We Were is the sequel to this film.

The same character growing up?

They're the same characters, and they're going on to the next story.

Can I ask what happens? What happens to Ivan?

At the beginning of the film, Ivan is applying to an institute. Later a tragic event takes place, connected with the war.

Again the war.

This is based on a true story that happened to my friend. During the war, during the famine, one night, he mistakenly drank a glass of phosphorous that was used to make matches, and he died of leukemia.

Do you like using nonprofessional actors?

Quite often. Because it's very important to me that the character looks like a particular type of person in real life—it's a kind of "typing." The visual aspect, such as creating the right atmosphere—if you create an atmosphere but no one recognizes what you're trying to convey, it doesn't work. In film there's a concept called an awareness of the time [when the film takes place]. This depends on how readily recognizable the "typing" of characters is as a reflection of a particular historical period. So many of my characters are taken from the streets, because they're more representative.

Well I think it was a success. Another scene that caught my attention relates to personal matters and there always remains a subjective element in seeing a film, and that was the "Spin the Bottle" scene. I had a similar experience such as you presented in the film.

It's a story that many people could relate to since they went through this when they were young.

I didn't know that game existed in the Soviet Union.

It's an international game. Love is the same everywhere.

But it was a well-done scene. One other question about the film. There is a scene where the neighbor dances with the visiting soldier who Ivan thinks is his father. And she suddenly stops dancing, takes his hat and gives him his hat, and he leaves. Again, I think I have an idea of what that scene meant, but could you explain?

This was a very typical dramatic situation that many women experienced when their men didn't return from the front. Naturally, the young woman needed love. She was languishing without her husband. Four or five years without a man. On the other hand, there was the hope that just maybe, her husband will return. She can't cross this moral threshold and give up all hope, so she asks the man to leave.

I think that was well done too. Here and there I noticed a picture of Stalin, which of course suggests to those who knew the period, the extraordinary role or image of Stalin. Did you purposely avoid considering that whole question, or was that your way of addressing the question?

It was impossible to explore that period of time and not include Stalin in it. That would be untruthful. At that time, Stalin was part of our daily lives. But for a kid, Stalin didn't hold the significance that he did for the older generation. He was more of a symbol. So since I'm telling this story through the eyes of this boy, we developed the story of Stalin as a political entity. Even though when the solar eclipse happens, the people in the Soviet Union who remember this moment know that it's connected with certain specific events. This eclipse took place in 1954 when Beria was arrested. And those who remember the eclipse will make that association.

So it had a symbolic value as well.

The eclipse happened on the same day that Beria was arrested.

That's interesting. That is a wonderful historical point. Would you say your film is a "Ukrainian film" and can one speak of the tradition of Dovzhenko?

I think that this story, this film couldn't take place anywhere else. This story could only take place in Ukraine. Because the results of the German occupation that were shown in the film existed only in Ukraine. As for the influence of Dovzhenko's poetic language, I don't think it's present here.

How would you define that tradition? In general?

In general I think that in Dovzhenko's poetics there were many mistakes. What truly interests me in Dovzhenko are his early works, such as *Earth, Aerograd,* and *Arsenal.* Not *Michurin.* During this early period, the national character and spirit of the people forms the basis of his work. Many interpret the poetry of Dovzhenko during this period by judging only the external elements of his work. I think that themes such as national awakening aren't external qualities—they're not apples, or sunrises and sunsets. Some people think that Dovzhenko can be reduced to a horse running through a field. The early works of Dovzhenko are interesting because they perfectly captured the Ukrainian national character.

And that's the part that you identify with?

I don't know, maybe.

OK. Let me take up a couple of subjects that we discussed earlier. And that of course is the impact of the decisions of the Fifth Congress of Filmmakers. And, in a general sense, the influence of the 27th Party Congress and glasnost and perestroika. Let's discuss a couple of issues related to this. Would you have made the film differently if you had made it today?

No. I think that I would have done it the same way. My film didn't try to be controversial, to address burning social issues. As for the events you mentioned, the 27th Congress and the Fifth Congress, I don't think their results are as important as what will follow.

I agree. And have you seen any changes recently?

Yes. I wanted to talk about it. Over the last ten years, bureaucrats have been in charge of the film industry. Bureaucrats who had no connection to the creative process, and they had no right to have such authority. Nonetheless, they were the ones who determined the release of so many films.

And you're now working in a new environment?

No, the environment hasn't radically changed so far. But there are certain radical measures that have been adopted, first of all by the Union of Filmmakers. This gives us a chance to take a different approach to the question of a filmmaker's creative independence. The filmmakers have been granted the right to influence legislation. The state apparatus—Goskino—is being reduced. The Editorial Council at Goskino, which used to censor screenplays, and which weighed heavily upon us, is being eliminated. Now studios have much greater freedom. This is a great victory.

So you're breaking down a tremendous barrier between you and the public.

There's a second step of *perestroika* in cinema. The second step will mean that if we truly demand independence and say that we will be in charge of everything, then we will also be responsible for financing our films, for ensuring that a film is profitable.

So it's up to you now?

Yes. And this is the problem. If we don't resolve this, then the bureaucrats will be only too happy to get their hands on the film industry once again. They'd have a very good argument—they'd say "we gave you freedom, but you weren't able to handle your freedom."

I wish you success. Last question. What film plans do you have?

I witnessed the events in the Crimea which took place in 1986. Chernobyl,[1] the catastrophe on the Admiral Nakhimov.

As an actual witness?

The sinking of the Admiral Nakhimov? No. Not literally a witness. It's just connected with Ukraine. During that year Ukraine had a high number of catastrophes. We have a huge environmental problem with the Dnepr River. The Dnepr River is totally polluted. And taken all together, this makes you realize that people have become victims of the environment we ourselves created.

And certainly all this is rich material for films.

We don't want to speak literally of the Chernobyl catastrophe.

We just want to show how modern man has put himself in a corner. And when he tries to save himself from one catastrophe, he ends up in another.

So you're reasserting a tradition of the Soviet cinema as a political voice?

No. Human nature is always in some way connected with the social environment in which a person lives.

[1] Belikov's Chernobyl film, *Raspad*, is discussed in Chapter I.

Nana Djordjadze

"Georgians love remembering their past, they love their history — all history, ancient history, recent history."

Menashe: *I came to Soviet cinema through my interest in history. I use Soviet films in my classes to illustrate historical themes, and I must tell you that I hope to use your film,* The Robinsonada, *in my course on the Civil War. Is it based on an original story?*

Djordjadze: We invented this story ourselves, but it has a lot of references to things that actually happened.

An extrapolation from the discovery of this grave of Christopher Hughes?

That's how the story originated. The telegraph lines were still there. We saw the grave, and the telegraph poles were still standing. You could even see some English notes hanging on these poles. And then we just extrapolated and invented the story line.

This question of dealing with the past in Soviet cinema — the critic Plakhov said, "in our country, the retro style found the most fertile style in Georgia." Is that true?

Yes. Because Georgians love remembering their past, they love their history — all history, ancient history, recent history. It is a nation that greatly respects its traditions, which go back for centuries. And for the Georgians it's very important to have a sense of your roots.

Would you say this is true of young Georgians as well? A sense of nostalgia?

Yes. Of course there are elements of nostalgia. But the most important thing is to know where you came from, to know your past.

This is very striking to Americans, because an American critic once said that "America equals amnesia." And the historical consciousness is something that often does not affect Americans. Let's say that that's a strong part of Georgian cinema. What other parts would you assign to it? Can one speak of a Georgian cinema?

There are certain tendencies. We also speak very specifically of a Georgian cinema as a phenomenon that is different from Russian cinema.

How is it different?

It's a different point of view. It's a different style, actors have a different way of carrying out their roles.

Specifically, how?

More specifically? For example, the Stanislavsky method which is very popular in Russia—the actors here know it, but it doesn't complement the Georgian character. Because the Georgian character is very emotional and impulsive. He's unpredictable, in his expressions and emotions. And that's why the logic of behavior behind the Stanislavsky method isn't logical with the Georgian character. In general, the Georgian character—the people of Georgia— are very artistic. When they're talking they're always playing some role. Not because they're fakes. They're just artistic. For example, when they're at table, the table is set in an artistic way. Because this is a special ritual. We have someone called a *tamada* who is the "table director." He's like a film director. Everything depends on him. The *tamada* is always chosen from people who are talented, full of energy. He must know poetry, know how to sing and dance. The director has to have a sense of every person in the film crew and open these people up. So I'm simply explaining to you how this is part of our national character. And he is totally unpredictable. Because Georgians are very individualistic. These artistic tendencies and the way actors approach their roles make Georgian cinema different.

As for the development of the story line, the building of the subject, even in the most tragic situations in life, Georgians will try to find the brighter, ironic side of things. And they have a great sense of self-irony. They hardly ever laugh at others—they like to laugh at themselves. Because it's not right to laugh at others. I can laugh at myself as much as I want, making fun of my shortcomings, but I can't do that to others—it's immoral to hang out another person's dirty laundry. This also distinguishes Georgian cinema from the rest. Another thing I'd like to add is that this sense of humor has helped lighten even the saddest things, because this nation over the course of its lengthy history has always lived at extremes. The nation has always been on the verge of tragedy. It's probably our sense of humor, not only that, but our sense of humor, sense of freedom, this national character has helped us survive. It's a form of self-preservation.

That was something I was going to suggest, but you presented it much better than I could. I too have noticed this ironic element in Georgian films. Last year I saw, and liked, and laughed at [Eldar] Shengelaya's Blue Mountain. *On the other hand, one of the saddest films I ever saw—as well as one of the most beautiful films I ever saw—was [Georgi Shengelaya's]* Pirosmani.[1] *How do you reconcile the two? This deep, deep sadness, as well as the constant joy and irony?*

Pirosmani, it seems to me, was a great artist. Even in that film there was a lot of irony. It might be a different kind of irony, a sad sense of irony. But the person who played the part of the Georgian artist Pirosmani was himself an artist, [Avtandil] Varazi. He magnificently portrayed a very tragic destiny. He was also an alcoholic and also died of alcoholism. He poured his own spirit into the character of Pirosmani. This film—I love this film—and Pirosmani's paintings even had a great influence. Because all the compositions in the sets for the film were taken from his paintings. The world of his paintings was recreated on the screen. The world of the Georgia in which he lived.

What did you see as ironic in the film?

In *Pirosmani*? First of all, the relationship of Pirosmani to himself, as an artist. How he sees himself. A person who had no egotistical tendencies. He was an artistic genius who for a glass of wine would paint things on a tablecloth, on the walls. It's a national characteristic of Georgians that they let their talents spill out freely. In Georgia you can find a lot of people who are wonderful storytellers. They have this great talent of telling stories. But they're too lazy to write them down. This could be wonderful literature. But no, they could tell these stories left and right, and other people could take these stories and create their own literature. And each time you're sitting at the table, it's like a variety show—poetry springs forth and then disappears, because no one writes it down. There are improvised competitions in verse. Songs are made up as people go along. No one ever records this on a tape recorder. So you get this feeling that everything is simply hanging around you in the air. And from one generation to another this state of grace, and all the air around is filled with this grace.

I look forward to going to Georgia and improvising at your table! Actually, that's all very interesting as a way of interpreting the film, Pirosmani. *Another aspect of Georgian civilization is its very patriarchical character. But in cinema, I notice, there are many women directors.*

There's always been a cult surrounding women in Georgia. You could even say that Georgia's renaissance took place when Queen Tamara was in charge. Women have always commanded great respect and always held the place of honor in Georgian society.

It seems that in the films that I've seen there is always a strong woman playing a part. In your film, for example, in The Robinsonada, *Anna is a very strong woman. She violates her brother's politics and policy and she goes beyond the tradition of staying in the village, shows up with a rifle in the bedroom scene. Were you conscious of making a powerful woman in your film?*

You know, it's very difficult to speak about Georgians without speaking about the women as well. She plays a very important role in life.

So you're not consciously a feminist as we say in the West, but you're presenting the natural order of things.

I'm not a feminist. I think—since women have always been free in Georgia—the issue of feminism never arose. The woman has always respected the man and his sphere of activity—he always had his sphere and she has always had hers. He always had his place and she always had her place. Men always respect women. It's very closely connected. Neither side felt privileged. But each person knew his or her place.

I've heard many Russian women talk about the need for a feminist movement in Russia.

I don't understand these women. For me they're like a bunch of girls, it's nothing I relate to.

There may be a big difference between Georgia and Russia in that regard.

I can speak about Georgian women, but let the Russian women speak for themselves.

The film was quite interesting as a kind of fantasy the way you switched time, the intermingling of time, the alternation between black-and-white and sepia and color. All of that I think is very evocative of the question of memory and the past, and I think you did that very well. Still, certain problems of realism come up. Mr. Hughes, for example, does not look like an Englishman, he doesn't talk like an Englishman.

He speaks like an American. This was a mistake—the way he talks. At that time a wonderful American was working at a university here in Georgia. He was a very artistic person and he was studying Georgian. He spoke both English and Georgian, and this worked out well for me. And he wasn't someone who has learned English—it was his native language. I didn't understand the nuances—I couldn't hear the nuances in the British and American accent. But I think that it's not that significant.

I agree.

Because this story is so mixed up in time and place. It seems to me that he could have spoken any language, because the modern-day hero—the grandson—projects his image onto the image of his grandfather. When he thinks of his grandfather he sees his own orchestra around him. When people try to imagine what their great-grandmother was like, they imagine that she looked just like themselves. You identify with her that way. That's why this contemporary composer could have spoken any language. Languages are always criss-crossing in this world. Americans travel to Europe, Americans borrow words from the European languages. Languages are no longer pure. Everything has gotten mixed together.

True. One last question about the general film industry. Would you have made this film differently if you made it today?

I wouldn't have filmed it any differently. But I might have experimented a bit more with the form. Because what I have done here with this system of collages, I was afraid that people wouldn't understand it. But now I know that there were parts of the film that

I tried to smooth out a bit, to make a story line out it, when I should have mixed up the time periods even more. If I were doing it again now, I would have edited it differently. But it's always easy to speak about the past. If I did it the way I did, then it's done and over with. Let's see what I'll do next time.

And what will you be doing?

I'm now completing a documentary film on Tbilisi.

For television?

No. I have an idea to do a project with the French and the Canadians.

What exactly?

A co-production. I don't like to talk about my films before they're finished. I'm superstitious. I also have a screenplay that I wrote with my husband, Irakli Kvirikadze, waiting for me in Georgia. But I'll get to it at the right time.

I wish you great success and good luck.

---

[1] *Pirosmani* is reviewed in Chapter VI.

Elem Klimov

"Society faced an accumulation of problems and a growing desire to solve these problems. I think this is a historical process that led to a great desire among the people for serious changes. The filmmakers were among the first who really wanted these changes."

Menashe: *Let's begin with your film, which here in the U.S. was called* Rasputin: The Real Story. *[Reviewed above, in Chapter III.] Was it your way of commemorating the sixtieth anniversary of the Revolution?*

Klimov: I didn't choose this theme in order to commemorate the anniversary. I began this film in 1966. And for quite some time I tried to get this film off the ground, but wasn't able to. The cinema leadership deeply feared this film.

Why?

Why were they afraid? They kept saying, "why should we talk about this filthy guy?" For Soviet cinema Rasputin was a closed subject. By the way, this alternative title for the film isn't accurate. It was renamed for commercial reasons. They renamed *Agoniya* as *Rasputin*. Yet it's not a film about Rasputin but about the phenomenon that he represented. This phenomenon is a concept all its own—the final stage of the degradation of the tsarist regime.

And is that what attracted you to the subject?

Rasputin? The degradation itself? It's a film about the end of an entire era. Which ended with such extreme, phantasmagorical forms of disintegration.

The writer Valentin Pikul treated the same subject in his novel of 1978. Was your film an influence?

Maybe. Because he used the same historical materials. But we interpreted them differently. Pikul tried to produce a book for the average Joe on the street, for the uneducated reader who is interested in the petty details of [the tsarist family's] personal life and its depravity.

You said something about how the authorities might have considered this a representation of the cruder aspects of Old Russia. Is that why the film wasn't released for ten years?

This too is a reason.

What else?

The fact that the film wasn't done along stereotypical lines. Our point of view on events focused on what was happening at the highest levels of power, the breakdown of the institutions of power, but as far as the revolutionary theme, it's simply present as a background, through documentaries. The revolutionary events that happened underground didn't enter our field of vision. So some people felt this was lacking in our film.

Let me say that you would make a wonderful historian.

I think that a person of any occupation—if at all possible, it should be required that he get an education in history. His second occupation can be whatever he wants, but only on that foundation, especially someone who is directing films. History is our greatest teacher—and we're the worst students. That's why throughout the whole history of mankind we repeat the very same mistakes.

In a manner of speaking, one might say. We won't get into the history of mankind, however. Let me conclude our discussion of **Agoniya**. *Here in the U.S. we speculated why the film wasn't shown. Here are the reasons that I have heard others express and that I myself might have thought, too. One: There was, for a Soviet film, too much sex. Including shots of nudity.*

This is reason number fifteen why my film wasn't released.

OK. Secondly, this is a rumor I heard from a friend who heard it in Moscow, that your portrait of Badmaev, which was extremely satirical, offended his great grandson, who was a famous, celebrated and important doctor in Moscow.

The thing is that besides that great grandson, Badmaev has many other relatives. They all protested even without seeing the film.

So was that a factor, perhaps?

I don't know for sure, but I heard of their protests. But I directed them to documents, to encyclopedias, in particular. You can't summarize Badmaev in a word. Actually, he was a very gifted doctor, a very intelligent person. He had two educations. He was baptized by Tsar Alexander II. He himself used to say that he lived his life under three tsars—Alexander II, Alexander III and Nicholas II. He was the only person whom Rasputin feared. Badmaev backed Rasputin. He was Rasputin's strategic intellect. All the encyclopedias say that he was an incredible thrill-seeker.

Your portrait of Badmaev and especially the relationship between Badmaev and Rasputin is quite striking.

I used a great deal of intuition in uncovering their secret relations because I read Rasputin's diaries, which almost no one knew about.

Finally, a third reason that has been offered. The portrait of Nicholas II. This is the most common explanation. That it is a sympathetic portrait, unlike the official Soviet portrait.

I wouldn't say it's positive. But it's not a caricature. We didn't want to make a caricature of him. We wanted to portray a living human being, who as everyone knows was a wonderful family man. He was fairly well-educated. But he had little talent as a leader. I've seen thousands of photos he took and none of them are any good. I held his watercolors in my hands—they're all without talent. But due to historical circumstances, this untalented, spineless man was put in charge of a government. And when a leader has no will or talent for leading a great country, a great people, especially at a historical moment like this, then others begin ruling in his place. They make a business out of it. As a result of this the government goes against the interests of the people. And it leads to great crimes, bloody crimes.

Despite himself.

Yes, because he was a nonentity. It creates a deep complex within him. And it's not by accident that the people made nicknames for the tsars. One was "Lame," another was "Great," another was "Terrible." But Nicholas II received the nickname "Bloody." And the actor played his part on the basis of this complex formula.

I think Anatoly Romashin played his part wonderfully. Once again, historiographically speaking, I think you portrayed him and the situation accurately. You mentioned his watercolors; Nicholas also loved the cinema. He had films shown to him all the time.

And he liked to be in the movies. There are some totally idiotic sequences of him. He bathes nude with his comrades.

But the scene in which you showed him painting that watercolor was extremely beautiful. And it reminded me of something that I see in many Soviet films, in Mikhalkov's Oblomov, *for example. A presentation of pre-revolutionary Russia which is extremely sweet and gentle and beautiful.*

In this case, we had a different rationale. We were focusing on the decadence of this art, this painfully beautiful art. It was the art of decay. This is where the color scheme and general creative direction of the film springs from, especially its overall dull coloring.

I can see that.

This art arose from a sense of spiritual decadence.

Do you understand what I mean by citing Mikhalkov's film?

I understand, but in this case, I repeat, we had a different rationale. Because I think that Mikhalkov idealizes that life.

Svetlana Alliluyeva, who has lived here for many years, said she decided to go back to the Soviet Union after she saw the film, Oblomov.

The idealized "good old days."

You have made several films: Farewell; Sport, Sport, Sport; Adventures of a Dentist; *And* All the Same, I Believe. *These have very diverse, seemingly diverse themes. Would you say, however, that there is some central idea that prompts your work in these films?*

God knows if there is any central idea to them. Maybe the only central idea has to do with the fact that they were all made by one and the same man, who was constantly developing, undergoing certain experiences, changing, and who never wanted to repeat himself, who was interested in producing everything in a new way, searching for new paths, new genres, new ways of expressing himself. But if we took the six films I've done, the first three films are one thing, but starting with *Agoniya*, *Farewell*, and *Come and See*, this is the second part of my creative life. Now the third part is beginning.

What do you project for that third stage?

A few more days and I'll announce it. I can only give you an aviation metaphor. Let's say I were a pilot in a fighter plane who flew different planes but at the speed of sound. Now he's interested in supersonic planes. So he wants to do something entirely new, and as I said, impossible.

Good luck.

But when the plane breaks the sound barrier, there's a blast, and the wings should take on a different angle. The plane flies according to different aerodynamic principles. As an aeronautics engineer, I know that. Now I'd like to break that barrier.

That's a wonderful metaphor. But I would still love a clue on what you would find on the other side of that barrier.

As Platonov wrote to his wife, "The impossible is the bride of mankind. The impossible is where our souls are flying to." I'm interested now in shooting what cannot be shot. Simple cinema is of no interest to me.

Is that why you decided to seek a functionary's office as head of the Filmmakers' Union?

No.

We'll return to that subject in a minute. I want to ask you a very interview-like question. What influences have operated in your work—Soviet as well as international?

As far as my directing is concerned? I always tried to avoid any strong influences, since each person must try to realize himself. I grew fond of Fellini, Orson Wells, Jean Vigo, our Boris Barnet, Kurosawa, Milos Forman. But honestly, I consider my teachers to be Michelangelo, Alexander Pushkin, and Fyodor Mikhailovich Dostoevsky. These are my geniuses.

Let me say, coming back to another of your films, which I just saw and was very moved by—Come and See—*I thought of several Soviet films actually. One that comes to mind because of the obvious parallels, is Eisenstein's* Alexander Nevsky. *Secondly, Donskoy's* Raduga. *Thirdly, Ivan's Childhood, by Tarkovsky, and finally, his* Andrei Rublev. *They all present Russia at the mercy of a cruel invader, and I wonder if you in either a conscious way or indirect way were influenced by any or all of those four films.*

I don't think so and moreover, this film was made as a form of inner protest against those films. In all those films you can see the director. Our inner aim in this film was to make ourselves invisible. A defect of *Agoniya* is that you could see the director, the cameraman, and the director of photography. In our latest film we tried to solve this problem in the film.

Would you say that your model was documentary film?

More so.

Did you use in Come and See *villagers, nonprofessionals?*

For the most part. Ninety-five percent.

I found the film to be the most powerful film in a war setting that I have ever seen. And I think perhaps the reason is that you use the techniques of a suspense film. Or even stronger, what we call in the United States a horror film.

We didn't think about that.

Because there were moments of great buildup, of suspense, when you knew something was going to happen, scenes in the forest, sounds of the plane overhead. And I felt that some great horror was about to take place, and in fact it does. So the structure of the film seemed to me like that of a thriller or horror film.

I can answer this in one phrase—this is war. Total horror, everywhere. To recreate the sensual image of war, to convey this image to the viewer, especially the young viewer who has never seen war, but plays at war. That's one of the aims of our work.

I see the production of films set during the Great Patriotic War continues. How do you respond to the observation that some people make, particularly in the West, that there seems to be an obsession with the theme of the war in the Soviet Union?

It's simple to explain. War became part of our genetic memory. It's our most important, most tragic historical experience. This is the greatest emotional experience our people have ever gone through. Such things are not forgotten. And by the way to a great extent they explain our desire to preserve a peaceful life. That's truly the way it is. People in the West don't always understand. Because the war didn't happen on U.S. territory, and Europe experienced the war, but not to the same degree as Russia did.

Let me now turn to your new role as—forgive the term—functionary. I've collected some quotations from the Fifth Congress of the Union of Filmmakers. Mikhalkov said, "why are there so many dull films?" Shengelaya said, "Today films are made from screenplays that have been reworked dozens of times at all stages of a multilevel structure. This creates an atmosphere of collective avoidance of responsibility, an atmosphere alien to the very nature of art as an act of authorship." Valery Kichin, film critic, said that "this Congress is a turning point in the history of our cinema." Etc. And you were there of course. My question to you is why now? Why all of this now?

Society faced an accumulation of problems and a growing desire to solve these problems. I think this is a historical process that led to a great desire among the people for serious changes. The filmmakers were among the first who really wanted these changes. They were tired of living and working in an atmosphere of bureaucratic supervision. They were tired of living in an atmosphere of perverted standards, when bad is called good and everybody is trying to convince himself of this. When honest, good things have nowhere to express themselves. We are tired of living in an atmosphere of duplicity, when one truth is spoken in the hallways and another from the podium. But the unique character of this period is reflected in the fact that the Party proposed a new path for the country. And it acted like the trail blazer. The 27th Party Congress attests to this.

So there is a direct correlation—what you're saying is that this is a set of accumulated grievances, but it requires the role of the Party and the new leadership under Gorbachev to break the ice. Would you characterize it that way?

Yes. Both the Party and Gorbachev have been acting very consistently over the past few months. A larger and larger number of people in our country have shifted to their point of view, although a certain percentage still wants to live in the old way. There are people who talk more loudly than others about *perestroika* but who actually don't want it to take place.

Both in the Party and among filmmakers?

It's easier for me to speak about filmmakers. I've seen many of this kind of people in film. They'd prefer to just talk about it but actually hope nothing will change. These days I sense a rather significant opposition to the changes in the film establishment. But the Filmmakers' Union is ready to act decisively. And what we've accomplished over the last four months [in 1986] has already changed a great deal in film. And I hope we'll be able to follow through on this to the end. We have enough honest and talented and active people who will carry this out.

As I understand it, two bodies have been formed so far. One group is responsible for reviewing films that were not released; the second group is addressing the question of structure, the relationship between Goskino and the studios. Is that correct?

No, that's a simplification. The activity of the Filmmakers' Union has already influenced our relationship with Goskino. After the Congress, the activity of the Filmmakers' Union has radically changed the relationships between the Union and Goskino. The thing is that the position of the Filmmakers' Union has become more active and decisive, which wasn't the case before. Now not a single serious matter can be decided, without consulting us.

Without the concurrence of the Union? Does this cover budgetary matters as well?

So far it doesn't cover the budget. But we're creating a new structure for our cinema, which will make budgetary matters dependent upon the studios and the Filmmakers' Union. As for censored films, the Union has in fact created a Conflict Commission that will reexamine these censored films.

How many are there?

Fifteen are already being released. About the same number—or even more—are being prepared for release. These are not only fiction films, but documentaries, television films, etc. Though frankly speaking, not all of them are deserving of being released. There are some films of very low quality.

Assuming that budgetary matters are not a problem, that you feel you're getting as much money as you need, does it mean that the Union or the studios will have full artistic control over a film and have the right to release it?

The studios themselves will create their own artistic guidelines, they will approve the scripts themselves, will produce and approve or disapprove the films themselves. Then they will promote their films to distributors. If any disagreements or conflicts arise, then the Union will intervene.

This represents a rather radical change from the past. Was it a struggle for you to be elected?

The Union elected a new board, and the elections were very dramatic. The board elected me as First Secretary. And the next morning I proposed fifty names for the Secretariat. I spent all night putting together that list. And these fifty members now occupy the most important positions in the Union leadership.

Just a personal question, a personal political question: You have said that Gorbachev and his wife are the first leadership family in a long time that might be considered intellectuals and who associate with the intelligentsia, and are especially interested in films, I think. Does that have any bearing on the current situation and the changes that are taking place?

Two weeks ago I had a conversation with Gorbachev. I was elated by our conversation. Among other things, we spoke about cinema, literature and theater. He very carefully analyzed the film *Farewell*. He gave an interesting analysis.

An accurate analysis?

The analysis was accurate. I'd also like to add that he had a very high opinion of the film, which pleased me. Though when it was released this film provoked protests from the film leadership.

Too gloomy, was one criticism?

Yes. And by the way—I found out that Gorbachev has read every work written by Valentin Rasputin. He has read many serious literary works. I also confirmed that he goes to the theater regularly, which I knew before that conversation, actually. He analyzed the performances that he had seen and gave very precise, critical analyses which I agreed with. In addition, he said he loves going to the movies.

Maybe I can interview him one day! When we speak in the West of a generation of outstanding film directors in the USSR, we usually include Klimov, Tarkovsky, Mikhalkov, Konchalovsky. Let me take three of those, and there are three different models here. One is Klimov and Mikhalkov, working very successfully in the Soviet Union. Konchalovsky, living in the West, still a Soviet director but living in the West. And Tarkovsky will always be a Soviet director but who is cut off from his homeland. Would you comment on these figures?

I would rather not talk about myself. As for Nikita Mikhalkov, he's a very gifted, artistic person. Some people like him, some don't. Some people take him seriously and others not. As for Konchalovsky, his brother, I saw his two American-made films. To me, these are Hollywood productions, and not in the best sense of this word. I already saw both of Tarkovsky's foreign films—*Nostalghia* and *The Sacrifice*. It seemed to me that Andrei could have easily made the same films in his homeland. No one would have prevented him.

Why, then, is he in Italy?

I still don't understand why. He had no reason to leave for the West. Second of all, no one ever prevented him from returning to his homeland. And to this day the door remains open to him. I for one think he should be working in his own country. Because he's a great artist, a great master. And I am convinced that a true artist can only realize his potential working in his own country.

Will you make any special effort to invite Tarkovsky back?

First of all, he must resolve this for himself. But I'd like him to know that there are no problems regarding his return and his work here. And that his colleagues respect him for his creative work. And that he will be totally free to work and do whatever he'd like.

I speak to you finally as a historian. Will you or other Soviet directors deal with important historical themes that don't get treated on the Soviet screen? Stalin? Stalinism? Of the many themes I can pick: Stalin, Stalinism, and the brutality and horror of collectivization, which I thought of indirectly, when I saw Come and See.

I think you're a bit late with this question. A film has just been completed on this subject. I've seen it—it's a very serious film based on Vasily Bykov's novel, *A Sign of Disaster*. [*Znak Bedy*.] It's a novel that recently received the Lenin Prize. It portrays in very tragic and dramatic terms the collectivization and occupation which followed. It's a fine work by the Byelorussian director, Mikhail Ptashchuk. It's a very dramatic and powerful film. Tengiz Abuladze, a very talented Georgian director, will soon release a new film. It's called *Repentance*. It's a very original artistic approach to Stalinism and the way it perverted basic values in society. But at the same time there are good people who struggle against this. I don't think that future directors will be able to avoid these issues.

I look forward to seeing those films and wish you great success.

Irina Kupchenko

11. Irina Kupchenko, rather more glamorous in this 1991 Sovexportfilm calendar photo than in many of her drab, type-casted film roles.

"But as for change in terms of the meaning of art, there can't be changes in this sense, because those who had talent are still talented now, and those who didn't have talent don't have it now. And no political changes can help them."

Menashe: *I've seen several of your films, and I'm a great admirer of yours. I've seen you in* Nest of Gentry, Uncle Vanya, Forgotten Melody for Flute, *and* In Private. *What caught my attention is that you're always playing an unhappy woman. And in this last film too*—Single Woman Seeking Relationship. *Why is that? And is that true of all the films you play in?*

Kupchenko: Yes, absolutely all. Except one or two films. Don't ask me but ask the directors who proposed such roles to me. I've always dreamed of playing in comedies, and Eldar Ryazanov, director of the film *Forgotten Melody for Flute*, gave me a role. I was so happy that I'd have a part in a comedy, because Ryazanov is our greatest comedy director. But in this comedy I also play a dramatic role. It's my fate.

In it, you are a married woman and you are unhappy there too. That's called typecasting.

Yes, typecasting. I'm so tired of these roles. I'd rather play another character, someone optimistic, funny, without all these dramas, but...

What are you working on now?

Now I'm working on some new films. One film by the Hungarian director, Paul Erdesz. It's a story about a schoolteacher. This is also a very heavy, dark, black drama. And the other film is directed by our Soviet filmmaker—but it's a co-production with Germany. The director is Alexander Proshkin. He made *The Cold Summer of 1953*. This is a story about our great scientist, Vavilov, who was imprisoned during the Stalin era.

And you also play an unhappy woman?

Yes, I have no future.

Both those films are co-productions. More and more Soviet films are co-productions. How do you feel about that?

On the one hand, it's very good. First of all, it's good for our cinema, because you have the equipment, which is much better than ours. Then, it's a chance to work with foreign directors and actors—they have an influence on you. It's interesting, and in a professional sense, it's a good thing. But on the other hand, if you are working with a foreign producer, then he begins to control you. Except we also have had control, but now I must say that there are no controls on directors in the Soviet Union. If some years ago our Goskino could say "no, you can't include this scene in the film, or you can't say these words in the film, or in general, this script can't be produced"—now nobody can say that and you can do whatever you want. But the producer who provides the funding for a film—he will say something. But in general, it's good—more good than bad.

So you're saying that control over these co-productions comes from the Western side?

It depends on the contract who is the most important partner in the co-production, their side or our side.

Whoever controls the finances controls the film.

Yes of course. Whoever gives the money makes the music.

Right. Who pays piper calls the tune, we have a saying. So it's another form of control.

Yes another.

True freedom doesn't seem to exist.

It can never exist, anywhere.

But what changes have you seen since the Fifth Congress of Filmmakers in 1986? Since glasnost *and* perestroika?

They are different things, the Filmmakers' Congress and *glasnost*, absolutely different things. After this Congress—this is my personal opinion, I may not be objective—I don't see any changes, because nothing changed. But *glasnost* created a lot of changes. For example, you're absolutely free to do whatever you like, except maybe pornography or military secrets, but basically, whatever you like. A lot of scripts that were written in the past can now be made. Many films that haven't been seen in public are now shown...

Films that were formerly on the shelf.

Yes. You have seen *Commissar*, one of Konchalovsky's first films, *Asya's Happiness*, and many, many others. Not many, but a lot more. I think that this is a great change, of course. But as for change in terms of the meaning of art, there can't be changes in this sense, because those who had talent are still talented now, and those who didn't have talent don't have it now. And no political changes can help them.

So you can't create great art through an ukaz.

Those who had freedom inside them made their films and they were shelved.

Are you disappointed with the films that are now being made?

Disappointed? No. Why?

Let me say that in the West, we expected that since glasnost opened up so many possibilities, there would be great new films coming from the USSR, but it seems that the great films were the ones that were made earlier.

The talent of any artist—a painter or musician or director—depends not on the political system but on God. And if you have it you have it. If you don't have it, nobody can help you. And another thing, if everything is forbidden, and you want to do something, you can't say it openly, but you can say it in a way that everyone who's sitting and watching your film will understand what you intended to say.

Between the lines.

Yes, between the lines. It's interesting, it was very interesting. They made films that had not one bottom, but four bottoms, and because of that they were very deep. They seemed very deep. But once you can say everything, it seems that you can say nothing. It's very difficult when you can say everything. Freedom is a very dangerous thing. And for artists it's especially so.

Why?

Because you see, you must have something very serious, some great idea to show everyone. If you have only a few thoughts inside you, but you can say them openly, you try to show that you have some deep thoughts, when in fact they're really simple. But because they're forbidden you think they're very deep. When you can express them openly, I can see that these thoughts were simple, they were just forbidden. And it's very difficult.

I've heard that opinion expressed by many Soviet artists. In Leningrad I spoke to Alexei Gherman.

He's a very good director but he isn't doing anything now. Why?

He says he finds it very difficult to work in conditions of freedom.

You see, freedom can exist only when there are slaves. If you have nothing to struggle with, freedom doesn't exist. What is freedom? Freedom is the opposite of something else. If this something else doesn't exist, you have no freedom.

That is very dialectical, very Marxist. Well, would you prefer no freedom?

No, I prefer freedom of course. But you see what's much more interesting is the path to freedom, the way you approach freedom.

Yes, I think I know what you mean.

The process is always more interesting than the result.

The journey is more interesting than the destination. So do you think that it's paradoxical that more freedom in Soviet cinema has not produced better art?

No, you see, it's natural. What I've said about them not doing anything now—it's natural, of course. Because they now must stop and think where they'll go next. They knew their way—we knew our way, where we had to go—to freedom, to openness, to *glasnost*. Now we have this. Now we must stay still for a moment, think, be calm, and discover where we should go next.

It's confusing, isn't it? Well, freedom is one characteristic of the new Soviet cinema scene. Another characteristic is the struggle for profit, khozraschyot. I know that this is now the concern among moviemakers. For example, Mosfilm Studios in 1988, of some 38 films, I believe, only three showed a profit. There must be great pressure now to make films that are commercially successful in the Soviet Union. How do you see that?

Yes, there is that. But as for studios that are supported by the government, it's not a big problem now. Because, for example, at Mosfilm Studios, there are some—maybe they're called departments, I don't know—of feature films, and in each department there are three or four films produced per year. Films for young people, comedies—*obiedineniia*—I don't know what they're called in English.

Production units? Associations?

So, if for example, of these four films, one is commercially successful, it will provide the funds for the other films, and they can be artistic films. But now some films are produced by "cooperatives", on private funds. I borrow money from some cooperative, make a film, and return the money. This film must be commercially successful. This is both good and bad. It's good because you aren't dependent on anyone. But it's bad because you're dependent on money. You've borrowed money and you must pay it back. The films produced on private funds recently are totally commercial, for a very wide audience. But maybe in the future, maybe even now, we'll see philanthropists appearing, people who will provide funding for art, but without expecting any return or profit. "Metsenat"—I don't know what it's called in English.

"Maecenas?" We say a patron, a sponsor or an angel.

A sponsor, but a sponsor who thinks about spiritual matters, not money. We had Morozov, who built the Tretyakov Gallery. He bought paintings from unknown painters to help them survive. It was he who built Russian culture in his day.

Like the patrons of the Renaissance.

More than half of Bergman's films aren't commercially successful. But somebody gave him the funding.

So you hope that this will happen in the Soviet Union too?

Maybe.

What examples of these independent productions can you give me?

Recently Vasily Pichul made *Little Vera*. He made his second film on private funds.

You mean V gorode Sochi, temnye nochi. [Dark Nights in Sochi].

I haven't seen this film, so I can't say anything, but he produced it on private funds. There are a lot of films—I don't know their names because I haven't seen them.

You mentioned Little Vera. *It was very popular here in the United States as well. When I was in the Soviet Union I asked people about the film, and practically everyone I spoke to—one woman, an older woman, said she didn't like it, she said it was offensive, but everyone else I spoke to, especially young people, said they liked it. They said that it was an authentic portrait of life among the working class. And there too, there are unhappy women. And you play unhappy women. And there are many Soviet films where there are unhappy women. Do you think, apart from the typecasting of you, do you think this is a general cinema statement about the reality of Soviet women?*

You see, the reality of our life, economically, is not good. Of course we're under stress, we're tired of everyday problems. But unhappiness doesn't just arise from that. I am sure that you know beautiful, rich, absolutely wealthy women who are unhappy. You can have a family, children, a wife, and be lonely. You see, unhappiness can happen to anyone. In the film *Little Vera* the director tried to make this social analysis of our life, of one class, of the working class. Our film, *Forgotten Melody*, is a psychological story. We tried to produce a psychological analysis of the relations between people. It's two different things, you see. And to say that she's unhappy because she lives poorly in an economic sense—this isn't true. Materially, she has everything. She has a job that she likes, money, an apartment, but she doesn't have happiness. Why? And we tried in this film to answer this why. Because many women were struggling for independence, and when they received it, they didn't know what to do with it. She has everything, and she thought that this was happiness. To be free of men, to have anything she wishes, to live the life she wants, but then she realizes that she's lonely, and that she has nothing, because the apartment, the money, the job are nothing. And she tries to find something in a relationship. She tries to find this not only in life, but inside her, because the people who are the most unhappy are those who don't feel anything inside. Not that somebody likes them, but they don't like themselves. Their soul is empty.

So you think the film tried to show that an independent woman who has everything is still unhappy because she doesn't have a satisfying relationship?

Yes, of course, because the woman has a biological need to have someone close to her that she can think about, who needs her. A man, a child, someone. That's a woman's nature.

I ask this in particular after having seen your film, and I also just saw a BBC documentary shown on public television, called Miss USSR.

About our girls?

Yes. And one young woman there talks about how miserable women are in the Soviet Union. We work eight hours a day, then we have to come home and do the shopping, do the cooking. The men don't help, the men are drunk, husbands are alcoholics. I have eight or nine abortions before I have a child. And then I get divorced. Is it an accurate picture?

Yes it is. It is. Our everyday life is very hard. For economic reasons women wanted to be free, to be equal to men. Then they had their women's problems in their life. But after this struggle they simply added men's problems to their women's problems. Now they have two problems—men's and women's. And that's why their life is so cruel. Because she has a job, but she's not working—she's thinking "where is my child after school? Is he playing outside, in the apartment? Has he had anything to eat?" Then she goes food shopping, then she goes home. She doesn't work the way she should and she doesn't keep the house up the way she should. And the result?

And some of this comes through in Soviet films.

I think this exists not only in the USSR—it's just that in the USSR it's more difficult for us under the circumstances of our life. But even in other countries, if a woman has a child, how can she be a good worker? It's very difficult for her. She can and she will because she has character, she wants to achieve something in her life, but it's very difficult. She's really a heroine, keeping all her problems inside her, because no one at her job is interested in them. But she has these problems.

If you're talking about marriage and children, then what about the man? The man could help.

The main thing in a man's life is his job. I don't know how Americans divide responsibilities between men and women.

Let me tell you, the phone call I just made was to my wife, to tell her I have an interview now and I'm going to be home for my boy. My son is thirteen years old and we have to prepare dinner for him. She can't make it, so I have to go. That's how we do it.

Congratulations to your American women. They are lucky if you help them in this way. Yes, there are Russian husbands who also help, but even if the man helps the woman, she feels all these problems more deeply than he does. It's natural, it's biological.

Have you ever spoken to Western feminists about this?

No, I hate feminism in general.

OK. There is another area in which women are prominent, and that is the film industry, as directors. Of course as actresses and others in films, but there are many women directors in Soviet film, Shepitko and Muratova, Djordjadze and many others. Do you ever have any intention or desire to direct?

No.

And do you think the films of women directors are special?

The films of Larisa Shepitko are not "women's" films. If you saw these films you wouldn't say that a woman made them. They are men's films. Because Larisa was a very strong woman, with a strong character, a strong will. Kira Muratova…you see, they're talented. They're good directors. And for me, it's not important whether they're men or women. Because their films are interesting.

Coming back to the film, this most recent film, it was made in 1986 at Dovzhenko Studios. And where is the city, Kharkov, Ukraine? We can't speak of it as a glasnost *film, but it has certain things in it that are unusual. It shows the liquor lines, people waiting on liquor lines. Previously that was difficult to show.*

No, no. Don't think that everything was forbidden.

Well, the boss, your boss, at the sewing shop. She has medals. She's clearly a "nachalnik," right? And she says to you, "you should—the collective is interested in you, and you should respect the collective." That implied criticism of the boss is also unusual.

No. You exaggerate. I don't think that this film couldn't have been produced [earlier]. It could have been. If somebody in Goskino forbade something, it was something politically more serious, or a naked woman, from a moral point of view, but not such little things.

But I thought those were important nuances.

Nuances, maybe. I don't know. It seems to me that it could have been allowed.... Maybe not.

Also, it was made at the time when there was a big anti-alcoholism campaign, right after Chernenko had died...

The struggle against alcoholism was waged everywhere. It was waged in private families. Wives waged it. Then the government began. We've always had this problem in our country. It's very common and very understandable.

I understand. But here is another interesting nuance that I saw. I don't know if it was intended this way. The character, the man in the film, when he talks about drinking, he says "there's always a reason. People drink for a reason." So it wasn't so simple. Drinking is a symptom of some social or psychological disorder, he was saying.

A psychological disorder, oh yes, I agree with you.

And consequently, it's not enough to ban the sale of alcohol or limit the sale.

Of course, and because of that, our anti-alcoholism campaign ended.

It was a failure.

Yes. Because of that. Because you must eliminate the cause and not try to get rid of the symptoms.

And he says another thing in the film, that we need more compassion, sympathy for each other. I thought those were all important elements in the film. And to me, that made it a new-style film rather than old-style film. Do you know what I mean?

Yes, maybe. Because there are some true things in this. You see, it's simply a picture of our life, as it is. It's truly a picture of our life. Maybe the story is a little bit of a fairytale, but the picture shows the truth about how people live. And it seems to me that it's interesting to people, because people are interested not only in politics. They're interested in how other people live.

That I think explains why Little Vera *was so popular too. Documentary films in the Soviet Union are quite striking now. They're doing what you're talking about.*

This is the main result of *perestroika* in Russian cinema. They [the documentaries] are really very good. Better than feature films, because you can take the camera and simply look through it at the life around you. In feature films you have something in your head, your soul, something inside you, but here you simply record what you see.

Kinopravda! What documentary films do you recommend?

I don't know all of them of course, because I'm not a specialist in documentary films. But of the most recent films—you've seen it in America, it seems to me—Is it Easy to be Young? The Muzhik of Arkhangelsk. A lot of films.

Pain, *about Afghanistan.*

Oh, *Bol*, yes. And about Chernobyl. A lot of very good films.

So the main fruits of glasnost *seem to be documentary films.*

This is natural. It had to be.

Has this recent film of yours been popular in the Soviet Union?

Yes, it's popular, because it's a story that people can identify with. It was interesting for them. This film gives hope to sick people that they can be cured.

Both men and women.

Both men and women.

That was a good ending, but I have one more question. You've worked with Konchalovsky on several films. Of course he is now making films in the West, and he's an interesting example of someone who liberated himself from Soviet cinema and found freedom—of course he had to find money as well—but found freedom to make films. Have you seen his Western films? Have you seen all five of them?

Not all five. I have seen *Maria's Lovers, Runaway Train,* and *Shy People.*

Then there's Duet for One *and most recently,* Tango and Cash, *which is playing here [in New York]. Go see it tonight. Do you think that his films are different in the West? Are they better, are they worse?*

You see, everyone develops and changes during his life, of course. If he made the films in the USSR, and I have seen his first film and his last film, there would be a great difference in them, even if he stayed in Russia. So in America I see the difference, of course, but it's an absolutely natural difference.

Better or worse?

Not better, not worse. Different. The most important thing for me is that he has remained true to himself here in America. That's the most important thing. Because it's very easy to lose yourself in a new land, in new circumstances. It's very easy to lose yourself and to adapt, to change color like a chameleon. This didn't happen with Konchalovsky. He remained true to himself.

Interesting. What Western films do you like?

I like the films of old directors: Bergman and Fellini, I like very much. I like films by Bertolucci, by Godard—Europeans. I like the films of Forman very much. It's the only example for me of a successful combination of a commercial and an art film. From what I know, the only one who has commercial success and real artistic success is Forman. Scorsese is professionally a very good director, there are a lot of them.

You know Tarkovsky has a following here—not with mass audiences.

Tarkovsky's popular here? I think with some special audiences. Because he can't be popular for everyone.

What of the two films that he made in Italy and Sweden?

They're not worse and they're not better—they're different.

And he remains Tarkovsky.

Yes, he remains Tarkovsky.

Gleb Panfilov

"That's what we call 'collective responsibility.' No one said 'no,' but no one said 'yes,' so *The Theme* film sat around for seven years."

Menashe: *I like your work very much, especially historical films like* Vassa, *but also* The Theme, *which gives us a portrait of contemporary* *life. And now you're working on a film based on Gorky's* Mother? *What will you do that is different from the Pudovkin and Donskoy versions?*

Panfilov: My film will be completely different. First of all, I have a different script. It's based on several of Gorky's works, including *Mother*, and *The Life of an Unnecessary Man*. Its underlying idea differs from that of Pudovkin and Mark Donskoy.

Not sentimental?

No. I live in different historical circumstances and have a better understanding than they did in their day. Besides that, I've structured my goals a bit differently. I decided to use materials from three works.

Are you trying to say something about today in dealing with a historical theme?

Definitely. My interest in the past is definitely dictated by the problems of our time. That's why I'm looking to the past to gain a better understanding of what's happening today and a better idea of what awaits us tomorrow. It helps me get a better sense of our lives today. I'm not a historian, and simply studying history in and of itself isn't interesting to me.

You were an engineer?

I still am.

You graduated from an institute?

The Ural Polytechnic Institute in Sverdlovsk. It's in the northern Urals, north of Magnitogorsk where I was born.

And your first films were made in Sverdlovsk, correct?

Yes. *The Theme, Valentina,* and *Vassa* were made at Mosfilm.

Others were made in Leningrad. What makes Mosfilm and Lenfilm different?

Mosfilm Studios has better facilities. In addition, it's a big studio and they don't keep tabs on every director there. This allows you to do your job without being bothered by anyone. At a small studio, there's too much attention focused on each director, but when you're at a big studio, there's less interference in your work.

Do Mosfilm and Lenfilm have different theories of filmmaking?

Leningrad has its own esthetic, its own particular profile. Mosfilm is like a modern-day Babylon, with all sorts of tendencies springing out of it. Leningrad does differ from Mosfilm. But I feel better working at Mosfilm, because I feel more personal freedom there. I'm free to do what I want. I prefer the conditions at Mosfilm over Lenfilm.

Can one say that a single idea or theme runs through all your films? What do you think?

I'm not sure. I've only seen Vassa, The Theme, *and* Valentina, *but I noticed strong women in all three, plus an emphasis on the need for honesty and integrity. Do you agree?*

Probably. Although the women have different personalities, they're women capable of acting independently. You could say that about Tanya Tiotkina. Though she's a very kind woman with certain idiosyncrasies of her own, she's capable of taking action, even heroic action. She has fears like any normal person, but is able to overcome them. It's the same with Barbara in *I Request the Floor*.

And Sasha, in The Theme, *of course, played by your wife Inna Churikova. Who came first, Sasha or Inna?*

Inna came afterwards. But Inna was the only one who could play the role in *The Theme*.

I found Vassa *quite interesting as an historical footnote about the rising bourgeoisie in pre-Revolutionary Russia, but the character Vassa — also played brilliantly by Churikova — is a powerful presence in the film. I notice you based the film on a play by Gorky. Of his two versions, one in 1911 and one in 1935, why did you chose the 1935 play?*

You know, the character of Vassa in the second version was more interesting. She had greater integrity than in the first production. And in the second version there's a reference to the Revolution — in Rachel — which enriches the play and gives viewers something to think about. That's why I chose the second version. Though I think that specifically for that reason many people nowadays would base their works on the first version, because I don't think they would know what to do with Rachel. Rachel isn't very clearly described in the play — there are inconsistencies in her portrayal. You get the impression that Gorky knew what he wanted but wasn't able to carry it out, because at that time he was quite sick. He died in 1936. I simply don't think he had enough time to polish the play's rough edges. I took it upon myself to complete Rachel's character. She's a character that I understand very well and it seems to me that my approach worked out OK.

So we have, in a symbolic sense, the revolutionaries against the antirevolutionary merchant class.

Theirs [the merchants'] was as democratic a path as there could be at the time. It was [Pyotr] Stolypin's path.

But both Vassa and Rachel are likable characters.

Of course. How could it be otherwise? That's also something new in my film, because usually Vassa is cast in a negative light. That's not the whole truth—it's only one side of the story, a simplification. I couldn't let that happen. Vassa's tragedy lies in the fact that she's a wonderful person and a deep person. She loves only her husband, she's a person of depth and integrity. And yet she finds herself tragically powerless in the face of her life. She has her whole life at her feet and yet can't do anything.

Gorky wrote a great deal about that situation.

No one has written it in this way before. No one was able to do this before with Vassa's character.

Is it true that you want to make a film about Joan of Arc?

Yes, I'd like to make this film and am waiting to do so, though Inna is a bit too old for this role, and I would have liked to have her do it. The script was written with her in mind. That's why it's hanging in mid-air to a certain extent. Although I'm continuing my work on that.

Let me turn to The Theme *again. In the episode with the gravedigger, the emigrant, the writer, he says that he discovered the papers of Radishchev. Why did you pick Radishchev? Any significance?*

You know, Radishchev was a great thinker in his time, a great advocate of liberty, and there has always been a lot of interest in him as a historical figure. The fact that a young historian is researching his works, his short stories, his letters—this reveals the character of this historian and makes him interesting.

I also noticed that there was a photo of Shostakovich in one of the scenes.

And Stravinsky—he was on the left. I simply love both of these composers, both Stravinsky and Shostakovich. That is, Sasha loves them, but I do too.

And so do I! The émigré, *was he Jewish or not?*

In this version, he's Jewish, because he's going to Israel at his father's behest. He's Jewish.

Was the film originally banned because it showed a Jewish émigré leaving Russia?

This is a complicated topic. For me, this was the first time I'd ever touched upon this theme in a film. It wasn't the theme of the whole film, but it was rather daring, so there were problems. I think the fact that the scene had such emotional impact on the viewers influenced the fate of the film.

And did the Union of Soviet Writers...?

That's the second reason. In fact the Union of Soviet Writers was the first reason. The leadership of the Union of Writers was upset that two writers were portrayed in such an unattractive way. "Where did you find such hacks? We're not like that—we're better than that!"

I heard that Romanov—the First Secretary of the Leningrad Party Committee—didn't like the film. Is that true?

No, it was another film that he didn't like. Maybe he didn't like this film, but I wasn't aware of it, because I made it in Moscow. It was another film that he didn't like: *I Request the Floor.*

Why?

He didn't like the way I portrayed the Secretary of the City Party Committee. He also felt that people like that don't exist.

In The Theme, *Chizhikov was a poet. Was he based on a real figure?*

Yes, this was an actual person, with an actual life, Alexander Baldyonkov. Before the Revolution he was an artist from Palekh, an artist's community. The artists paint miniature works and icons there. He painted icons before the Revolution. The people in Palekh knew him. After the Revolution he stopped painting icons and started writing poetry about the new life. I used some of his poetry and parts of his diary in my film. He was a very interesting figure—a self-taught poet, from a humble background, who had a keen sense of the truth and a gift for speaking the truth regardless of the consequences. This caused him a lot of pain—people despised him because of this.

He's not like the Kim of your film. Many of your films are set in small towns—Vladimir, Suzdal...

Yes, I like to focus on central Russia. Central Russia is very typical—the people, the air, the sense of life—this is the Russian heartland, the true Russia. I love it.

In The Theme, *Vampilov and Rasputin are mentioned as writers who live in the village…*

This is northern Siberia, a different atmosphere, but also part of Russia. This land was acquired by Russia only in the 18th century. But it's also part of Russia. I'm a man of the Urals—and the Urals share something in common with eastern Siberia.

Let's discuss the process of preventing films from being shown. The Writers' Union didn't like The Theme. *Romanov didn't like* I Request the Floor. *But who exactly gave the word that no one could see a particular film?*

No one. That's what we call "collective responsibility." No one said "no," but no one said "yes," so *The Theme* film sat around for seven years. Someone will say that of course the film is worthy of attention, that he supports it, but by himself he can't do anything. If only… and on and on. So when they say that the Union of Writers was against it—it's like saying New York was against it. Who do they mean? You understand? Whom do you turn to? So you couldn't find out who was responsible. Though it was clear that it was the leadership of the Union of Writers that was against it.

Two years ago, who said "yes?"

Who said "yes?" Yegor Ligachev [of the Politburo]. At a Conference of Cultural Workers. I wasn't there myself, but I was told about it right away. He said "we are ready to release *The Theme*. It was shelved—for reasons that are understandable. We don't like the film, but we'll release it." And that was it. He said he didn't really like it but that he'd release it.

Would you have made the film differently today?

You know, I wouldn't make such a film today, because circumstances have changed so much, and I've already moved beyond that point. But if, nevertheless, someone told me I could make it the way I wanted to, I still wouldn't change a thing. Of course I'd return to my very first notes about it, to study the kind of film I'd done at that time. It was a film from that period. That's the way it should be interpreted. It's not a film of 1987, but of 1979. That's how it should be interpreted. And I must say that I wouldn't redo a single one of my films. Because at that time—I can see the mistakes I made in retrospect, but it's a film of the seventies. That's how I see it. Whether it has any impact today is another question.

But now we have glasnost. *That's important. That's why I thought perhaps it would have been conceived differently or made differently. You said something very interesting at Lincoln Center last week. You said that* glasnost *is more important than* perestroika. *What did you mean by that?*

I meant that at this point, *glasnost*—not *perestroika*—creates the conditions for good films to be produced. To provide filmmakers with the material means for making a film isn't as important as providing *glasnost*. Secondly, we do need to improve our facilities. It's way behind the Americans. That's of course a very important issue, but *glasnost* is more important.

Letting someone speak the truth is more important than giving someone all the equipment he needs but forbidding him from speaking the truth. So *glasnost* is primary, the main condition necessary for good work in film. And not only in film, but I don't want to go off in another area. In addition, each production unit is now paying its artistic council—that's the way it should be, a paid artistic council. So then you're a member of the production unit's staff. Now all of us are in the same boat.

There are great possibilities and great dangers in the new system.

We still have problems. But the greatest achievement was *glasnost*. As for the logistical problems, we're approaching them carefully, or more accurately, boldly but not always successfully. They created nine production units instead of seven, and all of them will be paid. And they're all run by young directors, like [Sergei] Solovyov. We need to focus on *glasnost* now, because everything else is just as crummy as it ever was.

In terms of our organization, we have many, many problems. And people are already feeling this. They're just "restructured" themselves, and already they have to do everything differently, because it used to be that the production units would join together and present their grievances to the Union as a single entity, but now they're all divided. And it's the lower-level people who will suffer. The bigwigs will take over the new positions of power and their lives will be in order—they'll have their own organizations, their own private dining rooms.

How do you feel about co-productions with Western units?

Co-productions are incredibly complex. They require a huge amount of energy and don't produce much in return.

Do you know that Gorbachev loves films?

Yes, he's basically a real theater-goer. I saw him myself at a production at MKhAT [The Moscow Art Theater]. He was there with his wife. He goes to the movies a lot, knows the directors. I visited the Politburo in February, there was a meeting of representatives of various unions. He recognized me, said "Panfilov is here," and of course I was astonished. I realized that he remembers people's faces. He's a very educated person. Both he and his wife. That's a good thing for film.

3 After the Fall, 1993-1994

Leonid Gurevich

"Documentary film had less room for lies than any other occupation."

Menashe: *What's your background and how did you enter the film world?*

Gurevich: I have a degree in chemical engineering from Voronezh State University. That's my hometown, where I went to school and then college. To be honest, I was always more interested in the humanities. I thought I'd like to be a journalist or work in the theater, and secretly I dreamt of working in film, but I didn't have the confidence to pursue this, because I didn't think I was talented enough.

I graduated from college—Voronezh State University—in 1954. I received a Gold Medal award at college, which allowed me to enter any graduate school I wanted. So, I thought, why not travel to Moscow and apply to the film institute, even though I'd have to take the entrance exams? My mother went to Moscow ahead of me and said, "son, it's very dangerous there. There are anti-Semitic trials going on." There were even executions. They shot Peretz Markish and Lev Kvitko. My mother got scared and begged me not to go. So I decided not to go to Moscow. So I got a job at a chemical factory. Since early on I had been a "true believer" in Stalinism, the authorities planned on making me the head of the Komsomol [Communist Youth League] organization at Voronezh University, and they were preparing me for that.

What does that mean, a "true Stalinist?"

It seemed to me that socialism was in fact the pinnacle of social development, that communism was the only idea that should become a reality in the world. When Stalin died, I was in my third year of college, and a policeman pulled me off the sideboard of a train that I was riding on to get to the burial. To this day I thank that policeman, because who knows whether I would have been one of those who were crushed trying to see Stalin lying in state. But in March 1953 I sat on that sideboard, intending to go from Voronezh to Moscow. It was an eleven-hour train ride, and I considered it a duty to go and witness the funeral of my idol.

I'm not ashamed of saying this nowadays, because basically I was just a trusting person. But two years later, I put on an amateur student production, without any idea that it could be considered anti-Soviet. In fact I felt that it was helping society rid itself of unclean elements. But after that production, no one would consider me for the Komsomol organization, and I left for Saratov, where I worked at a factory for four years, producing car batteries. But during this time I began making amateur films, and by my second year in Saratov, I began applying to the State Institute of Cinema (VGIK) on a regular basis.

Where did they show these films, at the factory, at a club?

They showed these films at amateur film clubs. The best of these clubs could show the films at actual movie theaters. One of the films I produced with my friends was accepted for distribution in movie theaters. But there was a huge network of film clubs.

Where did the equipment and money come from?

From the trade unions. They had a lot of money. It's interesting to note that the trade union bought us a 16mm camera. But we got our 35mm camera from fighter pilots—it was used during the war. We had a great film club. VGIK didn't accept me for a variety of reasons. The first time, they rejected me because I'd only been working for two years. Russian law required me to work for three years in my field before I was free to pursue a different career.

When was that exactly?

I applied for the first time in 1956. I was rather successful. I got a mark of twenty-three out of twenty-five. And I had every right to be a student. But the commission decided that I hadn't been working long enough in my field. In 1957, when I think I was even better prepared, and encountered the same examiners, I was stunned when I received only two points [a failing mark] on the first exam. I was in Moscow in 1957 to celebrate the First International Youth Festival. It turned out that they rejected me because the Saratov KGB had denounced me. For some time they had been investigating our film club. We spoke our minds in that club. So I was rejected because people at VGIK knew what I had been saying. But a year later, I was simply expelled from the Komsomol.

Does that mean that you stopped being a Stalinist?

No, Louis, I thought that the excesses were due to individual weaknesses, that it was a perversion of the original idea.

How did your disillusion take shape, little by little, or all at once?

Of course it was over time, and the 20th Party Congress in 1956 really marked the turning point; it shook me up quite a bit. But nonetheless, my position was something like this: that Leninism was a wonderful idea which was perverted by the insidious Djugashvili [Stalin]. And I clung to that idea for a long time. Life tempered me well, because in 1957 I was expelled from the Komsomol. I was expelled for organizing a screening at the film club. There was a Disney film, which in 1937 had received the Gold Medal at the Moscow Film Festival. But the ideologues in the provinces denounced it as a cult of death. And I was denounced as someone who was luring young people into this. But I don't think that was the real reason they expelled me. I think it was because I carefully concealed the people who had given me a copy of this film so we could we could have three minutes of fun watching it. They had brought it back from Austria like a trophy, and didn't realize that it could be dangerous to them. They were professional filmmakers and I was just a chemical engineer. So I refused to say where I got it from. I lied about where I got it from. I was expelled for preaching bourgeois ideas and deceiving the Komsomol. It was incredibly funny.

But was it good for your career?

Of course, for my growth. For my career too, because when I went to Moscow in an attempt to rehabilitate myself, when I told people in film circles this story, everyone had the same reaction. They all laughed hysterically and then tried to help me out. Mikhail

Romm, Sergei Yutkevich, Rostislav Yurenev. They said, "that guy over there created a mini institute in Saratov, and because he screened this film—this is ridiculous." And in great part thanks to this support, I was restored to the Komsomol. I was rehabilitated. But the VGIK rejected me a third time.

Was the third time the last time?

No, there was a fourth attempt. Imagine my situation: when I was expelled from the Komsomol, the Institute washed its hands of me. I was living on my own, my parents were far away, I had no job, and VGIK had rejected me. I wasn't going back to Saratov. So with the help of my friends, I got a permit saying that I was in fact a student at VGIK. Moreover, I morally had a basis for this. I had gotten twenty-three points out of twenty-five on the entrance exams. There was no way for them to reject me. But they did reject me, because, even while knowing that I was being reinstated into the Komsomol, the chairman of the Komsomol Central Committee nonetheless stated before VGIK's commission that "Gurevich is excluded from membership." I said, "how can I be excluded? I have the documents on my rehabilitation." "As long as we haven't restored your membership, you're excluded," [he replied]. They voted on the matter, VGIK rejected me, and ten days later, I was reinstated into the Komsomol.

Was this the Institute's commission?

The Institute's official commission. But I again started making my rounds, showing people that the Komsomol had reinstated me, that I'd gotten twenty-three points on the exam, that it was illegal for them to reject me, but this holiest of holies, the Dean of the Institute said, "you'll get in here over my dead body."

Who was that?

Groshev. [Alexander] Groshev, the old head of VGIK, who said, "we accept only the leaders of the ideological front. You don't size up." "But I got twenty-three points," I told him. When I approached them in 1960 for the last time and got twenty-five out of twenty-five, they reminded me that I had some time ago forged a VGIK document. And VGIK got hold of this. Could they admit me after I had forged this document? "You forged this document." For a long time they concealed their true motives for rejecting me. It was ridiculous. I had twenty-five out of twenty-five—how can you reject someone? The reasons they gave were ludicrous: "You haven't done an apprenticeship." That night I flew to Moldova and got a document verifying that for two years I'd worked on a newspaper. The Dean told me, "sorry, you're late." This was the fourth time. I'm happy to say that now I often serve on VGIK's examination board. I am a professor at VGIK.

That's called "the irony of history."

"Irony of fate."

And absurdity.

And absurdity as well. For me that's a great triumph, Louis. I received an invitation to serve on the examining board. At the same institute that once wouldn't let me in the door. And so, when I got out of the chemicals industry, fate brought me together with a woman that I fell in love with and married, and I ended up in Moldova and began working at a newspaper there.

In Kishinev?

Kishinev. As a journalist, for two years at a youth-oriented newspaper.

There were surely other film institutes.

Not in Russia. There were in other republics, but that wasn't an issue. I got married and had to raise a family, we wanted to have a child. I couldn't just go off and study somewhere.

And without a degree from VGIK, you couldn't find work?

I tried and succeeded. That's the thing. It worked. Because the last time I applied to VGIK, I already had experience working in the newspaper business in Kishinev, and the story is really funny in that they admitted my wife to the institute, but rejected me. She was able to study there but I couldn't. We were living in Moscow—she was a legal resident…

That's difficult for maintaining a relationship…

You're right. She was a legal resident, as a student, but I had to invite the local warden over for some drinks so that he'd close his eyes to the fact that I didn't have a permit to live in Moscow. And when my friend, the daughter of a famous director, Grigori Roshal, who knew me as an amateur filmmaker (he was the head of the Russian Film Clubs, and he knew that I'd approached him three years earlier) his daughter said, "you know, I'm going to Kirghizia to shoot a fiction film." But this was as yet an untamed land.

It wasn't bogged down with bureaucrats yet. "Do you want to go with me?" she asked. And I said, "yes." So I went.

That was 1962. I went to Kirghizia. And made the best start a person without a degree can make. I began as an assistant director, but I did the work of an executive producer, on a film produced by me and Grigori Roshal. It was a children's movie shot in a distant region of Kirghizia, where the film industry was just developing and was not very good overall. But God sent me good people to work with. I'll always remember and cherish the head of the local studio, Sharshen Soboleev, a man who had been through the war, who was bold and courageous, not only during war—it's easier to be bold in times of war. It's very difficult to be bold in normal times, and then you meet someone with a sober, clear-headed philosophy, and a sense of what's good and bad, and he says, "those people who are coming here will work with us, and they'll be producing the films until we can produce our own." And as a filmmaker without any degree, I got my training in Kirghizia. I had to learn quickly as an assistant on an independent film. The most interesting thing about my fate is not the fact that only a year and a half later I received my own feature film to direct, and shot it—it was called, *The Most Obedient Girl* [1965]. The most exciting thing for me was that I became the leader of Kirghiz documentary film.

Why documentary film? That wasn't your first love, was it?

No. I always wanted to be a director of feature films. It took me a long time to realize that I was more interested in documentary film. I had to shoot a feature film to realize that. But my friends came and worked on my film. Boris Galanter served as assistant cameraman. Ilya Gorelick worked as an editor. And little by little, the studio was no longer able to give everyone a feature film to work on. But they did have documentary films that were available to direct. Sharshen asked me if I would shoot one. I said yes, but not the one he proposed. And together we created—it was a great moment in the history of cinema—we created the Kirghiz school of documentary film. There was a sense of camaraderie at the studio, which at that time, the early 1960s, occupied a position of leadership in the Soviet Union's film industry. The only group that was on a par with us was the studio in Riga, with its Baltic traditions, its strengthened European tendencies. And the Riga-Frunze connection, which I frequently wrote about in the press, was very active.

Wasn't Konchalovsky's First Teacher *shot in Kirghizia?*

Of course. I brought Andron in. After I'd refused to do the film because the screenwriters had drained this work of Chingiz Aitmatov of any social significance. I told Aitmatov—"they've drained it of its substance. How can I do anything with it?" And he said, "then you're not behind me. I'll have to wage this battle alone with the Secretary of the Central Committee." I said, "Well I can't shoot this." Aitmatov didn't care. The head of the studio told me to find someone else. I told him that I had someone, Sergei Mikhalkov's son, a young man with a good film to his credit. He said, "will you vouch for him?" I said, "I'll vouch for him. I've seen his work." So he said, "bring him in." I brought him in. When I saw his film, I thought, "what kind of idiot am I? Look at how this guy found a way to get his message across more clearly than I ever could have, even without any social commentary. He brought it out in another way." This was a big lesson for me, and by that time I'd become a regular anti-Soviet guy.

Could you tell me what a "regular anti-Soviet guy" is?

Someone who's finally understood a thing or two about the system. But it's also someone who's been wounded, because anger and hatred for the social system replace natural human values. But I gained experience. I directed a feature film. I worked as a film critic for a Russian-language newspaper, one of the best in Kirghizia. It was basically the work I did and the articles I wrote that enabled me to become a member of the Union of Filmmakers in 1962, though at that time I entered the Union as a film critic. I became someone who was able to direct films despite my lack of a degree in it. There's a clause in the tax laws—it was written in my work records that I should be taxed as a low-budget, [grade B] director. But I didn't need to be a fat cat. I needed to abide by the law.

What does that mean? Does it mean that if you aren't in that category, you can't work, obtain funding, equipment, and so on?

Right. Since the government holds all the cards when it comes to financing—the government determines who will get what project. This involves an official system of values in which people with degrees get more money than people without degrees. Someone who's shot three films is better than someone who's shot just one. That's a bureaucratic approach, because the guy with no degree can shoot a brilliant film, but it will still be stuck in the lowest category.

I'm not talking about myself. My film wasn't great. In fact it was a film I made at age 33. I didn't have the strength and courage to produce it the way it should have been because there would have been a huge uproar.

The desire to do it the way it should be was eating at me, but one of my friends—I won't name him—and the screenwriters for my film—I also won't name them—brilliant filmmakers, now known the world over, said to me, "what are you messing with that for? You better not do that." And I hate myself for following their advice. Because literally anywhere from four to seven scenes that I could have included in the film would have catapulted it to another level, where it would have caused an uproar. And while it would have created all sorts of problems for the studio, and for me, I'd be the one at the center of all the uproar. I didn't find the courage to go through with. And I'm not accusing my older colleagues—I like them, they're great artists.

That was under Brezhnev?

No, that was under Khrushchev, but I completed the film in 1965. And I could have made my decision in peace. But some very great, famous and talented people said, "your film will be lacking these elements, you shouldn't do this, and the esthetics of the film will be out of step." And I followed their advice. I was a fool! Nonetheless, the film gained recognition. I earned my reputation as a filmmaker. I received my certification. And I headed for Moscow.

Could you describe the situation in cinema during those years?

Of course. It was a strange and wonderful turning point, when we were able to express differing opinions, when at least an esthetic that didn't fit socialist realism had the right to exist. It was a time when after a long, humiliating existence, the generation that had proved itself could enjoy the banquet. Vasily Ordynsky, Marlen Khutsiev, Grigori Chukhrai, Alexander Alov, Vladimir Naumov and many new people who had paid their dues as assistants during a period of the Stalin era when few films were being produced. But of course they somehow found the funds to produce films.

It was an incredible time. Sergei Nikolaevich Kholosov, one of the leading figures in today's cinema, who directed the film, *The Schism*, called me over after watching my film, and he said, "I liked your film. Here's a script I'd like you to direct." Imagine, Louis, a guy from Kirghizia, someone who'd directed only one film, a chemical engineer, now at Mosfilm Studios, receives a major three-part television film, and Kholosov says, "take it."

What was your reaction?

Of course I grabbed the script, without even knowing what was in it, mainly hoping to shoot a film. Nonetheless, once I read the script, I realized that I didn't have the right to and wasn't able to produce it. I approached Kholosov and said—"the story of an aristocrat who betrayed his class in the war of the Bolsheviks and the secret police isn't the kind of movie I want to produce." He looked at me like I was nuts and said, "are you sure of what you're saying, do you take responsibility for it?" I said, "yes." "Then I can no longer be associated with you." He actually used a cruder expression.

I lost any possibility of future film work in Russia, but Chukhrai lent me a helping hand, and said, "why don't you work on the editorial board? You've got standing as a critic. In a year and a half, I'll give you a script to produce." That was a very interesting proposal, because he was in charge of an experimental studio—it operated differently from other studios. Vladimir Pozner ran it, the famous persona that everyone knew was basically a spy. [*Not to be confused with his son, also Vladimir, well known as a television personality later.*—LM]

Did that studio operate according to self-financing [khozraschyot]?

Yes, it was the period of self-financing, and Pozner was one of its pioneers. By that time he had little use for his command of four languages and experience as a secret agent—during World War II he was the head of a war-time studio in Hollywood. Vladimir Alexandrovich also looked upon me with suspicion, but nonetheless, I became a member of the editorial board at that studio. It would be a very long story to tell you everything. I didn't quite fit in with this studio either. Pozner, an energetic and daring guy who wasn't half bad, made a critical mistake: he hoped to create an oasis of capitalism within the socialist system. That's where he failed. And I'll always feel sorry for him. Besides that, he made a big mistake in choosing Chukhrai as his art director, someone spineless, someone, despite all the courage and decisiveness he exhibited during the war, who turned out to be unable to stand firmly in confrontations with the authorities. So the experiment was a luke-warm attempt, and made an impact mainly in the economic sphere, by violating the basic principle of Marxism, that ideological and economic spheres must be linked.

When I was chased out of that studio, the Deputy Minister [of Goskino], Baskakov, pounded on the table and said, "who gave you the right to pervert an economic experiment into an ideological one?!" I said, "Vladimir Ioannovich, you're a terrible Marxist. Marxist theory gave me the right to do that. It's the economic substructure and the ideological superstructure." I was quickly chased out of that studio because I helped bring about the production of the first film dealing with the 50th anniversary of Soviet power. The studio had a very good Editor-in-Chief, Vladimir Fedorovich Ognev, a brilliant critic, who supported the idea of producing a film about the dawn of an unknown era—that's an expression by Konstantin Paustovsky—an exploration in film of the writings of great writers, Babel, Olesha, Platonov, Paustovsky, Malyshkin.

I was the editor on this project. So we began producing this film, *The Beginning of an Unknown Age*. Babel and Malyshkin were eliminated, but Platonov, Olesha, and Paustovsky remained. And two of them were to be produced under my editorial supervision, and that of my friend, Andrei Smirnov. The one by Platonov was to be produced by my beloved friend, Larisa Shepitko, whom I'd known half my life. Genrikh Saulovich Gabai, who now lives in New York, was to do the third one [*Motria*]. The film was a bit of a hybrid, because it consisted of fictional novellas that also included documentary materials which I produced. This film was shelved and was the reason for my expulsion. That was the next hole I ended up in, because someone had to take the hit, and Chukhrai chose me.

An interesting title for what turned out to be a trilogy that the bosses wanted to keep "unknown."

Despite all their efforts, they didn't manage to destroy the original negative of this film—they destroyed the original negative of Andrei's film, *Angel*. Pasha Lebeshev, one of the best cameramen in Soviet cinema, managed to create a copy of this film by working from the film positive. It was hellish work. Larisa also had a great cameraman—for her *Homeland of Electricity*—Dima Korzhykhin, may he rest in peace. He died very soon after that film.

I was expelled from the film industry because of that trilogy, in a serious way and for a long time. But that's when I realized that I'd gained a certain amount of experience. This was a great experience for me, because I was young. I was the youngest member of the editorial board.

Why exactly did they suppress the films?

Because—even in the liberal period of the '60s—of the ideology they represented. What was *Angel* in Smirnov's interpretation? How happy we were to be able to express what we thought about that regime, that history, the rank criminality of it, and the impotent, doomed nature of that regime. And when at the end the fallen angel smashed the commissar's skull, no one was upset about it. He deserved it.

It certainly wasn't Chapayev.

[Laughter]. As for Larisa Shepitko's *Rodina Elektrichestva*, these people owed their lives to God and the rain from above, and not to any earthly authorities. So I was expelled from the studio again. Even though I was one of the people attracting others to this studio. Neither Chukhrai in terms of age, neither the charming, intelligent, and slight man who'd survived a jail term, my friend, Vladimir Lychenko, no one else could attract people the way I could. And all around us things were bubbling—with Shepitko, Klimov, Soloveev, Yashin, Todorovsky…

And would you put Tarkovsky in a separate category?

Andrei was with us. He began with us, but then went his own way. The film, *The Mirror*, was being discussed in its early stages, and Andrei was very interested in learning about the Kirghiz school of cinema, and from the very first shoot, he recruited a cameraman from Kirghizia. Andrei Arsenevich began *The Mirror* at our studio.

But Tarkovsky was a unique phenomenon, and his work…

As a director he is unique. But he was looking for the best people to carry out his ideas. And initially he looked for people in the documentary sphere, among my friends, Margachov and Vedugeris, the heads of the Kirghiz school, who shot some footage for Andrei of his mother on vacation in Bolshev, because he realized that his mother would be the main character in his film. Tarkovsky carefully weighed the authenticity, the unobtrusiveness and exactness of the documentary style, but he preferred to estheticize his images, and he was right. He decided not to work with Margachov and Vedugeris but with Rerberg, who didn't shoot in a basic documentary style but incorporated a certain esthetic to it.

The Mirror has a documentary dimension to it.

Of course. You see, when Andrei decided to cast his mother instead of an actress in his film, whatever his artistic vision was, he couldn't escape the fact that it would have a documentary feel.

I meant that it's almost like a historical chronicle marking the major events of the time like the Spanish Civil War...

Of course. I don't think it's a sin to discuss the influence of the documentary esthetic. It was apparent in Andron's work, who came of age in Kirghizia alongside our documentary films, who shot *Asya's Happiness* in that style, and who influenced Andrei Arsenevich to a certain extent.

So then what? What happened to the studio and its experimentation?

Then they began to break our group up. With my departure, the Experimental Studio decided it would mainly pursue an economic experiment and not an ideological one. Gurevich was gone—good riddance. They pushed hard to produce a commercial hit. Gaidai's *Twelve Chairs* appeared, then along the way was Todorovsky's *Magician*, a brilliant film. The Ministry had turned the studio into a purely commercial venture. I realized that the Experimental Studio would be too scared to take on certain projects. So I left to work in documentary film.

A documentary filmmaker at long last!

At last. I realized that this was my destiny.

How did you realize that?

You see, I realized it because documentary film had less room for lies than any other occupation. In documentary film, I didn't have to think every time I shot a subject how I could deceive the authorities. We always lived by the principle of reading everything between the lines. Andron [Konchalovsky] described this best: it was, "how many white dogs should you include in a film?" There were at least three levels a film had to go through: the studio director, Goskino, and the Central Committee of the Communist Party. And despite all this the film had to retain its integrity. So the intelligent director would include some blatant taboos in the hopes that the censors would be distracted by them and let other, more substantial things, slip by. I was sick of playing this game. So in 1968, as a sick, jobless Cossack, I started working out of my home, and strangely enough, I was more successful at this than at anything else. I realized that I had a talent for documentary film.

Tell me a bit about the situation in documentary film at that time.

Of course there was a long documentary tradition in the USSR. In the U.S. I got tired of hearing "Dziga Vertov, Dziga Vertov, Dziga Vertov!" And they don't know anything about Dziga Vertov, they only know his name!

I understand, though you might be exaggerating.

There was a young guy with me, Sergei Miroschnichenko, a talented guy who started yelling at them, "and what's so great about Dziga Vertov. Look at the way he filmed churches being destroyed, icons being burned. What are you, out of your mind? Dziga Vertov is Dziga Vertov—take a look at his work." But what do I really think of him? He was a sincere person, moved by emotion, and a religious person. He realized only later what was happening around him, but you can't incriminate him for that, no matter how much you might not like him, and I don't. He was a sincere, honest person. But little by little, with the influence of Dziga Vertov, documentary film came to serve as propaganda. It's a paradox that is worth studying—it's a sublime paradox. Documentary film thrives only in countries where ideology puts it into service.

I think I know what you mean, but please explain that "paradox."

A paradox in that it is specifically in totalitarian regimes that documentary film truly flourishes despite everything, when you must deceive the authorities, when under the banner of serving the regime, only the best, most interesting, daring, and most courageous pursue this vocation. The Soviet documentary filmmakers of the sixties were brilliant. When they had to weave their craft against the backdrop of patronage and panegyrics. Sometimes they [the authorities] would say, "do a film glorifying this," and they'd glorify that. But they'd slip in a couple of nuances and the film no longer would be serving the interests of the state. The state still believed it was. But in fact it was serving the interests of humanity.

What was the fate of the sixties generation? The human being re-emerged in cinema. We started paying attention to individual characters. We became interested in talented personalities. We slowly started the process of regeneration—like old skin peeling off after a burn. Amid the glorification of the state, the newsreels on the achievements of the state, an interest in individual human beings started appearing. That period marked the awakening of a fresh, pure voice calling attention to the individual, to each person's character, to conflicts that existed. It was the beginning of the break with the glossy, beautiful patriotic documentaries. It all started in Kirghizia and in Riga. That was in the 1960s. It was a wonderful time.

Did it last through the seventies?

The late sixties and early seventies. But no one noticed how during the second half of the seventies, the situation began changing, and the state began suppressing attempts at nonconformism. I myself was a victim of that process, when it seemed like you could say whatever you liked, but turned out not to be the case. Of course, the first wave of the sixties gave us a greater understanding of what documentary film could be if it wasn't serving the state. At the same time, people let their guards down. It seemed that talking about love, happiness, the capacity of the human being, creation, we were able to speak the truth. But the authorities knew that they'd diverted us to a carefully monitored detour, that they kept us off the main road. It's a very interesting dialectic. Because until the mid-seventies, there were sweet stories about everyday life, but we didn't notice that the sleepy hand of the state was taking control of everything again.

Let's jump to the present situation in documentaries.

Now no one wants to wants to talk about politics. Now the pendulum has swung to the other extreme, and everyone again, just as in the late sixties, wants to talk about simple, eternal emotions. It's natural. I analyze my own actions. Actually, I never made any political films. I don't know if that's something to be proud of or not, maybe on the contrary. But already over the last two years, I've been trying to promote films about love, about charity, about compassion. It's not always accepted, we don't always have the artistic resources to realize our ideas. But I know that, beginning with [Viktor] Kossakovsky, who tries to comment on the good by showing us evil, who calls for greater compassion by drawing attention to the lack of it in our lives—well, that's an artist's approach. But alongside this, there's film that defends compassion, compassion with a capital "C." That's what our viewers need.

Soundtracks: Interviewing the Filmmakers

12. A relaxed Leonid Gurevich in New York, 1991. Gurevich (1932-2001) was a prolific documentary filmmaker and scenarist, as well as an eloquent and energetic promoter of Russian non-fiction cinema, at home and abroad. (Photo: Anne Borin).

13. Anne Borin, scout and coordinator for American films to the "Message to Man" Film Festival, with its director, Misha Litvyakov, St. Petersburg, 1996.

Yuri Khashchavatsky

"But Russia is a great country because we absorb other cultures, including American culture. Don't you see how many films are shown here? But you've got to understand that people are now sick of Schwarzenegger."

Menashe: *We're recording now in St. Petersburg's Dom Kino with Yuri Khashchavatsky. Yuri, tell me a bit about yourself.*

Khashchavatsky: I know that you're very interested in talking about Arkady Ruderman,[1] so I can talk about the two of us. Both of us are from the KVN [literally, the "Club for the High-Spirited and Resourceful"—"Klub veselykh i nakhodchivykh"]. But I was a director from the Odessa branch of the KVN. And he was the head of the Minsk KVN. That was until they removed him as a Jew, because Jewish people weren't supposed to head such clubs. But it wasn't so bad, because the current head of the Minsk club, Oleg Bykhovsky, who took his place, is a terrific guy, whom everyone loves, and Arkady loved him too. I don't know whether he's better or worse. I don't have the right to say whether he's better or worse. It's simply that Arkady, since he was Jewish, couldn't be the head of the Minsk club.

When was this?

That was about 1970. Before that, in 1966 and 1967, I was the director of the Odessa club. That was the best KVN branch. We're about the same age. We're both very young and that's why I can remember the time I won a medal at the KVN. We played against the team from Baku. The entire Soviet Union was backing us. They also supported Arkady and he loved being in this role. He loved to be loved. Both of us graduated from the technical school. I graduated in Odessa and he in Minsk. He graduated from the Polytechnic Institute as an electrician. I'm a mechanic. And my wife—her name is Tamara—practically predetermined our destiny. I'm speaking honestly, because if Arkady were alive and sitting here with us, he'd say, "yes, that's the way it is." Because you see, when both of us, as Jews...

So you're Jewish?

I'm not Jewish by origin, but I always considered myself to be

Jewish. I'm in a truly idiotic situation. My mother is Russian, my father is Jewish. For Jews I'm Russian, but for Russians I'm a Jew. I'm in an idiotic situation. My wife, who is a marvelous woman, is Jewish. Thank God my son is Jewish. That doesn't mean I prefer Jews. I'm just glad he's somebody, at least. My wife told me that because we're Jewish they wouldn't let us enter a specialized school in Byelorussia; they really didn't let us in specifically because we were Jewish. They canceled our exams because we were Jewish. That's the truth, that's what they told me. My wife called Leningrad. Now, thank God it's St. Petersburg, though it's hard for us to cross this language barrier, calling it Petersburg. She told us that we needed to go to Leningrad. So we traveled here together with Arkady in 1976. We arrived here with Arkady and entered the Leningrad State Institute of Theater and Film. No one asked about our nationality. It's an institute of brilliant professionals. At that time Tovstonogov still worked at this institute. To my mind he's one of the best theater directors in the world.

What was your first film?

Let me tell you about Arkady's first film, then about mine. Arkady's first film was made as part of Minsk television's young people's programming. His film was called, *Reaching the Flag*. This was a film about two teams, one from a civil engineers' institute and one from an athletics institute. The teams were thrown into a swamp that was impossible to cross. They were supposed to lay gas pipes in this swamp, to perform a feat similar to that portrayed in the film, [Nikolai Mashchenko's] *How the Steel was Tempered*. These kids—there's something about Russian kids—they actually did it. They established a certain principle: each morning they took a flag, carried it to a point one kilometer ahead, so it could be seen from all over, and planted it there. Then they wouldn't stop laying pipe until they'd reached that spot. Hence the name of the film, *Reaching the Flag*.

It was a documentary film?

Yes. It aired on TV.

Did you work on any documentaries with Ruderman?

You know his famous film, the film that made him famous, *Theater in the Times of Glasnost and Perestroika?* I worked on that film. By that time, I was quite a respected director. I wouldn't work under

Arkady. But my friend came to me, you see, he came to me and asked me if I could help him. When Arkady died, people approached me and spoke with me as if I'd lost the closest friend I'd ever had. And I used to tell them, "he's not my closest friend, he's like my brother, whom I had the right not to love, and who had the right not to love me." But what united us was something powerful.

What were the circumstances of Arkady's death? I know his car was targeted at some point.

It was an ordinary catastrophe. They simply—to this day its not clear—either the steering failed or the driver lost control of the wheel himself.

But they weren't shot at?

Two hours earlier, they had been surrounded. They escaped.... That's when they were shot at. You know, it was the camera that killed him. I know that the camera killed him. When the cameraman—Yuri Koruliov—was shooting a sequence, Arkady told him to hold the scene a bit longer. He said, "I know what narration will accompany this scene." Yuri shot a very long take. It lasted about four minutes. It was four minutes of a military unit in Tadjikistan.

Was this close to Dushanbe?

It was very close to Dushanbe, very close to where military operations were taking place. And Arkady said, "Yuri, shoot just a little longer. I know what narration I'll put in this scene." Yuri kept shooting and passed the camera back to him [Arkady]. It was a big Betacam SP camera. Two minutes later the vehicle tumbled over. And in the back there was just twisted wreckage where the camera had been. You know, from my point of view, unfortunately, we all hate to see our friends, those close to us, our loved ones die, right? But when they die, we want them to die a romantic death. We want them to die from a bullet. But life is more complicated than that. It's more complicated, and always more cynical—it kills us in a different way. It usually kills us in a very mundane, commonplace way. That's how we die—in our bed, or in an overturned car. And the situation in Tadjikistan is very difficult right now. That's why I emphasize the fact that the Tadjiks are in no way to blame for Arkady's death. It's terrible. The people there are engulfed in tragedy. It's crazy, it's a land that gave Zoroastrism to the world. So probably what we're talking about isn't so important. And let's hope that it isn't so important. Because the greatest meaning in all this is what is happening now.

This film was about Davlat Khudonazarov?

Yes, he was at the center of the film, it was called *From One Prayer to the Next*. In principle, I served as the director. It was difficult for Yuri Koruliov to shoot anything after that. It seems me that after the accident he couldn't shoot any more. Nobody wanted to go there after that. Not a single cameraman. We can't blame them. They're normal people. Try to understand this terrible tragedy. As I'm editing Arkady's film, I see the military leader shaking hands with people. I know what's going to happen if this sequence is shown in Tadjikistan. The opposition will be sitting and taking note of everyone he shook hands with, everyone who extended a hand, and they'll kill every one of them.

It's a well-intentioned film, a film that was meant to put an end to the bloodshed, but can you see how even a well-intentioned film can bring about suffering, bloodshed and death? That's the most terrible thing. That's what we were afraid of. That's why I'm very grateful that they didn't show it in Tadjikistan, because fewer people were killed. We ourselves don't understand what terrible weapons we have in our hands.

Thank you for your reminiscences about yourself and Ruderman, but I must ask you about your film, Russian Happiness. *Were you poking fun at your subjects?*

I'll explain. That kind of criticism has come up. But the critics who say this are not farsighted. Because this is a tragic, searching film. And it's silly to blame me for taking a superficial approach—it's a tragedy. Yes, you know about "holy fools" in Russia. I was trying to convey the sense of being a holy fool in this film. I tried to convey that kind of character. Many critics said the opposite. They said that the film was too ironic, frivolous.

There's some confusion about the end of the film, the guy climbing—what was the intention?

The end of the film is the end of the film. It's impossible to explain. The end of the film is—like Russia—impossible to understand. I realize I've closed myself off to you, that it's an easy answer, but you know that famous Tiutchev poem.

But literally, what did he think that he had done?

He thought one thing. He thought that we were filming him, that he'd climb the church, to the belltower and that we were filming him, and that everybody would see it. And for him that was very important that everyone saw him climbing the belltower. He was an incredible person.

He thought he was getting closer to God?

That's a Russian tradition. Let's talk about Russia. In Russia, it seems to me, when we talk about godless Russia or people now like to say that it's god-loving Russia—well, it's nothing of the kind. It seems to me that the Russian *muzhik* has always loved God, but he loved him in his own way. He loved him without the church. He didn't need an intermediary to love God. There's a certain national trait in this. The Russian peasant always considered himself to be equal to God. He was climbing the belltower because he considers himself to be equal to God. It's both wonderful and terrible. You can both admire this man and fear him.

I felt that. He mentioned something about land.

They still haven't given the peasant any land. We only touched upon this briefly in the film, because we understand this—it's evident. Despite *perestroika* and the whole market economy, people aren't being given any land. Moreover, when there are decrees ordering them to be given the land, they're given land in a different place or at a different time. "OK, we'll give you land. Go over there and get it. But we need this piece of land." It's terrible. This will go on for a long time.

So you conceived of Russian Happiness *as a kind of folk-tragedy rather than a comical evocation of local folkways?*

I'm happy that you understood that. Because I'm always trying to convey that. It seemed like I was shooting a very light, folkish film, but in reality I draw people into a tragedy. You know, the story behind this film is very funny. This film was commissioned by the Japanese TV company, NHK. And when the Japanese producer saw this film, he said it was shameful to shoot films like this.

Well, fine. But you can't impose your own rules on a foreign culture. In Russia there's a great saying: "Don't bring your own rules into a strange monastery." But Russia is a great country because we absorb other cultures, including American culture. Don't you see how many films are shown here? But you've got to understand that people are now sick of Schwarzenegger. Why? Russia needs its own Schwarzenegger, its own heroes. Russia is a fantastic part of this earth, but it's a part of this earth that needs repentance.

I've always done my best to understand Russia, but I'm often perplexed.

My dear, you're not a Russian person. You can't understand Russia. We're Russians, and we can hardly understand her! Because as Tiutchev said, "One cannot grasp Russia with reason, nor measure her by conventional means. In Russia one can only believe."

Thank you for this poetic, very Russian conclusion!

---

[1] Ruderman (1950-1992) died at the height of his career as a documentary filmmaker strongly committed to democratic values in the late Soviet and post-Soviet years. I worked with him on Sherry Jones's award-winning documentary for PBS, *In the Shadow of Sakharov* (1991), and he remains in my memory as an engaging, smart, and resourceful film person whose socio-political interests led him to Tadjikistan. His death there gave rise to speculation that he was assassinated or caught in the crossfire of a Civil War that erupted after the collapse of the USSR. Khashchavatsky, his friend and colleague, corrects the record here in this interview. Davlat Khudonazarov, the subject of the film Ruderman was working on at the time of his death, was a cinematographer and director, a former head of the old Filmmakers Union, and was active in reformist politics of the late Soviet period and in his native Tadjikistan. Khashchavatsky himself has been a courageous figure, with his films and political activity, in the opposition to the authoritarian rule of Alexandr Lukashenko in Belarus. He was kept under surveillance, and suffered a savage beating in 1997, but he continues undaunted in the struggle for basic freedoms in the former Soviet republic.

Mikhail Litvyakov

"Wise governments that fund documentary film are supporting a visible record that will last forever."

Menashe: *Tell me a bit about yourself—your background, career, and so on.*

Litvyakov: I'm a pre-war baby, born in 1938. My father was in the army, and the war forced us to live in the Staraia Rus' war camp. We lived through the bombings, the occupation.... Basically everyone figured I'd end my days on the Volga. I thought I was going to die, but somehow the Lord God—I survived and thank God I am still alive. Then I lived the normal life of a Soviet schoolboy, a young man. The Pioneers wouldn't accept me, but I was the head of a school detachment. And for me, submitting to hierarchy always seemed silly. I never wanted to be a slave to people above me. After high school, I tried to get into medical school to be near my girlfriend.

Where was that?

Here, in what was then called Leningrad. I tried to get into the theater institute, but wasn't accepted. So I began studying at the railroad institute. It was about that time that I started thinking about things. I completed a certificate course and went to work on geological expeditions in the Far North as a geophysics technician. I was looking for uranium deposits, and was afraid of finding them, because as an inexperienced technician, I was afraid that if I found these deposits I'd have to perform more in-depth analyses of them. For two weeks the equipment had been registering second-degree radiation, for two weeks we'd been exposed to a high level of radiation. I was worried, and only afterwards, much later, did I learn that the authorities had been performing nuclear tests at Novaia Zemlia. And now we're surprised how few people are left in the Far North. They're all slowly dying off. They don't use that equipment any more.

And when does film enter your life?

I got my first taste of film in the army. Because the happiest time for any soldier is time spent watching movies at the club. For the first time I got to see Roman Karmen's incredible documentary films, which had a powerful effect on me. They made me cry, they charged my emotions. I realized that this was a kind of art I'd never experienced before.

What were these movies about?

They were about oil workers in the Caspian Sea, about people, their destinies, real people whose lives on the screen moved you by their honesty. And for the first time I learned about the existence of the Cinema Institute in Moscow [VGIK]. For the first time I learned that Gerasimov was one of the professors there, and that his class was shooting *The Young Guard*. I realized that I really wanted to apply there. This is because we all were raised on films. Films introduced us to a whole new world. We watched *Tarzan* and shouted like savages.

I served in the army in 1957. There were all kinds of trials and denunciations going on. I served in many units, and I completed my service just as the Gary Powers incident broke [in 1960]. Our unit was sent to intercept him, because they [the authorities] knew that a spy plane was flying over, and they sent us there. We completed our service at Baikonur. They fired the shots from there. And if you look at his flight course, when he started zig-zagging, sensing he'd been spotted by the enemy, we were sitting right under that zigzag. When I finished serving, I went into cultural work, ran radio shows, and prepared for a life's work in the cultural sphere.

But you hadn't made any films then.

No, I still didn't know what a movie camera was. But I sent my documents to the Cinema Institute. By the time the Institute was holding entrance exams, I still hadn't received a reply. So I sent a friend of mine who'd already completed his service and lived in Moscow. He went to the Institute and told me to come right away. But I got sick at that point with dysentery. Then the invitation arrived from the Institute. I told the doctors, "for God's sake, let me go and the first film I make will be about doctors." And I kept my word. My first film, *The Eternal Struggle*, was about a surgeon.

When I got to Moscow I went straight to the Institute, and it was as though I'd walked into a temple of culture—assistant directors, assistant cameramen, composition, frames—I was in heaven. I felt I had nothing to lose. Many students simply wrote down their creative ideas, for screenplays or film proposals that they'd been working on. But I turned to my life experience—after loosening up with a quick drink. I wrote about how our boat capsized during one of our expeditions. I basically recounted my life. That helped me a lot. That was my education. To this day I thank God that he blessed me with the feelings I've experienced throughout my life.

When did you return to Leningrad?

I passed all the exams with top marks, but the results on the basic skills exam weren't so good. But I didn't wait for the results, because they'd accept students who'd gotten even lower marks. I was getting bored, so I left for Leningrad and went to work as an assistant director at the Leningrad Documentary Film Studio, it was called "Lenkinokhronika" at that time. On the very first day I worked with a camera and shot a scene for the first time in my life. It was at the Pushkino-to-Leningrad [line]. I stood there with an Eyemo Camera—the kind used during the war—and my heart was beating so, I thought everyone would hear it, but there I was, camera in hand. I started shooting, and the stills got into the newspaper. For me it was a real coup. A year later I entered the Cinema Institute. I got good marks. For me it was a wonderful time. At the Institute I shot a student film, as cameraman and director. I did some journalism and photography; I have a whole photo album from the Institute during the sixties. Kolya Gubenko lived with me. Vasily Shukshin hung out with us. Larisa Luzhina, Zhanna Prokhorenko, they were all my friends and colleagues.

So that began your long career in documentary film.

I was lucky that I'd begun my work in film in the sixties, during the Thaw. People were hoping that there would be a democratic revival in our country. The rehabilitation of innocent political victims. My grandfather was repressed, and my uncle perished in Magadan. My grandfather was First Commander of the tsarist court's Georgiev Cavalry at Tsarskoe Selo, and he wouldn't let anyone loot the palace. For me, the early 'sixties was the first time I started making films about people, and my first film was about a surgeon. Then I shot a film about delinquent kids. *Goodbye, Mom* was a film about abandoned kids, about parents' responsibility towards their children. During this time I was trying to produce films that didn't mythologize the ruling structures, that focused their attention on the individual, on personality, on feelings. That was my credo.

And at that time this was possible.

Yes. This was a very happy time for me. I was basically bought by the Soviet authorities. I received a number of Russian and Soviet awards, was named a Respected Artist of the State, and so on. For a certain period of time I was able to travel abroad. I played all the games. But I don't look with regret upon the past. Because I think I was incredibly lucky to be able to work in documentary film. What other career would allow me to travel throughout the entire Soviet Union and to many countries?

But later?

Later I—

Things got more difficult?

No. Now it's quite difficult to produce a movie. We didn't realize that documentary film has to be subsidized by the state. Wise governments that fund documentary film are supporting a visible record that will last forever. Though video won't last forever. I worked in the film archives. I realized what an incredible treasure our former filmmakers and cameramen had left us. They left behind the great history of the Romanovs, war newsreels, the Leningrad blockade. It's an incredible feeling how documentary films become better with each year, just like good wine. They become more delicious and more valuable with time. I realized what a crime it was that the authorities had cut off funding for newsreels. Because...

You're talking about what's happening today?

Today. Because the production levels at the film studios have dropped 90 percent. And now people must organize their own little studios, seek out funding sources, etc. Many studios have to rent out their space to pay for utilities, heating bills. We've become so corrupted by the state structures built on lies, because we were sold sausage for twenty-five cents when in reality it cost much more to produce. It was a huge deception. And now we finally understand that the loaf of bread that kids used to play soccer with has a certain price, and it's rather expensive. It's difficult, but we're beginning to understand that everything has a real value. And we've begun trying to adapt—it's very difficult—to adapt to this system of value.

How did you get into the administrative side of things, especially heading the Petersburg Festival?

So I was Secretary of the Leningrad Union of Filmmakers. They decided to divide the Moscow Film Festival into three parts: documentary, children's and fiction films. I was often in Moscow visiting the Union of Filmmakers because they held professional competitions that involved representatives from studios from throughout the Soviet Union. There were people from Kiev, Sverdlovsk, etc. They took part in certain exercises—taking the role of director, etc. And each group proposed its own program. I came from Leningrad with my own proposed program. I was sent to the International Center for Cinema and Television, which had its own hotel, movie theaters, etc. I had a great proposal—everyone liked it. Well, I'm from Leningrad. I decided to organize a festival in Leningrad. As they say, God gave me a mission.

And when I began this—because I had absolutely no experience in doing this kind of thing—I'm a documentary filmmaker. Though I could measure up to any feature filmmaker, because life forces us to take on the responsibilities of producer, director, and screenwriter; because as life presents new situations for us, we have to adapt on the set. If you can't get in the door, try the window, if the window is closed, we'll get a ladder. Life shapes us, we're molded by life. This proved very important when I began organizing the festival. The first festival we coordinated in 1989 was a town-wide, even nationwide, celebration. Were you there?

No, unfortunately.

It was marvelous. In fact, I have a video of it that you can watch. We thought we'd hold the festival once every two years. But by the time of the second festival, *perestroika* had begun, there were funds to support it, and it was difficult, but we pulled it off. We had festivals in 1989, 1991, and 1993. And after 1993, when we'd organized the Third International Goodwill Festival, we hadn't taken into account the fact that documentary film studios were making the transition to self-financing. That was a strategic error. No one wanted to invest money in documentary film. It's not profitable.

With all the trouble, especially financial trouble, that you were facing, why did you decide to expand this year's festival [1994]? There were many new categories apart from documentaries.

Why did I create these categories? Because at that time, very few documentary films were being shot. And they weren't showing up in theaters. It became very difficult to put together a program.

Personally, I think that when people say, "Russia is in economic decline. Do we really need any festivals and celebrations?"—I think there will be no economic revival in Russia if Russians don't grow culturally; Russia will experience no spiritual rebirth. And during the Goodwill Festival, I found a verse in the Bible, in the Letters to the Corinthians, I realized that this was a message of goodwill, not to people in general, but to each individual, each human being. Be it a good person, a bad person, a criminal—I want to send a message to each and every person, because for many years we said, "we are the Soviet people," and millions were sacrificed to communism, to the camps, because human life had no value. I want our festival to rekindle an understanding of kindness, mercy, compassion, love in the hearts of people, universal principles. And if only our respected government would finally understand. I don't need a handout from them. Just adopt a single law, and everything will experience a renaissance. Money that's invested in culture should be tax-deductible. No taxes. I'm talking about culture: libraries, museums, film, theaters, that kind of thing. I'm certain that it will produce an economic miracle.

Let's hope so. I was told that two days before the festival you didn't know whether the funding would come through. What did you do?

Literally two days before the festival's opening date, when the American delegation had already arrived, including Anne Borin.[1] That's our coordinator. A very active woman with a great American can-do attitude. I asked our mayor—we had letters stating that we'd receive 300 million rubles from the federal budget. But the money wasn't there. And our mayor, Anatoly Sobchak—God bless him, because he was the only person who understood the role of art and culture in the spiritual rebirth of Russia and our city. In a single day he carried out what normally would have taken two weeks to get through—in half a day, he personally decreed…

You didn't have to organize a fundraising campaign?

Nothing, no one. He simply decreed it. He stated it grandly. On Friday, which is a short working day, he said, "if by 1pm you don't transfer 100 million rubles to Litvyakov, I'm firing three people in your agency. If you don't transfer it by tomorrow, I'll fire another three. And so on, until someone takes action on this." I don't understand Byzantine methods—you need to get things done immediately, and that's how it was done. I could see the mayor exercising his authority.

He was your savior. Did he transfer all the funds you needed?

No. He transferred 100 million to me. I'm closing this festival with a debt of 80 million rubles. Now I'll have to figure out how to pay this debt over the next month or two.

Were you satisfied with the festival this year?

In dealing with these kind of technical problems, I've had to spend less time with my dear guests and more time running back and forth between the hotel, the bank, the mayor's office, and the patrons' offices—to ensure that this festival would actually get off the ground. I'm witness to all our shortcomings, our poor equipment. Our equipment, like everything in the Soviet Union, is on its last leg. So our respected Anne Borin's hopes for a certain level of film screening technology—we simply don't have the equipment for it. We were really counting on JVC, which we were negotiating with, and which offered as part of its sponsorship some pretty heavy-duty equipment. Then at the last minute, they said, "next time." What if we suddenly found a company that could sponsor of our festival and provide equipment?

What kind of equipment are you looking for?

We need good 16mm movie projectors, we need good quality film and video projection and screening equipment, so we could show videos on a large screen, some kind of JVC system.

Of the new categories in this year's Festival, I thought one was particularly interesting: "Russia in the Eyes of Her Friends."

When I was in Germany visiting a TV station there, one guy said to me, "you're losing so much. They're shooting so much over there, there's so much interest in Russia—you should create a special category for that." I said, "sure, let's do it." So we did. The Germans, the French, the Americans, the Dutch, the Finns—these are the countries that have the greatest interest in Russia. Maybe we called it "Russia in the Eyes of Her Friends," but it included all kinds of interpretations. The "friends" could be in quotes. We wanted this category to go beyond the usual superficial image of destitute people living in a dump and to convey a deeper understanding of Russians. Russia is filthy only on the outside right now—inside she's quite rich, and she has much greater spiritual wealth than in the West. I tell you that because I've been to the West. And I'm sure that Western producers will come here and try to dig a little deeper and not just skim the surface. Otherwise, they're doing the same thing that the Soviet propagandists did in the Communist period: "look at the slums of New York! Look at the streets of the Bowery, the bums." They're saying the same things as our propagandists. But there are films in the festival that portray human beings with concern, compassion, love. I think that without love, you can neither organize a festival nor make a movie.

[1] Borin is a prominent figure in New York film circles (e.g., as head of "New York Exposition of Short Films and Video" for many years), and has long been active in promoting Soviet- and Russian-American relations through film. She was an important facilitator for bringing U.S. films to the Petersburg Festival, and has served as a valuable consultant to Litvyakov and other leaders of the "Message to Man" Festival from its inception.

Alexander Rodnyansky

"Culture—it's something multinational. There are no borders in culture, especially in film, in documentaries."

Menashe: *By way of identification, how do you describe yourself, and your work?*

Rodnansky: I'm a film director and producer. Today it's called an independent producer. I'm from Ukraine, Kiev, which is my native city, but now I'm also working in Germany. And I'm trying to combine all the financial resources for my projects in Germany, Ukraine and Russia.

How did that happen, the German connection?

It happened after my last project about Raoul Wallenberg and his mysterious fate in Russia. It was my first project produced by foreign TV companies together with a Russian TV company. Swedish Television was a partner—Inkop Productions—and there was a German company. After this project, I met some television people, producers in Germany, I established some contacts there, and now I have the possibility of finding some support for my next project.

It seems to me that that's what every Russian, Ukrainian and directors of other nationalities dream of these days—to work out co-productions with foreign, especially Western, companies. So I congratulate your success in that regard. But explain exactly what it means to be engaged in a co-production with, for example, a German company. What is it that they're doing that you can't find here in Russia or in Ukraine?

I can't find enough money for my projects here. There's high level of inflation in our country and I can get some money from the Ministry of Culture of Ukraine, which is responsible for the development of film in our country, but the inflation rate in our country is approximately 7% every day. That means that money means nothing to us. That's why, I'd like to be, first of all, sure that everything is going ahead on my project. Secondly, we are a part of the European film process, something like that, or we have to be a part of that process.

What do you mean by being a part of the European film process?

When we were citizens of a closed society, as documentary filmmakers, we were supposed to be, as everyone knows today, the so-called "ideological agents" from the state to the audience. And now that we're independent, the state has lost all interest in our work. That's perhaps why we've lost the interest of a big part of our audience, but we should find our place in the cultural context. Culture—it's something multinational. There are no borders in culture, especially in film, in documentaries. And when our country is trying to find its place on the new geographical map of the world, it should be in documentaries. The number of documentary filmmakers may be very small, but they're very independent, and a very unique part of the international documentary film process. I hope that we can accomplish this.

So firstly, you cite financing, money, as coming from your co-producers abroad. Secondly, you're happy to enter, at last, world culture, again. Any other reasons why you seek joint production?

I'm looking for an opportunity to establish a strong structure that could support different documentary projects in my own country. That's why I should learn about all the opportunities available for obtaining funding or selling documentaries on the international market, because nobody can recoup their investment upon completing a film if they try to market it here. That's why I should be in cooperation with different foreign TV channels. That's very important, because today, there is nothing backing us up. If you compare it with the time when the state supported us... sometimes that was very bad, if we talk about ideological pressure. But they still supported us. And today, there's no support. That's why we must do it ourselves.

Interesting. Do you think that documentary film in the world market will meet with a big reception? My impression is that documentary film plays a much greater role in Russia, or the former Soviet Union, than it does, certainly in the United States, where the place for most documentary film is pretty much strictly television. But here, it seems to me, documentary film has always had a place among the filmgoing public in general. There are special theaters for documentary films, and so on. So what makes you think that documentary film will be—especially coming out of production here, or even with joint production—what makes you think that there will be a reception for it in the West?

First of all, I agree with you. But I didn't say the U.S. market. I don't have confidence in the U.S. market for documentaries. I'm very afraid, to tell you the truth, to be in co-productions with Americans. Except, of course, for some specific cases. But if we take the European market, it's feasible. I know at least three or four channels that could be very interested in our projects or with cooperating with us. In Germany, that's CDF, the second German TV station; VDR, a very big channel, which is very interested in documentaries, and I know a lot of people who work there. In Great Britain, there's Channel 4, and sometimes BBC. There's the prospect of developing a project there. In France, there's the Cultural Channel, "La Sept." Now it's called the Cultural Channel, and the new European cultural channel, Arte. There are a lot of opportunities for working together.

Yes, I think you're right. And there's tremendous interest in Russia at this point.

The second point. We don't need as much money as Americans.

Well there aren't huge amounts of money in America. People have that impression. Just talk to American documentary filmmakers, who are always struggling and always trying to find money.

You're right, but when there is the prospect of co-production, the possible promotion of our films on the European market, I can immediately get—the next day—financial support here. I know a lot of independent, commercial structures that could support our documentary project in the case of a co-production. That's why we don't need a lot of money. That's my personal strategy, and sometimes, I succeed. It's not always documentaries. It can also work with feature films.

Are you interested in doing any feature films?

To produce, not to direct them.

The films that I've seen of yours, that you directed—Wallenberg; Meetings with Father; *the film that was screened here at the festival,* Goodbye to the USSR—Part I, Personal, *all deal directly or indirectly with Jewish themes. Would you say, therefore, that you are a Jewish filmmaker?*

No, never. I am not a Jewish filmmaker. I am a filmmaker. But I spent the last five years making very personal films. It was a time when I had to find something for myself, my place in this world, in this country, to tell you the truth. I had to find out what connected me to this country, to all my friends, to the people, to the history, in general.

That's five years ago, meaning since the Gorbachev period?

The Gorbachev period. But it's not because of policy, because of Gorbachev. It's because everything is over. Not because the USSR, in a geographic sense, like a political empire, is over. The system of human relations is over, and that's the most important thing. I was forced to find a way out, like all my friends were.

Are you saying the system of human relations was destroyed under that regime?

Not under the regime, but under the process of *perestroika*. Because over the last five years, there was not only the process of destroying the political structures, but the destruction of human relations. At times this system wasn't very bad. At times it was very good. The special atmosphere that prevailed in the small circles of friends we had.

You're not talking about the "kollektiv?"

No, I mean relations among friends, the cultural underground.

You felt very together because you were committed to a common cause in opposition to the state system?

Absolutely. Together we had a common enemy, and we were together in opposition to this enemy. We were very close.

Wouldn't you say that this is a very Jewish characteristic? That Jews too, historically, have survived by experiencing solidarity.

Probably you're right. But you know, I didn't make all Jewish films. You haven't seen some of my films that weren't about Jewish themes. For example, *Tired Cities*, a film about the ecological disaster in our country. It became well-known here. It won many prizes.

It was my first film to become known among the professionals in the audience. And now I'm going to make a new film that isn't connected with Jewish topics. But it was absolutely necessary for me to establish my identity. I didn't feel like a Jew ten years ago. You know the situation in our country, when every Jew had strong pressure on him. Sometimes people were ashamed of being Jewish, including some of my relatives. That's why it was very important for me to establish my identity. My Ukrainian friends—it was a very painful process for them to find their national identity.

You mean for Ukrainians to find their national identity as Ukrainians. One of the fascinating things about your film—Part I, Personal, is the different ways in which Jewish identity is defined. A couple of people in the film say that they're really more Russian than they are Jewish. And yet, they still are Jewish. In another case, someone says that when he learned of the tragedies and catastrophes of the Jewish people, that's when he became Jewish. And Zaslavsky says that he's genetically Jewish, but culturally not. As a matter of fact, he's even Orthodox. (By the way, I must tell you that in the translation, it says "Orthodox." Now when people see that, they will think he means "Orthodox Jewish," because the same word is used in English for Orthodox Jew and Orthodox Church. That was confusing to some of the people I was sitting with, and I pointed out that Zaslavsky is Jewish, converted to Russian Orthodoxy.) Anyway, so there are a variety of ways in which people define themselves as Jews, and I wonder how you define yourself, which of those definitions do you most connect yourself to?

That's a difficult question. I've observed all these people with a special purpose. Just to try them on, to see how they avoid all the obstacles in this country, how they find their own way. I have a very close friend who's a set designer, who works here in this country, and it all sounds very simple. It's not, of course, so simple. He wanted to be a famous set designer, and he has the opportunity now in our country, because he is the number one designer. He works with all our rock stars, music stars, with everyone who wants to do something very expensive and exciting. I share his position that we should be very connected to our culture, to our roots...

To which culture, Russian?

Russian culture. I would say Russian language culture.

Not Ukrainian?

Not Ukrainian. I'm a Ukrainian citizen. I live there. My family lives there. But I'm a member of the Russian "intelligentsia."

Why do you consider yourself a member of the Russian "intelligentsia?"

Because I was raised on Russian culture, with roots in Russian language. That's why I'm a member of this special culture or social group.

Not Ukrainian, though. Now again, was that conscious, or did it just happen that your family was oriented...

It just happened. Conscious? That's also important, but...

You didn't make a decision, "I'm putting aside Ukrainian culture. I want Russian."

It happened... it happened because Kiev was like the southern capital of the Russian empire. It was a very strong island of Russian culture, that region.

Your family was not religious, Jewish religious, or Jewish conscious, they didn't speak Yiddish?

No. And in fact, my family was... of course secularized... but they were members of the Russian "intelligentsia" for three generations. My family, my grandfather and great-grandfather were lawyers in the Russian empire. They were involved in administrative processes. They had what's called "honorary citizenship" in the Russian empire. When Jews performed a great service but refused to convert to Orthodox Christianity, they could receive this status.

Fascinating. These were lawyers? Were there any other professions in the family?

My grandfather was the first documentary filmmaker. His father was a lawyer.

And all in Kiev?

Kiev in Ukraine. And Kharkov. Kharkov was a very important city in Ukraine.

I can see that, and I can see why you identify with this particular guy in the film. Except he said, when you ask him, "what do you want to be?", he says, "I want to be a foreigner." Now, he was being ironic?

Of course. He's always kidding around. That's why I like him. He never speaks without irony. I always laugh at his way of speaking.

At the same time, he was aware of the problems of living here. He said,

"I have to leave this apartment because I don't have a residence permit," *and so on. So one can understand why people would want to leave.*

But he's aware of the difficulties of living in the United States, for immigrants. We're thirty years, thirty-one years old, and we have to work. We would like to—I don't mean to get money—but to work as well as we can. That's why it's important for us to be here. By the way, to achieve success here, it's more possible than in the United States.

I agree. Let me just continue on the Jewish theme, if I may. I've noticed in the last few years that there have been quite a few Jewish films, both documentary and feature. There have been some of your films, there are Arkady Ruderman's films, which also, directly or indirectly, deal with Jewish themes.

We were friends. That's why we were close, because of these topics.

There are Aranovich's films. I just saw his Great Concert of the People. *There's a feature film—Astrakhan just made the film,* Izydi. *There was another film based on Babel,* Sunset/Zakat. *So in short, it looks like, at long last, filmmakers are able to present Jewish themes. Is this something that's going to continue? How do Russians react to this? And one additional question I have is, are there non-Jewish filmmakers who are making films about Jewish themes?*

There are some. I'll start from the end. There are some non-Jewish filmmakers who are making Jewish films. Because for us to make Jewish films, it gives us the possibility of creating a very dramatic story. Because the Jews have interesting stories, with their strong conflicts that provoke the audience to think about the society around them. Because the Jewish question is not a question of Jews. The Jewish question is a question of the people they live with. It's not a question for Jews. The Jews live here in this country. The problem with the attitude toward them is a problem with Russians. And I would say that the Russians should make the Jewish films more than Jews. So for us, for Sasha Zeldovich, who made *Sunset*, and for Aranovich—I didn't talk to him—and for me, for Arkady Ruderman, it was very important, the personal statements, of course, because we are Jews, and we had to identify ourselves. So it was an interesting topic for the audience, because it was an absolutely forbidden theme before. Of course, we thought of it before. And the third very important thing—there was a major traditional Jewish culture in this country. At times we met people who remained after these whole fantastical problems...

...you mean the attempt to destroy the Jewish culture...

I mean the attempt to destroy the Jewish culture. And sometimes I feel I'm doing this out of a sense of duty.

Also, the Russian Empire and the Soviet Union was always a very national-conscious society. Everyone identified themselves in national terms. So it's natural for Jews, who were identified as a nationality according to Line 5 [of the internal passport], it's natural for them to be dealing with Jewish themes. But I think what you said is kind of interesting, that the Jewish problem is not really a Jewish problem as such.

Right. I don't think there would be a Jewish problem without the anti-semitic activity around me. I can interact with you without any mention of national problems. It's not your or anyone's business. It's my own personal background. It's my personal life. It has nothing to do with anybody, except maybe my family or something like that. It's my personal story, my personal experience, that's all.

Have you experienced—have your films experienced any anti-semitism? Pamiat attacks?

At times I've met with different responses, but I've gotten used to it. Because after the Wallenberg film, there were different responses from different people. *Meeting with Father* was a very strong film. It was shown in prime-time on Ostankino TV. The film was about 20 minutes. There were a lot of responses, very positive and very negative, which were written by absolutely anti-Semitic people. This film is about Jews who don't leave for good. They stay here in this country. And they say, "we are Russian citizens, we are Russian cultured citizens, and we work for Russian culture." It's a very Russian film, by the way.

What constitutes a Russian film?

That's very reflective.

Somewhat melancholy?

Sometimes. But I try to do it so it won't be boring.

Yes, that's what I know Americans expect of Russian films, that they're always sad, that you always have to bring several handkerchiefs with you to wipe away the tears.

No, that's not what my film's about. I hope not.

One last question about the film. I liked the way you used two themes that kept repeating themselves through out the film. One was Babi Yar, the other one was the figure Shaia. I found that quite fascinating. I remember in Riga you showed a fragment of Shaia, and now you've integrated it into this film. Tell me what it is you thought you were doing by having Shaia there.

You know this story of Shaia is a kind of mythological theme for me, because it's the story of a lonely old man who is kept from the genocide by German Nazis in Babi Yar, in Kiev, and has disappeared in a big city like Kiev. Everybody saw him but no one knows where he is now. And this goes on throughout the whole film, for several years. For me, it's like a biblical motif. But very documentary. That's important for me. In this line, every detail means something for me, when somebody is sweeping hair up off the floor. Every detail means something. And of course I tried to find this old man, but I didn't find him. And for the film, maybe it's bad to admit that, but maybe it's better. Because it's like a symbol that for me is very close to a permanent structure—it's beneath all the people who are portrayed in this film, including myself.

Somewhat mysterious, fugitive, almost like a Chagall man floating in the air. Last question. This film was Part I of Farewell to the USSR. *Just tell us what Part II is about.*

Part II has nothing to do with Part I. That's the first thing. There is no national Jewish motif in Part II. It's a story about a few very general worlds. It's a film about the twentieth century. It's a film about the fate of the USSR in the twentieth century. That's why it's based on two events in Russian history. The first event is from the very beginning of this century, 1914, the beginning of the Great War. And the second event, which in my opinion, is the close of the twentieth century, is the breakup of the Soviet Union, recent events. It's connected to the fates of Russian soldiers in Germany both at the beginning of this century and today, when Russian troops are withdrawing from that country.

It sounds like a powerful historical theme.

Right. And I'd like to make a story about the fate of generations of citizens of this country, who were forced to overcome all these difficulties, who were doomed by this fate.

And have you located actual families who lived from that period, right through the present?

Absolutely. I've got three heroes. One of them is Russian, the second one is Ukrainian, and the third is Caucasian.

Georgian?

No, he's Daghestani. I've got two generations, one from the very beginning of the century, and young soldiers of today—they're the same, absolutely. They're very similar processes and very similar events. There was a third line in my structure: episodes from the famous Russian silent movie from the twenties—[Friedrikh Ermler's] *Fragment of an Empire*—which work very well with the first two [segments].

That sounds terrific, if I may comment as a historian.

Aleko Tsabadze

"It's not a good thing to make movies and be in politics."

Menashe: *I am here with Aleko Tsabadze, who is in New York for a few days in connection with his interesting film,* Night Dances.

Tsabadze: Well, OK—my name is Aleko—actually my name is Alexander. But my mom likes to call me Aleko.

OK—I'll call you whatever you prefer. You say your mother prefers Aleko. Is that for Georgian nationalist reasons?

Well, you know, I mean, she's just my mother. She likes to say Aleko.

Both your parents are Georgian?

Yeah, sure.

You're not Jewish?

No.

The reason that I ask that is because one of the characters in the film is.

The reason is that I like the Old Testament very much, better than the new one. It's closer to the nature of mankind.

You mean the picture of life that it presents?

Yeah. They say an eye for an eye...

...a tooth for a tooth...

That's what I mean.

You think it's closer to what we experience today?
Exactly. Well actually it was in the former Soviet Union. And that's what going on now in Georgia. An eye for an eye and a tooth for a tooth.
Blood is being shed in Abkhazia, Ossetia. Is that why you left?
Yes. I don't want to be depressed. I don't want to be a killer. I don't want to be killed. I just want to work.
You don't consider yourself a political man?
No, absolutely not.
And life forces you to be political in Georgia these days?
Yes. You have to be—you have to carry a revolver or gun with you all the time if you want to survive. I want to stay alive.
Are you from Tbilisi originally?
I'm from Tbilisi.
And you're living and working in Germany now. Why did you choose Germany?
Just by chance. I had no choice. I just didn't want to go back, and the only possibility I had was Berlin because I had been living here for eight months.
In New York?
No, in Atlanta and Chicago and San Francisco. But I didn't speak any English at that time. And after that I was invited to the festival in Berlin. So I stayed there.
You prefer Berlin to Chicago?
Well, what can I do in Chicago? Who needs me in Chicago? Nobody. But in Berlin, I got a scholarship. 3,000 marks. It's not so bad.
When I was in Berlin two and a half years ago, in 1990, I visited a friend there, an American, who was on a generous German fellowship. They gave him a beautiful apartment, money every month, and so on. So that's enabling you to survive now in Berlin?
That's the only chance now I have. But when the script is ready, I'll get another chance to survive. I know a few people who are interested in the script, in my new project. But we'll see.
What is it about?
I don't know yet myself. It's about me, actually, about my being in Berlin. It's about Germans. It's about how rough they are.
Why do you say that? How do you mean?
Well, in daily life, I mean. If you want to get a bus or something,

they just push you away. I don't know. It's hard to explain. You have to be there, or you have to be with them to really understand.

And you don't want to have anything to do with your rodina *any more?*

No.

Why?

"Moia rodina." Well, I lost my country. I lost everything that I had. Because my friends—and I love them very much—but they've changed now. They became killers or... I don't know. They've changed. On the other hand, they envy me. That's what I don't like, really. They envy me. Because they think that I'm living sometimes in Berlin, sometimes in America, that I have a lot of money. That's not true. I'm doing what I want to do.

And you don't intend to go back?

No.

That strikes me as a very dramatic decision on your part.

And it's very hard now. I mean, it's a strange culture that surrounds me now in Berlin and it's not so easy to make a movie, being in my condition.

Are your Georgian friends all involved in politics?

Not all, but you have to be that way if you want to survive in Georgia. If you want to get some money, to eat something. If you want to get some food. Well, actually two years ago I left my country. Later I tried to—I visited there. I wanted to stay there for two weeks, but I couldn't. I left after four days.

This was after you made the film, Night Dances? *You had completed it? And essentially it's a Georgian production?*

Yes. I left my country in September, and in October the fighting began.

And your film opened, or you don't know, or you don't want to say?

Nobody cares now in my country about *Night Dances.*

Why do you say that? Do you think Georgians are not interested in films any more, or not interested in films of a certain kind?

It's hard to say. I mean—I don't exactly know what's going on there. I don't know.

The Georgian film tradition is an extraordinary one, and it's sad to see this break, your conscious break from the Georgian film tradition. I know that certain Georgian filmmakers are very politically engaged. *Shengelaya, for example, and others, as you know. And you, on the other hand...*

It's not a good thing to make movies and be in politics. It's not professional.

But, one can say that your film is very political, in the sense that it presents a definite picture of life in more or less contemporary Georgia. It's a very depressing picture. I know you think there are moments of humor.

No, it is. I agree with you. It is depressing. It's depressing for me, first of all. That's why I don't like to talk about it, about my movies. Because I was depressed while I was working on it.

It shows. [laughter] And the new film that you're working on—at least the script—tell me exactly how that's being produced. Who is involved and who is financing it? Who is the production company?

Actually I don't know yet. I'm a lucky guy. I think so. I know a few people who like *Night Dances*, and if I have a new script, I'm sure they'd want to work with me. That's the only thing I know, that I can be sure about.

There's no production group that you knew, that you worked with in Georgia? I know that many Russian directors are working with German companies in co-productions, and I thought maybe you had established a relationship.

No, nothing. Just money to live on—I got the first prize in Greece.

From Night Dances?

Yes.

And Night Dances *was produced entirely in Georgia—it was a Gruziafilm production, in the traditional way? Except that Gruziafilm is now independent of the state, or—I'm not sure how these things are working in this peculiar period.*

What is independent Georgia? I don't know. They are not independent. What is independence? To be free, to be at peace, to have what you want, what you need. This is independence. They have nothing. They are killing each other.

And the studio itself? Where does it stand?

I don't know what's going on at the studio. I saw a few people from Gruziafilm Studios in Berlin, at the last festival. They said that they were OK and that they are still making movies. I don't know how they can make movies. If you go out with your camera…

You mean it's physically dangerous?

Yes. It's depressing. But before, you have to have a script—you have to write one. How can you do that if you're at home and outside people are being shot? It's crazy. But at the same time I know some people who like it somehow. It sounds crazy.

It's history.

It's like when you're a drug addict, you need your fix. That's what I mean about them. They need that situation to feed themselves.

Speaking from the point of view of filmmakers—they might be speaking of precisely this kind of situation.

You mean to make movies about the situation?

And to take an active part in the political battles. I can understand what you mean about danger. I don't know if you know a Byelorussian documentary filmmaker, Arkady Ruderman? He was killed in Tadjikistan, with the civil war going on. And of course in Riga in 1991 in January, when Soviet troops attacked the television tower. I think Yuri Podnieks' cameraman was killed in that event. Podnieks himself was killed. But that I think was a pure accident. So life for the filmmaker can be dangerous. And I can understand your sense of depression about it and your desire to get away from it.

Well, the only thing—I have to go back. I have parents and I love them very much. They are the only friends I have, the only ones. Because nobody wants me. I told you about my friends who have changed. I don't like them.

They understand why you left?

I don't think so. But they want me to be with them, to be the same way. With a gun in my hand. "Why don't you come back here, because you're Georgian?"

Do they look at you as a traitor?

Oh, traitor. Yes, it could be.

May I ask which side your friends are fighting on?

They don't know themselves. To survive. That's the only thing they know. I'm sure. Because, this is crazy, this war.

I won't ask you the political complexities of the Georgian situation. Let's get back to film. The reason I ask you if you are Jewish is obviously because one of the main characters of the film—Moshe—is Jewish. And there are some Jewish themes throughout the film. And I've noticed that Jewish themes are reappearing in Russian films, in Russian documentary films, features, etc. So I thought this was perhaps a part of a general revival of Jewish themes in post-Soviet cinema. But you didn't intend it that way.

I told you—the only reason they are Jewish is that I read the Old Testament before writing the script, and I loved it. It was very inspirational to me. And the feelings I got after having read the Old Testament—this is *Night Dances*. Plus the conditions in Georgia. Plus my personal... it's always hard to say. A lot of things happen by themselves, emotionally. I never think about it. If I did, I think that my films would be worse.

If you were too analytic about them, too intellectual?
Right.
So they come directly from the heart.
From the heart, from emotions. I like this way the best. Making movies is like playing the guitar. You never think about it, you just act upon feelings. And I know when I need a certain sound or when I have to—in *Night Dances* they just appear suddenly, or disappear. I don't know why I do things.

In the film you often hear sounds of the ocean, but there is no ocean.
No, there is no ocean. It's Rustavi, 25 kilometers from Tbilisi, and the town was built by Stalin. There are a lot of factories. But it makes the film more poetic. That's what I mean about playing the guitar.

The Old Testament is very down-to-earth, but your film is often surreal.
Well, the Old Testament is surreal too, isn't it?
I think in certain passages. I know—you quoted one passage. You said "what is the film about? It's about vanity. All is vanity."
My favorite book from the Old Testament is *Ecclesiastes*.
And Moshe is a kind of Old Testament figure. He's a very tough guy.
He is.
He doesn't tolerate immorality. The first time we see him—he sees a beggar and says, "what are you doing here? Get out of here and get some work." He's a tough guy, yet he's very loyal to his friend and he tries to save him in the end. But I fear that's hopeless.
It's hopeless, yes.
Often Russian films are compared to Dostoevsky, and it seemed to me that your film fits. There's great squalor, poverty, rage, murder, and then there's even a reference to epilepsy, and you know that Dostoevsky suffered from epilepsy, as did Prince Myshkin in The Idiot.
I remember Prince Myshkin, and I like very much Dostoevsky—

I *liked*. Not now. When I was living in Georgia it looked to me like Dostoevsky's world. And it's not Myshkin but another one, who kills a woman. In *Crime and Punishment*. Raskolnikov. I think Raskolnikov is me somehow. Who I was—not who I am. When I think about certain things, I'm able to do them. But not in reality.

You're a lucky man. I think all artists are lucky, especially the filmmakers. Because they can realize their fantasies on celluloid, on film.

What I cannot do in reality, I can do in my films. If I don't like someone, I can kill him. It's funny, you can play games with people.

That's why artists are like God, filmmakers are like God, you create a whole world with characters, you give them birth, you kill them. But you're a special kind of god—you're an Old Testament god. You're strong, very vengeful.

No, I'm not that way.

So maybe you're more a New Testament—maybe the New Testament is really you, and not the Old Testament. Are you a musician?

I was.

You played guitar?

Yes.

That was a wonderful sequence with that character who doesn't appear again, the guitarist.

He's great. I wanted to bring him with me—but he has a lot of problems and complexes. Which happens from living in the Soviet Union. They are kind of scared.

Why don't you say a little more than that. What do you mean by someone who lived in the Soviet Union?

Well, we used to say "don't do that." That's what I mean, that they're scared.

And that continues today, even after the destruction of the Soviet Union?

Yes. I know a lot of people—I saw them in Berlin—and sometimes they don't know what to do, even to cross the street. How to cross, whether they're allowed to cross.

That's sad. You haven't been back to Russia, have you?

No, just at the airport. It was very depressing.

Why was it depressing?

The situation I saw around me at the airport. The people, they were so scared.

I haven't found them to be scared in the same sense, but down and depressed, yes. "Bez nadezhdy". Not everybody. Some people were elated by the recent events. They feel freer, free to do business.

I mean insolent. They're either scared or insolent. There is nothing in between, when someone can simply enjoy life. It's either insolence, among those who are earning big bucks, or people are simply down.

That's maybe what I saw. And do you find this among East Germans at all?

Oh, yes. They still hate each other. And I still saw those holes on the walls from bullets after the war. It's so funny.

I'm a historian, and I write on film and history. And it's very strange for me. I can't get used to it that there is no Soviet Union, no Berlin Wall. Communism has died. Whether it's permanent or not, we can't tell. But its still very, very strange. And I wish that everyone could be more hopeful. But the whole situation seems so gloomy. "Grustno." I would say that if we were to put your film into a category, it's in the general category of what Russians call chernukha. *Would you agree?*

There was a time when the Communists were still in power, when I sent my script to them, to Moscow, because we had a rule to make sure... And the answer I got back...

This is what year?

1987 or 1989. They said, "This is *chernukha*. What the hell do you want to make a film like this?" But the Communists were on their way out. This helped me a lot. And I managed to make my movie, without Russians, without Communists.

Well, of course Repentance *had already been shown at that time, and that was the breakthrough film. But in every regard, your film belongs to that category.*

Unfortunately.

There's only one element that is not in your film that is in so many recent films: no sex. No nudity. That is not in your film.

I hate it. I hate movies with sex. I hate them. It's not esthetic. It's a private thing. You could be really great in your bedroom, but not in the script.

But there is a certain eroticism in your film, a certain sex, beneath the surface.

The mannequins...

The mannequins—that was not beneath the surface. That was obvious.

When Stella comes back and she pokes fun at her former husband. Clearly, he was having sexual problems. Let me ask you one last, slightly technical question about your film. Darkness plays a part in your film. You saw Canby's review yesterday in the New York Times? *He said the difference between night and day [in your film] is that night is a little darker. So there's darkness during the day as well. So clearly that sets some of the mood. Also, I notice you only used medium and long shots. You never have close-ups. Why?*

I don't like them. It's not natural. Now I'm looking at you, right. I see the whole figure. I like that more than close-ups.

Index

Note: Page references in bold refer to film reviews. Page numbers followed by "n" refer to endnotes.

A

Abdrashitov, Vadim, 234
Abrash, Barbara, 188, 263n
Abuladze, Tengiz, 42, **49–55,** 170–172, 199, 338–339
Adam's Rib (Krishtofovich), 36, **182–185**
The Aesthenic Syndrome (Muratova), 201
agitation films *(agitki),* 73, 79, 162
Agoniya/Rasputin (Klimov), **125–136,** 170, 172, 276, 329–331
Akhmatova, Anna (born Anna Andreevna Gorenko), 47–48, 71
The Akhmatova File (Aranovich), **45–48,** 213
Alentova, Vera, 233
Alexander Nevsky (Eisenstein), 89, 197
Alexandra (Sokurov), 150, 267
Alexandrov, Grigori, 195–196, 271, 272
Alliluyeva, Svetlana, 111–113
Alov, Alexander, 93, 171
American Association for the Advancement of Slavic Studies (AAASS), 44, 185–186
American Historical Association (AHA), 44
Anderson, Brad, **284–285**
And Nothing More (Sokurov), 215

Andrei Rublev (Tarkovsky), 134, 142, 165–166, 274, 294–295
And The Past Seems But A Dream (Miroshnichenko), 154
Angel (Smirnov), 76
Angi Vera (Gabor), 253–254
Animated Soviet Propaganda (Borsten and Vidov), **282**
Anna (Mikhalkov), **31–33,** 214
Anna Karenina (Soloviev), 267
Annaud, Jean-Jacques, 97
anti-Semitism, 64–65, 82–84, 87. See also Jewish issues
Aranovich, Semyon, **45–48,** 213
Aristov, Viktor, **12–15**
Arnshtam, Leo, 89
Arsenal (Dovzhenko), 74
Artemyev, Eduard, 142
The Ascent (Shepitko), 95, **153**
Ascuks, Bruno, 243
Askoldov, Alexander: *Commissar,* 76–77, **82–88,** 171, 304–308; interview with, 300–308
Astolphe, Marquis de Custine, 116
Astrakhan, Dmitry, 3, **19–20;** interview with, 308–318
Asya's Happiness (Konchalovsky), 171–172, 295
At Home Among Strangers, a Stranger at Home (Mikhalkov), 78–79

Autumn Marathon (Danelia), 158–159, 166, 199, 256–257

B
"Babi Yar" (Yevtushenko), 82–83
Balabanov, Alexei, 212, 229, 230–231
Ballad of a Soldier (Chukhrai), 92–94, 168, 198, 253
Barak (Ogorodnikov), 230, 260
The Barber of Siberia (Mikhalkov), 224, 238n, 254–255, 265–266
The Bear's Wedding (Eggert), 193
Beatty, Warren, 297–298
Bed and Sofa (Room), 193
Before Exams (Krishtofovich), 183
The Beginning of an Unknown Century (or *Age*), 76, 366
Bekmambetov, Timur, 267
Belikov, Mikhail, **17–18**; interview with, 318–324
The Belovs (Kossakovsky), 216
Bergkraut, Eric, **285–286**
Beria, Lavrenty, 52–53, 54
Bertuccelli, Julie, 273
Bjorsmark, Carl, 240
Black Rose the Emblem of Sorrow, Red Rose the Emblem of Love (Soloviev), **6–7**, 201
Black Square (Pasternak), 154
Blanchet, Narda, 26
Bliss (Mansky), 216
Blockade (Loznitsa), **105**
Blue Mountains (Shengelaya), 198
Bobrova, Lidiya, 3, **15–16**, 230
Bodrov, Sergei, **100–104**, 231
Bogatyrev, Yuri, 158
Bondarchuk, Sergei, 93, 170, 198, 298
Bontoc Eulogy (Fuentes), 218
Boogie Nights (Anderson), 230
Borin, Anne, 219, 371, 383–384, 385n

Boris Godunov (Bondarchuk), 170
Borodyansky, Alexander, 229
Borsten, Joan, 282
Bragarnik, Svetlana, 14
Brashinsky, Michael, 201–202, 203
Brauns, Uldis, 240–242
Brief Encounters (Muratova), 171–172
Brigands, Chapter VII (Ioseliani), **34–36**, 232
Brodsky, Joseph, 268
The Brother (Balabanov), 229
Bukharin, Nikolai, 50, 67
Burnt by the Sun (Mikhalkov), **55–60**, 71, 214, 231, 254, 265
Buttner, Tilman, 114, 117–125
Bykov, Rolan, 77, 85, 88, 159–160, 175, 198, 227

C
Cameron, James, 225
The Captain's Daughter (Proshkin), 233
Cargo 200 (Balabanov), 267
The Castle (Balabanov), 231
Chalimon, Andrei, 284
Chapayev (Vasilyev and Vasilyev), 74–75, 76, 195
La Chasse aux Papillons (Ioseliani), **26–29**
The Check (Giller and Borodyansky), 229
Checking Out (Bjorsmark), 240
Checkpoint/Trial On the Road (Gherman), 93, 171, 172
The Chekist (Rogozhkin), **29–31**, 72–73, 231–232
chernukha, 229, 257, 264, 267, 401
Chiaureli, Mikhail, **69–70**
Chiaurieli, Sofiko, 40
Children of Ivan Kuzmich (Goldovskaya), 182

Index 405

Children of the Arbat (Rybakov), 83
Children of the Iron Gods (Tot), 261
Chkheidze, Rezo, 94
Chukhrai, Grigori, 74, 92–94, 167–168, 198, 231
Chukhrai, Pavel, **33–35**
Churikova, Inna, 183–184, 351
Cinema and Soviet Society (Kenez), 192–193
cinéma vérité, 162, 179
Circus (Alexandrov), 195
Clear Skies (Chukhrai), 167–168
Close to Eden (Mikhalkov), **22–24**
Cold War films, 90–91
The Color of Pomegranates (Paradzhanov), 275
Come and See (Klimov), 95–96, 128, 334–335
Commissar (Askoldov), 76–77, **82–88**, 171, 304–308
Comrade Stalin Goes to Africa (Kvirikadze), **5–6**
Confession (Sokurov), 147, 149–152
The Confession (Costa-Gavras), 61, 64, 66
Cossacks of the Kuban (Pyriev), 197
Costa-Gavras, 61, 64, 66
Countersuit (Ruderman), 216
The Cranes are Flying (Kalatozov), 91–92, 168, 198, 253
Cserhalmi, Gyorgy, 106
The Cuckoo (Rogozhkin), 97
Curtiz, Michael, 63

D

Danelia, Georgy: *Autumn Marathon*, 158–159, 166, 199, 256–257; on Mosfilm, 223–224; *Passport*, **3–5**
Dapkounaite, Ingeborga, 58
Dark Eyes (Mikhalkov), 158, 169, 186

Darkness at Noon (Koestler), 64
Days of Eclipse (Sokurov), **9–11**
Day Watch (Bekmambetov), 267
Deneuve, Catherine, 68
Depardieu, Gerard, 233
de-Stalinization. *See* Stalin, Joseph
Desyatnikov, Leonid, 103
Dialogues with Solzhenitsyn (Sokurov), 150
Directed by Andrei Tarkovsky (Leszcylowski), 135–136
Disbelief: A Documentary Composition in 12 Parts (Nekrasov), 277
Disgraced Monuments (Lewis and Mulvey), **268–270**
A Disgusting Anecdote (Alov and Naumov), 171
Djordjadze, Nana, 40; interview with, 324–329
DMB-91 (Khaniutin), 214, 216
Dobronravov, Ivan, 245
"Doctors' Plot" (Rapoport), 83
documentary film: *Anna* as, 30–32; Aranovich on, 46, 48; *cinéma vérité* style in, 162, 179; coherence in, 188; funding for, 211–213, 381–382; and *glasnost*, 163–164, 177–179, 240, 263n; Goldovskaya on, 178–179; Gurevich on, 362, 367–370; historical documentary, 61, 186, 187, 189; International Documentary Film Festival, 209–218, 283; Latvian, 240; Litvyakov on, 380–382; old Soviet, 161–162; and *perestroika*, 146, 179, 185, 188–189, 215–216, 263n; Rodnyansky on, 386–387, 393; as Russian impulse, 214–215; Sokurov on, 146–149, 152; in the world market, 386–387

Dondurei, Daniel, 222, 224
Donskoy, Mark, 89–90, 197
Dovzhenko, Alexander, 74, 75, 153
The Downfall (Hirschbiegel), 97
Dreiden, Sergei, 116
Drumroll (Ovcharov), 232
Drygas, Maciej J., 207
Dubcek, Alexander, 61
Dvornitchenko, Oksana, 214
Dvortsevoy, Sergei, **40–41**, 217

E
Early on Sunday (Mamedov), 216
Eastern Elegy (Sokurov), 215
East Side Story (Ranga), **270–272**
East-West (Wargnier), **68**, 236n
Easy Money, 298–299
Efron, Sergei, 55–56
Eggert, Konstantin, 193
$8 1/2 (Konstantinopolsky), 229
Eisenstein, Sergei, 89, 191, 197, 269
Elegy of a Voyage (Sokurov), 117, 148, 149
Elegy of the Land (Sokurov), 147
"Elegy" series (Sokurov), 215
The End of St. Petersburg (Pudovkin), 73
Enemy at the Gates (Annaud), 97
Envy of the Gods (Menshov), 232–233
Erkenov, Hussein, **107**
Eternal Memory: Voices from the Great Terror (Pultz), **69**
The Eternal Struggle (Litvyakov), 379
The Evening Sacrifice (Sokurov), 146, 164, 215

F
The Fall of Berlin (Chiaureli), **69–70**
A Family Celebration (Pirosmani), 274

Farewell (Ioseliani), 238n
Farewell (Shepitko and Klimov), 95, 127, 153, 169, 172, 254, 337
Fate of a Man (Bondarchuk), 93, 198
Father of a Soldier (Chkheidze), 94
Fear and the Muse: The Story of Anna Akhmatova (Janows), 48
The Ferry (Pakalninja), 240
Filmmakers Union, 165, 174, 203, 226–227, 301, 336–337
Final Verdict (Frank), 154
First Teacher (Konchalovsky), 172, 363
Fokin, Vladimir, 232
Forgotten Melody for Flute (Ryazanov), 171, 344–345
The Forty-First (Chukhrai), 168
The 41st (Protazanov), 74
Forward March Time (Mayakovsky), 282
The Fountain (Mamin), 176
4 (Khrzhanovsky), **264**
Franks, Hertz, 154, 240–242
Freedom is Paradise (Bodrov), 100
Freeze, Die, Come to Life (Kanevsky), 260
A Friend of the Deceased (Krishtofovich), **36–39**
From One Prayer to the Next (Khashchavatsky), 375
Frumin, Boris, 234, 238n
Fuentes, Marlon E., 218
funding for films: and collapse of Soviet Union, 178, 211–212, 215; cooperatives and sponsors, 343–344; co-productions, 242, 340–341, 355, 387; for documentaries, 211–213, 381–382; in *glasnost*, 200; at Goskino, 224; independence in, 212; for the "Message to Man" film festival, 215–216; at Mosfilm, 221, 223, 343; in the present,

267; from the West, 180, 212, 222, 239, 242–243

G

Gabor, Pal, 253–254
Galichenko, Nicholas, 200, 203
Garage (Ryazanov), 171, 198
The Gardens of Scorpio (Kovalov), 232
Garvin, Tom, 242
Geislerova, Ana, 106
Gelovani, Mikhail, 70
Get Thee Out! or *Go Away!* (Astrakhan), 3, **19-20**
Gherman, Alexei: *Checkpoint/Trial On the Road*, 93, 171, 172; *Khrustalyov, My Car!*, 230, 254; *My Friend Ivan Lapshin*, 171, 172, 201, 254; *Twenty Days Without War*, 95. See also as Guerman, Alexei.
Giller, Boris, 229
glasnost: Astrakhan on, 310, 312, 314–315; and *Black Rose the Emblem of Sorrow*, 5–6; *chernukha* films in, 229, 257, 264, 401; and collapse of the Soviet Union, 156, 187, 192; and documentaries, 163–164, 177–179, 240, 263n; encouragement of film under, 155–156, 164–166, 169–175, 199–204, 216, 220, 355; film distribution in, 227; importance of film in, 43; Kupchenko on, 341–343, 346, 348; Lawton on, 200, 202–204, 236n, 265; Panfilov on, 354–355; portrayal of Stalin in, 45; reasons for, 164–166; recognition of earlier films during, 76, 157, 196, 198; and *Repentence*, 51; and Soviet Jews, 82–88; taboo themes in films in,

263n; worker portrayal in, 255, 259, 261. See also *perestroika*
Glasnost: Soviet Cinema Responds (Galichenko), 200, 203
Glasnost Film Festival, 146, 154, 161–164, 178
Go and See (Klimov), 95–96, 128, 334–335
Go Away! (Astrakhan), **19–20**, 308–318
Gogoberidze, Lana, **39–40**
Golden Centaur, 216–217
Goldovskaya, Marina, 163, 177–182, 213, 214–215
Goldovsky, Yevsei, 178
Goldstucker, Eduard, 62, 64, 65
Golovnya, Anatoly, 73
Gorbachev, Mikhail, 82, 337, 355–356
Goskino, 170, 174, 224, 227, 295, 323, 336
Govorukhin, Stanislav, 213, 239n
The Grand Illusion (Renoir), 125
The Great Concert of the People (Aranovich), 213
The Grey-Bearded Lion (Khrzhanovsky), 217
Grossman, Vasily, 83, 87, 99, 304–306
Grozny. May 95 (Yakubson), 215
Guerman, Alexei, 310, 312–314. See also Gherman, Alexei.
Gumilyov, Lev, 47
Gumilyov, Nikolai, 47
Gurchenko, Liudmila, 139
Gurevich, Leonid, 219, 371; interview with, 357–370
Gusinsky, Vladimir, 223, 225–226

H

Hammer and Sickle (Livnev), 232, 258–259

Happiness (Dvortsevoy), 217
Happiness (Medvedkin), 133
Happy Guys (Alexandrov), 195
Happy New Year, Moscow! (Piankova), 234
Heavy Sand (Rybakov), 83
Heifitz, Iosif, **286–287**
Heights (Zarkhi), 253
The Heir of Genghiz Khan (Pudovkin), 74
Heuman, Susan, 187
Hey, You Wild Geese! (Bobrova), 3, **16–17**
Hirschbiegel, Oliver, 97
His Wife's Diary (Uchitel), 233–234
Honkasalo, Pirjo, **107–108**
Horton, Andrew, 190, 201, 203
Hot Summer of 1968, 271
House of the Rich (Fokin), 232–233
The House With Knights (Goldovskaya), 180
Hubert Robert: A Happy Life (Sokurov), 149

I
Ibragimbekov, Rustam, 23, 58
Ilyenko, Yuri, **8–9**, 168–169
Imaging Russia 2000: Film and Facts (Lawton), **265–266**
The Inner Circle (Konchalovsky), 196
Inside Gorbachev's USSR (Menashe), 189
In That Land (Bobrova), 230
In the Dark (Dvortsevoy), **40–41**
In the Shadow of Sakharov (Jones), 188
In the Town of Berdichev (Grossman), 87
Ioseliani, Otar: *Brigands, Chapter VII*, **35–36**, 232; *La Chasse aux Papillons*, **26–29**; *Farewell*, 238n
I Request the Floor (Panfilov), 353
Is It Easy to Be Young? (Podnieks), 213, 240
Ivan's Childhood (Tarkovsky), 92, 97, 143
Ivan the Terrible, Part I (Eisenstein), 197
Ivan the Terrible, Part II (Eisenstein), 168, 197
I Was Stalin's Bodyguard (Aranovich), **45–48,** 213

J
Jancso, Miklos, 80–81
Janows, Jill, 48
La Jetée (Marker), 132–133
Jewish issues: anti-Semitism, 64–65, 82–84, 87; Askoldov on, 305–306, 388–389; Astrakhan on, 20, 308–311, 313–317; and films of the Russian Civil War, 72, 76–77, 82–88; Justman on, 60, 63–65; Khashchavatsky on, 372–373; Panfilov on, 170–171, 352–354; Rodnyansky on, 212, 388–392
Jones, Sherry, 188, 377n
Justman, Zusana, 60

K
Kalatozov, Mikhail, 91–92, 168, 198, 253
Kamalova, Kamara, **24–26**
Kanevsky, Vitaly, 260
Karelov, Yevgeny, 77–78
Karmen, Roman, 100
Kavan, Jan, 64–65
Kenez, Peter, 192, 194, 196
Kerensky, Alexander, 126
Khaniutin, Alexei, 214, 216
Khashchavatsky, Yuri, interview with, 372–377
Kholosov, Sergei Nikolaevich, 364–365

Khotinenko, Vladimir, 231
Khrushchev, Nikita, 70, 167–168
Khrustalyov, My Car! (Gherman), 230, 254
Khrzhanovsky, Andrei, 163–164, 217, 268
Khrzhanovsky, Ilya, **264**
Kindergarten (Yevtushenko), 95
Kinfolk (Mikhalkov), 33
Kingsley, Ben, 284–285
Kinoglasnost (Lawton), 200, **202–204**, 236n
Kino-Glaz (The Film Eye), 162
Kino-Pravda (Film Truth), 162
kinopublitsistika, 163
Kleiman, Naum, 209, 228
Klimov, Elem: *Farewell*, 95, 127, 169, 172, 254, 337; on the Filmmakers Union, 174; *Go and See*, 95–96, 128, 334–335; interview with, 329–339; on Mosfilm Studios, 211; *Rasputin/Agoniya*, **125–135**, 170, 172, 276, 329–331; *Sports, Sports, Sports*, 128; use of color by, 96; *Welcome*, 127
Koestler, Arthur, 64
Kolya (Sverak), **283–284**
Konchalovsky, Andrei: *Asya's Happiness*, 171–172, 295; *First Teacher*, 172, 363; *The Inner Circle*, 196; interview with, 291–299; *Siberiade*, 58, **136–140**, 254, 292–294
Konstantinopolsky, Grigory, 229
Korzun, Dina, 248–249
Kossakovsky, Viktor, 216, 217
Kovalov, Oleg, 218, 232
Kravchenko, Alexei, 96
Krishtofovich, Vyacheslav: *Adam's Rib*, 36, **182–185**; *Before Exams*, 183; *A Friend of the Deceased*, **36–39**; *Lonely Woman Seeks Life Companion*, 183
Kupchenko, Irina, interview with, 339–349
Kuprianov, Sergei, 14
Kutuzov (Petrov), 197
Kvirikadze, Irakli, **5–6**

L

The Lady with The Dog (Heifitz), **286–287**
Land of the Deaf (Todorovsky), 249
Landsbergis, Vytautas, 215
Landscape with Juniper (Khrzhanovsky), 163–164
Larina, Anna, 67
The Last Bolshevik (Marker), 133
The Last Day of a Rainy Summer (Sokurov), 147
Last Resort (Pawlikowski), **248–252**
Lavrentiev, Sergei, 224
Lavronenko, Konstantin, 244, 245
Lawton, Anna: *Imaging Russia 2000: Film and Facts*, **265–266**; *Kinoglasnost*, 200, **202–204**, 236n
Lebedev, Nikolai, 97
Lebeshev, Pavel, 102, 158, 184
Lenin's Body (Mansky), 212
Leszcylowski, Michal, 135–136
Letter from Siberia (Marker), 133
Letter to Anna (Bergkraut), **285–286**
Lewis, Mark, 268–270
Liberation (Ozerov), 94–95, 170
Life and Fate (Grossman), 83, 99, 305–306
Little Vera (Pichul), 160, 199, 257–258, 261, 344
Litvinenko, Alexander, 276–279
Litvyakov, Mikhail, 371, 377–385
Living with an Idiot (Rogozhkin), 231–232
Livnev, Sergei, 212, 224, 225–226, 232, 258–259

410   Index

London, Artur, 63, 64, 66
London, Lise, 62
The Lonely Voice of a Man (Sokurov), 146
Lonely Woman Seeks Life Companion (Krishtofovich), 183
Losev (Kossakovsky), 217
Loznitsa, Sergei, **105,** 217
Lucky to Be Born in Russia (Goldovskaya), 181, 214–215
Lugovoi, Andrei, 278
Luna Park (Lungin), 260
Lungin, Pavel, 199, 232, 260–261

M

Magambetov, Marat, 217
Magnitogorsk–Forging the New Man (Smit), 263n
Makharadze, Avtandil, 42, 52
Mamedov, Murat, 216
Mamin, Yury: on the esthetics of the ugly, 235; on the Moscow Film Festival, 221; *Sideburns,* **175–177,** 260; *Window to Paris,* 232
Man of Marble (Wajda), 253
Mansky, Vitaly, 212, 213, 216
March of the Living (Rodnyansky), 217
Margolius, Heda, 63, 65
Maria (Sokurov), 216
Marker, Chris, **132–136,** 148
Martin, Steven M., **283**
Mayakovsky, Vladimir, 282
Medvedkin, Alexander, 133
Meeting with Father (Rodnyansky), 392
Mekhralieva, Susanna, 103
Melnikov, Vitaly, 233
Menshikov, Oleg, 57, 68, 102, 103, 255–256
Menshov, Vladimir, 174, 232

"Message to Man" International Film Festival, 209–219, 283, 371
Midnight Review (DEFA), 272
Mikhalkov, Nikita: acting in *Siberiade,* 139, 254; *Anna,* **31–33,** 214; *At Home Among Strangers, a Stranger at Home,* 78–79; *The Barber of Siberia,* 224, 238n, 254–255, 265–266; *Burnt by the Sun,* **55–60,** 71, 214, 231, 254, 265; *Close to Eden,* **22–24;** *Dark Eyes,* 158, 169, 286; on the Filmmakers Union, 226–227; *Kinfolk,* 33; *Oblomov,* 32, 113, 158, 198, 332; "A Slave of Love," 73, 77, 78–80, 169, 199, 299; on theatre conditions, 225; *Unfinished Piece for Player Piano,* 158, 169
Mindadze, Alexander, 234
Miroshnichenko, Sergei: *The Marriage Sacrament,* 217; *And The Past Seems But A Dream,* 154
The Mirror (Tarkovsky), 148, 157–158, 367–368
Misiano, Viktor, 270
Mission to Moscow (Curtiz), 63
Miss USSR, 345
Molokh (Sokurov), 238n
Monnikendam, Vincent, 218
Mortimer, Emily, 284–285
Moscow (Zeldovich), 229
Moscow Does Not Believe in Tears (Menshov), 174, 232, 255–256
Moscow Elegy (Sokurov), 148
Mosfilm, 211, 221–223, 227–229, 350
Mosgovoy, Leonid, 20
The Most Obedient Girl (Gurevich), 362
Mother (Panfilov), 254, 349–350
Mother (Pudovkin), 73, 194
Mother and Son (Sokurov), 150, 230

Mother Dao, the Turtlelike (Monnikendam), 218
Motherland of Electricity (Shepitko), 76
Motyl, Vladimir, 75
Movies for the Masses (Youngblood), 192
Mulvey, Laura, 268–270
Muratov, Sergei, 162
Muratova, Kira, 171–172, 201, 230
musicals, 270–273
The Muslim (Khotinenko), 231
My Friend Ivan Lapshin (Gherman), 171, 172, 201, 254
My Wife Wants to Sing, 271–272

N
Naumov, Vladimir, 93, 171
Negoda, Natalya, 160
Nekrasov, Andrei, **276–279**
Neptune's Feast or *Neptune's Holiday* (Mamin), 175–176, 232
New Economic Policy (NEP), 166, 193
Night Dances (Tsabadze), 396–402
The Night Is Short (Belikov), 318–322
Night Watch (Bekmambetov), 267
Ninth Company (F. Bondarchuk), 268
The Non-Professionals (Bodrov), 100
Nostalghia (Tarkovsky), 112, **279–281**
Nykvist, Sven, 135

O
Oblomov (Mikhalkov), 32, 113, 158, 198, 332
Of Freaks and Men (Balabanov), 230
Ogorodnikov, Valery, 230, 260
One Day in the Life of Andrei Arsenevich (Marker), **132–136**

One Day in the Life of Ivan Denisovich (Solzhenitsyn), 132, 167
100 Days Before the Command (Erkenov), **107**
Orlova, Lyubov, 272
Out of the Present (Ujica), **206–209**
Outpost (Rogozhkin), 238n
Ovcharov, Sergei, 232
Overture (Yakubson), 214–215
Oxenberg, Jan, 218
Ozerov, Yuri, 94–95, 170

P
Pakalninja, Laila, 240, 242
Pamuk, Orhan, 148
Panfilov, Gleb: interview with, 349–356; *I Request the Floor,* 353; *Mother,* 254, 349–350; *The Romanovs,* 233, 254, 265; *The Theme,* 84, 170–172, 183–184, 352–354; *Vassa,* 166, 254, 351–352
Paradzhanov, Sergei: *The Color of Pomegranates,* 275; *Shadows of Forgotten Ancestors,* 165–166
Particulars of the National Hunt (Rogozhkin), 231
Passport (Danelia), **3–5**
Pasternak, Joseph, 154
Pawlikowski, Pawel, **248–252**
Peace to Him Who Enters (Alov and Naumov), 93
The Peasant from Arkhangel (Goldovskaya), 179
Pechonkin, Pavel, 217
perestroika: acceptance of earlier films in, 166, 204, 215; Askoldov on, 303–304, 306–307; Belikov on, 323; documentaries in, 146, 179, 185, 188–189, 215–216, 263n; encouragement of films during, 1, 43, 131–132, 148,

215; and human relations, 388; Khashchavatsky on, 376; Klimov on, 337; Kupchenko on, 349; and *Repentence,* 51; Rodnyansky on, 388; Stalin portrayal in, 54. See also *glasnost*
Perestroika from Below (Walkowitz and Abrash), 188–189, 263n
Pervila, Kristiina, **107–108**
Peter I (Tolstoy), 89
Peter the First (Petrov), 233
Petrov, Vladimir, 197, 233
Piankova, Natalya, 234
Pichul, Vasily: *Little Vera,* 160, 199, 257–258, 261, 344; *Sky Studded with Diamonds,* 229
Pikul, Valentin, 330
Pirosmani (Shengelaya), 165–166, **273–275,** 326–327
Pirosmani, Niko, 274–275, 326
Platonov, Andrei, 146
Podnieks, Juris, 213, 240
Poisoned by Polonium: The Litvinenko File (Nekrasov), **276–279**
Politkovskaya, Anna, 285–286
Politsch, Barbara, 218
Polyakov, Yuri, 107
Potemkin (Eisenstein), 191
Pozner, Vladimir, 365
The Prince is Back (Goldovskaya), 182
A Prisoner of the Caucasus (Tolstoy), 102
Prisoner of the Mountains (Bodrov), **100–104,** 231
Private Life (Raizman), 199
Professor Mamlock, 83
Proshkin, Alexander, 233
Protazanov, Yakov, 74
Ptashchuk, Mikhail, 338
Pudovkin, Vsevolod, 73–74, 194
Pultz, David, **69**
Punin, Nikolai, 47

Putin, Vladimir, 44, 277–278
Pyriev, Ivan, 197

R
The Rainbow (Donskoy), 89–90, 197
Raizman, Yuli, 199
Ranga, Dana, 270–272
Rapoport, Yakov, 83
Raspad (Belikov), **17–19**
Rasputin/Agoniya (Klimov), **125–136,** 170, 172, 276, 329–331
Reaching the Flag (Ruderman), 373
Rebellion: The Litvinenko Case (Nekrasov), **276–279**
The Red and the White (Jancso), 79–80
Redgrave, Vanessa, 67
Reds (Beatty), 297–298
Reed, Rosemarie, **67**
Repentance (Abuladze), 42, **49–55,** 170–172, 199, 338–339
Requiem (Akhmatova), 47
The Return (Zvyagintsev), **243–248**
The Robinsonada (Djordjadze), 324–329
Rodionov, Alexei, 96
Rodnyansky, Alexander, 212, 217; interview with, 385–394
Rogozhkin, Aleksander: *The Chekist,* **28–30,** 72–73, 231–232; *The Cuckoo,* 97; *Living with an Idiot,* 231–232; *Outpost,* 238n; *Particulars of the National Hunt,* 231
The Romanovs (Panfilov), 233, 254, 265
Romashin, Anatoly, 332
Room, Abram, 193
A Room and a Half (Khrzhanovsky), 268
Ruderman, Arkady, 163, 216, 372–375, 377n, 391

Run Lola Run (Tykwer), 117–118
Russia at War (Werth), 95, 99
Russian Ark (Sokurov), 114, 115–125, 146, 149
Russian Civil War: films about, 71–81; and Soviet Jews, 82–88
Russian *émigrés*, 111–113
Russian Happiness (Khashchavatsky), 375–377
The Russian Idea (Selianov and Kovalov), 218
Russian Popular Culture (Stites), 203
Russian Ragtime (Ursulak), 234
Ryazanov, Eldar, 171, 198, 344–345
Rybakov, Anatoly, 83

S
The Sacrifice (Tarkovsky), 135
Saleem, Hiner, **272–273**
Samoilova, Tatiana, 92
Satan (Aristov), **13–16**
Saunders, Mark, 243
Scarecrow (Bykov), 159–160, 175, 198
Schnittke, Alfred, 88, 131
Schoss, Nancy, 188
Sculpting in Time (Tarkovsky), 136
The Second Circle (Sokurov), **11–13**
Second Class Citizens (Muratova), 230
Selianov, Sergei, 218
Shadows of Forgotten Ancestors (Paradzhanov), 165–166
Shakhnazarov, Karen, 201, 227
Shakhverdiev, Tofik, 213
Shlapentokh, Dmitry, 196, 262n
Shlapentokh, Vladimir, 196
The Shattered Mirror (Goldovskaya), 180–181
Shchors (Dovzhenko), 75
Shengelaya, Eldar, 198
Shengelaya, Georgy, 165–166, **273–275**

Shepitko, Larisa: *The Ascent*, **153**, 169; *Farewell*, 95, 127, 153, 172; *Motherland of Electricity*, 76; *Wings*, **153**
The Shining Path (Alexandrov), 195–196, 272
Shlapentokh, Dmitry, 196, 262n
Shooting Range (Tarasov), 282
Shy Boy (Kamalova), **24–26**
Siberiade (Konchalovsky), 58, **136–140**, 254, 292–294
Sideburns (Mamin), **175–177**, 260
Siegelbaum, Lewis H., 189
A Sign of Disaster (Ptashchuk), 338
Since Otar Left (Bertuccelli), 273
Sklansky, Yasha, 170
Sky Studded with Diamonds (Pichul), 229
"*A Slave of Love*" (Mikhalkov), 73, 77, 78–80, 169, 199, 299
Sling, Maria, 62
Smirnov, Andrei, 76
Smit, Pieter Jan, 263
Smith, Hedrick, 187–188
socialist realism, 74, 162, 167, 195
Sokurov, Alexander: *Alexandra*, 150; *Confession*, 147, 149–152; *Days of Eclipse*, **9–11**; *Dialogues with Solzhenitsyn*, 150; *Elegy of a Voyage*, 117, 148, 149; *Elegy of the Land*, 147; *The Evening Sacrifice*, 146, 164; *Hubert Robert: A Happy Life*, 149; *The Last Day of a Rainy Summer*, 147; *The Lonely Voice of a Man*, 146; *Maria*, 216; *Molokh*, 238n; *Moscow Elegy*, 148; *Mother and Son*, 150, 230; *Russian Ark*, 114, 115–125, 146, 149; *The Second Circle*, **11–12**; *Spiritual Voices*, 147, 149, 150; *The Stone*, **21–22**
Solonitsyn, Anatoly, 77–78, 143

Solovei, Elena, 79, 158
Solovetsky Power or *Solovki Power* (Goldovskaya), 163, 179, 213
Soloviev, Sergei, **6–7**, 201
Solovky Power (Goldovskaya), 179
Solzhenitsyn, Aleksandr, 152, 167
Some Interviews on Personal Matters (Gogoberidze), **39–40**
Soviet Cinematography (Shlapentokh and Shlapentokh), 196
Soviet Toys (Vertov), 282
Spanish Civil War, 63
Spiritual Voices (Sokurov), 147, 149, 150
Sports, Sports, Sports (Klimov), 128
Stalin, Joseph: disowning son on battlefield, 93; and *The Fall of Berlin*, 69–70, 90; filmmaking under, 195–197; and *I Was Stalin's Bodyguard*, 48; on patriotism, 89, 90; portrayal in Khrushchev's regime, 167–168; portrayal under *glasnost* and *perestroika*, 45, 54; in *Repentence*, 49, 52–55, 87; and Russian Civil War, 72
Stalingrad (Varlamov and Karmen), 100
Stalingrad (Vilsmaier), **98–100**
Stalin is With Us (Shakhverdiev), 213
Stalker (Tarkovsky), **140–145**
The Star (Lebedev), 97
"Staring Back" (Marker), 148
State of Weightlessness (Drygas), 207
The Steamroller and the Violin (Tarkovsky), 254
Stites, Richard, 193, 203
The Stone (Sokurov), **21–22**
Storm over Asia (Pudovkin), 73–74
The Story of Turin, A Painter and a Victim (Pechonkin), 217

Streep, Meryl, 69
Strugatsky, Arkadi and Boris, 140–141
The Sun (Sokurov), 267
Sverak, Jan, **283–284**
Sverak, Zdenek, 284
Swan Lake. The Zone (Ilyenko), **8–9**

T
Tarasov, V., 282
Tarkovsky, Andrei: *Andrei Rublev*, 134, 142, 165, 274, 294–295; Gurevich on, 367–368; *Ivan's Childhood*, 92, 97, 143; Klimov on, 338; *The Mirror*, 148, 157–158, 367–368; *Nostalghia*, 112, **279–281**; and *One Day in the Life of Andrei Arsenevich*, **132–136**; *The Sacrifice*, 135; *Sculpting in Time*, 136; *Stalker*, **140–145**; *The Steamroller and the Violin*, 254
Tarkovsky, Arseny, 142
Taxi Blues (Lungin), 199, 260
Ten Days That Shook The World (Eisenstein), 269
Thank You and Good Night (Oxenberg), 218
Theatre in the Time of Perestroika and Glasnost (Ruderman), 163, 373–374
The Theme (Panfilov), 84, 170–172, 183–184, 352–354
Theremin: An Electronic Odyssey (Martin), **283**
The Thief (Chukhrai), **33–34**, 231
Third Meshchanskaya Street (Room), 193
This Shaking World (Goldovskaya), 182
The 3 Rooms of Melancholia (Honkasalo and Pervila), **107–108**

Three Songs About Motherland (Goldovskaya), 182
Three Stories (Muratova), 230
Time of the Dancer (Abdrashitov and Mindadze), 234
Tired Cities (Rodnyansky), 388–389
Tisse, Eduard, 239
Today We Are Going to Build a House (Loznitsa and Magambetov), 217
Todorovsky, Pyotr, 95, 249
Tolstoy, Alexei, 89, 102
Tot, Tomasz, 261
The Train Rolled On (Marker), 133
Trajan, Ondrej, **105–106**
"Transit Zero," 239–243
Transsiberian (Anderson), **284–285**
A Trial in Prague (Justman), **60–66**
Trial on the Road (Gherman), 93, 171, 172
Tsabadze, Aleko, interview with, 394–402
Tsar (Lungin), 267
Tsarevich Alexei (Melnikov), 233
12 (Mikhalkov), 268
Twelve Angry Men (Lumet), 268
Twenty Days Without War (Gherman), 95
The 28th Instance of June 1914, 10:50 A.M. (Politsch), 218
Two Comrades Were Serving (Karelov), 77–78
235,000,000 (Franks and Brauns), 240–242

U
Uchitel, Alexei, 233–234
Ujica, Andrei, **206–209**
Unfinished Piece for Player Piano (Mikhalkov), 158, 169
The Unvanquished, 83
Urga (Mikhalkov), **22–24**

Ursulak, Sergei, 234
Urusevsky, Sergei, 74, 91

V
Varlamov, Leonid, 100
Vasilyev, Georgy, 74, 195
Vasilyev, Sergei, 74–75, 195
Vassa (Panfilov), 166, 254, 351–352
Vertov, Dziga, 73, 162, 282, 369
VGIK (State Institute of Cinema), 146, 301, 358–361, 379
Videograms of a Revolution (Ujica and Farocki), 206
Vidov, Oleg, 282
Vilsmaier, Joseph, **98–100**
Viva Castro! (Frumin), 234
Vodka Lemon (Saleem), **272–273**
Volga, Volga (Alexandrov), 195, 271
The Voroshilov Marksman (Govorukhin), 239n
Voznesensky, Andrei, 83

W
Wajda, Andrzej, 253
Walkowitz, Daniel J., 188–189, 263n
Ward No. 6 (Shakhnazarov), 268
Wargnier, Regis, **68**
A Wartime Romance (Todorovsky), 95
The Wedding (Lungin), 232, 260–261
Welcome (Klimov), 127
Werth, Alexander, 95, 99
White Bird With Black Markings (Ilyenko), 168–169
White Sun of the Desert (Motyl), 75–76
Why Am I Alive? (Dvornitchenko), 214
Why Are You Alive? (Dvornitchenko), 214
Widow of the Revolution: The Anna Larina Story (Reed), **67**

Window to Paris (Mamin), 232
Wings (Shepitko), **153**
Woman on the Rails, 272
"Working Group on Cinema and TV, the Soviet Union, and Eastern Europe," 185–186

Y
Yakubson, Felix, 214
Yeltsin, Boris, 104, 181, 262n
Yevtushenko, Yevgeny, 49, 50, 82–83, 95
You Cannot Live Like This (Govorukhin), 213
Youngblood, Denise J., 190, 192–194

Yufit, Yevgeny, 230

Z
Zarkhi, Alexander, 253
Zelary (Trajan), **105–106**
Zeldovich, Alexander, 229, 391
Zero City (Shakhnazarov), 201
The Zero Hour (Horton and Brashinsky), 201, 203
Zhurbin, Alexander, 238n
Zhvanetsky, Mikhail, 201
Zoya (Arnshtam), 89
Zvenigora (Dovzhenko), 74
Zvyagintsev, Andrei, **243–248**

Also by New Academia Publishing

Cinema

AMERICA REFLECTED: Language, Satire, Film, and the National Mind, by Peter C. Rollins

HERETICAL EMPIRICISM, by Pier Paolo Pasolini

PIER PAOLO PASOLINI: In Living Memory, edited by Ben Lawton and Maura Bergonzoni

EVERY STEP A STRUGGLE: Interviews with Seven Who Shaped the African-American Image in Movies, by Frank Manchel

IMAGING RUSSIA 2000: Film and Facts, by Anna Lawton

BEFORE THE FALL: Soviet Cinema in the Gorbachev Years, by Anna Lawton

Popular Culture/ Visual Culture

RUSSIAN FUTURISM: A History, by Vladimir Markov

WORDS IN REVOLUTION: Russian Futurist Manifestoes 1912-1928 A. Lawton and H. Eagle, eds., trs.

SHOPPING FOR JESUS: Faith in Marketing in the USA, Dominic Janes, ed.

SUPER/HEROES: From Hercules to Superman, Wendy Haslem, Angela Ndalianis, and Chris Mackie, eds.

WE'RE FROM JAZZ: Festschrift in Honor of Nicholas V. Galichenko edited by Megan Swift and Serhy Yekelchyk

TERROR ON THE SCREEN: Witnesses and the Reanimation of Terrorism as Image Event, Popular Culture and Pornography , by Luke Howie

REMEMBERING UTOPIA: The Culture of Everyday Life in Socialist Yugoslavia, Breda Luthar and Maruša Pušnik, eds.

Fiction

RED STAR, CRESCENT MOON: A Muslim-Jewish Love Story, by Robert A. Rosenstone

TO KILL A TSAR, by G. K. George

ON THE WAY TO RED SQUARE, by Julieta Almeida Rodrigues

Memoirs

THROUGH DARK DAYS AND WHITE NIGHTS: Four Decades Observing a Changing Russia, by Naomi F. Collins

JOURNEYS THROUGH VANISHING WORLDS, by Abraham Brumberg

Read an excerpt at: www.newacademia.com

www.ingramcontent.com/pod-product-compliance
Lightning Source LLC
Chambersburg PA
CBHW021758220426
43662CB00006B/100